Dyslexia

Research and Resource Guide

Carol Sullivan Spafford
American International College

George S. Grosser
American International College

Allyn and Bacon
Boston • London • Toronto • Sydney • Tokyo • Singapore

This book is dedicated to Ken, Harry, Barb, Ray, Mylan,
Christine, Tobi, and Maryfrances as they helped
to make this book a reality.

Library of Congress Cataloging-in-Publication Data

Spafford, Carol Sullivan
    Dyslexia : research and resource guide / Carol Sullivan Spafford, George
S. Grosser.
        p.   cm.
    Includes bibliographical references and index.
    ISBN 0-205-15907-9
    1. Dyslexia—United States.   2. Reading—United States—Remedial
teaching.   3. Dyslexic children—Education—United States.
4. Dyslexics—Education—United States.   I. Grosser, George S.
II. Title.
LB1050.5.S63   1996
371.91′44—dc20   95-13738
                                                                       CIP

Printed in the United States of America

10   9   8   01

Contents

Preface

Dyslexia is one of those mystifying problems that affects approximately 3% of the population. Dyslexia is a reading disorder whereby an individual fails to attain reading skills commensurate with age and ability levels despite adequate educational opportunities. Although dyslexia cannot be cured in the sense that some medically-based illnesses can, dyslexia can be helped to the extent that the individual can function relatively well. Famous dyslexics who have overcome or compensated for their problems include Thomas Edison, Hans Christian Andersen, George Patton, Woodrow Wilson, Nelson Rockefeller, Bruce Jenner, Tom Cruise, and one of George Bush's children.

Dyslexia has been addressed by a number of authors in a multitude of ways because a definitive causal link to this disorder has not been found. Therefore, one will encounter many and varied approaches to the problem in the popular and professional journals. Currently, linguistic explanations seem to dominate the professional journals with causation attributed to various linguistic deficiencies. More recent research in the visual realm has resulted in specific factual and objective information concerning the role of retinal receptors in the processing of visual information. This has led to some exciting new avenues to explore in searching for causative explanations behind the dyslexic's reading problems. We provide some recent correlating factors in this regard along with several other challenging and interesting schools of thought. Although we endeavor to be as objective as possible, the authors' presentations of some of the other researchers' points of view reflect our own interpretations.

The format of this book is unusual in that it is intended to reach a broad spectrum of professionals to include diagnosticians, researchers, teachers, college students, and anyone else interested in this problem. Most books tend to be overspecialized and address only a specific aspect of dyslexia. It is our belief that this important reading problem be addressed from many dimensions—definitions, subtyping, assessments, remediation, social aspects, and neurophysiology. We believe that in looking at any child, one must look at the overall well-being of the individual.

The following questions are frequently asked by parents, classroom teachers, professionals in the field such as speech therapists and psychologists, administrators, and others. While some tentative answers can be given at this time, these answers are subject to further refinements as relevant data continue to be gathered and the knowledge base increased. These questions are

What is dyslexia?

What is it **like** to be dyslexic?

How did the term *dyslexia* originate?

Are there subtypes of dyslexia?

What are some other forms of learning disabilities?

What are some physiological correlates of dyslexia?

What is the effect of the environment?

What is important in a dyslexia assessment?

What is portfolio assessment?

How effective are current remedial measures?

What is the role of motivation?

How does one's cognitive or learning style impact reading proficiency?

Are there gifted dyslexics?

How can school administrators ensure appropriate programming decisions and placement?

What can parents do to help their dyslexic child?

What can the regular classroom teacher do to assist the learning of dyslexics?

What are some specific remedial reading, language, and writing strategies professionals can use with students with dyslexia?

How can teachers become involved in research?

What is the impact of inclusionary practices on educational program planning for dyslexics?

What agencies can be contacted to provide assistance for dyslexics and their parents/caretakers?

Do dyslexics have optimistic chances of completing college and professional careers?

What kind of technological assistance is available to individuals with dyslexia?

What kind of computer software, CD-ROMs, and multimedia are available for the disabled?

March 6, 1995 saw the historic first of NASA providing computer access to the public in its recent shuttle flight by allowing occasional dialogue between "earthlings" and the Endeavour's seven astronauts in space. Some of the fortunate Internet users on earth were able to receive pictures and audiotapes of the crew via Internet. Messages like "One small step for NASA, one giant step for the 'Net' " and "Absolutely amazing, beam me up!" were exchanged (Dunn, 1995). Internet is one source of technology access that can enhance learning for individuals with dyslexia. The United States House and Senate reauthorized technology-related assistance in a conference version of the 1988 IDEA (Individuals with Disabilities Act) which resulted in funding increases for assistive technology for individuals with dyslexia. Approximately $50 million in grants to states has been allocated through 1998 for advocacy training, technology training, and other related services. It would be prudent to keep abreast of these developments, as your school system might qualify for grant money training funds. It is common knowledge that technological training and familiarity with technological advances are lagging in the education field and such funding availability could help close the knowledge gap.

Because much of the terminology in the education field can be a jargon all unto itself, a comprehensive glossary is provided at the end of the book. Case studies are also included to serve as a concrete hand-hold. Additionally, chapter summaries, and a comprehensive reference listing will assist the reader in obtaining the greatest possible knowledge base a single, small book can provide.

This book is meant to present a comprehensive overview of one of the most puzzling problems educators confront—that is, why do dyslexics have reading problems and what do we do to help them? We are not suggesting we have the definitive word, but rather, we aim to provide some additional insight into this problem with the hope that with further research and study, the nature and causes of dyslexia can be found. We carefully document all material with research in the field. It is vitally important to substantiate theory with practice, and practice with theory.

No one remedial technique has been proven to be the answer, and several suggestions/techniques/methods/assists have been documented with several graphics and examples. As you will see, we have chosen an eclectic perspective. We are recommending that professionals have "a bag of tricks" or various alternatives to use when a particular approach doesn't work. Common sense should always prevail. Be wary of approaches and treatments which claim to have the cures and the definite answers to this reading problem. We are taken by Janet W. Lerner's words from 1971, "The search for the perfect package to teach academic skills and foolproof programmed materials can be viewed as an attempt to minimize the teacher's need to make decisions." The teacher should always assist in determining any remedial actions for students with disabilities, as they must implement and evaluate any academic programming efforts. It is incumbent upon all who are involved with individuals with dyslexia to *Read, Review,* and *Reason* with a critical eye. It is important to note that we are encouraged by the progress educators are making in providing quality programs to students with disabilities and other learning difficulties. As an example, the 1994 College Board report released at year-end cited significant strides in math and science performances over a five-year period for some previously underachieving groups.

We believe that this cyclopaedic presentation of dyslexia is the most comprehensive and up-to-date source on the subject of dyslexia, with substantive research given as documentation every step of the way. We hope that researchers, graduate students, and other professionals will continue to to seek answers through stringently controlled research. We have only dented the surface in trying to present and resolve the myriad of issues raised in both the diagnosis and treatment of this perplexing problem. Keeping a sense of humor and an "effective-affective" perspective helps to keep us focused with our feet on the ground.

A project of this magnitude necessarily entails solicitation of advice, resources, and time from colleagues. First we wish to thank our friends from Allyn and Bacon publishing. Foremost, we were extremely privileged to have had the input and wise counsel of Ray Short, Senior Editor; and Mylan Jaixen, Executive Editor. Ray was key in moving this project forward. His dedication to excellence and constructive suggestions provided the insights we needed to complete the book. Mylan Jaixen provided creativity and an appealing format for the book at the beginning stages of this project. Mylan's reviews helped keep the quality of the book a prime concern at all times. For the guiding hands of these two professionals, we are most grateful. Additionally, Virginia Lanigan was always there when we needed advice—many thanks Virginia! Susan Hutchinson, Nihad Farooq, and Lori Smith were with us at the beginning of the project and were most helpful and accommodating. Last, but not least, Christine Shaw carried this project through the final stages. Christine's expertise, patience, and wonderful disposition were greatly appreciated.

The valuable contributions of Dr. Barbara Dautrich were essential as she provided guidance for many of the graphics in Chapters 10 through 12. Barbara brought refreshing new looks and style to many of the appealing tables and graphics and generously gave of her time and expertise. Maryfrances Peters created, completed, and edited most of the outstanding visuals throughout the book. Maryfrances was a graduate student at the beginning of the project and now is a high school teacher. We are proud of her! A special thanks goes to these two fine professionals as they were instrumental in making an important dimension to the book a reality. We have also been fortunate to have several individuals generously support our efforts. In naming those who helped, we apologize in advance for any omissions. First, we are grateful to the following people for their unconditional support in making our research/writing efforts possible: the Courniotes, Blake, Falconer/Sokolowski, Sprague, and Abdow families. The Blakes, in particular, have founded schools, fellowships, and programs dedicated to improving the lives of individuals with dyslexia. As far as mentors/professionals/friends are concerned, Dr. Harry Courniotes is tops in our book! We are especially grateful to have had the computer expertise of Maria Cahillane (who did not leave the computer for two solid years), Andre Houle, Betty Gandi Tobin, Marguerite Genest, Judy Dumont, Mary Lanz, Annette Krzyzek, Madelyn Orozco, and Bea Roberts.

Professionals who provided lesson ideas, inspiration and other advice include Dean Charles F. Maher, Dr. Richard C. Sprinthall, Dr. Augustus Pesce, Dr. Ann Courtney (excellent input on portfolios), Dr. Henry Benjamin, Ben Swan Sr., Drs. Celeste Budd and Art Jackson, Kathy Sullivan, Marie, Angela, and Phil Coburn, Nancy Cabana, David Ardito, Dr. Mary Allen, Robin Bailey, Eleanor Balboni, Hilda and Lisa Bartnik, Susan Blackington, Karen Ciempa, John and Cloretha Coleman, Charles and Judy Collins, Linda Cooling, Glenn Coolong, Ingrid Cuevas, Sally Curtis, Michele D'Amour, Eileen Donahue, Opal Dillard, Nancy Farrell, Melody Forbes, Dr. Tulius and Marsh Frizzi, the Golzmanes, Craig Greenberg, Edwina Grimaldi, Richard Hansen, Lisa Hayden, Barbara Hayes, Michelle Hervieux, Dr. Betty Hukowitz,

Melanie Jennings, Erroll Jones, Pat Jones, Christopher Klukas, Manisha Lalwani, Michelle LaVallee, Doris LeBlanc, Lena Lefebvre, Kathy Lynch, Chris Marek, the Mc-Clures, Cindy and Barry McCormack, Kathy Mayo, Lee Mitchell, Todd Mongeon, Pauline Mortenson, Maureen O'Connell, Eileen Tremble Pisarski, Jeanne and Edna Proulx, Liza Quirk, Dina Rossi, Paula Rozkuszka, Linda Rozolsky, Miriam Santiago, Kim Scofield, Dave Sokol, Lisa Sotirion, Mary Stacy, Dr. Cheryl Stanley, Hilda Supernaut, Tina Toohey, Brian Welch, and Stephanie Wilson. Dr. Carol Spafford also extends a special thank you to Sister Mary Caritas, the Trembles, the D'Amours, Ada King, the Momnies, Dr. Beverly Miller, Dr. Joe Donatelli, Dr. Steve Squillace, Dr. Jon Dana, Dr. Carol Ammons, Dr. Judy Voress, Dr. George Hynd, Dr. George Pavlidis, Dr. Margaret Cassidy, and Dr. Georgia Parafestas. Brian Snook provided wonderful graphics for the "kite" multicultural visuals—Brian is an artist in the true sense of the word. Another creative individual, Mary Saltus, graciously shared personal correspondence in Chapter 7. Susan Guay and Joanne McClain provided great study skills ideas. Cathy Meadows, graduate assistant, pounded the pavement for those hard-to-find resources as did Matt Pappathan and Ira Glunts. Cathy unfailingly attended to every research request and Matt had a knack for finding "impossible" journal references. Manisha Lalwani assisted with last minute details. Despite the death of her spouse, Marie Stevens, our graduate assistant, always gave us her best. She also is a teacher and we're so proud. Office staff member Mildred McKenna, now retired, kept us organized and on track. The Springfield Public School System provided professional expertise/opportunities for observing teacher excellence.

Susan Swanson provided copyediting support at the "homestretch" that was of the highest quality. Michael Bass and Associates with Tobi Giannone, in particular, also assisted with manuscript preparations. Tobi's expertise in publishing helped us improve the book. The computer skills of James L. Mayrand Jr. and Sara Hibbard are also thankfully acknowledged. We greatly appreciate the timely and professional contributions of these individuals.

Several individuals provided case study information which enhanced the ability of the authors to discuss sympotomologies, correlating factors, the diagnostic process, and specific recommendations. The following people are gratefully acknowledged for their invaluable contributions: Dr. and Mrs. Sarkozi and daughter, Carrie; Debby and Paul Fortini and sons, Joseph, Thomas, Edward, and Matthew; Liz Nystrom and daughter, Stephanie; Sonya Martinez and son, Joel; Dr. Solveig Pflueger and son, Bobby; Toni Spinelli-Nannen and children, Matthew and Stephanie; the Pattersons and son, Jack; Neta Maddox and son, Clifford; Tom and Ruth Garbett; Tom Sullivan and son, William; Betty Bonfitto and daughter, Marla; the Bednarzyks and son, Billy; the MacNamees and son, Robert; the Herlihys and son, Tim Sunstrom; Jill Rollend; the Momnies; the Conlins; the Filips; and the O'Neills; Laurie Bobskill and son, Bobbie; and Frank Vargo. We are especially thankful to Laurie as she willingly provided a forum for our work early on.

Finally, we thank our family members and friends for their many kindnesses and support. To our family members, Ken Spafford, Kenny Spafford, Richard Spafford, Irene Spafford, Richard and Carol Sullivan, George, Pat, and Janice Sullivan, and Eleanor Grosser, thanks for your support and for sharing so much of your time, patience and resources—you're the best. The authors may be reached by: E Mail on the Internet at 71650.677@Compuserve.Com and Fax #1-413-525-1901.

$$ C\ h\ a\ p\ t\ e\ r\quad 1 $$

Introduction

Overview of the Field

The Challenge . . .

In every school there are children who do not learn to read and spell satisfactorily . . . increasingly, however, conscientious and discerning teachers and anxious parents are realizing that there are intelligent non-readers [and troubled readers] who try very hard, and that such children present a challenge which customary teacher-training does not enable the teacher to meet . . . —(GILLINGHAM & STILLMAN, 1966, P. 1).

As Gillingham and Stillman note, adaptations, methods, materials, and resources are required to meet the special needs of individuals with dyslexia. As you peruse and digest the many suggestions throughout the book, you will see that adaptations can be made to all age levels; dyslexia is a condition which persists through to adulthood. This book is rich with resources, teaching assists and ideas, and strategies for individuals with dyslexia and other learning disabilities.

Dyslexia is a specific type of learning disability involving a severe impairment in reading ability which affects and disrupts a person's language development and functioning. It is estimated that at least 2.625% to 5% of the entire population suffer from dyslexia, the most prevalent type of learning disability (see Figure 1-1). In regard to numbers of students who are learning disabled, 5.25% have been identified as learning disabled of a total of 10.25% disabled students being served in our schools (U.S. Dept. of Education, 1995). At least half of these students would be classified as dyslexic. As a specific type of learning disability, dyslexia falls under Part B of the Individuals with Disabilities Education Act (IDEA) of 1990, P.L. 101–476:

". . . a disorder in one or more of basic psychological processes involved in using language, spoken or written, which may manifest itself in an

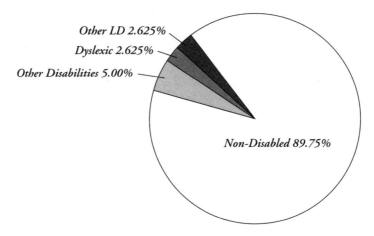

FIGURE 1-1   Percentages of Disabled Students—1995

imperfect ability to listen, think, speak, read, write, spell, or do mathe-
matical calculations. The term includes such conditions as perceptual
handicaps, brain injury, minimal brain dysfunction, dyslexia, and de-
velopmental aphasia. The term does not include children who have learn-
ing problems which are primarily the result of visual, hearing, or motor
handicaps, of mental retardation, of emotional disturbance, or of envi-
ronmental, cultural, or economic disadvantage . . ."

The Individuals with Disabilities Education Act (IDEA) of 1990 is a reautho-
rization of the more familiar P.L. 94-142 (1975) federal legislation, which was called
the Education of All Handicapped Children's Act (EOAHC). IDEA includes a 1983
(P.L. 98-199) and 1986 (P.L. 99-457) amendment to P.L. 94-142 (see Chapter 2). Essentially, IDEA is a federal law which provides detailed specifications as to how
special services will be administered to disabled children. All disabled children are
guaranteed a free and appropriate education under this act. The Federal Office of
Special Education Programs, directed by the Deputy Assistant Secretary, is responsible for its implementation. A major change in the P.L. 94-142 (U.S.O.E., 1977) legislation involved deletion of the use of the term, *handicapped,* replacing it with
the term, *disabilities.* Additionally, IDEA now requires that transition services for
students leaving high school be written into a student's individual education plan
(IEP). Typically sections 617 and 618 of the regulations are referred to by professionals when looking at EOAHC (P.L. 94-142), and sections 1417 and 1418, with
IDEA (P.L. 101-476).

Majority of LD Population Is Dyslexic

It is necessary to distinguish the problem of dyslexia from other learning disabilities. Learning disabilities in general can refer to a number of problems including
difficulties in reading (dyslexia) and language, math, memory, and non-verbal communication problems. However, in most instances learning disabilities are almost

always diagnosed with the use of a reading assessment battery and almost always refer to some type of reading disability or dyslexia (Aaron & Baker, 1991). Many writers use the term learning disability interchangeably with dyslexia, reading disability (RD), severe reading disability (SRD), severe reading disorder (SRD), and remedial reader. There are no firm figures regarding the percentage of individuals experiencing learning disabilities who are identified specifically as dyslexic. However, a majority would indicate at least 50% or 2.625% of the total 5.25% learning disabled identified in our schools (U.S. Dept. of Ed., 1995). Of the total 10.25% disabled being served (see Figure 1-2), the learning disabled comprise the largest category followed by speech and language impairments (2.32%), mental retarda-

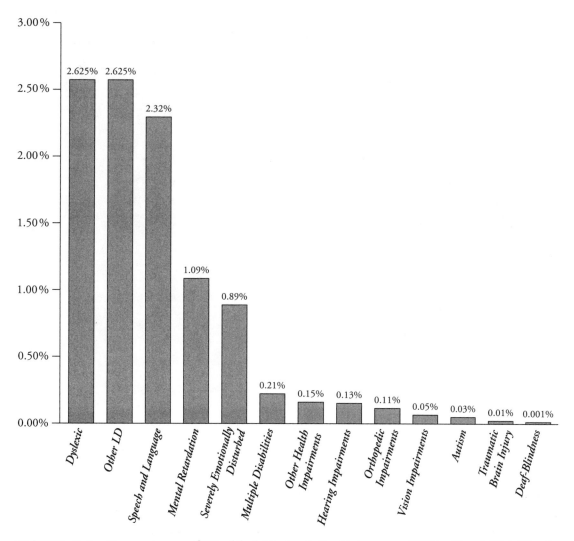

FIGURE 1-2 Percentages of Disabled Students by Category—1995—Total 10.25% of Entire Population

tion (1.09%), severely emotionally disturbed (.89%), multiple disabilities (.21%), hearing impairments (.13%), orthopedic impairments (.11%), other health impairments (.15%), visual problems (.05%), autism (.03%), traumatic brain injury (.01%), and deaf-blindness (<.01%).

In order to further set the stage for the content of the book, we have summarized the *What?*, *How?*, and *What Else?* of affective and instructional dimensions of strategic procedures for dyslexics at the outset (see Table 1-1). The reader can check the table of contents and index for particular references.

TABLE 1-1   Affective and Instructional Dimensions of Strategic Procedures for Dyslexics

What?	How?	What Else?
Reading Phonics Vocabulary Comprehension Integrated Writing Activities Leisure Reading	*Study Skills* Selecting Material Outlining Memory Devices Spaced Practice Review	*Social Skills-Contextual* Appropriate Language Appropriate Behaviors Body Gestures Reciprocity Listening
Math Concepts Facts Algorithms Problem Solving	*Metacognitive Strategies* Constructivism Self-Instruction Self-Monitoring Self-Correcting Self-Reflecting Self-Questioning	*Time Management* Planning Schedules Planning Alternatives Planning Appropriate Loads Planning Locales Planning Support Systems
Language Spelling Syntax Vocabulary Comprehension Writing Prosody Communication	*Cooperative Learning* Peer Tutoring Peer Coaching Adult Tutoring Adult Coaching Mentoring	*Desired Outcomes* Positive Self-Concept Positive Social Life Positive School Experience Positive Career Directions
Physical Overall Physical Health Eye/Ear Exams Dental Exams Postural Screening	*Interventions* Language Training Math Training Reading Training VAK Training	*Additional Challenges* Developing Multicultural Literacy Establishing an Inviting Classroom Portfolio Development Integrating Across the Curriculum

We will take both a current and historical perspective in looking at the problem of dyslexia after considering the words of some prominent experts in the field:

> ". . . the history of thought regarding the . . . basis of . . . dyslexia [defined as a reading disorder], is consistent with contemporary research findings . . ." (Hynd, 1992, p. 110).
>
> Additionally, . . . "it must be admitted, . . . that no one [person] . . . in previous history advocated or combined all the elements of sound method; but taking the course of history as a whole, we are able to cull out here and there principles and devices which, when combined, match the best thought and practice of the present generation . . ." (Taylor, 1912, p. 119). It is well known that many of today's education practices are easily traced to "ideas expressed much earlier, including prescribing instruction based on the child's characteristics, carefully sequencing tasks from simple to complex, emphasizing stimulation of the child's senses, and tutoring in functional skills" (McNergney & Herbert, 1995, p. 60).

We hope you enjoy the historical excerpts that we have included at the beginning of each chapter. As you will see, much contemporary thought regarding the nature of dyslexia has its roots in the minds of well-regarded and brilliant individuals. It would be important to reflect on just how new "new" thoughts and approaches are.

Historical Basis for Term "Dyslexia"

Awareness of the dyslexic condition can be traced to the works of Dejerine (1892) and Bastian (1898); they, along with current researchers, have found a variety of congenital neurological problems, which may account for various subtypes of dyslexia. Dejerine (1892) connected neurological injury to reading disabilities by inferring that they were caused by damage to specific areas of the brain, the corpus callosum and the visual cortex of the dominant hemisphere. Hinshelwood (1917) later described the genetic component to this problem by discussing several children with reading disabilities who experienced what he termed as, *congenital dyslexia*. The following chapter takes a closer look at the use of the term *dyslexia*.

Kirk (1963) Brings LD Problems to the Forefront

It was Kirk in 1963, who propelled dyslexia and other forms of learning disabilities to the forefront of educator's minds as he delivered a speech to the Conference on Exploration into Problems of the Perceptually Handicapped Child. At this conference, Kirk coined the term *learning disability* to describe ". . . a group of children who have disorders in development, in language, speech, reading, and associated communication skills needed for social interaction . . ." (cited in Kirk & Kirk, 1976, pp. 255–256). As practitioners in the field, parents, and other interested parties search for clues and answers, we are confronted with additional challenges, e.g., to evaluate various theories and models, to assess suggested treatment modalities, and to evaluate remedial educational programs.

Correlates of Dyslexia

Several correlating factors have been used by professional diagnosticians in the field in order to properly identify individuals with this problem. These are frequently used as diagnostic indicators by psychologists, practitioners, and school professionals. Because dyslexia is considered a developmental condition, that is, one develops this condition throughout one's lifespan (see, for example, Grosser & Trzeciak, 1981), these correlates would co-occur with dyslexia or developmental dyslexia (Ellis, 1984). Many of the following correlating symptoms and behaviors can be seen in individuals who are described as dyslexic:

1. Delayed language development and/or language-related problems (Mattingly, 1972; Mann, 1986, 1991; Richman, Stevenson & Graham, 1982; Wiig, 1990)
2. Late talkers (Naidoo, 1972)
3. Verbal processing deficits involving phonological and/or auditory processing deficits (Tallal, Sainburg, & Jernigan, 1991; Liberman, Shankweiler, Liberman, Fowler, & Fisher, 1977; Snowling, 1980; Zigmond, 1967)
4. Reduced naming rates of colors, numbers, and objects in pictures (Denckla & Rudel, 1976a, 1976b; Wolf, 1986)
5. Relatively good peripheral vision (Grosser & Spafford, 1989a, 1989b, Dautrich, 1993; McKiernan, 1990)
6. Relatively poor peripheral light sensitivity (Grosser & Spafford, 1990, 1993a, 1993b; Spafford & Grosser, 1991) and reduced sensitivity to sinusoidal gratings at certain spatial frequencies (cycles of visual angle per degree) Grosser, Spafford, Donatelle, Dana, & Squillace, 1995)
7. Errors in oral reading (Whittey & Kopel, 1936; Aaron & Simurdak, 1991)
8. Serial order and sequencing problems (Myklebust, 1965; Myers & Hammill, 1990)
9. Familial history (Orton, 1937; Eustis, 1947; Critchley, 1963; Rutter & Yule, 1975; Manzo & Manzo, 1993)
10. Motor sequencing problems (Pavlidis, 1986)
11. Problems in writing and spelling (Bryan & Bryan, 1986; Interagency Committee on LD, 1987)
12. Slow recognition of individual letters and words (Clark & Chase, 1974; Ellis & Miles, 1981; Grosser & Trzeciak, 1981)
13. WISC-R Verbal-Performance IQ discrepancy differences (Spafford, 1989)
14. WISC-R ACID (low arithmetic, coding, information and digit span) profile for males (Spafford, 1989) and males and females (Young, 1993; Vargo, 1992) and an AVID (low arithmetic, vocabulary, information and digit span) profile for females (Spafford, 1989)
15. Overall IQ's in the low 90s (Stanovich, 1986 a, 1986b)
16. Confusion between right and left (Rutter, Tizard & Whitmore, 1970)

17. Reduced reading rates as adults (Ellis & Miles, 1978)

18. Time and directional confusions (Bryan & Bryan, 1986)

19. Lack of adequate problem-solving strategies (Palinscar & Brown, 1987; Stone & Forman, 1988)

20. Problems with attention (Interagency Committee on learning disabilities, 1987)

21. Diminished on-task behaviors such as completion and follow-through of assigned tasks; understanding and following directions, and completing tasks independently (Gresham & Reschly, 1986)

22. Social behavior problems to include more negative peer interactions, lower social standing, diminished self-concept, external locus of control and learned helplessness, unawareness of social conventions (Spafford & Grosser, 1993; Leary, 1992; Vaughn, 1991; Vaughn & LaGreca, 1988; Pearl, Bryan, & Donahue, 1983)

23. Memory deficits (Torgesen, 1988; Torgesen & Kail, 1980; Swanson, Cochran, & Ewers, 1990)

24. Erratic eye movements (Pavlidis, 1985a, 1985b, 1985c; Rayner, 1983, 1986)

25. Neurological anomalies/disruptions (Geschwind, 1982; Geschwind & Levitsky, 1968; Hynd & Hynd, 1984; Hynd, Obrzut, Hayes, & Becker, 1986; Hynd & Semrud-Clikeman, 1989b; Hynd & Willis, 1988; Galaburda, 1988, 1989; Livingstone & Hubel, 1988; Obrzut & Hynd, 1991; Obrzut, 1989)

The 1988 National Joint Committee on Learning Disabilities (NJCLD) has agreed that there is a link between dyslexia and central nervous system dysfunction. This connection is not easily explained by professionals in the field. There are early warning signs of dyslexia that relate to the correlating symptoms mentioned (see Table 1-2). Certainly when parents or professionals notice a child exhibiting several of these behaviors, a referral should be made to an appropriate professional/facility for a proper evaluation and diagnosis.

After remedial efforts are undertaken, most adult dyslexics have learned how to read and adequately use oral and written language. However, remnants of the problem still exist in adolescence and adulthood. As an example:

> *". . . How I do hate writing letters! was the exclamation of a youth of fourteen years of age, as he sat down before a sheet of fine letter-paper, prepared to do what he considered the most difficult of all his duties. With an excellent pen, just made for him by his uncle, and good ink, and lines under his paper, and plenty of thoughts in his head, there he sat like one stupefied; and after scrawling over his blotting-paper, trying his pen again and again, and waiting so long between each trial that the ink dried in the nib, he threw it down in despair, muttering the foolish wish that the art of writing letters had never been invented . . ." (Farrar, M.J., 1836, p. 1).*

No Definitive Answers

One can clearly see from the research that there are no definitive answers and there are certainly conflicting reports regarding correlates of dyslexia. As our definition of dyslexia becomes more fine-tuned, screening procedures more standardized and

TABLE 1-2   Early Warning Signs of Dyslexia

Parents and professionals need to make note of the following:

- Delays in speech and language development
- Difficulties in reading, math, writing, and spelling
- Difficulties in time and space concepts
- Difficulty copying work
- Disorganization in thinking through a problem, planning ahead, and following directions
- "The Clumsy Child Syndrome"
- Poor self-image and poor self-confidence
- Poor or less than satisfactory peer interactions
- Mood swings
- Hyperactivity, impulsivity, inattention, and low frustration tolerance
- Familial patterns
- Slowness in completing tasks
- Memory problems
- Poor study habits
- Poor test performance
- Excessively distractible

uniformly utilized, and research efforts tightened up, especially in regard to subject selection, only then will we see more of a consensus as to the nature and causes of dyslexia. In addition, it is important to welcome new perspectives and insights into this problem, especially in the realm of physiology. We now see more and more disorders being linked to physiological explanations. A good example would be recent evidence demonstrating that the disorders of schizophrenia and autism are related to a genetic and biochemical basis. Previously, many believed the home and the child's environment to be the predisposing causes of these problems.

Identifying Characteristics

The discussion thus far has centered on what dyslexia is and some of the better documented correlates. The variety seen in these correlating factors points to a very heterogeneous group of individuals, which raises the next question: Are there different types of dyslexia? We believe there are, based on the research promulgated to date. There are data that help to substantiate our subtypes, and remedial efforts need to be firmly linked to possible causes. As you will see, there are no definitive answers, only good solid hunches based on empirical evidence. Are there good points or strengths that may also differentiate dyslexics from proficient readers? Kean, of the Center for the Neurobiology of Learning and Memory at the University of California at Irvine (as cited in Ricks, 1986), has done research that points to "uncanny spatial skills" or the ability to understand abstract ideas and concepts as well-developed in dyslexics. Additionally, this research has uncovered what appears to be the dyslexic's superior ability in performing map tasks. Certainly, identified strengths could also lead to substantive correlates or indicators for the dyslexic.

Subtypes

Just as the condition of dyslexia is narrowly defined to specify brain/cognitive deficits specific to reading (Stanovich, 1986 a, 1986b), the concept of dyslexia, "requires that deficits found in such readers must not exceed too far into other domains of cognitive functioning" (Morrison & Siegel, 1991, p. 83). It is important to note that there are different types of learning disabilities and we would agree with Morrison and Siegel (1991) that the failure to differentiate among the various types of disabilities can lead to faulty conclusions and probably at times less than satisfactory remedial strategies. We believe that there are three distinct types of dyslexia: (1) a **visual-dysphonetic type,** (2) an **auditory-linguistic type**, and (3) a **mixed typed** with symptoms from both (1) and (2). We have established a factual basis for the visual-dysphonetic type by research in the area of visual anomalies (see Grosser, Spafford, Donatelle, Dana, & Squillace, in press). Current research does not yet support the prescription of specific techniques for different subtypes with validating research for any subtyping scheme at the infancy stage of development. For additional information on subtyping schemes in the field of learning disabilities, see authors Petrauskas and Rourke, 1979; Satz and Morris, 1981; Pirozzolo, Dunn, & Zetusky, 1984; Satz, Morris, and Fletcher, 1985; Weller & Strawser, 1987; and Newby and Lyon, 1991.

Other Types of Learning Disabilities*

It should be noted that the identifying symptoms discussed should differentially define dyslexia from other types of learning disabilities.

Memory Disorders

Memory disorders are characterized by the inability to recall what was experienced in terms of sensory stimulation (i.e., what is seen and what is heard). Memory dysfunctioning can interfere with language development, and individuals with dyslexia and other learning disabilities have been shown to display less efficient short-term and long-term memories and the ability to efficiently utilize memory strategies. Short-term memory (also called working memory), and long-term memory systems for tasks that require the processing of information, appear to be clearly deficient in individuals with learning disabilities as compared to that of non-learning disabled peers (see Swanson, Cochran, & Ewers, 1989; Swanson, 1989). The relatively poor memory performances of individuals with learning disabilities has been attributed to a number of problems, including difficulties in phonological encoding of information (Torgesen, 1988), the use of rehearsal strategies and retrieval cues (Wong, 1980), and organizational and evaluative strategies (Palinscar & Brown, 1984; Pressley & Levin, 1987). Thus, there is the failure of the individual with dyslexia to reflectively monitor cognitive progress

*See Appendix for Attention Deficit Problems.

and growth as well as non-disabled readers do. Swanson (1988) believes that there are particular memory subtypes which can characterize the learning-disabled population. Swanson's theoretical premise is that particular subtypes of learning-disabled children will consistently evidence poor performance on verbal and nonverbal memory tasks and on material which requires the encoding of information for short-term memory recall.

Mathematics Disabilities

Definition of Terms
It would appear that there are individuals with **mathematics disabilities** alone (without reading/language disabilities, and involving some type of right hemispheric dysfunctioning) and other individuals with reading and language disabilities who have math disabilities as well (with left hemispheric dysfunctioning) (Rourke & Strang, 1983; Ozols & Rourke, 1988). The entire study of math disabilities and math problems has been an area of research neglect for years. Spafford (1995, submitted manuscript) recently reported that 61% of an 8th grade population studied (N = 210) displayed math performance below the 45th percentile on the Wide Range Achievement Test-Revised. Certainly the math problems of our youth are a cause for intense and continued study.

Math disabilities are developmental or acquired problems in one or more of the general areas of number sense or numeration, computational ability, problem-solving, symbol interpretation, algorithm application, and visual-motoric-task completion (e.g., alignment problems). Math disabilities can occur alone or concurrently with other reading/language disabilities and are presumed to be due to central nervous system dysfunctioning in either/or both the visual and verbal realms. Math disabilities occur on a continuum with severity ranging from mild (a discrepancy of one standard deviation or **standard score** unit below one's measured general intelligence, e.g., IQ score) to severe (three or more standard deviation or standard scores units below one's measured intelligence).

Major Categories
There have been inconsistencies in the terminology used when defining various types of math disabilities (Sharma, 1986). However, there appear to be two major types of math disabilities supported by the neurophysiological school of thought—**acalculia** and **dyscalculia** (Keller & Sutton, 1991).

Acalculia.   Acalculia is an acquired math disorder resulting from brain trauma or injury after birth. It involves a failure in math ability in many areas (Kosc, 1974). Specific subtypes of acalculia have been described in the literature. The first of these is primary acalculia, also called **anarithmetia** and/or **true acalculia** (Benton, 1987; Spiers, 1987; Gaddes, 1985). This math disability involves difficulties in applying algorithms to basic math operations although memory and language skills appear relatively intact. In other words, calculating abilities are impaired across the board. A second form of acalculia is also called **aphasia acalculia**. The third variety is **acalculia with alexia**, visual-spatial acalculia. This disorder involves problems related to the visual placement and alignment of numbers resulting in math errors. A fourth type is Gerstmann's acalculia. This is a mathematics disability that has been frequently described in the literature since 1940. Individuals with **Gerstmann's syndrome** have been described as disabled in mathematics calculations, lacking in the ability to identify which finger was stimulated (finger **agnosia**), lacking in the ability to distinguish between left and right, and having **dysgraphia**. Some authorities insist that one type of Gerstmann's system can be an innate, developmental condition. Kinsbourne and Warrington (1963) have found that these individuals evidence higher incidences of left-handedness, with Verbal IQs higher than Performance IQs, and with females outnumbering males. Gerstmann's syndrome has also been considered a type of dyslexia.

Dyscalculia. Kosc (1974), Novick and Arnold (1988) and others, discuss developmental math disabilities they designate as **dyscalculia** whereby the individual lacks math proficiency in one or several areas. Specific types of dyscalculia have been identified in the literature:

1. **verbal dyscalculia** (oral language)—a math disorder in retrieving mathematics labels, terms, and symbols
2. **practognostic dyscalculia**—(gnostic=knowing; practo=doing; i.e., knowing by doing) a math disorder in applying math concepts when using manipulative objects in the environment (either visual or three-dimensional)
3. **lexical dyscalculia** (reading)—a math disorder which involves impaired reading of math vocabulary and symbols
4. **graphical dyscalculia** (writing)—a math disorder which is an impairment in the writing of mathematics symbols, equations, and other relevant language terms
5. **ideognostical dyscalculia** (ideas)—a math disorder which centers on impaired mathematical thinking or impaired conceptualizations (the ideas) in mathematics
6. **operational dyscalculia** (operations)—a math disorder focusing on impaired applications of algorithms to the four basic math operations (e.g., addition)

(Major source: Kosc, 1974).

Math Subtyping Schemes Based on Limited Study

"We believe a stronger case is made for the heterogeneous presence of math-disability subtypes than against them" (Keller & Sutton, 1991, p. 561). However, the little available research in this area has many methodological weaknesses, " . . . [and math measures are used which] are often of unknown quality psychometrically or of known poor quality" (Keller & Sutton, 1991, p. 561).

Seemingly more prudent than listing six subtypes with fine distinctions among them would be the broad delineation of math subtypes into verbal, visual, and mixed subtypes. At the present time, there is little empirical research evidence to justify the use of multiple subtyping categorizations of mathematics disabilities. When there are subtyping schemes offered, performance-based measures do not offer the breadth and depth of coverage as those offered by comparable reading assessments.

It would appear that there may be visual and verbal math disability types based on the schemas listed previously. It would be difficult to determine if individuals in a verbal deficit category are generally different from individuals who are dyslexic or language disabled. Work is much more preliminary and tentative compared to the subtyping research in dyslexia. This is due partly to a lack of interest and partly to low subject numbers (lack of subjects certainly can cause a lack of interest, especially among graduate students hoping to do research for degrees).

New Math Subtyping Scheme Offered

The authors suggest three broad conceptualizations of math disabilities based on a review of the research. We must use broad brush strokes in painting this picture as there are limited numbers of individuals identified as math-disabled to involve in research endeavors. Keeping in mind that the major reasons for subtyping any disorder involve identification for (1) research pursuits and (2) remediation efforts. Therefore, we offer a (1) visual mathematics disability type (similar to Gerstmann's acalculia), a (2) verbal mathematics disability type which would include all of the above subtypes which involve oral and written language symptoms, and a (3) mixed mathematics disability type which would include symptoms from the first two categories. Certainly the case study format offered by Warrington (1987) would shed light on specific and comprehensive math problems experienced by individuals with math disabilities. As you will see in Chapter 8, we follow mathematics research and intervention measures from a developmental perspective while keeping in mind specific error patterns and algorithmic approaches.

Non-Verbal Learning Disabilities

Johnson and Myklebust (1967) were one of the first research teams to describe non-verbal types of learning disabilities. The term *non-verbal learning disabilities* implies intact language functioning. Non-verbal learning disabilities (NVLD) are also known as developmental right-hemisphere syndrome (DRHS) because right-hemispheric brain lesions are thought to precipitate this disorder. Gross-Tsur, Shalev, Manor, and Amir (1995) cite the core symptoms of "emotional difficulties and disturbances in interpersonal skills; poor visuospatial ability; academic failure, especially in arithmetic; and left-sided neurological findings" (p. 80). Social knowledge of conventional behavior, the language of gestures, and facial expressions is lacking in this population. This is a relatively new syndrome cited in the literature with few diagnostic criteria available for differentially diagnosing this population. A majority of researchers would probably agree that non-verbal learning disabilities such as **social misperception** are concurrent symptoms to other types of problems or disabilities (Spafford & Grosser, 1993). Another type of non-verbal disorder, **attention deficit/hyperactivity disorder (ADHD)**, is considered by some to be a learning disability but most would agree ADHD is a secondary problem for only some individuals with learning disabilities. Although many individuals with attention deficit disorders (ADD) do not experience hyperactivity, ADHD will be described in depth, as a large percentage (3–5%) of all children suffer from ADHD (both LD and non-LD individuals).

Attention Deficit/Hyperactivity Disorder (ADHD)

Attention Deficit disorders should not be confused with dyslexia. Many individuals with dyslexia **do not** have attention deficits. Fowler (1992) estimates that 25% of children with learning disabilities have attention deficits. Further, Lerner, Lowenthal, and Lerner (1995) suggest that **most** children with learning disabilities who experience attention deficits **do not display hyperactivity** (the *H* in ADHD). Attention deficits can be correlating behaviors for a number of disorders including dyslexia. ADHD will be described as a separate syndrome with the primary presenting problems of attention-deficits and hyperactivity. Individuals with dyslexia can have attention deficits; however, these deficits would be considered secondary manifestations of the primary problem, which is reading. Stanford and Hynd (1994) caution that children with learning disabilities have distinct symptomatologies from those children with ADHD.

Attention deficit/hyperactivity disorders generally follow three types according to the American Psychiatric Association's, *Diagnostic and Statistical Manual*, (**DSM-IV**, American Psychiatric Association, 1994): (1) attention deficit/hyperactivity (ADHD) inattention type, (2) attention-deficit/hyperactivity impulsive type, and (3) a mixed type containing symptoms noted in (1) and (2).

ADHD Inattention Type (ADHD-IA) (Formerly called Undifferentiated ADD and ADD without hyperactivity)

The ADHD inattentive type involves at least six of the following symptoms which have persisted for at least six months:

1. carelessness in schoolwork or other work activities
2. difficulty in maintaining attention during play activities
3. often cannot listen to others for sustained periods of time
4. does not follow through with assigned tasks to include schoolwork (not due to oppositional behaviors)
5. experiences difficulty in organizing tasks and assignments
6. will avoid or strongly dislike tasks which require sustained attention (e.g., schoolwork, job requirements)
7. will lose necessary learning tools required for task completion (e.g., pens, books)
8. is easily distracted by environmental stimuli
9. forgets to complete expected tasks during daily routines both in and out of the school setting

ADHD Hyperactivity Impulsivity Type

The Diagnostic and Statistical Manual (DSM-IV, American Psychiatric Association, 1994) of the American Psychiatric Association states that the ADHD Hyperactive Impulsive type must display at least four of the following symptoms over a period of six months:

1. fidgets with arms or legs or constantly moves in his/her seat
2. leaves the classroom or other situations unexpectedly

3. will run, jump, or climb in situations where such behavior is inappropriate and unwanted
4. has difficulty becoming involved in leisure activities
5. will blurt out answers in class to questions inappropriately
6. will often have difficulty waiting his/her turn or waiting in line

ADHD Mixed Type

According to DSM-IV, a combined type of attention- deficit/hyperactivity disorder would involve symptoms from the first two types listed (i.e., inattentive and impulsive).

Ross (1976, p. 61) suggests that attention deficit disorders are "the result of delayed development in the capacity to employ and sustain selective attention." There are a substantial number of children who are diagnosed as ADHD with some estimates keying in on 5% of all elementary school age children (Wolraich, Lindgren, Stromquist, Milich, Davis, & Watson, 1990). It is important to stress that ADHD and academic learning disabilities are not synonymous. There are many learning disabled children who do not have attention deficits or hyperactive symptoms (Samuels & Miller, 1985). "Likewise, numerous children who display impulsivity, inattention, and/or hyperactivity do well in school" (Heward & Orlanski, 1992, p. 142).

Interventions for Individuals with ADHD

All ADHD types occur before the child is seven years of age with behaviors noted previously occurring both in and out of the school situation. ADHD students do have impaired social, academic, and emotional functioning that might require medical and/or behavioral interventions. Generally, two types of interventions are used with individuals who experience ADD or ADHD; namely, medical and education. Medically speaking, medication is recommended only as a last resort and generally takes the form of psychostimulants or antidepressants (Reid, Maag, Vasa, & Wright, 1994). Educationally, three distinct types of remediation can be identified in the literature as successful treatment modes for individuals with ADHD: (1) behavior modification interventions (DuPaul, Guevremont, & Barkley, 1991); (2) cognitive interventions (Fiore, Becker, & Nero, 1993); and (3) cognitive-behavior modification strategies (Lloyd, Landrum, & Hallahan, 1991) (see Table 1-3).

Language Learning Disabilities

The Education for All Handicapped Children Act specifies that written language disorders be considered as a type of learning disability. Alley and Deshler (1979) report that children with such problems also experience difficulties in speaking and listening. Language disabilities can be either in the written or oral realms.

Aphasia

The term **aphasia** refers to a "breakdown in the ability to formulate, or to retrieve, and to decode the arbitrary symbols of language" (Holland & Reinmuth, 1982, p. 428). Aphasia can involve both expressive (verbal encoding) and receptive

TABLE 1-3 Treating ADHD (and when appropriate, ADD)

Recommendations of Spafford and Grosser: Treat ADHD by (1) a combination of behavior/cognitive interventions with consideration given to the age, developmental level, and individual academic/social needs of the individual—what works for one individual might not work for another and (2) medication only if prescribed by a physician and after other avenues have not alleviated the ADHD to the point where the individual can satisfactorily function in academic and social situations. Also recommended would be those activities which foster positive interactions and growth as opposed to negative reinforcers or punishments.

Medications Prescribed and Treated by Medical Doctors Only

Remember: Check to see if ADHD student is taking any medications, as prescribed, in the nurse's office and check for such side effects as appetite and digestive problems, tics, lethargy, depression, headaches, nervousness, irritability, sleeping difficulties, etc. Consult with family and school medical personnel if side effects are seen.

Psychostimulants   Antidepressants

Education Interventions

Behavior Modification Methods

Positive Reinforcement
   reinforcement for desired behaviors (e.g., praise)

Negative Reinforcement
   removal of an unpleasant stimulus (e.g., removal of objects/situations causing inattention)

Punishment
   providing an uncomfortable stimulus/situation following undesired behavior(s) (e.g., issuing demerits)

Time Out
   removal from distracting/interfering Activities
   —time out within the classroom by moving assigned seat
   —time out of the classroom (e.g., time out room or the principal's office)

Contingency Contracting
   providing rewards or reinforcers contingent upon desired behaviors via a contractual agreement

Shaping
   rewarding behaviors that get closer and closer to the desired behaviors

Non-Reinforcement or Extinction
   not rewarding or responding to undesired behaviors hoping they will fade or be eliminated by the lack of attention or reinforcement

Token Economies
   therapeutic reinforcement of behaviors which can be exchanged for goods (e.g., pencil), services (e.g., free-time to play games), or privileges (e.g., being a hall monitor)

Cognitive Methods

Self-Management of Behaviors
   self-monitoring, self-evaluating, self-instruction, and self-reinforcing behaviors

Problem-Solving Training
   (1) defining problem areas, (2) hypothesizing

about causes and possible solutions, (3) implementing a plan of action, and (4) self-evaluating the plan for future actions

Relaxation Training
   self-talk, self-instruction

Cognitive Behavior Modification

Self-Monitoring Activities
   involving reinforcement systems and cognitive training (e.g., after a reinforcer has been given, ask, "Was I paying attention?")

Parent Organizations
   CH.A.D.D. or Children with Attention Deficit Disorders, 499 Northwest 70th Avenue, Suite 109, Plantation, Florida 33317 (1-305-587-3700; fax 305-587-4599)
   Parent Training Programs—call your local school department for details

problems (auditory decoding). Kleffner (1964) described disorders in understanding receptive language or the understanding of verbal symbols (Spradlin, 1967) as **receptive aphasia**. Problems in spoken language or expressing oneself in writing are called **expressive aphasia**. The reading act is different from these specific language components. As examples, "the reader can regulate his[her] speed, going slower or faster as his[her] purpose and the difficulty of the material dictate, while the listener's speed of listening [receptive language] is set by the speaker. The listener has additional clues of voice, gesture, and appearance, and emphasis of the speaker, while the reader cannot derive such supporting information from the printed page . . . the term reading implies comprehension of the reading act" (Lerner, 1971, p. 161). Generally individuals who are considered to be dyslexic do not have severe receptive and expressive language problems. The term **dyslexia** is reserved for those individuals who experience primary deficits in the reading area.

Expressive Aphasia. Expressive aphasia is characterized by difficulties in using oral or written language. Agraphia is a type of expressive aphasia which involves an impaired ability to express language in writing with dysgraphia, a specific form of agraphia, which involves underachievement in spelling ability. Dysgraphia many times occurs with the condition of dyslexia. This co-existing phenomenon appears to occur across language cultures (Duane, 1991).

Receptive Aphasia. Receptive aphasia refers to an impaired ability to understand or receive the components of our written or spoken language. Two other types of general aphasia include agnosia, or the inability to understand or recognize certain sensory stimuli, and apraxia, the inability to execute learned motor movements not due to sensory or motor disturbances. Strokes frequently induce aphasia in adults, with children acquiring such a disorder after a head injury. Mild aphasics typically have word finding difficulties with more severe instances characterized by communication and language dysfunctioning. Language disabilities range from the relatively minor language dysfunctioning of dysgraphia to severe language comprehension impairments as in the instance of autism.

Autism

A severe language disability as noted under the 1990 (P.L. 101–476) amendments to P.L. 94–142 is the condition of **autism**. Besides severe language problems, autistic individuals display abnormal behavior patterns. Autistic individuals lack the language comprehension and awareness necessary for successful adaptation to school, home, and the environment. Autistic children can learn to read words quite well but have been shown to lack appropriate comprehension skills for sufficient understanding of presented reading material. Dyslexics when presented with the same material as autistics will exceed the comprehension performance of the autistics even though the autistics' phonological decoding skills are intact (Frith & Snowling, 1983).

After considering the different correlating symptoms and behaviors associated with dyslexia and other learning disabilities types, it would be important to be sensitive to the ethnicity of the individuals tested. There are factors to consider when testing individuals from different ethnic backgrounds. Our rich cultural diversity demands that there be an understanding of the unique cognitive and psychological strengths and weaknesses of all (Graham, 1992).

Subcultural Factors and Considerations

First and foremost, it would be important to identify dyslexic children from all backgrounds as the condition of dyslexia affects individuals from all cultural backgrounds and languages (Lerner, 1989; Lerner & Chen, 1992). There is no research consensus as to the over- or under-representation of certain minority groups in classrooms for children with learning disabilities (McLeskey, Waldron, & Wornhoff, 1990). Certainly one must consider the causes for depressed test scores in some groups of minority children cited in the literature (see Hale, 1983). However, as Eysenck (1984) and others point out, there are not innate cultural differences in intelligence or other academic abilities borne out in the research. Therefore, one must look toward factors which involve test preparations, test administrations, and educational programming.

Meaningful activities that promote multiculturalism include printed materials that are authentic and positive portrayals of the rich cultural heritages of today's families. For example, books written that capture the rich Central American lifestyle include: *Family Pictures-Cuadros DeFamilia* by Garza, Children's Book Press, San Francisco, 1990; *My Aunt Otilia's Spirits* by Garcia, Children's Book Press, San Francisco, 1987; and *The Banza* by Wolkstein, E.P. Dutton, New York, 1981 (Casper, 1994). For the student with dyslexia, repeated readings, retellings, and so on would be needed (see chapter 6) to reinforce presented materials. It is recommended that structured lesson activities be used that incorporate a multi-sensory interactive approach for the full benefit of enrichment for the student with dyslexia.

Personality Factors to Consider

Oakland and Glutting (1990, p. 90) recommend that when testing minority children that "cautious . . . test interpretations" be made when the personality traits of good attention, self-confidence, and a high degree of cooperation are not observed.

Cultural Differences

Culture-Free Tests Not Recommended

Cultural differences are considered in this book in terms of sensitivity to the individual differences, interests, and backgrounds of students when planning education curriculum. However, it is important to keep in mind that innate cultural differences in abilities and disabilities have not been proven. This point has been a matter of discussion in the area of testing. Although some tests are more culturally loaded than others (e.g., WISC-III versus the Bender-Gestalt), it is neither possible nor prudent to expect minority children to undergo culture-free or culture-fair tests (Sattler, 1992). After all, intelligence and academic measures of assessment do measure our ability to function in the culture in which we live. As such, we take the position that examiners be sensitive to the rich cultural diversity and special needs of all individuals, but that screening be as uniform as possible in order to ensure equal education opportunities and subsequent job opportunities for all.

Special Considerations Involved in Test Administrations with Individuals from Different Cultural Backgrounds

There are special test considerations for ethnic minorities which can be used in order to optimize test performance. These would include providing verbal reinforcement (Witmer, Bornstein, & Dunham, 1971) and the establishment of good test rapport, a positive and affirming test atmosphere, and the use of native language (e.g., Spanish) or dialect (e.g., black dialect) (Bernal, 1984). Such measures have been shown to improve test performances of minority children (Bernal, 1984). Additionally, "observations of the [minority] child's behavior during the actual assessment coupled with other assessment tools, including environmental observations and personal interviews, are encouraged and allow the clinician to gain the most knowledge and form the best possible hypothesis regarding the child's cognitive strengths and weaknesses" (Black, 1993, p.10). Certainly the measures listed would be considered common sense and good solid testing for all individuals. Special sensitivity, however, to the cultural diversity and ethnicity of others can only optimize the educational experiences for the children and individuals we serve.

Curriculum Planning

There is a lack of appropriate educational programs for students of culturally diverse backgrounds in the LD area (Smith & Luckasson, 1995). Chapters 4 through 7 provide many instructional suggestions for individuals who work with students with dyslexia, and we would recommend adaptations within bilingual programs by bilingual professionals and that cultural considerations always be involved. Several graphics have been provided which could be used across the curriculum. The key to any planning effort is to make the instruction integrative and relevant to the learner's interests, strengths and deficits, cognitive learning style, and developmental level. Figures 1-3 and 1-4 depict semantic maps or webs of how concrete/abstract subject matter at all levels can be integrated across the curriculum before specific strategies/materials are implemented. Chapters 4–8 will provide specific curriculum materials and suggestions for professionals and parents alike. As in any well rounded program, the overall health and well-being of all children need special attention.

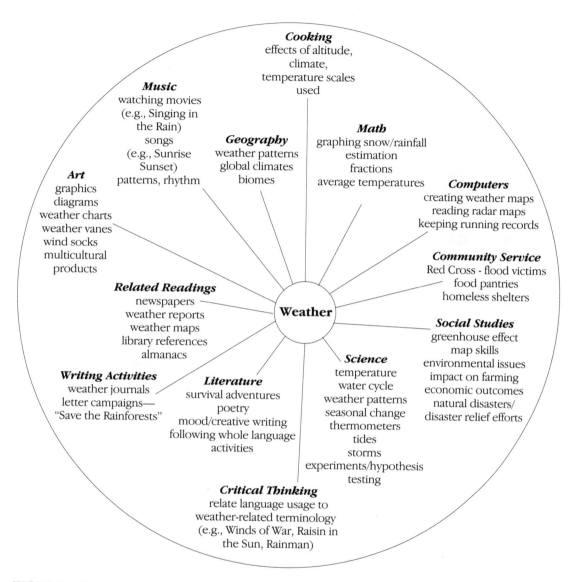

FIGURE 1-3 Integrating Across the Curriculum, at the Elementary Level

HIV/AIDS—Implications for Students with Dyslexia and Other Special Needs

Greg Louganis... born January 29, 1960 and only 16 when he won a silver medal at the 1976 Olympics. Louganis won 4 of 4 Olympic gold medals in both platform and springboard diving competition at the 1984 and 1988 Olympics. He has also won 47 United States diving titles and 6 of 6 Pan American gold medals in 1979, 1983, and 1987. Shortly before the 1988 Olympics, Louganis discovered he was HIV positive. The revelation of Olympic gold medalist Greg Louganis

Medical

The medical world has made tremendous progress in understanding genetics. The use of amniocentesis to determine chromosome abnormalities is outstanding. The students are exposed to this by actually arranging a karyotype of normal human chromosomes and comparing it to abnormal human chromosomes. Also, the students, in an independent research project, trace family diseases, i.e., heart disease, cancer, and find if they have a predisposition for the disease.

History

History plays a large role in genetics. The work of Gregor Mendel in the 1800's led to the discovery of genes. T.H. Morgan in the early 1900's was the first person to actually understand the dynamics of the gene.

The history of genetics also plays a more individualized role in each student's life. The students have to go into their family's history to make a pedigree of a certain trait.

Math/Probability

From Gregor Mendel's early experiments with pea plants, he mathematically figured out the ratios of expected traits by using probability mathematics. Later on in history, chromosome mapping of the fruit fly was determined by the use of mathematics. In this unit, students figure out ratios of crosses using the Punnett square, much like that of Mendel.

Business

The world of business houses genetic progress. Such processes as selective breeding help in the cattle industries to produce the most productive animals. Genetics helps in the business area of agriculture to produce the most productive crops.

Genetics

Art/Expression

Genetics touches the art world in the sense that diagrams and figures must be represented in text books. In an assignment, entitled, "Walk a Mile in My Genes," the students are asked to put themselves in the position of someone who is genetically different from themselves. They must express some of the paper in words, but art or any form of expression is acceptable.

Current Events

Genetics is very much in the news, e.g., techniques such as gene splicing, cloning, recombinant DNA, genetic counseling, etc. In an effort to enrich the students' minds, they are asked to bring in articles from newspapers/journals about current topics in genetics for class discussions, and as a part of this unit's bulletin board.

Counseling

The field of counseling is of major importance in the field of genetics. The students actually role model a genetic counselor, specifically a karyotypist. Also, the pros and cons of amniocentesis is a class discussion in which the students are able to view both sides of the issue.

Special Education

As genetic studies continue, we find that children with learning disabilities are the product of inheritance. Today, scientists are actually looking for the genes for learning disabilities.

FIGURE 1-4 Using the Language of Genetics Across the Curriculum

Source: Maryfrances Peters

(who is dyslexic) of contracting the HIV virus prior to some of his Olympic successes raises several questions regarding the "who will?" "what?" and "when?" of HIV/AIDS education with all populations, and in particular those with special needs. "Students with special needs cannot be ignored in the designing and implementing of HIV education programs" (Prater, Serna, Sileo, & Katz, 1995, p.72). The National Forum on HIV/AIDS Prevention Education for Children and Youth with Special Needs has suggested that children, especially those with disabilities, need health education that includes HIV infection prevention education (Byrom & Katz, 1991). The National Commission on AIDS (1994) believes that AIDS education must include (1) important factual knowledge for students, (2) skills building, (3) interpersonal explorations of attitudes and beliefs, and (4) access to health services. In discussions with students with dyslexia regarding the subject of HIV/AIDS, teachers and parents need to: provide oral and written materials on the subject; re-word and repeat key concepts; become knowledgeable about legal, religious, ethical, and medical issues surrounding the problem; consult with the "experts" for clarification and verification of "the facts;" and always be available to answer questions or to provide guidance when needed. Certainly school district policies (especially in regard to curricular materials) should always be consulted before any actions are taken. Local libraries; medical, physicians, and nursing associations; teaching hospitals, health agencies, public health departments, and so on should be able to provide tips, content, and presentation modes for HIV/AIDS materials to teachers and parents alike. Additionally, journals such as *Teaching Exceptional Children, Intervention in School and Clinic*, and the like have provided sample HIV/AIDS curriculum scope-and-sequence guidelines and written and audio-visual materials currently on the market.

Conclusion

Dyslexia has become known as a specific type of learning disability which is characterized foremost by difficulties in acquiring the reading skills necessary for age-appropriate reading success. The term dyslexia is used by the authors throughout the book to refer to all subtypes or types of this disorder, whether acquired (accident or injury) or developmental (inborn or congenital) in nature. Specifically, dyslexia is defined as "an inability to read which is inappropriate to the individual's level of general intelligence." In other words, there is a discrepancy between an individual's innate abilities (i.e., as measured by IQ tests) and reading/language performance. Dyslexia is thought to: (1) co-occur with social (e.g., more negative interactions with others) and behavioral (e.g., attention deficits) difficulties; (2) last a lifetime, with residual symptoms in adulthood after successful interventions (e.g., spelling problems, reduced reading rate, etc.); (3) be caused by some type of neurological dysfunctioning; (4) be genetically based or run in families; (5) involve different subtypes, with your authors favoring a visual-dysphonetic subtype, an auditory-linguistic subtype, and a mixed subtype (i.e., with visual/auditory-language deficiencies); and (6) require specific educational strategies and interventions as well as assistance from other professionals when needed (e.g., medical, psychological, etc.) (see Grosser & Spafford, 1995, p. 74). When establishing a dyslexia diagnosis, substantial "importance [needs to be] attached to the examiner's need to verify hypotheses with multiple sources of data (Kaufman, 1994 p. 279).

It should be kept in mind that conditions such as ADD (attention deficit disorders) are not synonymous with dyslexia but can co-exist with such problems. Individuals with dyslexia more often experience attention problems or ADD without hyperactivity and only 25% of those with dyslexia experience ADD. Certainly treatment modes are complicated by the existence of two problems and both need to be addressed. Remember the primary presenting problem of the dyslexic is reading and remedial prescriptions need to include reading techniques (see Chapters 4–7).

The reading problems of dyslexics probably result from a combination of factors with causation attributable to neurological anomalies which are either enhanced or intensified by environmental and social factors. The heterogeneity of this population (Spafford & Grosser, 1993) could result in subtyping categorization schemes; individualized assessment procedures, and remedial interventions (see Chapters 4–7). It is also apparent that dyslexia and other types of learning disabilities persist through to adulthood (White, Schumaker, Warner, Alley, & Deshler, 1980). The following chapter more closely defines dyslexia as we chose in this chapter to survey the field of learning disabilities in order to give the reader a broad overview of the field.

We will be looking at the problems of the dyslexic from a holistic point of view throughout the book. The social, emotional, academic, and psychological well-being of the individual with dyslexia need to be considered as " . . . happiness arises from the harmonious operation of all the sentiments of a well-organized and unified personality, one in which the principal sentiments support one another in a succession of actions all of which tend toward the same or closely allied and harmonious ends . . ." (McDougall, 1912, p. 156).

Keep in mind the "Wise Tidbits" in Figure 1-5 for students who have great difficulty learning.

Just to think about . . . [Making Learning Fun]

" . . . Making education a process of self instruction, and by consequence a process of pleasurable instruction . . ." (p. 159)

" . . . To educate rightly is not a simple and easy thing, but a complex and extremely difficult thing; the hardest task which devolves upon adult life . . ." (p. 215)

FIGURE 1-5   Herbert Spencer's Tips on Teaching

Source: Herbert Spencer, (1861). *Education: Intellectual, Oral, and Physical.*

C h a p t e r 2

Dyslexia Defined

> *". . . Reading is, indeed, a most intellectual accomplishment. So is music, too, in its perfection. We do by no means undervalue this noble and most delightful art, to which Socrates applied himself even in his old age. But one recommendation of the art of reading is, that it requires a constant exercise of mind . . .*
> —(MCGUFFEY'S SIXTH ECLECTIC READER, 1896, P. 59).

However, not everyone can enjoy this "most delightful art" as can be seen from the following passage:

> *". . .Again he thought of the Bible. He would never read. The Franciscan who had tried to help him had gone, spreading hands in impotent regrets. The taunting letters eluded, sliding away into futility. They would never be mastered. Lost lands could be regained but letters would rebuff him until the end . . . Talvas was baffled. Alain had once pointed to a row of letters and spelled out 'The rain falls in the valleys.' At another time seemingly identical letters had become 'They strewed branches in the way,' and yet later were transformed into, 'the wet road below was covered with fallen twigs'. . .*—(VANSITTART, 1964, PP. 87–88).

Dyslexia—Still an Elusive Disorder

Why is reading so frustrating and baffling for so many individuals who appear to have normal intellectual ability and educational opportunities? The answer many times will be that such individuals are afflicted by what has come to be named dyslexia. Dyslexia is an elusive reading disorder for many that afflicts up to 5% of our population. Elusiveness in the sense that it is difficult to capture or grasp the true nature and causes of this perplexing problem. Only after a careful review of

TABLE 2-1   Correlating Behaviors of Dyslexia

- Delayed Language Development
- Late Talkers
- Verbal Deficits
- Visual Anomalies
- Oral Reading Miscues
- Sequencing Difficulties
- Familial History
- Gross Motor Problems
- Written Expressive Language Deficits
- Spelling Errors
- Reduced Reading Rates as Children and Adults
- Verbal-Performance IQ Discrepancies
- ACID Profile for Males (lowest scores on Arithmetic, Coding, Information, and Digit Span of WAIS or WISC)
- AVID Profile for Females (lowest scores on Arithmetic, Vocabulary, Information, and Digit Span of WAIS or WISC)
- Left-Right Confusions
- IQ Average = 90s
- Time and Directional Confusions
- Lack of Problem-Solving Strategies
- Attention Problems
- Less On-Task Behaviors
- Less Follow-Through
- Less Independent Behaviors
- Social Behavior Problems
- Memory Deficits
- Erratic Eye Movements

the literature and research available to us can we draw some educated hypotheses and conclusions regarding definition, possible causes, appropriate assessment tools, and effective remedial procedures or methods. Remember the correlating behaviors covered in the last chapter as listed in Table 2-1.

Keeping an Open Mind

As with many major issues, opinions and prejudices run rampant, and unfortunately, the public that would benefit finds itself confused and perplexed. Research efforts need to be undertaken to help resolve many issues confronting educators who must provide service options/opportunities for students with dyslexia. One of the most controversial topics in today's education establishment is the determination of an appropriate educational setting for students who are dyslexic and learning disabled. Essentially, there are those professionals who wish to move toward a full **inclusionary model** which would involve placing students with dyslexia in a regular classroom situation with support services available within the classroom setting (e.g., the resource teacher or consultant would work in the regular classroom). The second school of thought is considered a **mainstream approach** which accepts special education placements into the regular classroom generally without services; services may be provided if those involved in the educational planning of the child deem these services to be in the best interests of the child.

The Learning Disabilities Association of American (LDA) in their July/August 1994 newsletter puts forth the position of its leadership regarding inclusion. It states that a continuum of services should be available for those with learning disabilities and that responsible inclusion should (1) operationally define responsibilities and roles of education professionals, (2) promote professional staff development, (3) identify collaborative teams for training and consultation, (4) ensure that individual education plans (IEP's) meet the individual learning styles and needs of the student, and (5) be accepted by a consensus of staff members. Tables 2–2 and 2–3 summarize some similarities and differences of these two approaches and the pros and cons of full inclusion models. We would agree with Roberts and Mather (1995) that, "regardless of whether an individual with LD is educated in the regular education or resource room, the demand for individualized instruction remains constant . . . and full integration programs are not effective for **all** students" (pp. 50–51).

When healthy discussions are offered by those who have knowledge of the subject, "such discussion brings benefits to the public needing information and clinical assistance . . . and to the involved clinicians who need all possible explorations of concepts and procedures" (Getman, 1985, p. 505). Getman so aptly conveys one of the basic features of this book. Alternative, opposing, and even far-reaching hypotheses for, methods of research in, and treatments for dyslexia will be presented in the interest of discussion, acquisition of knowledge, reflection, and furthering the positive growth of research in the field. Getman, in particular, has been dismissed even though his work can be considered a building block for much of the progress in visual field studies. The increased interest in the subject matter of dyslexia in part stems from the fact that many famous individuals in history and recent times have had this disorder.

TABLE 2–2 Mainstream and Inclusion Proponents— Similarities/Differences

Similarities

- Both support REI (regular education initiatives return students to regular classroom) to the maximum extent possible
- Both believe social benefits occur when integration takes place
- Both believe cooperative learning and community living can be enhanced
- Both believe gainful employment opportunities are enhanced with REI initiatives
- Both lack a subtantial research base to affirm that one approach should be used to the exclusion of the other

Differences

- Inclusionary Programs are "In-Class Models" and mainstream practices allow for "Pull-Out" classes for academic/social remediation where necessary
- Mainstream proponents emphasize integration after students prove they can handle the work/classroom environment. Inclusion efforts don't require students to keep up with their peers; classroom adaptations are made.

2-3 Pros and Cons to Fully Integrated In-Class Models

Pros	Cons
1. Colleague consultation, collaborative teaching, and cooperative ventures provide a rich diversity of teaching methods/materials.	1. Lack of adequate physical space can result in an uncomfortable classroom environment where there are just too many people in the classroom.
2. All students can receive individualized education plans with smaller student–teacher ratios.	2. The average student can be educationally shortchanged if instructional efforts are not even-handed.
3. Socialization opportunities and social skills acquisition can move forward in positive ways with increased occasions for interactions for all students.	3. Severely disabled, behaviorally impaired students can disrupt the education of other students if they aren't socially equipped to handle an integrated setting.
4. Responsibility is shared in program planning, curriculum choices, and implementation efforts. Having classroom professionals and paraprofessionals in the classroom provides assistive consultation teaching/involvement in specialty areas in which most regular teachers lack intensive training/study.	4. Hierarchial responsibilities have not been well defined for teachers. Staff development efforts regarding inclusion implementation have been slow in coming. Sometimes there is a feeling of "shoving programs at teachers" who are not adequately prepared to handle children with disabilities even with other professionals present.
5. Opportunities to build self-esteem and self-concepts can present themselves when students are made to feel as though they are an integral part of the classroom.	5. Students who are self-conscious about their learning disabilities may be reluctant to volunteer or participate in class.

Famous Individuals with Dyslexia

There is an ever growing list of famous individuals who have been described as dyslexic and who have been extremely successful in the reading world. Several of these were mentioned in the preface and the list includes: Winston Churchill, George Patton, Woodrow Wilson, Charles Darwin, Thomas Edison, Emile Zola, Hans Christian Andersen, Albert Einstein, Galileo, Leonardo da Vinci, Carl Jung, and Michelangelo. These individuals were considered gifted and also dyslexic. Certain identifying characteristics portray this population (see Table 2-4).

Posthumous Diagnoses

Adelman and Adelman postulate that some individuals have posthumously diagnosed some famous individuals as dyslexic because of documented instances of "developmental delay, illness, unhappy school experiences, or anomalies related to learning to read, spell or do math" (Adelman & Adelman, 1987, p. 270). They further decry these posthumous diagnoses as fund-raising gimmicks that actually

TABLE 2-4   Identifying Characteristics of Gifted Dyslexics

I. Learning/Cognitive

1. Generally, Full Scale IQ = 110 or above
2. There are Performance – Verbal IQ discrepancies in some cases
3. Oral vocabulary advanced for age or grade level; reading average or below grade level
4. Quick thinkers; able to reason through a problem; analytical thinking excellent
5. Inquisitive and constantly questioning (can be misinterpreted as a challenge to the teacher)
6. Reading/Writing/Spelling Skills are not commensurate with intellectual potential
7. Math Skills frequently above average
8. Has a particular hobby (e.g. baseball cards) that she/he will thoroughly research

II. Creativity

1. Creates novel or original solutions to problems
2. Risk taker—willingly enters into adventurous situations
3. Sensitive to others, the environment, and the fine arts
4. Understands subtle humor
5. Can be unconventional and/or nonconforming to standard expectations

III. Social

1. Tends to be independent with a small circle of friends; generally introverted, quiet, and shy
2. Is persistent and can be stubborn
3. Can irritate others by frequent questions and self-absorption in his/her own lifespace
4. Can become narrowly focused or miss the "big picture" of what's going on outside of his/her lifespace
5. Self-critical and easily frustrated by unfinished and incorrect work
6. Concerned with black and white answers to unresolved questions/issues; has difficulty with open-ended social situations requiring social finasse/aptitude
7. Can have low self-esteem, low self-concept and diminished view of self-worth
8. External locus of control syndrome
9. Will have difficulty accepting giftedness and how to best utilize talents/gifts
10. Often will not share work because of the fear of rejection

draw attention away from the fact that the definitions and diagnostic criteria that led to the designation of these individuals as dyslexic were less than satisfactory. We hope to unmuddy some of these waters by carefully reviewing the research and clearly stating the issues. Before defining terms and issues and providing substantiating research, we would like to provide a birds-eye view of some dyslexics' thoughts, feelings, problems, concerns, hurdles, compensatory strategies, family lives and personal issues, as these insights will provide the foundation for your understanding of what dyslexia is and what it is like to be dyslexic. There is an old Indian saying that to understand someone we should walk a mile wearing his moccasins. We can never pretend to know what it's like to be in those shoes, but we can do our best to walk those miles to bridge the gap of understanding and empathy.

CASE STUDY

An Adult Coping with Dyslexia

Self-Realization of the Problem

Jill is a 45-year-old successful businesswoman who is treasurer and manager of a family commercial quick-print business. Her expertise and business acumen have assisted her husband in increasing their small company's earnings 40-fold. As part of her responsibilities, Jill proofs many of the jobs in press. A few years ago, she had to approve the final copy of a booklet on dyslexia for a local college. In reading this booklet, Jill confirmed that she too, was dyslexic. She describes experiencing "fear" and "excitement" as well as a "sense of a relief" for she had in writing, "a description of me—that's the easiest way to put it."

Frequent Misinterpretations of Symptoms

Jill now could come to terms with her problem as she went through life unsure of why she encountered so many problems in learning how to read. She was frequently told as a child by teachers that she was "lazy," "stupid," "unmotivated," and that she "just didn't work hard enough." Her parents were perplexed and nonverbal about this situation and decided to pull her out of school after a dismal first-grade experience. They placed Jill in a remedial reading program which, unfortunately, did not result in substantial growth on Jill's part. In fact, the year's absence from the public schools was essentially considered a retention which reaffirmed to Jill and the public school system that she was "stupid."

Coping

Effects of Positive Reinforcement

Jill vividly remembers being "super-good" in the classroom so that she could obtain an *A* in something—classroom behavior. She remembers never being praised and when praised "would hold on to the praise for dear life and not let go of it" because praise from teachers was never there—she couldn't read. Jill vividly recalls an incident in science class in the third grade which involved a teacher stating in front of the entire class, "Jill, you asked an excellent and intelligent question." Jill relays that, "I was so thrilled to be called intelligent that I didn't shut up for the rest of the class—I remember that incident like it was yesterday."

The Heart of the Problem

Reading problems were at the heart of Jill's painful school career.

> *I always remember having trouble with reading. I would have difficulty sounding out words—I couldn't sound out words—the words never fit to-*

gether right. If I heard the word said first, then I could learn the words. I did best in classes like science when the material was presented verbally. I had a hard time comprehending because I had a hard time sounding out words. I remember making reversals like "96" for "69" and "dod for bob." Spelling was my best subject if I could memorize the words just before the test. Afterwards I would forget the spellings and start all over again. For years, I spelled, "those" as "thoughs" and anything with a "f" sound incorrectly, like "phone" as "fone." I remember never learning how to spell "spaghetti." I would have to use a dictionary to assist me in spelling "spaghetti" even today. I don't write anything without a dictionary next to me.

(When asked to spell "spaghetti," Jill spelled s-p-a-g-e-t-t-i.)

Peer Relations

Lack of Confidence

When under pressure, my spelling and reading abilities get much worse. I remember becoming frustrated when discussing test scores with my peers all through my school years. This is because I remember working harder than the other kids. So I withdrew from people because I was ashamed—I would try to hide my test scores. However, I was never teased by kids and I always had a few close friends. In my family, my sisters didn't think I was intellectual enough. It was never anything verbal but it was in the way they related to me.

Lowered Self-Esteem

I remember being made fun of in a cute way in school at times. For example, I had trouble with the words, "subscription" and "prescription." I made the comment one time that I had to go to the pharmacy and have a "subscription filled." They told me that you get a subscription for a magazine and prescription for medicine. Boy, that dredged up memories.

Depressed School Performance

I can remember in high school I paid a lot of attention in class. As long as it was presented verbally and placed on the chalkboard, I could get Cs. When I had to read and study without that verbal help, I was lost. It just didn't make sense to me. I think that's why I had so much trouble in math, chemistry, English, term papers and just about everything else. But I loved French and had a tutor in French. I couldn't get any higher than a C because I had so much trouble conjugating verbs and things like that. I did best in class when the teachers talked a lot and put work on the board and summarized our books. I had a lot of trouble with classes when we had to do the readings all on our own. I would panic and freeze up. My biggest frustration came with my greatest love—my figure skating."

Dyslexia Affects All Facets of Life

Outside Interests
Figure skating was my love. I spent four to five hours every day skating—before school, after school, weekends—you name it, I was skating. But figure skating was an overwhelming frustration. I mean being left-handed and having problems with directions did it. (An aside: My Dad was left-handed but he didn't have any learning problems. He went to an Ivy League College.) When you learn how to skate you learn to jump and spin in the same direction because you should be spinning in the same direction whether you are on the ground or in the air.

Orientation and Directional Problems

I never learned how to spin and jump in the same direction which is alien to the nature of figure skating. I learned how to jump in what was alien to me—in the wrong direction. Although I learned how to spin turning to the right which was normal for me, but I was taught jumping rotating to the left. This caused problems as the jumps got more difficult because the rotation became confusing for me—rotating in the direction which was confusing to me, I became disorientated when landing. It wasn't until I was older that I could understand why I never became became a good jumper. Looking back on that, anything more than 1-½ rotations in the air I couldn't do.

College Failure Not Forever

I pursued figure skating for a year after high school and then went to college. I went to college for three-quarters of a year. My grades were so bad they wouldn't allow me to continue. It was too frustrating. But I did get an "A" in marketing class because it was a lecture class. The final presentation was an oral report which I did well on. Math killed me. I got a 37 on the first test and then dropped out. I can remember freezing completely—choking. It was just like high school all over again. But I'll get this degree; I want to prove it to myself. I have such a fear of failure. It paralyzes me from doing it, but come hell or high water I'll get my degree. My husband says I deserve this degree based on my life experiences.

Support Systems

My husband is extremely supportive and has encouraged me to improve my reading. This kind of support is critical in order to go on. From the standpoint of someone else reading this, the most paralyzing thing for a dyslexic is to be handed something to read and then to try to make sense of that in front of other people. I have learned that if I take this material on my own and then read and re-read it and then share it with my husband, I can be successful. Dyslexics need someone to lean on who understands them. I've also learned to say I'll get back to you. For the dyslexic, there is a lot of panic when confronted with something to read and possibly not knowing what's there—the fear, the anger.

Self-Concept Related to Environmental Feedback

Developing Reading Strategies Boosts Self-Confidence

I always thought there was something wrong with me. I didn't realize until I was about 40 years old that there was nothing wrong with me. In fact, I'm glad to know that the more I try to read and understand, the better I get. When I read, if I have to comprehend, I make sure there is dead silence and that I'm not too tired. There can't be any confusing things going on in the room. Then I look at each word—word for word. I'm proud of that. I'm working hard to force myself to do things right in reading like reading from left to right.

Empathy a Necessity

I hope people can relate to what I'm saying because there are a lot of people out there like me and that they don't have to reach the age of 40 before understanding that they aren't stupid. It might not just be them. It could be another family member. My brother has reading and spelling problems like me and it took him six years to go through a two-year college. He is extremely successful now.

Developing a Positive Attitude

Facing the Realities

I wish I knew at 8 years old what I know now. I'm extremely proud of what I have done on my own. I hope people who are dyslexic reading this and don't know it will learn about their problem before the age of 40 like me. I've not given up and have taken the attitude: I can do it! I got this attitude from my parents. They always told me I could do it. I hope this helps someone else to become more confident. That's the reason I'm dredging up so many painful memories.

Professional Support Needed

But now I also have to look to my future. I would love a tutor to help me to read better. Dyslexics need to seek that help and not be ashamed. Do you know a tutor that can help me? I guess I can say that I love to read now because I know that I'm not stupid and I'm a successful business-woman. If I can manage 20 people and a small business, I can learn how to read better.

Summing It Up

To summarize in Jill's words, ". . . I was so thrilled to be called intelligent that I didn't shut up. . . . I would hold on to praise for dear life and not let go . . . the most paralyzing thing for a dyslexic is to be handed something to read and then try to make sense of that in front of other people . . . dyslexics need someone to lean on—someone who understands them . . . "

Now that the reader can feel and sense what dyslexia is all about, we can now delve into the "cold hard facts and figures."

Dyslexia Defined

Reading is one of the central difficulties of students with learning disabilities that can lead to behavior problems, anxiety, and a lack of motivation. Even reading habits are less than satisfactory with such overt behaviors noted as losing one's place, lateral head movements, the holding of reading material too close to the face, and an obvious lack of confidence during the reading act itself (Mercer, 1987). As such, reading problems and dyslexia in particular, can greatly impact the quality of one's academic, social, and psychological well-being.

Word Origin

The word dyslexia can be broken down into the letter-groups *dys* and *lexia*, or *distorted words* in reading and writing. The literature in the 1890s and early 1900s tended to focus on the terms **word blindness** or "alexia" which would indicate a total lack of reading and/or writing skills (Spache, 1976a, p. 179). Hinshelwood (1896) reported that Kussmaul in 1877 identified adults who had an acquired inability to read or word blindness and that a similar phenomenon was described in 1877 by Berlin (cited in Hinshelwood, 1896), who coined the term dyslexia.

Word Blindness

Although W.P. Morgan (1896) is many times credited with introducing the concept of word blindness, his description of a typical dyslexic is really the foundation for our current definition. In 1892, Dejerine published a case study of an individual who, after a stroke, developed an inability to read. Dejerine described this condition as alexia and after the death of the patient, discovered a lesion in the left angular gyrus which might have caused the reading problem. Dejerine's alexia is different from dyslexia in the sense that the individual lost a previously held ability to read. With the dyslexic, reading skills are impaired from birth. Orton's 1925 critical paper entitled, " 'Word-blindness' in School Children," brought this focus on neurological implications to the forefront and his report of the neurological correlates of childhood dyslexia remains "one of the best clinical descriptions of the disorder" (Shaywitz et al., 1991, p. 29).

Dyslexia—A Learning Disability

Kirk Introduces "LD" Terminology

Although dyslexia has been described in various forms since the late 1800s, it wasn't until the 1960s that this condition was called a learning disability. Mercer (1987) describes the frustration parents experienced during the 1950s and 1960s when some reading/language disabled children weren't permitted to attend special education classes because they weren't blind, retarded, physically impaired, or named in some other special needs category. A 1963 national conference was held in order to address this problem. Samuel A. Kirk introduced the term *learning disability* at the conference as one that could be used as a special needs category for children who didn't acquire language/reading skills commensurate with their age and ability levels. According to Kirk and Kirk (1976), there are children ". . . who are not receptive to language but are not deaf, some are not able to perceive visually but are not blind, and some cannot learn by ordinary methods of instruction but are not mentally retarded . . . [this group of children] come under the heading of 'specific learning disabilities . . .'" (pp. 3–4).

World Federation of Neurology Definition

Critchley's Influence

The Research Group on Developmental Dyslexia of the World Federation of Neurology provides a basic definition which is still embraced in most education circles today. "Dyslexia is a disorder manifested by difficulty in learning to read despite conventional instruction, adequate intelligence, and socio-cultural opportunity. It is dependent upon fundamental cognitive disabilities which are frequently of constitutional origin" (Critchley, 1970). The alert reader will have noticed that the hardest, basic aspects of this definition are the exclusionary ones; in other words, dyslexia is being defined on the basis that it is not a matter of poor instruction, low intelligence, or sociocultural deprivation. This definition does not venture into subtypes nor does it point to a definitive cause. Critchley (1981) refocused this definition in the 1980s to what he termed **developmental dyslexia** which he defined as follows: "Developmental dyslexia: a learning disability which initially shows itself by difficulty in learning to read, and later by erratic spelling and by lack of facility in manipulating written as opposed to spoken words. The condition is cognitive in essence, and usually genetically determined. It is not due to intellectual inadequacy or to lack of socio-cultural opportunity, or to faults in the technique of teaching, or to any known structural brain defect. It probably represents a specific maturational defect which tends to lessen as the child gets older, and is capable of considerable improvement, especially when appropriate reme-dial help is offered at the earliest opportunity" (pp. 1–2).

Critchley's 1970 Definition Preferred

We would prefer the more general definition Critchley offered in 1970 as opposed to his 1981 conceptualization. Recent neurophysiological evidence would indicate that some dyslexics do indeed evidence different anatomical brain structures and this condition appears to have a physiological basis. Additionally, in some cases the symptoms associated with dyslexia do not lessen and there is not a great deal of evidence to point to maturational defects.

DSM-IV Criteria

The Diagnostic and Statistical Manual IV (DSM IV, American Psychiatric Associa-tion, 1994) doesn't define the term dyslexia as such but rather discusses reading disorders under subsection 315.00 of Learning Disorders (Academic Skills Disor-ders). Three conditions are listed which parallel the NJCLD (National Joint Com-mittee for Learning Disabilities) (1988) definition and in a general sense, Critchley's basic premises. These conditions are:

> A. *Reading achievement, as measured by an individually administered standardized test of reading accuracy or comprehension, is substan-tially below that expected given the person's chronological age, mea-sured intelligence, and age-appropriate education.*
> B. *The disturbance in A significantly interferes with academic achieve-ment or activities of daily living that require reading skills.*
> C. *If a sensory deficit is present, the learning difficulties are in excess of those usually associated with it.*
>
> (DSM-IV, 1994, p. E:1).

A five-axis system is used by DSM-IV to classify and categorize presenting prob-lems.

Orton's Contributions

Orton (1925) believed that dyslexics had average intelligence with traditional in-telligence tests not fairly measuring their true IQ potential. He compared the prob-lems of dyslexics to those of acquired alexics with agraphia (loss of basic reading and writing skills) and he assumed that the disturbance was a functional one; that is, no visible structural abnormalities would be seen in the left hemisphere. Orton also noted the elevated number of dyslexics who were stutterers and that a dis-proportionate number of dyslexic were left-handers. He further found that dyslex-ics were preponderantly male. The belief that a greater percentage of dyslexics are left-handed and male has been steadfastly held up through the 1980s. However, recent discussions have contradicted these long-held beliefs.

Causation Linked to Cerebral Dysfunctioning— 1802 to Present

According to Wiederholt (1974), Franz Joseph Gall in 1802 and Bouillaud in 1825 attempted to link certain brain activities with specific loci in the brain which led to the hypothesis, by an opthalmologist named Berlin, that cerebral disease was the culprit for a group of patients who experienced great difficulties in the reading area. He, like many other medical practitioners, saw dyslexia as a type of aphasia. Today, causation is thought to be linked to some type of cerebral hemispheric dysfunction either in the language area, the vision area, or both.

Dyslexia-Aphasia Link

The term aphasia refers to a loss of speech/language functions which can usually be traced to cerebral disease or damage of some type. Wiig and Semel (1980) define the aphasic individual as one who has, "an acquired language disorder caused by brain damage with complete or partial impairment of language comprehension, formulation and use" (p. 443). Historically, there have been two primary types of aphasia which have been studied for over a century: (1) Broca's aphasia (1865) which implicates the posterior portion of the left frontal lobe which is involved in speech production (the individual understands speech but is unable to reproduce accurately intended communications); there are articulation difficulties and a paucity of speech and (2) Wernicke's aphasia (1874) which is a type of receptive disorder characterized by faulty speech comprehension seen in the "nonsensical" speech uttered by the afflicted individual.

Speech Dysfunctioning in Aphasia

Jackson (1874) was one of the first to trace the hemispheric functioning of speech production and comprehension to specific hemispheres; he assigned speech production to the left hemisphere and speech comprehension to the right hemisphere. Certainly, the speech dysfunctioning of the aphasic individual would be expected to impact the reading process. However, there is not any type of consensual agreement that dyslexia is a type of aphasia. The view that defects localized in specified brain regions such as Broca's and Wernicke's areas result specifically in motor or sensory language abnormalities, respectively, in turn causing dyslexia, is in itself open to debate. This localization position has been supplemented by a more comprehensive view of language.

Current Conceptualizations Tied into 1896 Definition

The current conceptualization of dyslexia, which is somewhat universally accepted now (Melikian, 1990) refers to the reading problems of these individuals despite average to above-average intelligence; this implies a failure to obtain reading skills commensurate with age and ability (Spafford & Grosser, 1991). This view is consistent with Morgan's (1896) basic premise that there are individuals who are word-blind or who experience difficulty reading despite adequate intelligence. For dyslexics, causation does not appear to be consistent with the apparent brain damage incurred by aphasic individuals and their subsequent speech production and comprehension problems. Although some dyslexics may exhibit aphasic symptoms, the primary presenting problem is a reading deficiency, not a speech and language disorder. The current definition of dyslexia many times is discussed in reference to other types of learning disabilities under the term, *reading disorder*. The National Joint Committee on Learning Disabilities (NJCLD) offers a comprehensive and research-based definition of learning disabilities which includes dyslexia under the umbrella of reading disorder.

Inclusionary Focus—NJCLD 1988 Definition

The National Joint Committee for Learning Disabilities (NJCLD) whose membership includes representatives from the Speech–Language–Hearing Association, the Association for Children and Adults with LD, the International Reading Association, the Orton Dyslexia Association, and others has proposed an *inclusionary* definition (not to be confused with *inclusionary classrooms* described in Chapter 9) of learning disabilities as opposed to the more traditional exclusionary definition cited in the Federal Register (1977). The definition proposed by the NJCLD reads as follows:

> *Learning disabilities is a general term that refers to a heterogeneous group of disorders manifested by significant difficulties in the acquisition and use of listening, speaking, reading, writing, reasoning, or mathematical abilities. These disorders are intrinsic to the individual, presumed to be due to central nervous system dysfunction, and may occur across the life span. Problems in self-regulatory behaviors, social perceptions and social interaction may exist with learning disabilities but do not by themselves constitute a learning disability. Although learning disabilities may occur concomitantly with other handicapping conditions (for example, sensory impairment, mental retardation (MR), serious emotional disturbance (ED)) or with extrinsic influences (such as cultural differences, insufficient or inappropriate instruction), they are not the result of those conditions or influences (NJCLD, 1988, p.1).*

IDEA Definition PL 94-142

(Note: this law has been renamed the Individuals with Disabilities Education Act [IDEA] of 1990 under PL 101-476 of Learning Disabilities.)

The proposed definition of LD can be compared to that which is most commonly accepted:

> *"Specific learning disability" means a disorder in one or more of the basic psychological processes involved in understanding or in using language,*

*spoken or written, which may manifest itself in an imperfect ability to lis-
ten, think, speak, read, write, spell, or to do mathematical calculations. The
term includes such conditions as perceptual handicaps, brain injury, minimal brain dysfunction, dyslexia, and developmental aphasia. The term
does not include children who have learning problems which are primarily the result of visual, hearing, or motor handicaps, of mental retardation,
of emotional disturbance, or of environmental, cultural, or economic disadvantage (Federal Register, December 29, 1977, p. 65083)."*

The NJCLD definition presents several advantages according to Hammill, Leigh, Mc-
Nutt, and Larsen (1981). It (1) includes adults over a life-span, which is an improvement inasmuch as traditional emphases have been with children, (2) avoids
the wording of "basic psychological processes," "minimal brain dysfunction," and
"perceptual handicaps" as these are nebulous and controversial terms; (3) eliminates spelling disabilities as these are actually one segment of written language disabilities; and (4) clearly articulates that LD may occur with other handicapping
conditions such as MR and ED. Hammill (1990) asserts that the NJCLD 1988 definition is the most widely used and commonly accepted definition of learning disabilities today. The fact that learning disabilities persist over a life-time could be
due, in part, to the "**Matthew Effect**."

The Matthew Effect

The Matthew Effect as described by Stanovich (1986b) possibly adversely impacts
the cognitive development of the individual with dyslexia. According to the
Matthew Effect, students with dyslexia experience more intense symtomatologies
as they get older. That is, reading and language difficulties (e.g., spelling problems)
intensify because of increased vocabulary/language demands as one progresses
through school. In the words of Stanovich, "the rich [proficient readers]-get-richer"
and "the poor [deficient readers]-get-poorer" (p. 382). The Matthew Effect is particular evident in the slight decline of IQ scores over time (Full Scale and Verbal IQs)
with children who experience dyslexia (see Schmidt, Kuryliw, Saklofske, & Yackulic, 1989). When looking at IQ scores, researchers and practitioners in the field
typically limit dyslexia diagnoses to those individuals with IQs over 80 (average IQ
score = 90–110).

Standard Score Discrepancies or "The How of Determining Discrepancy Differences Between Intelligence and Achievement"

What is a Discrepancy Difference? It is crucial to the differential diagnosis of the
dyslexic individual!!! (Please note: The following section was designed for use by
School Psychologists or others with a mathematics/statistics background.)

Background

Test standardization adds greatly to the usefulness of test results. If both intelligence and an academic performance (e.g., reading comprehension) are measured with standardized tests, the student's performance on the intelligence test can be compared with that student's score on the reading comprehension test (one type of performance test). In making this comparison, the examiner can tell whether the two test scores are consistent or whether, on the other hand, one of those scores is out of line with the other (thus, a discrepancy). When academic test scoring is well below the student's measured ability level, we refer to this as an ability-performance discrepancy. Frequently a numerical criterion is used to decide whether this discrepancy is large enough to indicate that a learning disability or problem exists. Such a criterion is a reading comprehension score that is *1.5 standard deviation units* (or more) below the student's tested ability level.

Comparing Unlike Test Measures—That Is, Intelligence and Achievement

How can two different tests be compared numerically? Isn't this like trying to add or subtract five apples and seven oranges? True, the original score units on the reading comprehension tests are not identical with the sum of the subtest scores on a test of general intelligence. What we compare are not scores stated in the original test units, however. Instead, we compare two standard scores; a standard score is the number of standard deviation units above or below the mean (on each test) where that score is to be found. For standard scores to be computed, the data from many tested individuals (the standardization sample that appears in a test manual or technical manual for a test) should form a normal curve when the frequency of each score (e.g., how many people were tied at each score) is plotted on the Y-axis with the size of a score plotted from left to right on the X-axis. Such a frequency curve will tend to have a bell shape. Extremely low and extremely high scores tend to be rare; they will have low frequencies. Scores toward the middle of the scoring range will have higher frequencies and the scores at the very center of the range will have the highest frequencies of all. The bell-shaped curve is called the Gaussian or normal curve.

Determining Basic Statistics

The Mean

The mean or average performance of a group taking a test is equal to the sum of all their scores divided by the number of scores there are. The number of scores will be equal to N which is the sum total of all the score frequencies. If one person scored 5 out of 100, the frequency of that particular score of 5 is equal to 1. If three people scored 7, the frequency of that score is 3. Adding frequencies up to this point, we have 1 plus 3 or an N of 4. If the entire group had an average score of 78, and a given person scored 85, this person scored 7 points above the mean. That 7 points cannot be used directly when we compare one person's performance on that test measure with the same person's score on another test. We do use this score as a starting point, though. What we need to do is to look up the size of the standard deviation (a measure of variability around the mean of 78). That raises a new question, "Where do we learn what a test's standard deviation is?"

Finding Standard Deviation Information

To find the standard deviation of a test we look in the same place that gives us the mean or average performance for the standardization sample tested. Typically, publishers of tests provide a pamphlet or small book that is a test manual. The mean and the standard deviation of the entire group of people who were given the test are presented in the manual. This group is called the standardization sample, which should be updated from time to time as demographics change. The manual reports demographics or relevant facts (i.e., the percentage of Asians, Hispanics, African Americans, and so on taking the test) about people in that group (also age, gender, special needs, grade levels, socioeconomic status, total numbers per category, and so on). A test manual should report the correlation coefficients indicating the test's reliability (consistency over time) and validity. Specific types of reliability reported are test-retest, parallel forms, or split-half and specific types of validity reported include concurrent and predictive. For our present purpose, though, what we need are the test's average or *mean* (M), its *standard deviation* (SD), and the *student's score* on the test.

Converting a Raw Score into a Unit of Standard Deviation called the Standard Score or (z),   -
which is scored in standard deviation units.

What we will do now is convert the student's raw score on a test of general intelligence to a standard score (z). Take the difference $(X - M)$ between a student's hypothetical score $(X = 85)$ and a hypothetical mean score $(M = 78)$. The difference is +7. Suppose the standard deviation (SD) for the test from the test manual is 3.5. Dividing $X - M$ by the SD = $+7/3.5 = +2$. The result is the student's z-score, i.e., the standard score for this student on this test. Incidentally, the normal curve will show that the student is scoring higher than 97.5% of all the people who took the test (as inferred from the performance of the standardization group). Now, don't just look at this as following a recipe in a cookbook. If one SD is 3.5, then 2 SD are 7. Instead of setting up the calculation as a division problem, we can do equally well by directly perceiving how many SDs make up the difference between the student's score and the average score. We admit that we picked the numbers so that the z-score of 2 would be easily obtained and would come out to 2. Of course, you might run into examples where it's harder to get a count of the SDs by eyeballing the numbers. In such cases, it would make more sense to do the math and be sure of the accuracy of your result.

CASE 1   A Non-significant Discrepancy Between Reading Achievement and Overall Intellectual Ability *Discounting* PERHAPS the Presence of a Learning Disability or Dyslexia.

Subject: Duane

Test Results:

I. Determining Reading Achievement Standard Deviation WRAT-R (Wide-Range Achievement Test-Revised) Reading Subtest.

Duane's WRAT-R reading standard score from manual = 88. WRAT-R mean score for original standardization group = 100 and standard deviation = 15 (information from manual).

Now relate Duane's reading test score to unit normal curve which has a mean of 0 and SD = 1.

Duane's score of 88–100 (mean of standardization sample of 100) = –12. Now divide that deviation score (–12) by the standard deviation of the original sample of 15 = –.80.

Duane's reading WRAT-R subtest performance score has been converted to a z score or standard score in units of standard deviation to –.80.

II. WISC-III (Wechsler Intelligence Scale for Children—Revised)—Determining General Intellectual Ability Standard Deviation.

Manual Facts from the WISC-III: Scale or mean IQ = 100; the standard deviation unit = 15 IQ points.

Note: Both the WRAT-R and WISC-III have mean averages of 100 and standard deviations of 15.

Duane's Full Scale IQ = 95. Standard score on unit normal curve = (95) – (100) = –5 and –5/15 = –0.33 standard deviation units.

Duane's WISC-III Full Scale IQ performance converts to –.33 standard deviation units.

III. Determining the Overall Ability (using the WISC-III)-Achievement Discrepancy (using the WRAT-R Reading Subtest). Subtract the difference between the two standard scores: –0.33 – (–.80) = +0.47.

IV. Evaluate the Resultant Discrepancy Difference.

Duane's discrepancy of +0.47 is less than 1.5 standard deviation units generally accepted as statistically significant. We therefore do not consider Duane to have a specific reading disability.

---

*Note: For example, a discrepancy of –2.5 should be considered significantly *greater* than one of –1.5 (though –2.5 is "less" than –1.5) because it is the **absolute value** of these numbers that is the important thing.

Finding the Two "z" Scores

This student also took a reading comprehension test. This test was also standardized: Again, a large group was given the test and the mean and standard deviation of the test scores were computed. Our student's score on this one is 15 while the group mean is 20, as examples. On the reading test, the SD = 5. Let's calculate our student's standard score on the reading test. Take the 15 and subtract 20. This yields –5; note that this is a negative score. But this score of –5 is in raw score

CASE 2 A *Significant* Discrepancy Between Reading Overall Intellectual Ability and Reading Achievement Indicating PERHAPS the Presence of a Learning Disability or Dyslexia.

Subject: Crystal

Test Results:

I. Determining Reading Achievement Standard Deviation WRAT-R (Wide-Range Achievement Test-Revised) Reading Subtest Crystal's WRAT-R reading "standard" score from manual = 82.

WRAT-R mean score for original standardization group = 100 and standard deviation = 15 (information from manual).

Now relate Crystal's reading test score to unit normal curve which has a mean of 0 and SD = 1.

Crystal's score of 82–100 (mean of standardization sample of 100) = –18. Now divide that deviation score (–18) by the standard deviation of the original sample of 15 = –1.2.

Crystal's reading WRAT-R subtest performance score has been converted to a z score or standard score in standard deviation units of –1.2.

II. WISC-III (Wechsler Intelligence Scale for Children—Revised)—Determining General Intellectual Ability Standard Deviation

Manual Facts from the WISC-III: Scale or mean IQ = 100; the standard deviation unit = 15 IQ points.

Crystal's Full Scale IQ = 108. Standard Score on unit normal curve = (108)–(100) = +8 and 8/15 = +0.53 standard deviation units.

Crystal's WISC-III Full Scale IQ performance converts to +.53 standard deviation units.

III. Determining the Overall Ability (using the WISC-III) - Achievement Discrepancy (using the WRAT-R Reading Subtest).

Subtract the difference between the two standard scores: +0.53 – (–1.2) = +1.73.

IV. Evaluate the Resultant Discrepancy Difference

Crystal's discrepancy of +1.73 is more than 1.5 standard deviation units generally accepted as statistically significant. We therefore consider the possibility that Crystal has a specific reading disability or dyslexia.

units for the reading test. We must divide by the size of the SD, which in this case is 5. The result is a z-score of –1. If we looked this result up in a normal curve table showing z-scores and percentiles, we would see that the student scored better than only 16% of test takers.

Determining the Ability (Intelligence)-Reading Discrepancy

Now our job is to check out our student's ability-reading discrepancy score in total SD units. Is it higher than our criterion of 1.5? Since the ability z-score is +2 and the reading z-score is –1; +2 – (–1) = +3, the answer is a resounding "Yes." This discrepancy score of 3 standard deviation units shows a serious reading problem may exist.

Other Standard Score Discrepancy Calculations

Let us examine two other examples of standard score discrepancy calculations. First, if a student has an ability z-score of –1.5 and a reading z-score of –2, the discrepancy is equal to .5. While this person's reading is very poor, it is not below expectations, given the low level of academic ability that the person has (as shown by the z-score of –1.5 on that test). This is a poor reader of the type described by Stanovich as a "garden variety poor reader." Our second example is a high-ability student scoring a z of +2 in ability and a z of +1 in reading. While we might have cause to wonder why this able student is doing better than only 84% of tested persons, the ability-performance discrepancy is still not great enough to raise a red flag. Remember, we are using a criterion of 1.5 standard deviations or standard score units of discrepancy and this person shows a discrepancy of only 1.0.

What "magic" gives us the ability to compare ability and reading performance scores? The process of calculating standard scores transforms the two sets of data into unit normal curves. Not only is the frequency curve bell-shaped, but in each case the mean is converted to 0 while the SD is converted to 1. When we subtract the mean from the score, we are zeroing out the size of the mean and getting some positive or negative number depending on whether our student scored above or below the mean. Note that if the student scored exactly at the mean, the difference score $(X - M)$ would be neither negative nor positive and it would be equal to 0. Now, how do we change the SD to 1 (from 3.5 and 5 in our examples)? Dividing by the size of the SD cancels out the size of that SD. Similar things happen when we convert a measurement in inches to its equal in feet. For example, 72 inches is divided by 12 (which is the size of the new unit, the foot, in inches) to obtain 6 feet. Again, when we get the equivalent in dollars of 637 cents, we divide by 100, the number of cents in a dollar to get $6.37 in dollar units. In the length analogy, we are cancelling out the size of a foot in inch units. In the money analogy, we are cancelling out the size of a dollar in cent units.

Prevalence

Dyslexia is a popular term for a common reading disorder which afflicts approximately 3% of our school-age population. Some researchers (e.g., Harris & Sipay, 1990) propose a much higher incidence rate of 10–15%. Conservative estimates would indicate that dyslexia affects up to 5% of the U.S. population (Hynd & Cohen, 1983; Hynd & Semrud-Clikeman, 1989a). The U.S. Department of Education reported in 1989 that 4.41% of the population between the ages of 6 to 17 could be classified as LD, with 10.25% in 1994. Most would agree that at least 50% of this LD population experience the problem of dyslexia or reading disabilities (or exactly 2.625%). Notice the significant increase in the number of students diagnosed as LD—a rate that doubled during a period of five years. It is possible that screening procedures have improved or perhaps we need to carefully examine diagnostic procedures which over-identify students. Regardless, the heterogeneity of the LD population alone would require identification of different types, correlating symptoms, and remedial practices specific to the disability. Our focus is on the problem of dyslexia; therefore, the remaining chapters primarily focus on addressing this disorder.

Sex Differences

There has been widespread understanding that boys outnumber girls 3-, 4- or 5-to-1 as having dyslexia. Lubs et al. (1991) have actually found sex ratios to be equal within families of dyslexics and suggest that one factor in the overreferral or over-diagnosis of males in the classroom is the more disruptive behavior of male pupils. Shaywitz and other researchers reported a 1990 study (Shaywitz, 1990) in which 445 Connecticut children were studied from kindergarten to third grade. The schools had identified the incidence of dyslexia in the ratio of 4:1 boys to girls, for the second grade. However, these researchers independently tested the school population, and they found that equal numbers of boys and girls could be objectively classified as dyslexic.

Sex Ratios

DeFries, Olson, Pennington and Smith (1991) have been connected with the Colorado Reading Project which has been funded by the NICHD (National Institute of Child Health and Human Development) continuously for over ten years. Their data also show equal numbers of female and male dyslexics.

The excess of identified dyslexic males over females has accordingly, been explained by a bias in the classroom referral system. Vogel (1990) notes that the referred samples of dyslexics do not represent the overall population. It appears that the notion that dyslexia affects males more than females must be questioned at the current stage of research.

Handedness

Another commonly held belief is that left-handedness is more frequently associated with reading difficulties (Benton & Pearl, 1978). As far back as 1925, Orton saw an elevated rate of left-handedness in dyslexics and their families. More recently, Geschwind and Behan (1982) linked left-handedness with developmental dyslexia and other disorders associated with certain immune-related disorders. However, there have been challenges to this premise since the 1950s with Malmquist as early as 1958, Belmont and Birch in 1965 and Helveston et al. in 1970. All concluded that non-right-handedness is *not* associated with reading problems to a significantly higher degree than it appears in the general population.

Hair Color

Even hair color has been alleged to be correlated with dyslexia. See Chapter 3, Controversial Theories, for a discussion of the research behind the claim.

Conclusion

Despite differences in presentation and discussion, we can agree that Critchley's (1970) definition of dyslexia which has been supported by the World Federation of Neurology and which nicely summarizes this perplexing problem:

> *[Dyslexia is] a disorder manifested by difficulty in learning to read despite conventional instruction, adequate intelligence, and sociocultural opportunity. It is dependent upon fundamental cognitive disabilities which are frequently of constitutional origin* (p. 11).

The Matthew Effect was briefly discussed as one way to account for the permanency of the dyslexia condition. Although the individual with dyslexia can learn how to read, study, and communicate adequately, remnants of the disorder persist through to adulthood (e.g., organization problems and spelling difficulties).

Placement options were briefly discussed in terms of the inclusion model and resource room placements. The United States Department of Education (1995) shows that the majority of placements for students with learning disabilities are still in more traditional resource room settings (54%) with 20% in substantially separate classes, 1% in separate facilities, and only 25% in regular classrooms (inclusionary placements). Chapter 9 more fully discusses placement options and as we approach the year 2000, we will probably see a substantial drop in resource room placements with programming efforts directed more toward inclusionary practices.

We have come full circle to the topic of dyslexia by historical references, definition, contrast with other disorders, and descriptive correlates. Please continue to read, review, and reason with a critical eye! Chapter 3 deals with controversial approaches and offers the caveat, "Buyer Beware."

C h a p t e r 3

Controversial Theories

> *". . . Moreover, opportunity for making mistakes is an incidental requirement . . . "—(DEWEY, 1919, P. 231).*

Most educators and researchers in the field would agree upon the importance of research in searching out the cause(s) of dyslexia. This necessarily means we'll make mistakes along the way; that is, some treatments or remedies might be initially recommended that further research will not bear out as fruitful endeavors.

Many practitioners would agree that the causal link to dyslexia is rooted in some type of constitutional neurological dysfunctioning which can emanate from various parts of the brain. This assumption would lead one to speculate that there can be various subtypes of dyslexia depending on the origin of the neuronal dysfunctioning. It is still the case that, "in almost every [instance] . . . , the exact cause of a child's learning disability is unknown . . . a wide variety of causes have been proposed" (Heward & Orlansky, 1992, p. 146). These include some very controversial approaches. We will present some of these perspectives as it is important to read, reason, and review so that reasonable and well-grounded educational planning endeavors result. It is important to be well-informed regarding those approaches which common sense tells us might not work or might not even directly impact the learning/behavior problems of individuals with dyslexia.

The Hawthorne Effect

The field of dyslexia research and the study of learning disabilities in general is rich with provocative, unusual, and inconsistent findings. Often, parents, teachers, and other concerned persons will search for miracle cures to relieve the reading disability of the dyslexic child. The major approaches to this problem have to be examined in order to assist those who seek to understand this problem and cure the disability. First and foremost, we must stress that no conclusive research has been provided by anyone to substantiate the idea that a final cure for dyslexia is at hand. The best we can hope for with our present knowledge and available technology is to produce a combination of alleviating measures, using an eclectic approach that will be keyed to the most effective instructional methods. This process can allow us to assist the dyslexic in acquiring compensatory approaches to reading and in developing the skills to function at a literate level. In some of the later pages, we will be discussing some helpful procedures for dealing with academic and social problems. In the meantime, it should be noted that as many as 80% of the medically reported disorders can be relieved without direct intervention (Clark, 1985). Even if this figure were conservatively to be cut in half, many disorders and deficits can be positively affected without formal remedial efforts. This is partly due to the **Hawthorne Effect**, or a positive change in behavior not due to the treatment mode, but rather to the individual's sense of participation in important research or desire to please an important supervisor, mentor, teacher, and so on. In a condition that has behavioral components, it may well be the case that the person's strivings and earnest efforts to do better may carry more weight than the supposed treatment for the problem.

Treatment Considerations

Several currently proposed but controversial approaches, cures, remedial measures, and quick fixes will be discussed in this chapter. Our intention is to enable concerned professionals and parents, as well as learning disabled individuals themselves, to make wise decisions among the many possible modes of treatment being offered. Table 3-1 lists criteria to consider when selecting a treatment for a learning disabled student.

Cerebellar-Vestibular Dysmetria (CVD)

Drs. Jan Frank and Harold N. Levinson (1977) are psychiatrists. Levinson states that left-handedness, mixed-handedness, and gender are not correlated with dyslexia. While we tend to agree with this, we do not support Frank and Levinson's view either. The theory of dyslexia they offer holds that the cerebellar vestibular (CV) system of balance functions unreliably in dyslexics. The neural pathway from the

TABLE 3-1 Criteria for Choosing a Remedial Treatment for a Learning Disability

- Weigh the likely positive and/or negative outcomes.
- Consider the theoretical support for the suggested therapy.
- Take into account the expense involved in using the treatment.
- Consider the feasibility of implementing the treatment.
- Apply your own common sense. To help deal with a reading problem, the therapy must be reading-related (Worrall, 1990a, 1990b).

balance organs of the inner ear to the cerebellum and the external eye muscle control nuclei of the midbrain is involved. Abnormal functioning in this part of the brain will not be revealed in any test of cerebral cortical malfunction. This, says Levinson (1988) accounts for the negative findings of diligent studies of the cerebral hemispheres of dyslexics. The investigators, he says, were simply exploring an irrelevant part of the brain!

Blurring, Scrambling, and Reversals Linked to CV System

Frank and Levinson (1977) say that the dyslexics' problems with ocular fixation and sequential scanning are analogous to the tracking difficulty we all have when trying to read signs from a rapidly moving vehicle. The impaired cerebellar-vestibular system, they claim, normally inhibits the rate at which sensory information is fed to the cerebral cortex. With a malfunctioning cerebellar-vestibular system, the rapid influx of data leads to the subjective experiences of blurring, scrambling, and reversals.

Internal Releasing Mechanism (IRM)

Motion sickness is hypothesized to be the result of an **internal releasing mechanism** (IRM) triggered by the excessively rapid inflow of sensory information to the cortex. This condition warns the organism that something is wrong. Seasickness medications such as Dramamine can reportedly restore the cerebellum to normal functioning so that it can perform its task of inhibiting and thereby slowing down the flow of sensory information into cerebral sensory areas. Accordingly, Dramamine should relieve dyslexia (Frank & Levinson, 1977). Confirming evidence by other researchers regarding the efficacy of this approach has not been forthcoming.

In Rebuttal

Levinson (1988) argues that his dyslexic patients nearly all showed attention deficits, and that ADD is to be expected in all dyslexics. Wilsher and Taylor (1987) have criticized Levinson's work on several accounts. First, there are many persons with cerebellar-vestibular difficulties who have no problems with reading. Second, a study of dyslexics by Brown et al. (1983) showed that this population had no greater percentage of people with cerebellar-vestibular dysfunctions than the general public.

Third, Levinson's research involved the administration of anti-seasickness drugs to all his reading-disabled patients. There were no placebo controls, because Levinson contends, it would be unethical to deny treatment to any patient (Levinson, 1980). Fourth, he claimed positive results for his treatment on the basis of the self-reports of the research subjects. This fourth point emphasizes the vital importance of the third: Children given prescribed treatment from a qualified medical doctor are bound to have either or both a placebo effect (faith in the treatment) or a Hawthorne Effect (a strong desire to produce an interesting result for the important person doing research on them).

Neural Organization Technique (NOT)

Ocular Lock Syndrome

Two chiropractors, Drs. Ferreri and Wainwright (1984) proposed a treatment for dyslexia that entails the manual manipulation of the skull bones in order to cure the problem. They attribute reading disability to a **sphenoid wing malfunction** (p. 79). This bone problem prevents the eye muscles from working freely, resulting, they say, in an **ocular lock.** The two important skull bones for this condition are the sphenoid and the temporal bones.

The Pelvic Girdle and Dyslexia

Ferreri and Wainwright (1984) feel that the pelvic girdle (the hip bones) also is involved in dyslexia. The pelvic bones have to be set right because they are related to the execution of the "cloacal reflexes," which, starting at the bottom of the spine, establish the reader's posture for either good or poor reading. The dyslexic's major problem, the ocular lock, is a neural deficit caused by an over-focusing of the eyes in certain directions, resulting in a weakening of the eyes. The eyes become heavy and are unable to follow a moving target; this applies to reading, because the task involves left-to-right tracking and return sweeps.

Chiropractic Interventions

Ferreri and Wainwright (1984) believe that the muscles of the eyes are attached to bones that have been "subluxated" for long periods of time. Since the eye muscles have been altered in length, the eyes can only work under "stress" involving "neural deficit" (p. 80). They hold that the key to treatment is direct chiropractic intervention involving the eye muscles. Part of the therapy involves locating indicator muscles and then strengthening those muscles by having the patient view stimuli in the direction of the "greatest weakness." Cranial manipulations are utilized which supposedly correct difficulties with cranial faults, cloacal reflex functions, and eye muscle imbalances.

Physiological and Psychological Inconsistencies with NOT

Some researchers (Worrall, 1990a, 1990b; Silver, 1987) have refuted the basic premise of the Ferreri-Wainwright approach by pointing out the physiological and psychological inconsistencies with this theory. For example, Ferreri and Wainwright (1984) claim that cranial bones move; standard biology texts indicate otherwise. There is very little if any substantiating evidence to confirm the validity of this treatment. According to Worrall, any attempt to manipulate the skull bones may produce positive injury to the dyslexic child (for example, pressure on the eyeball may be transmitted to the brain via the optic nerve, bringing on seizures). Clearly, this is one remedy that should **be avoided** by the intelligent consumer.

Megavitamins

Cott (1977, 1985) is probably the best known proponent of the use of massive doses of vitamins in the treatment of children with learning disabilities. The self-styled orthomolecular school of psychology holds that any behavioral or emotional abnormality is due to the existence of a chemical disorder in the brain. **Megavitamins** (and often, megaminerals) are said by the proponents of this view to have the capability of re-ordering the brain's chemistry and restoring neurological health. Learning-disabled terminology is used interchangeably with the term, *minimal brain dysfunctioning* which until the 1980s was considered an acceptable synonym.

Hypoglycemia, Hyperinsulinism, and Dysinsulinism

The basis for Cott's (1977) vitamin supplements is traced to his basic premise that, "many disturbed and learning-disabled children are found to have either hypoglycemia, hyperinsulinism, or dysinsulinism; cane sugar and rapidly absorbed carbohydrate foods should be eliminated from their diets" (p. 31). Cott maintains that wheat products and milk frequently occur in foods containing sugar and are the culprits for producing what he has coined the "cerebral allergies" seen in the disturbed behavior of overactive and learning disabled children.

Diet Eliminations and Supplements

Cott has recommended an elimination diet of wheat, eggs, corn and corn products, and beef. This diet is similar in theory to the one suggested by Feingold (discussed later in this chapter) recommending elimination of foods with naturally occurring salicylates, artificial flavors, and colors which occur in foods like sodas, frankfurters, apples, oranges, cucumbers, and so on. Cott also believes in a type of diet supplement whereby megavitamins are used to maintain the body's chemistry. His research has pointed to biochemical causes of learning disabilities, especially among low-income families.

Basis for Megavitamin Treatment

The basis for megavitamin treatment is rooted in the belief that minerals provided in megavitamin capsules such as zinc and selenium, for example, protect the individual against accumulating lethal doses of another mineral, in this case, cadmium. The accumulation of toxic metals, Cott contends, interferes with pyruvic acid levels and the subsequent curtailing of energy to the brain. We would agree that in some cases, e.g., lead overdoses, research has shown that toxic levels interfere with learning and normal everyday functioning. However, the use of mineral supplements **has not** been shown to be an effective preventive measure against the acquisition of physical conditions or dyslexia/learning disabilities.

American Psychiatric Association Task Force on Vitamin Therapy in Psychiatry

American Psychiatric Association Task Force on Vitamin Therapy in Psychiatry (1973) issued a report on the validity of megavitamin therapies. The report states that such treatments **are not supported** by scientific data. The unrestricted use of megaminerals and of the fat-soluble vitamins (vitamins A, D, and E), at least, may be damaging to one's health. Arnold, Christopher, Huestis, and Smeltzer (1978) found that in a sample of children with learning problems, there were no noticeable gains in academic performance with this treatment.

In looking for the positives of any approach, we would agree with Cott (1977) that, "children must learn the principles of proper nutrition" (p. 32).

Feingold K-P Diet (Kaiser Permanente)

Dr. Ben Feingold (1976), creator of the "Feingold K-P Diet" at the Kaiser-Permanente (K-P) Hospital Group in San Francisco has claimed that the learning disabled and hyperkinetic child has been affected by additives placed into our processed foods whether to sweeten the taste of the food or to dye the food with an appealing color. Dr. Feingold first used his diet in 1965 to assist a woman with an acute case of hives. Salicyclates (natural compounds found in some fruits and vegetables) were removed from her diet and supposedly cured the hives (Feingold, 1976). According to Feingold (1976), "The K-P diet, which eliminates all artificial food colors and flavors as well as foods with a natural salicylate radical, will control the behavioral disturbance in 30% to 50% (depending on the sample) of both normal and neurologically damaged children" (p. 558). In essence, Feingold is linking the ingestion of food colors and flavorings to learning disabilities and hyperactivity.

Feingold insists that since drugs should be the last treatment mode for learning disabilities and hyperkinesis, certainly improving the diet should be the initial treatment choice. His reporting of studies in an anecdotal and conversational manner never convinces the reader that the diet has proven itself scientifically as the best cure for the hyperkinetic syndrome.

Elimination Diet Program

Some cases of learning disabilities and most cases of hyperactivity should be approached with the **elimination diet** program, according to Feingold (1975, 1976, 1977; Feingold & Feingold, 1979). Synthetic chemicals, particularly those added to soft drinks, hot dogs, luncheon meats, and candies, for example, are the suspect items to be eliminated from the diet. Feingold presents recipes for homemade mayonnaise and candy, even for meat dishes, salads, cakes, soups, and other main dishes. He is a kind of crusader against the thoughtless methods of some of the major food processors. When discussing some cereal manufacturers, Feingold says, "I find it hard to believe that they are not aware of the dangers of high sugar content; or that the paint pot of colors inside many boxes is of absolutely no benefit and of possible harm" (Feingold, 1975, p. 79). The K-P diet eliminates these food demons along with natural salicylates.

Dietary Approaches and Cognition

There have been some case studies which have supported Feingold's basic tenets but these have been criticized for methodological problems, especially the lack of adequate controls (Spring & Sandoval, 1976; Sieben, 1977). Kavale and Forness (1985) have established that dietary approaches have little impact on cognitive functioning. However, face validity would tell us that excessive amounts of sugar or caffeine would over-stimulate (Powers, 1975) or under-stimulate (Firestone et al., 1978) central nervous system functioning. Harris and Sipay (1990) suggest that the key, in the instance of caffeine, appears to be the amount ingested in determining whether or not a child would be overstimulated or understimulated.

Healthy Diets Commonsensible for All

Much research needs to be done in the areas of diet and basic nutrition; it would be difficult for us to recommend any kind of dietary restrictions because of the limited and somewhat flawed research presented thus far. Although Feingold claims that his K-P diet is harmless (Feingold & Feingold, 1979), Conners, Goyette, Southwick, Lees and Andrulonis (1976) have found the diet actually is nutritionally lacking. On a more positive note, some of what Feingold is recommending resembles "good old-fashioned wholesome food." Certainly this type of approach is appealing to parents because of the additive-free healthful nature of the diet (Divosky, 1978).

Sound Treatment

Tuning-Fork Screening/Audiotherapy

A relatively unknown and unproven sound treatment method was developed by Johansen (1984). Johansen (1984) claims he is able to differentially diagnose individuals with dyslexia by using tuning forks. The tuning fork is struck close to an individual's ear. When the individual states that he/she can no longer hear the sound, the vibrating tuning fork is then touched to a bone behind the ear in order to determine if the sound can be heard through bone conduction. Johansen (1984) cites the work of Volf from the 1960s who believed that many males experienced dyslexia because of an undescended testicle which in turn hampered testosterone production and language development. Audiotherapy is applied after tuning-fork screening (in a wide stretch of the imagination) to stimulate the testicle to descend into the scrotum, thereby causing testosterone production to return to normal levels. This author leaps to the conclusion that reading/spelling problems will therefore be ameliorated. According to Manzo and Manzo (1993), thousands of individuals in Scandinavian clinics have received this **unproven** treatment.

Analysis of Mineral Levels

The analysis of levels of minerals, particularly heavy metals (i.e., lead, cadmium, aluminum, arsenic, and mercury) has been linked by a handful of researchers (Perino & Ernhart, 1974; Marlowe, Cossairt, Welch & Errera, 1984; Struempler, Larson & Rimland, 1985; and Thatcher & Lester, 1985) to reading problems. High levels of cadmium have been linked to behavior problems and high levels of magnesium and lead to both reading and behavioral difficulties.

Proven Toxigen—Lead

Lead has been the most researched toxigen, which when even in small amounts has been hypothesized to have a negative impact on learning ability (David, Hoffman, McGann, Sverd & Clark, 1976; Dubey, 1932; Marlowe, Cossairt, Welch & Errera, 1984). Needleman, Gunnoe, Leviton, Reed, Peresie and Barret (1979) studied first- and second-grade children from two suburban school systems and found that children with higher lead concentrations in the blood performed significantly more poorly on the Wechsler Intelligence Scale for Children (WISC) than children with similar socioeconomic backgrounds and lower lead blood levels. Perino and Ernhart (1974) similarly found a negative correlation between cognitive and sensorimotor abilities and lead blood levels with three- and six-year-old children. Although the Center for Disease Control established in 1970 that lead in "30 micrograms (30/1,000,000ths of a gram) per 100cc (cubic centimeter = 1/1000th of a liter) of blood" be considered biologically toxic for children (as cited in Marlowe et al., 1984, p. 421), there is a **shortage** of research sufficient to link dyslexia or learning disabilities specifically to toxic lead levels.

Lead Levels Considered Toxic for Children

A 1991 study of over 1000 Mexican-American children has persuaded the Center for Disease Control to lower the critical lead concentration to 10 micrograms (only 10/1,000,000ths of a gram) (remember that a gram is as small a weight as .035 ounces) per deciliter (100cc) of blood. The expected age-related increase in height was decreased for children with above-average lead levels in their blood. The height loss averaged four-tenths of an inch, and, in extreme cases, was as great as a full inch, according to A. R. Frisancho, one of the investigators (*Science News*, 1991, p. 189).

Landesman-Dwyer, Ragozin & Little (1981) found **no relationship** between blood lead levels and reading problems, lowered intelligence, and behavior disorders. These researchers studied several children in a factory area where lead was released into the environment. They determined that social factors were more related to the learning and behavior problems observed than was the released lead.

Chelation Treatment

Chelation treatment has been found to reverse the negative effects of lead poisoning (David, Hoffman, McGann, Sverd & Clark, 1976). The relationship between lead and learning disabilities is far from clear and too few studies are available to draw any conclusions at this point in time.

Hair Mineral Analysis

The relationship between high hair cadmium levels and learning disabilities was more recently introduced by Struempler, Larson and Rimland (1985). Careful examination of these studies shows that conclusions were based on only a few case studies. **Hair mineral analysis** is thought by a few researchers to be a valuable diagnostic indicator of medical and behavioral and psychological problems (Laker, 1982; Maugh, 1978). They believe that hair accurately reflects when the body absorbs excess minerals or lacks a sufficient intake of nutrient minerals.

Link Between Hair Mineral Concentrations and Learning Questioned

Silver (1987) doubts that hair mineral analysis results can be generalized to the amount of mineral trace elements in the body itself. Certainly internal excesses would have to be assessed in relation to cerebral metabolic functioning, as brain functioning **has never been** causally linked to hair composition; although, Thatcher and Lester (1985) found that higher lead and cadmium concentrations were associated with a decrease in EEG amplitude. Regardless, Sieben (1977) has reported that there are **no concrete data** to support the link between mineral concentrations and learning. Struempler, Larson and Rimland (1985) admit that "the state of the art (associations between mineral concentration and learning and behavioral problems) does not allow firm conclusions to be drawn" (p. 611). One might wonder what direction a researcher would take if the dyslexics studied were bald.

Hair Color and Handedness

Some researchers would answer "NO!" to the question, "Do blonds have more fun?" Schachter, Ransil and Geschwind (1987) looked at the association between hair color and handedness, and learning disabilities. They found that of 50 subjects they studied with LD, 10 or 20% were blond. In contrast, 120 out of 1067 subjects without LD were blond. They raised the possibility that melanin may be implicated in both the development of motor dominance (left-handedness) and in the development of other systems even to include the color of one's hair. Their association between increased left-handedness and the learning disabled population was not surprising based on Behan and Geschwind's previous research (see Geschwind and Behan, 1982, for example). These reported findings on left-handedness were obtained by self-reports and one might question the validity of such data.

Tomatis Audiological-Psycho-Phonology (APP) Method

Ontogeny—Up From the Fertilized Egg

Based on audiometric test results, A. A. Tomatis (1978) developed a new theory of hearing, according to which the ear continuously undergoes retraining in response to stimuli of various tones. He has found that loss of hearing for high frequency sound impairs the ability of sopranos to sing high notes. Children with ear infections become poor listeners and are set on the road to language problems and learning disorders. The proper training of the ear for hearing and decoding speech begins with the four-and-one-half month-old fetus. The sound of the mother's voice becomes differentiated from other environmental sounds. Warm and welcoming tones in the mother's speech invite the fetus to attempt to hear this voice again and to begin to communicate with it—the "first dialogue." If, however, the pregnancy is unwanted, or if the mother is ill or anxious, the fetus retreats from communication and shrinks back from the world. Tomatis has a remedial treatment of playing higher frequency sounds to the young child via earphones. He claims that autistic children can be stirred to remove the high walls that they have erected to protect themselves from the language world.

Ontogenetic Perspective—APP

Kershner, Cummings, Clarke, Hadfield, and Kershner (1986; 1990) conducted a one-year and two-year evaluation of the Tomatis Listening Training Program (LTP) with learning disabled children. These authors found only a single group effect; that is, children who were in the placebo group were superior in performance on a Seashore Rhythm test which is a measure of auditory discrimination. Essentially, these researchers report **negative findings** regarding achievement gains from the use of the Tomatis method. In fact, Kershner, Cummings, Clarke, Hadfield, and Kershner (1986, 1990) are rather harsh in their assessment of this program, ". . . such programs [as the Tomatis Listening Training Program] promise what readily available procedures cannot—optimism about reversing the academic deficiencies of LD children . . . [p. 43] . . . the LTP may delay or interfere with LD children's progress toward acquiring certain fundamental auditory skills . . ." (p. 50). In all fairness to this method, it should be emphasized (in the words of Kershner, Cummings, Clarke, Hadfield, & Kershner, 1990), " . . . the [findings pointing to the] ineffectiveness of the LTP . . . [are] limited to the specific conditions of the experiment[s] including the setting, the students, and the 100-hour modification of the LTP . . ." (p 50).

We would **hesitate** to endorse the LTP or APP approach primarily because so little research is available to support this method. The Tomatis Audio-Psycho-

Phonology (APP) approach can be considered to be an ontogenetic view of learning disabilities, particularly since it implicates the conditions prevailing in the womb. The next approach we will consider is based on a similar recapitulation idea.

Postural Rehabilitation—the Delacato System

As the old cliche of developmental biology goes, "ontogeny recapitulates phylogeny." **Ontogeny** refers to the development of an individual living organism whereas **phylogeny** refers to the evolutionary development of the entire species. The old saying is meant to suggest that as the human embryo and then the human fetus develops in the uterus, the little organism starts out looking reptilian, then becomes similar to a lower mammal, and gets to look human only rather late in gestation. Carl Delacato (1963), however, intends this phrase to mean something a little bit different. The lowly salamander swims with both right legs moving in the same direction and both left legs going the other way (the homolateral pattern). This is replaced later in development by a more mature cross-pattern kind of locomotion, with the left front and right hind legs moving forward at the same time. Delacato states that control of this pattern is in the midbrain (the structure forward of, and higher than, the pons). In mammals, the cerebral cortex controls locomotion. Finally, in humans, the left cerebral hemisphere is the main control system for movement. This evolutionary pattern is reflected in the growth and development of human skills.

Categorizing Learning Problems on a Continuum

What have been treated as separate learning disabilities, says Delacato, are not truly separate. Aphasia represents the lowest level of development of communication skill; it is not a unique problem but a stage of development. The next higher stage of development is delayed (or poorly articulated) speech. We make a serious error if we try to treat delayed speech in isolation, instead of attempting to deal with the child's total stuttering. Again, this is only a developmental stage. The next step is retarded reading. Developing past this stage leads to poor spelling and handwriting. When the child matures further, he/she reaches the level of reading below mathematical performance.

Establishing Cerebral Dominance

Two great mistakes made by the learning disabilities experts are these, says Delacato: (1) the equating of handedness with cerebral dominance; and (2) the equating of cerebral dominance with neurological maturity. The establishment of cerebral dominance, Delacato points out, requires that many parts of the body should be given practice simultaneously. For example, do not train the poorly developed, learning disabled children just to be right-handed. To quote Delacato, "we are not training a foot, an eye or a hand, but . . . we are in fact retraining a hemisphere of the brain. The retraining of one area alone cannot result in the establishment of hemispheric dominance" (Delacato, 1963, p. 122). Delacato's training procedures include creeping, walking, visual targeting, focusing the gaze at various distances, balancing oneself on a narrow beam, jumping up and down on the trampoline, among others.

Delacato Theory and the Test of Time

The original Delacato theory was based on a study of brain- injured children by Doman, Spitz, Zucman, Delacato, and Doman (1960); the entire report is reprinted in Delacato's (1963) book. No other empirical evidence has been presented since. Overall, the Delacato system **does not** seem to have passed the test of time. In 1995, in the United States, the theories of Doman and Delacato have fallen into disrepute. The ontogenetic theory is interesting, amazing even, but makes very little biological sense. At every stage of evolution, the whole animal, even the whole lowly salamander, uses all of its brain. The brain is reorganized at each new, higher phylogenetic level, but the animal at any level is always using the whole thing. Because we humans can pride ourselves on having a very large, complex cerebral cortex does not give us the right to claim that we have outgrown our pons or our midbrain. However, Maggie White of Australia revived this approach during the late 1980s.

Delacato System's Revival in the 1980s

Cathexis School of Transactional Analysis (TA)
The Delacato system was partially revived in the 1980s in the work of the Australian researcher, Maggie White (1988), who adheres to the Cathexis School of Transactional Analysis (TA). TA refers to the "I'm OK" school of psychological counseling. White (1988) cites Robert Lefroy of Western Austrailia, a Western Australian remedial teacher, as having modified the Delacato training system.

Lefroy-Delacato Program
Lefroy (1975) (as cited by White, 1988) has retrained dyslexic children with a set of basic physical "patterning" exercises that reenact the crawling or creeping stage of development. Seven dyslexics, Lefroy claims, all showed disturbances in that developmental stage. Progress was reportedly shown in these dyslexics.

Ayre's Program of Sensory-Integration Therapy
White (1988) also cites Ayre's Program of Sensory-Integration Therapy. The Ayres program, White claims works well with five- to seven-year-olds while the Lefroy-Delacato program is successful for older children (ages 8 to 16). White also supports the Strauss-Lehtinen (1947) recommendation of a well-structured and stimulus-reduced school environment. We would focus more on the training of

social relationships, as opposed to sterilizing the learning environment, which in essence, is what removing all extraneous stimuli does for the learner.

Unconditional Positive Regard

A further recommendation by White (1988), which is more positively embraced by the authors, is for therapeutic tutoring to occur in a nurturing environment or showing, in Carl Roger's phrase, "unconditional positive regard." Creative curriculum planning which keys in on the learning-disabled child's strengths is also a substantive recommendation.

Grief Counseling

However, we now draw the line if practitioners embrace White's (1988) belief that "grief counseling" should be available for the learning-disabled child at ages 13 or 14 and her/his parents so they can come to terms with the knowledge that the child is not destined to be socially-adept or a high achiever. We would ask why the learning disabled cannot become socially adept, if not so to begin with, and who has established that the learning disabled cannot become high achievers? Perhaps it is the practitioners who are not able to deal with the special learning needs of dyslexic and learning-disabled children.

Perceptual-Motor Approaches Linked to IQ/Academic Progress

It is true that many children with dyslexia exhibit lags in motor development and could benefit from motor training programs. However, not all children with dyslexia have motor problems. Therefore, administering motor programs routinely to children and individuals with learning disabilities **is not** warranted. As Janet W. Lerner so aptly stated, "motor training alone will not teach a child to read, any more than eyeglasses alone will instantly transform a nonreader into a bookworm" (1971, p. 107). Frostig (1968) also cautions against delaying academic remedial procedures in favor of motor-training programs alone. There are some perceptual-motor theories which directly link the learning problems and IQ/academic progress of individuals with learning disabilities to inadequate perceptual-motor skills development. Kephart and Barsch, in particular, seem to have taken the role of perceptual-motor skills development in developing cognitive skills (to include reading) one step too far.

Kephart's Influence

A perceptual-motor theory of learning disabilities was offered by Kephart (1960; 1971) who believed that perceptual-development activities allow children to develop stable and reliable conceptualizations about the world. So-called normal children develop adequate perceptual-motor patterns by the age of six, according to Kephart (1963, 1967). For the learning disabled child, the dimensions of time and space are unstable and interfere with school learning. Learning disabled children are supposedly disorganized cognitively, motorically, and perceptually.

Motor Generalizations and LD According to Kephart

Kephart believes that there are four motor generalizations that children must master in order to achieve academically in school: maintenance of posture and balance; contact; locomotion; and receipt and propulsion. When a child fails to integrate perceptual information with motor information, distorted perceptions result which can interfere with stored cognitive information. In this instance, Kephart states that a perceptual-motor match cannot be made.

Perceptual-Motor Training Programs— Academically Inefficient Alone

Kephart's teaching program focuses on ameliorating perceptual- motor deficiencies of children with learning disabilities by using walking boards and balance beams, jumping and hopping activities, identifying body parts, mimicking body movements, moving through physical obstacle courses, visual-ocular pursuit activities, copying geometric shapes, and other activities. Lerner's (1971) basic assessment that "there has thus far been little research evidence to indicate that practice in motor training directly results in increased academic achievement" (p. 100) is still true today. The research of Hammill, Goodman, and Wiederholt (1974) and Kavale and Mattison (1983) would confirm the **inefficiency** of such motor programs.

Barsch and Movigenics

The Movigenic Theory was proposed by Barsch in the late 1960s as another theory of movement related to the problems of children with learning disabilities. Barsch (1965, 1967, & 1968) looks at several dimensions that are supposed to impact learning in general: (1) children acquire information through their percepto-cognitive systems; (2) movement occurs within space and children must learn to move efficiently through space; (3) motor skills are acquired in a developmental sequential manner; and (4) language skills are derived from visual-spatial grounding (with movement efficiency being the key).

The Movigenic Curriculum—Lack of Research Support

According to Barsch, a motor curriculum must be developed for the child with learning disabilities in order to bridge the gap between motor skill development and academic skills acquisition. The child is initially supposed to develop a state of proprioceptive awareness, or an awareness of the environment and his/her movements in relation to the environment. Children are directed to touch objects in the environment and to locate and move body parts around environmental objects. The mechanics of movement are then relearned properly so that children can relate time to movement to learning. An example would be to teach children how to posture themselves so that they move their bodies in relation to gravity. Planned kneeling, sitting, standing, and walking activities are involved. More complex motor acts are introduced that develop shifting capacities in rates and patterns of movement. For example, children are instructed to walk and then hop, but to continue hopping after every fifth clap. As in the case of Kephart's program, there is **little research** to substantiate the Movigenic Curriculum.

The Eye Patch Treatment

Unstable Eye Movements

Unstable eye movement control is the prevailing deficit in dyslexia, according to Stein and Fowler (1985). In view of this hypothesis, they advocate the use of an eye patch to occlude the problem eye so that the dyslexic child can attain reliable "ocular motor/macular associations by eliminating the possibility of discrepant retinal signals being projected by the two eyes" (p. 72). Stein and Fowler suggest that the reading problems of dyslexics are characterized by letters and words that "move around, reverse themselves, or jump over each other" (p. 70). According to Stein and Fowler (1985), all reading problems involve errors in locating letters within words, letter reversals, letter rotations, etc. Even attempts by normal readers to read under difficult conditions can produce such errors (Grosser & Trzeciak, 1981). It is possible that a very few individuals are called dyslexics when their reading disability results from disorders of the external eye muscles, but they are probably the exception rather than the rule.

Eye Vergence (or The Zen of Oculomotor Maintenance)

Stein and Fowler (1985) report that 68% of a large sample of dyslexic children had unstable **vergence** eye movement control (unfixed reference) on the Dunlop test which measures the level of an individual's eye movement control. Almost all of a set of normal readers (matched for age and intelligence with the dyslexic subjects) showed good eye movement control.

They hypothesized that the dyslexic child could perform visual tracking successfully by having one eye occluded, so that confusion of the two retinal images is prevented. The experiment done to test the hypothesis was only partly successful. Stein and Fowler (1985) argued that the dyslexics who were not helped might have suffered from a non-visual subtype of dyslexia.

Dunlop Test

Stein (1989) postulates that the right posterior parietal cortex has the special function of associating sensory and motor inputs in order to maintain a representation of objects in three-dimensional spaces. In his later work, Stein (1989) added to the use of the Dunlop test. He measures the child's ability to hold fixation upon a small target during convergence at the child's own reading distance. Children with dyslexia are much worse at this task than good readers of the same age. Riddell,

Fowler, and Stein (1990) also compared the accuracy of spatial localization on a non-linguistic computer game by children having good and poor vergence control. Children with poor vergence control made significantly more errors than other children did.

Normal and Dyslexic Readers—Negligible Convergence and Stereopsis Differences

Wilsher and Taylor (1987) point out that normal readers are just as likely to suffer poor vergence control as dyslexics, citing a study by Newman et al. (1985). Another study, by Bishop et al. (1979), took the opposite tack, by examining a large sample of dyslexics. Bishop et al. (1979) found **no evidence** of an extra convergence deficiency or poor stereopsis in their dyslexic subjects. Both the Newman and Bishop studies found that the Dunlop test (used as an important response measure by Stein and his colleagues) **failed** to differentiate between good and poor readers (Wilsher & Taylor, 1987).

The Scotopic Sensitivity Syndrome and Irlen Lenses

The Scotopic Sensitivity Syndrome (SSS) is Helen Irlen's conception of the condition that most of us refer to as dyslexia. It is characterized by difficulties in reading and writing, painful sensitivity to light, and problems with perceptions of wavelength and black-white contrast. SSS is not identical with dyslexia, rather it is a complex state that can coexist with dyslexia, dysgraphia, dyscalculia, attention deficit disorder, or hyperactivity (Irlen Institute brochure).

Treating the Scotopic Sensitivity Syndrome

The Irlen Institute headed by Executive Director Helen L. Irlen has a number of treatment centers in several states. It is dedicated to the treatment of the Scotopic Sensitivity Syndrome, which has five major kinds of symptoms:

1. photophobia (sensitivity to glare, discomfort with fluorescent lights, etc.)
2. background distortion (an inability to work with sharp black-white contrast such as sheet music or pages of print)
3. visual resolution (problems with printed matter that moves or that alternates between turning on and turning off, as in advertising signs)
4. scope of focus (difficulty maintaining focus, with frequent blinking, squinting, or ceasing to read);
5. depth perception/gross motor (difficulty using stairs, tailgating when driving, poor at coping with a moving ball in sports, poor at height or depth judgment). (Irlen Clinics Brochure, undated).

The Institute's method for treating SSS is to provide the patient with a color filter either to be worn over the eyes like sunglasses or to place over a page of print. Each corrective color is said to be unique to the particular individual. The treatment is claimed to lead to improved accuracy and comprehension in reading, as well as a number of side benefits (Irlen Clinics Brochure). The technique for treating SSS essentially involves altering the wavelength of the light entering the eyes of the individual through the use of colored filters either worn as lenses or placed over a page of print. The exact color prescribed for the individual is as unique to the person as his/her fingerprints would be. It can only be selected by intense diagnostic testing (Irlen Institute brochure). This treatment is not equivalent to teaching the patient to read but is said to rectify a condition that impedes progress in reading.

Scientific Support Lacking for SSS

Harold Solan (1990) has stated that Irlen has offered **no scientifically sound evidence** to support the idea that SSS symptoms are related to reading disorder. Helen Irlen owns every set of Irlen lenses in existence (even those prescribed for the SSS patients). Testing for SSS is by the Irlen Differential Perceptual Schedule (IDPS), a test which has not been standardized or even made available for standardization research. The participation of an examiner trained and certified by Irlen is required for any attempt to validate Irlen's claims. Some recent research has not supported the benefits of the Irlen lens treatment with individuals experiencing dyslexia (Spafford & Grosser, 1995; Spafford & Grosser, In Press; Cardinal, Griffin, & Christenson, 1993; Lopez, Yolton, Kohl, Smith, & Saxerud, 1994).

The Blue-Gray Lens—An Alternative to Irlen

Mary Williams and her collaborators have reported that blue or gray lenses (or blue or gray transparent overlays placed over a page of print) result in improved reading on the part of reading-disabled subjects (Williams & LeCluyse, 1990). This differs from Irlen's claim that there is a unique preferred color for each individual SSS patient. Moreover, Williams has a theoretical basis for her claim. Williams and other members of her school of thought hold that dyslexics have a poorly-functioning transient visual nervous system. The task of this visual system in reading is to erase afterimages of past visual stimuli after a saccade, when the eyes have moved quickly to a new focal point on the printed page. The resolution of fine details needed for recognizing letters is the task of the sustained visual system. With a non-functional or even poorly functioning transient system the words being read may get jumbled with words seen at the previous fixation (stopping-place) preceding the saccade. Blue or gray lenses slow down the sustained visual system, thereby providing an artificial equivalent for transient system functioning.

Research Related to the Irlen vs. Williams Viewpoint?

Solman, Dain, and Keech (1991) used the Williams theory as the basis for their experiment on reading-disabled and normal readers. They tested for sensitivity (i.e., low threshold discriminations) at low, medium and high frequency, sine-wave brightness gratings. A brightness grating is a set of parallel dark and light lines of equal thickness. A sine-wave grating has fuzzy transitions between dark and light. The term for a grating with sharp, sudden changeovers from light to dark would be a square-wave grating. A low-frequency grating has very wide dark and light lines (few changes of brightness per degree of visual angle); a high-frequency grating consists of thin lines, hence many changes from light to dark and dark to light per degree.

Why use degree of visual angle instead of inches or decimeters? Because the optical size of a visual stimulus depends on both the size of the stimulus and the distance that stimulus is away from our eyes. The visual angle measure accounts for the result of both factors, size and distance. The data obtained by Solman et al. differentiated normal readers from disabled readers in a complex way that is hard to interpret as either supporting the Williams theory or refuting it. The color of lens that produced the best contrast sensitivity to the brightness gratings yielded the poorest visual search performance. Note that this concept of a "best" lens seems to be more relevant to the Irlen approach than the Williams.

Other Grating Data

Spafford, Grosser, Donatelle, Squillace, and Dana (1995) performed an experiment along roughly the same lines as that of Solman et al., but they presented the gratings on a stationary wall chart rather than in a continuously moving format as the Solman group did. These researchers found that the sine-wave gratings did lead to very different performances by reading-disabled subjects from those of normal-reading subjects. The poor readers had inferior sensitivity (i.e., higher thresholds) for both low-frequency and high-frequency gratings. Although various lens colors were used, each subject performed about the same with each pair of lenses worn. One of the pairs of lenses was clear. All the lenses were optically neutral. Their finding that lens color made no difference casts some doubt on both the Irlen and the Williams theories, but particularly so for the Irlen view. Still, there was no reading test involving different lens colors, so those views have not been definitively cast into doubt.

Syntonics

Two optometrists (R. Kaplan, 1983; J. Liberman, 1986) advocate syntonics as a system for the treatment of learning disabilities. Syntonics, according to Liberman (1986) "is that branch of ocular science dealing with the application of selected visible light frequencies through the eyes" (p. 6). This is a type of light therapy which is rooted in the work of Dr. Henning (1936), and that of Dr. H. Spitler (1941) who formed the College of Syntonic Optometry. According to this viewpoint, an autonomic nervous system imbalance will lead to learning disability. The sympathetic nervous system, when activated, puts us in a "fight-or-flight" readiness mode, hence it goes with a negative mood, or exophoria, in the jargon of the syntonic school. The other part of the autonomic nervous system, the parasympathetic, will, when activated, allow us to feel well-rested and satisfied. We find ourselves in a positive mood or esophoria. Either too much exophoria or too much esophoria will give us a restricted visual field, so we need to have a well-balanced middle-of-the-road mood. Now red light makes us exophoric and blue light makes us esophoric, so that we are dominated by the sympathetic or the parasympathetic nervous system, respectively.

The Effect of Blue and Red Lights

Visible light frequencies are thought by the proponents of the syntonics school of thought to interact differently with the endocrine system which is inhibited or stimulated based on the frequency of the light. Light frequencies which produce blue or red light are thought to elicit feelings of relaxation and lowered anxiety and hostility. Frequencies which produce the color red supposedly encourage tension and excitement. Wolfarth and Sam (1982) report that even blind subjects' behaviors are affected by selected colors. Subjects are exposed to different color filters based on the nature of the subject's autonomic imbalance. A sympathetic nervous system (SNS) predominance (i.e., exophoria) requires a treatment by a parasympathetic stimulant (blue light). A parasympathetic (PNS) predominance (i.e., esophoria) requires sympathetic NS stimulation with red light.

Theoretical Rationale for Syntonics

The theoretical rationale for the syntonics treatments is based on a visual NS pathway (not involved in visual functioning) that follows the inferior accessory optic tract via the midbrain's transpeduncular nucleus to the superior cortical ganglion, thence to the pineal gland, chemicals from which enter the cerebrospinal fluid of the third ventricle. This in turn affects the hypothalamus which connects to the pituitary gland. If you can follow this lengthy road map, give yourself an esophoric treatment!

Confirmative Research Weak in Methodology

The effects of the syntonic treatment in Liberman's study (1986) were determined from a **weak methodology** that is summarized as follows:

How the Experimental Ss Were Treated

1. Ss with constricted visual fields with minimal phoric deviation were given yellow-green light (500–590 nanometers) to normalize the visual field.

2. Ss with constricted visual fields and moderate phoric deviations first got yellow-green followed by either red (620–770nm) or indigo (400–500nm), the former if S was excessively esophoric, and indigo if S was excessively exophoric.

3. Ss with constricted visual fields and moderate to large phoric deviations got either red or indigo as appropriate.

Comparisons Questionable in Syntonics Study

"Control" Ss were not exposed to the viewer at all, as either blackness or white light would have some phoric effect. Liberman admits that this might have allowed the study to become biased. We must ask the question: Why weren't controls administered the treatments? Because of inadequate controls, the Liberman study is essentially comparing apples to oranges or rods to cones.

Howell and Stanley (1988) point out that there were a number of **design errors** and **procedural inadequacies** in the Kaplan and Liberman studies. Furthermore, the gains reported by Liberman for the experimental subjects might have involved mood and motivational factors rather than perceptual ones.

Conclusion

Determining the causative factors of dyslexia and the various subtypes of dyslexia is not an easy task. We have so far suggested that there are different dyslexic subtypes with neurologically-based dysfunctioning in either or both the linguistic and visual systems. Cerebellar-vestibular dysfunctioning, scotopic sensitivity, unstable eye movement control, exophoria/esophoria excesses, ocular lock syndrome, and hair-splitting mineral excesses are all interesting views of why dyslexics experience difficulties in oral and written language. However, at this point these hypotheses are speculative and accordingly, adhering to any recommended treatment would be questionable, especially when substances are ingested or physical manipulations are initiated with bone structures.

Theory should always beget practice and vice versa. It is our contention that remedial procedures should always include input from the medical and educational realms and that treatments follow a conservative and scientific route. **Educational** components should be a priority. If and when these don't suffice to alleviate the problem, interventions in the medical field can be considered only if and when the causation appears to be rooted in some physiological problem or dysfunctioning. Prescribing drugs, vitamins, lenses, or altering bone structures are avenues that can impact a child's physical well-being. Keeping that in mind, conservatism should prevail; there should be no medical interventions without good solid empirical evidence based on theory. Common sense should always prevail, as well as our 4 Rs of Reading, Reviewing, Reasoning, and Researching. The following chapters deal with remediation and support systems.

$Chapter$ 4

Developing Word Recognition Skills

*. . . there is only one thing in the world that you will need to
use oftener [than using sounds which form spoken words],
and that is the air you breathe . . . —(WATSON, 1876, P. 17).*

The development of a foundation for word recognition is dependent upon the
knowledge of sounds which form spoken words and phoneme-grapheme correspondences. For the individual with dyslexia, this ability is lacking. Generally, two
schools of thought emerge when discussing developing word recognition skills in
students with dyslexia: (1) traditional phonics approaches, based on the **bottom-
up model** of reading, which stress the learning of phoneme-grapheme correspondences to the point of automaticity, and (2) **whole language**/language experience approaches, based on the **top-down model** of reading, which place
minor emphases on phonics instruction and central focus on reading as a meaning-based process. We are recommending a combination of bottom-up/top-down
models in the teaching of reading to individuals with dyslexia or an interactive
model (see Rumelhart, 1977).

Theoretical Perspectives—Bottom-Up/Top-Down Models

"Although there is general agreement that the purpose of reading is getting meaning from print, how that occurs is the subject of debate" (Kavale, Forness, & Bender, 1988, p. 65). There are two distinct schools of thought regarding the acquisition of reading skills (see Figure 4-1); (1) the *bottom-up* (also known as *outside-in*)
theoretical perspective which adheres to the belief that beginning readers should
start from the bottom with sounds/letters and work up to the top (comprehension)
(Gough, 1972; LaBerge & Samuels, 1974). Students are instructed first in letter-

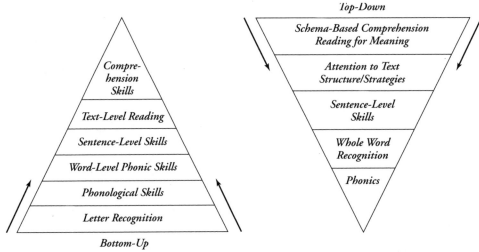

FIGURE 4-1 Models of Reading

sound correspondences before progressing to words and stories. Immediate and accurate recognition of sounds/words are considered necessary prerequisites to comprehension proficiency. (2) The opposing school of thought is called the *top-down theory,* also known as *inside-out,* and is based on the premise that higher level cognitive processes, such as understanding the gist and reading for meaning, should be stressed more than lower level word recognition skills, such as decoding. Those who follow this approach stress the reading of connected text as opposed to a skills approach (Goodman & Goodman, 1982).

Before determining an appropriate course of reading action, several issues need to be considered which include developmental concerns and affective dimensions (motivation, purpose setting, background building, sensitivity to multicultural issues, and establishing an inviting classroom environment). Sometimes subtyping classifications are considered before prescribing procedures/methods/techniques for the student with dyslexia.

Subtyping Considerations

We believe that there are three basic subtypes: an auditory-linguistic type, a visual-perceptual type, and a mixed type with symptomology consistent with the first two types combined. Our subtypes would be similar to those of Boder (1970) and Manzo and Manzo (1993) who believe that word learning problems can be categorized as (1) **dysphonetic** (poor understanding of graphemes or letter correspondences and phonemes or sounds) problems, (2) **dyseidetic** (poor ability to recognize sight words but able to use some phonics knowledge) problems, and (3) **dysphonetic-dyseidetic** (poor phonics/sight word knowledge) problems. Essentially these problem types serve as classification types for some students with dyslexia. Boder (1970) states that the majority of students with severe reading problems are of the dysphonetic type. Current practices and theory do not allow educators to definitively classify students with dyslexia into specific subtypes. There is yet to be a consensus in the field regarding a subtyping schema or how to remediate various subtypes. However, there seems to be a consensus regarding the belief that most students with severe forms of dyslexia have phoneme awareness deficiencies. In choosing teaching techniques/strategies/programs for students with dyslexia, we recommend providing intense decoding strategies which key the learner into phomenic awareness tasks. Actually, we agree with Manzo and Manzo's contention that, "most students tend to need a decoding program" (p. 234).

In determining specific areas to teach, we recommend using a word recognition diagnostic checklist (see Table 4-4) as it emcompasses a wide range of skills required for efficient word recognition. Very simply, the teacher or professional can check problem areas after using informal or formal assessments and then prescribe remediation based on activities related to the deficit area. We are recommending several word recognition techniques after a review of research which focuses in on successful use with dyslexic populations.

Developmental Issues

Developmentally appropriate practices have become widely embraced since Dewey (1899) first advocated the use of developmental information by educators. The National Association for the Education of Young Children (NAEYC) (see

Bredekamp, 1992) state emphatically that all curriculum goals and teaching strategies must be designed to take into account learning styles, development, and ability levels. The NAEYC (see Bredekamp, 1992) recommends presenting reading curriculum at least, in part, through learning centers, and projects that reflect children's interests and learning styles, especially up to the age of eight. Visually based programs (see VAKT below) which stress bottom-up processing seem to be effective with young children (Silver, Hagin, and Beecher, 1978) and students with severe forms of dyslexia and reading disabilities. When considering adolescent students, Deshler, Schumaker, Alley, Warner, and Clark (1982) emphasize the necessity of including cognitive study skills strategies in programs for students with dyslexia and other learning disabilities (see Chapters 6 and 7). Sprinthall, Sprinthall, and Oja (1994) stress the study of various developmental theories and approaches before implementing curriculum designs.

Teachers need to identify the student's current performance level so that instruction can be designed within proximity of the learner's ability. With instruction presented just at or above the learner's ability, students experience early and consistent success with each new skill or level. In this manner, the learner's developmental stage is used to determine appropriate curriculum and techniques. Bryant (1995) and others suggest a firm grounding in the works of Piaget and Vygotsky, as examples, in order to understand the development of children's understanding of relational concepts and specific abstractions.

Cognitive Learning Styles

Educators can look at learning styles and cognitive styles when discussing developmental issues as one's cognitions (thought processes) follow an ongoing process of development. Memory processes, as an example, are more highly developed in older children than in younger children probably because of increased language proficiency and the neurological maturing of the cerebral cortex. Current thinking views cognitive development more in terms of process as opposed to separate stages of development with distinct breaks (Morris, 1993).

Piaget (1952) specifically ties the development of one's thought capacities to teaching presentations. Concrete presentations are more appropriate for younger children as their experiences have not resulted in many opportunities for higher order thinking (e.g., making inferences). Certainly environmental influences have a great impact on how one responds to learning situations. Discussions of cognitive/behavioral responsiveness to the environment during learning situations have focused on: (1) *learning styles* or how students respond to various environmental influences—an individual's *external* responsiveness to the conditions under which learning occurs, and (2) **cognitive learning styles** or how individuals *internally* process information. Harris and Sipay (1990) have reviewed the literature and have concluded that there is little consensus as to what a learning style is or how one addresses learning styles in remedial settings. We have chosen to combine the terms, *cognitive* and *learning* into one encompassing descriptor, *cognitive-learning styles*. Cognitive-learning styles are really cognitive/behavioral correlates which are readily identifiable and overtly observed and

TABLE 4-1 Cognitive Learning Styles for Dyslexic Students with Unique Education Challenges

Cognitive/Behaviorial Characteristics	Strategic Environmental Accommodations
Dyslexic Students with Attention Deficits (see Chapter 1 for an in-depth discussion)	
Distractible	Provide environmental experiences which minimize visual/auditory distractions; modify classroom set-up if need be
Lack of follow through	Break tasks down into small steps; provide written step-by-step directions whenever possible; allow students to self-monitor progress by logging successes/completed tasks; modify expectations when necessary
Difficulty listening for sustained time frames	Minimize lengthy verbal exchanges; summarize whenever possible; be clear; repeat, rephrase, review to ensure understanding; encourage interactive, positive, and personally relevant exchanges for short time frames; ask the student to do an errand, move to another part of the classroom, shift gears, and change activities whenever you see attention is waning
Impulsive	Work on self-reflecting and self-monitoring behaviors and have students review the consequences of quick decision making; slow the individual down by using writing activities to summarize what needs to be done
Disorganized in planning for school and study as well as planning activities in personal life	Develop study skills/organizational skills (see Chapter 7); use assignment notebooks, calendars, notebooks, folders, chore charts, refrigerator reminders, bulletin board clips; encourage cooperative activities where good role models can emulate desired behaviors and outcomes
Difficulties in reading and written expressive language areas	Same techniques for other students with dyslexia mentioned in Chapters 6 and 7
Dyslexic Students with Special Gifts and Talents	
Intellectually superior in reasoning ability, analytical and holistic thought, metacognitive processing, and divergent thinking	Encourage sharing of learning outcomes and demonstrations to others; develop areas of giftedness and talent by providing enrichment activities which are highly personalized to the student's interests, aptitudes, and social/emotional/psychological needs; provide problem-solving situations (e.g., puzzles, mathematics problems, science experiments, analogies, etc.) which require divergent thinking
Inquisitive to the point of being irritating at times	Encourage positive interactive dialogues with others; develop questioning strategies (see Chapter 6); work on timing and appropriateness in questioning
Disorganized in planning for school and study as well as planning activities in personal life	Develop study skills/organizational skills (see Chapter 7); use assignment notebooks, and other activities mentioned above; encourage cooperative activities where good role models can emulate desired behaviors and outcomes
Prefers to work on independent assignments; likes to be alone; introverted	Balance independent activities with group assignments; encourage cooperative learning activities where the individual can serve as a coach or tutor

Continued

Cognitive/Behaviorial Characteristics	Strategic Environmental Accommodations
Dyslexic Students with Special Gifts and Talents	
Will dwell on shortcomings and negative environmental experiences, especially when wronged	Counseling if necessary; build self-esteem and self-confidence; provide as many opportunities for positive social interactions as possible to include group activities such as clubs (e.g., chess), the fine arts, and sports
Difficulties in reading and written expressive language areas	Same techniques for other students with dyslexia mentioned in Chapters 6 and 7; use reading/language materials which tap into special talents, interests, hobbies; encourage self-selection of library materials

TABLE 4-2   Famous Misjudged Gifted Individuals Who Were Dyslexic or Experienced Social/Learning Problems

Einstein—was thought to have learning problems because he did not communicate orally until age four and did not read until the age of seven.

Louisa May Alcott—was rejected by a newspaper editor as someone who could not write to the popular press.

Winston Churchill—was thought to be intellectually inferior when he failed sixth grade.

Werner von Braun—was thought to be a poor mathematician when he flunked 9th grade algebra.

Thomas Edison—was thought to be intellectually below average and uncreative when learning problems occurred as a young boy.

Beethoven—was thought to be totally lacking as a composer when he could not follow the directives of his music teacher.

Isaac Newton—was thought to be intellectually below average when he had very poor grade school performance.

Louis Pasteur—was thought to be very mediocre in chemistry when he demonstrated average potential in college.

F.W. Woolworth—was thought to be totally inept in business when his employers refused to allow him to wait on customers when he was twenty-one.

characterize how students internally and externally respond to environmental influences in a learning/teaching environment. We would agree with Harris and Sipay's (1990) contention that modality preference or matching a student's strongest learning mode with a corresponding teaching method is NOT supported by the research. Careful consideration of the research needs always to be a critical issue (Sprinthall, Schmutte, & Sirois, 1991).

Special characteristics which impact the learner with specific environmental accommodations seen as positively impacting adaptive learning/social functioning should be viewed (Durkin, 1989). Two special instances of dyslexia, students with attention deficits (ADD), and students with special gifts and talents, demonstrate well how consideration of the unique and special cognitive-learning styles of individuals with dyslexia and other disabilities can enhance learning experiences. Perhaps keying in to the cognitive-learning characteristics of individuals who are dyslexic or learning disabled may result in more appropriate diagnostic/remedial courses of action. The gifted learning disabled population is an excellent example of how some very gifted and imaginative people throughout history were overlooked or misdiagnosed because professionals did not assess their cognitive-learning styles/talents. Please refer to Tables 4-1 and 4-2.

Developing Affective Dimensions in a Reading Program

Motivation for Reading

"No object is more important than to gain the love and good will of those who are [to be taught] . . . In no way is this more easily accomplished than by a kind interest manifested in the students welfare; an interest which is exhibited by actions as well as words. This cannot fail of being attended with desirable results . . ." (Hall, 1829, p. 67). Hall sets the teaching stage for all of us—preparing teachers to cultivate individually the minds and affections of students, while creating a learning atmosphere that is personalized and enjoyable for everyone. The psychological and affective dimensions involved in teaching need to be researched and considered in terms of developmental issues and theoretical perspectives (Woolfolk, 1993).

Individuals with learning problems especially need to be personally invested in the reading setting. The reader will notice as research methods and general findings are mentioned, the terms *dyslexia, learning-disabled, poor readers, disabled reader, readers with word recognition problems,* and others are used interchangeably. The variation in terminology reflects the fact that there is little or no consensus in the field regarding finer differences in such terminology. Remember that many individuals with dyslexia, a type of learning disability, do experience word recognition difficulties. However, NOT all students with dyslexia experience word recognition difficulties. It is our belief that many of the recommendations listed in the following chapters would benefit all readers who experience difficulty acquiring the skills necessary to be proficient readers. As in any good teaching program, one has to have a bag of tricks that makes it easy for the teacher to shift gears when certain methods or techniques don't work. Moore, Moore, Cunningham, and Cunningham (1994) point out that it is critical to first establish the motivation necessary to make students with reading problems eager learners and to provide them with the prerequisite knowledge that will enable them to achieve a purpose for reading. The following examples illustrate how generating discussion/activating background knowledge can enhance purpose-setting/learning.

Background Building and Purpose Setting

As soon as words are learned they should be used in the context of personalized, meaningful sentences so as to foster a real purpose for the reading experience. There has to be background building in reading for purpose setting (Bartlett, 1932; Ausubel, 1960) especially in the case of the student with dyslexia.

Secondary
AMERICAN JUSTICE SYSTEM

Jurisprudence and the
Scales of Justice

What symbols do you see?

What do they mean?

Why are the scales balanced?

Why is she blindfolded?

What does her garment signify?

Elementary

What symbol do you see?

How do you feel when you
see this symbol?

When do you feel the happiest?

**FIGURE 4-2   Generating Discussion/Activating
Background Knowledge**

Because reading is usually slow and laborious for these students, purpose setting must occur at the outset.

According to Stanovich (1994), children who lack phonological awareness and have too much trouble with word recognition don't find the reading experience rewarding. "When word recognition processes demand too much cognitive capacity, fewer cognitive resources are left to allocate to higher-level processes of text integration and comprehension" (Stanovich, 1994, p. 281). It would be important for the child with dyslexia experiencing word-recognition difficulties to understand the nature of his/her problem so that remedial efforts make sense to the child. Teachers need to key in on the individual and specific word-recognition strengths and deficits of students with dyslexia by using a variety of informal and formal assessments. Children should know how important it is to identify words so that reading sentences and paragraphs is facilitated.

Sensitivity to Multicultural Factors/Literacy

". . . Developing language and literacy in multicultural content topics is based on the dual premises that learning is personal and that teaching provides opportunities for students to transact a wide range of meaningful, relevant, and functional learning experiences to flesh out their own world view and learn other world views while increasing their independent learning strategies . . ." (Crawford, 1993, p. 279). Strategies for teaching multicultural content topics apply especially to the social studies area. The growing presence of students with dyslexia in all classrooms calls for multicultural, process-based strategies to support students in "reading to learn." There are specific activities which can be used for multiethnic education classes and ethnic heritage studies.

Specific Activities for Multicultural Education

According to Jarolimek (1990), the major focuses of multiethnic education for all students need to be on " . . . truthful accounts of the multiethnic composition of this society; . . . [developing] a sense of pride in the multiethnic heritage of this nation; . . . [developing] a respect for the contributions of all groups to the life and culture of this nation]; . . . [developing] harmonious social relations resulting from the use of acceptable methods of resolving social conflicts . . . [and] [developing and understanding] that much of the strength of this nation derives from the diversity of its ethnic heritages and cultural origins . . ." (p. 192).

Jarolimek provides an excellent listing of specific activities teachers can use to accomplish the aforementioned goals in multiethnic studies. These include:

1. researching contemporary groups that have been established because of particular ethnic identities
2. creating scrapbooks of outstanding persons from different ethnic backgrounds who have made contributions in a particular area
3. creating or acting out puppet shows and plays that take a folktale or story from a particular ethnic group
4. learning folktales, poems, dances, songs, holidays, festivals, food items, etc. from different ethnic groups
5. encouraging students to tune in to radio or TV shows which focus on a particular culture
6. using the phone directory to locate names associated with particular ethnic groups
7. writing newspaper articles, stories, and poems about different ethnic studies
8. inviting representatives from the community to speak of their cultural heritages and roots
9. preparing bulletin boards and displays of different countries and ethnic groups

Focusing on particular words or terminology particular to a cultural group can enrich the learning environment for all as seen in the activities in Figures 4-3 and 4-4.

Jackson (1993/1994) is quick to point out that teachers must not stress "cognitive aspects of teaching . . . at the expense of developing the affective aspects . . ." (p. 299). Some icebreakers can be posed in the form of questions: "What generation in the United States do you or your parents represent?" "Have you ever seen

Name: _____

Be a Team Player

Think about this first:
Coach Taylor and Coach Powell always tell their players, "Whether you are in the classroom or on the court, a winner never quits and a quitter never wins!"

By drawing a line, match the Coaches 7 "Magic" basketball principles with the correct Kwanzaa principle.

Umoja   _____ Working as a team player for the good of all.

Imani   _____ Working collectively as a team to "become winners."

Nia   _____ Sharing personal items and other things needed for survival of the team and spirit.

Kuumba   _____ Knowing when to shoot the ball or when to make quick decisions on the court.

Ujamaa   _____ Making the community more beautiful by volunteering your services in ways that will make other peoples lives better.

Kujichagulia   _____ Setting long-term and short-term goals for the team and then reaching for your dreams.

Ujima   _____ Finding a purpose to work together on and off the court especially in the classroom where studying together can make you better students.

Bonus Essay: On the back of your paper, describe the Kwanzaa principles that best describe our Olympic gold medal "Dream Team."

FIGURE 4-3   Cross-Cultural Enrichment—Learning New Words

a family tree?" "If not, ask your parent(s)/guardian(s) if you can make a family tree." "From what country(ies) or where did your ancestors come from?" "What are some cultural customs your family might identify with (i.e., food, dress, social behaviors, special celebrations)?" "What holidays does your family like to celebrate?" "What occupations do some of your ancestors represent?" and "What makes you proud about your ancestors?" Certainly Jackson's (1993/1994) contentions that we have high

Cloud Crystal Ball

Look into your "Cloud Crystal Ball." What can you do in the future to make this a better world? Martin Luther King Jr. made this a better world by living, "I Have A Dream."

You can also dare to make your dreams come true. Write about your dream for a better world inside the "Cloud Crystal Ball."

Teachers: Use the Cloud Crystal Ball sheet for this bulletin board.

FIGURE 4-4 Applying a Cultural Heritage to Creative Writing

expectations for all students and ought to avoid stereotypical thinking that may impact student's perceptions need to be embraced along with the following general reading suggestions.

Establishing an Inviting Classroom Environment

The establishment of a comfortable classroom climate needs to occur in a supportive, nourishing, and individualized manner. While establishing a positive and affirming atmosphere, teachers need to organize the classroom as a literate community where readers and writers interact and share their work while communicating and learning from one another. A helping ethic, in our view, would be more beneficial than the particular method used, especially in light of the fact that students with dyslexia frequently experience low self-esteem and low self-image (Spafford & Grosser, 1993).

TABLE 4-3   Word Recognition Characteristics

Dyslexics	Proficient Readers	Remedial Strategies and Assists
Passive Learners—Low Self Concepts	Confident—Interact with Print	Helping Ethic Inviting Classroom
Lack of Sufficient Phonological Awareness	Effective Phonological Awareness	Predictable Books Phonetic Awareness Programs—A.D.D. and Reading from Scratch
Lack Automaticity in Word Recognition	Automaticity in Decoding	Technology Usage Multiple Readings Language Experience Word Bank Families
Limited Sight Vocabularies	Good Sight Vocabularies	Dolch and Fry Lists Games, Modeling
Ineffective Metacognitive Awareness at Word Level	Monitors Comprehension of Word Meaning	Self-Questioning Dictionary Usage Word Games
Limited Vocabularies	Good Expansive Vocabularies	Context Cues Semantic Mapping VSS, SCANR Vocabulary Overview Guide Vocabulary Circles Concept Maps Feature Analysis
Extreme Cases—Severely Dyslexic	Extreme Cases—Gifted Readers	Synthetic Phonics, Monroe, Fernald-Keller, Gillingham-Stillman, Reading Recovery Recipe for Reading Slingerland Writing Road to Reading

The classroom atmosphere should allow for the development of each student's awareness of his/her own thoughts and needs when reading so that a purpose can be set for the reading task itself along with strategies to achieve that purpose. Cognitive awareness and control of one's thoughts and strategies is known as **metacognition** and is requisite to reading success. Proficient readers have good metacognitive awareness when confronted with reading tasks whereby they can *actively* use strategies in a purposeful and independent manner (Mason & Au, 1990). Students with dyslexia on the other hand are often *passive* learners who lack the ability to produce and monitor adequate reading behaviors (Harris & Graham, 1985). Reading instructors of individuals with dyslexia need to be able to assist them in a positive manner with the active construction of meaningful text-knowledge, so they can self-monitor the comprehension process. Several techniques mentioned later in this chapter can assist in this regard.

Both the diagnosis of reading problems and the identification of strengths allow for the flexibility necessary in appropriate programming. Please keep in mind the reasons why individuals with dyslexia differ from proficient readers. This knowledge is key as there are differences in cognitive functioning that can be identified and targeted for remedial efforts. Learning to read is based on a wide range of linguistic and metacognitive skills, each of which is important to the reading process itself. It has been shown that individuals with dyslexia display language deficits in both the oral and expressive realms (Murphy, Pollatsek, & Well, 1988). The word recognition characteristics in Table 4-3 have been identified as problem areas for many individuals with dyslexia. Specific remedial strategies and assists will follow the discussions of these characteristics.

Initial Reading Challenges—Developing Word Recognition Skills

Ekwall and Shanker (1988) describe reading as a process of "recognizing and analyzing words and understanding words and ideas" (p. 73). The necessity for identifying word recognition strengths and weaknesses is particularly relevant to the student with dyslexia as fast and accurate word recognition abilities are frequently lacking in this population. Remedial programs should be matched to deficit areas as they are identified and remedial activities should always occur in the context of connected print (e.g., books). There are several word recognition strategies and remedial procedures mentioned in this chapter. These need to be matched carefully to the deficit areas noted on the diagnostic word recognition checklist (see Table 4-4). Some strategies work better with different children depending on the severity of the disability, intellectual capacity, social/emotional factors, and so on. Students need to be trained to be able to use several ways to recognize words. Typically, students with dyslexia can use the following basic sequence when encountering pronunciation difficulties.

1. Try to sound out the word using phonics.
2. Look at word parts like root words, prefixes, and suffixes:

TABLE 4-4 Diagnostic Word Recognition Checklist

Write "Yes" or "No" if Mastered

Use of Graded Word List for *Vocabulary Level* (e.g., WRAT-III, Informal Reading Inventory)

List used: _____

_____ Independent Level (no more than one error in ten words)

_____ Instructional Level (no more than two errors in ten words)

_____ Frustration Level (more than two errors in ten words)

Automaticity in Reading

(see comprehension checklist to calculate)

Reading Rate _____ words per minute

Word Identification Errors or Miscues

_____ guesses that distort meaning ("grass" for "snow")

_____ misuses context clues

_____ fails to self-correct

_____ skips unknown words

_____ substitutes meaning words ("grass" for "lawn")

_____ repeats letters, words, or phrases ("the nice, nice person")

_____ inserts words that don't belong ("and so" after each sentence)

_____ mispronunciations

_____ letter or word reversals ("tap" for "pat"; "lake" for "leak")

Phonetic Analysis

Consonants (one)

_____ initial position (**m**an)

_____ medial position (na**m**e)

_____ final position (Pa**m**)

Consonants (clusters)

_____ two-letter blends (**pl**)

_____ three-letter blends (**spl**)

_____ digraphs (**sh**)

_____ hard and soft sounds of c ang g (**c**ity, **c**at, **g**iant, **g**oat)

Consonants (silent letter)

_____ (**k**nife) Circle troublesome silent letters: wr, kn, gn, gh, mb)

Vowels (one)

short   a ____ e ____ i ____ o ____ u ____

long   a ____ e ____ i ____ o ____ u ____

y (cry) _____ (long)   y

Vowels (two)

_____ digraphs (ea in leap)

_____ diphthongs (oy in boy)

_____ final silent e (bike)

_____ vowel controlled by "r" (her)

Structural Analysis

_____ Prefixes (initial syllables; **re**set): a, ab, ad, al, anti, be, com, con, de, en, for, fore, ex, im, in, inter, intra, mid, mis, non, out, per, pre, pro, re, sub, tele, trans, un

_____ Suffixes (word endings; love**ly**): age, al, able, an, ance, ant, ation, en, ence, ent, er, est, ey, full, fully, ian, ier, ible, ily, ion, ious, ish, ist, ity, ive, less, ling, ly, ment, ness, or, ous, th, ty, ure, ward, y

Compound Words _____ Possessives _____

Syllabication

_____ VC/CV rule example: but/ter

_____ V/CV rule example: e/ven

_____ VC/V rule example: lim/it

_____ V/CLE or VC/CLE example: mar/ble

_____ prefix/suffix as separate syllables examples: re/set; love/ly

Sight Word Recognition

_____ List used (e.g., Dolch)

List troublesome words

_____

_____

_____

_____

_____

TABLE 4-4 *(Continued)*

Context Clues	**Oral Reading Behaviors**
_____ attention to capital letters	_____ observes punctuation
_____ attention to double letters	_____ reads in phrases
_____ use of word length	_____ uses word recognition strategies
_____ use of pictures, diagrams	_____ uses expression/appropriate tonal qualities
_____ use of graphs, pictures, charts	_____ adjusts rate to task at hand (e.g., reading p versus narrative text)
_____ use of maps	
_____ use of atlas	

Dictionary Skills

_____ finds words quickly

_____ knows a, b, c order

_____ alphabetizes to 2nd & 3rd letters

_____ uses guide words

_____ uses pronunciation guide

_____ understands parts of speech

_____ interprets multiple definitions

_____ uses cross references

_____ understands word origins

_____ after definition can use word in a sentence

Behaviors/Attitudes During Observations

_____

_____

_____

_____

_____

Additional Comments

_____

_____

_____

_____

3. Write down the word and look up the pronunciation later (unless immediate identification is important).
4. Ask someone for help.

The same sequence of word recognition pronunciation strategies could be used when students are trying to discern word meaning except for (1). In place of the use of phonics, students can use context clues such as sentence and paragraph meaning, pictures cues, and other visuals to assist in word meaning. Teachers should try to anticipate word pronunciation/meaning problems by reviewing potential problems before an oral/silent reading assignment.

Developing Metalinguistic Awareness

In relation to reading ability, it is widely accepted that the foundation of literacy is based upon a person's awareness and knowledge of language. The ability to recognize symbols and words as representations of spoken language requires awareness of metalinguistic concepts such as *word, sound,* and *sentence.* Moreover, the basis for making these early connections is believed to rest in primary experiences with oral language: hearing and saying sounds, following the acoustic sequence of words and strings of words, internalizing these phonological patterns, and perceiving the segmentation of speech into units of words, syllables and phonemes. In keeping with the bottom-up models, these fundamental skills are believed to underlie the reading process. Decoding the printed page begins at the letter/word level where students can develop phoneme (sound)/grapheme (written symbol) connections. Speed and accuracy of decoding or identifying sound/symbol correspondences quickly is critical to future reading and writing successes.

Consonant sounds should be taught first; vowel sounds should be taught afterward. Following the introduction of long and short vowel sounds, other phonics specifics can be presented: silent final *e* after a long vowel sound (*cake*), vowel digraphs (*ea* in *seat* and *ie* in *pie*), vowel diphthongs (*ou* in *out* and *oy* in *toy*), vowels controlled by *r* (*r* in *her*), special sounds (schwa sound—*o* in *police*) and letters (hard and soft *c* and *g*; as in the *c* in *city* and *cut*), and phonograms (*ight* as in *bright, light,* and *sight*). Syllabication of words should also follow a developmental sequence according to Rubin (1991b)—vc/cv, v/cv, c/cle, open and closed syllables, and finally how and where to accent syllables.

The corrective phonics approach differs from a whole language perspective, discussed later in this chapter, in which it is believed that students discover phonics rules and generalizations inductively as they read and discover the printed page. We advocate phonics/phonemic awareness/skills work in connection with whole language activities because students with dyslexia are often quite deficient in recognizing letter-sound correspondences. Such training has been found to assist in that regard. In fact, Wallach and Wallach (1976) have found that students who experience phonics training achieve more in reading than students who do not have such training. Teaching phonemic awareness can be beneficial to children with dyslexia (Aaron & Baker, 1991). Phonological training can enhance phonemic awareness and usage as seen in the following example.

Various programs for teaching the skills for phonological awareness often provide concrete manipulatives. The use of manipulatives allows the teacher to pair auditory stimuli with visual presentations. For example, using various colored cubes in which each cube represents a single sound (phoneme) and each color represents the different sound, students are asked to construct the left-to-right pattern of a presented sound of sequence:

/ t /   / m /   / t /   = | red | | blue | | red |

/ m /   / m /   / s /   = | blue | | blue | | green |

The skills are developed to gradually include representing phonemes in whole words:

	b	r	u	sh
"brush" =	blue	red	yellow	green

This practice with phonemic segmentation builds a necessary foundation of phonological awareness.

FIGURE 4-5   Phonological Training

Phonemic Awareness—Strong Reading Predictor

Phonemic awareness is causally related to reading achievement and can be considered a strong predictor of reading ability. It has been well established in the literature that the majority of students with dyslexia lack sufficient phonemic or phonological awareness. Bradley (1988) had emphasized that phonological programs should combine with spelling remediation so that students can keep on making new connections between sound and print. There are a number of commercial phonics programs which can be used to enhance phonological awareness and provide practice for children with learning disabilities. We will mention a few in the next chapter.

Automaticity in Reading

If students are to understand what is read, letter and word identification must occur automatically. Part of the decoding problem for individuals with dyslexia is the lack of automaticity (Perfetti & Lesgold, 1979). A distinction should be made between *controlled processing* versus *automatic processing* which is required for reading.

Controlled Versus Automatic Processing

Schneider and Shiffrin (1977) pointed out that controlled processing requires concerted attentiveness on the part of the individual to complete a task. This type of processing is likely to use most of the short-term memory capacity of the individual. Contrarily, automatic processing happens with little conscious effort and places few demands on short-term memory capacity. Most people can only attend to one task that demands controlled attention. On the other hand, one can attend to more than one task if processing abilities are more or less automatic (e.g., driving and conversing at the same time; driving should be automatic). Students who are proficient readers are able to decode automatically the written symbols of speech sounds (Rubin, 1991a, 1991b, p. 280), as reading depends on an automatic speech-to-print match.

Speed in Word Recognition

Speed or automaticity in word reading impacts reading rate—the number of words per minute a student can read. Reading rates are typically slower for the student with dyslexia who has difficulty adjusting to different reading situations.

Types of Reading and Speed Required

Richardson and Morgan (1994) list several factors which impact reading speed or rate such as the type of material used, familiarity with content, reader's motivation and purpose, size of type, and physical conditions (e.g., lighting, lack of sleep, presence of directions, and so on). Students with dyslexia will need to learn to adjust to different reading situations—a speed range of 100–200 words per minute (WPM) is required for reading material which requires a careful analysis of highly technical content (e.g., science texts) and poetry; a speed range of 600–800 wpm is needed for speed reading of newspapers, magazines, etc. Most reading material of the study-type nature requires 200–300 wpm (Richardson & Morgan, 1994). It has been shown that some of the techniques mentioned in this chapter such as multiple readings and predictable books improve reading rate.

Rauding

Carver (1992) has described "rauding" as the merging of reading (by looking and understanding) with auding (listening and understanding) into what is considered the reading process. For middle school students, an average rauding rate is 190 words per minute with a typical average of 300 words per minute for college students. A student with dyslexia would read below these rates meaning that the amount of reading materials a student with dyslexia could accomplish would be less than the proficient reader (Richardson & Morgan, 1994). Teachers need to reduce reading assignments accordingly and need to teach specific strategies for adjusting reading rates. The rate at which one reads depends primarily upon the purpose for reading. The following reading rates would be expected for students with dyslexia at the college level, remembering that success in college depends in part on how well the student processes the curriculum content via college texts.

Reading Style	Example	For the Dyslexic	Proficient Readers
Scanning	Finding Cue Words	400–500 wpm	600 wpm
Skimming	Proofreading	300–350 wpm	450 wpm
Rauding	Comprehension of Text	200–250 wpm	300 wpm
Text Mastery	Oral Report Prep	100–150 wpm	200 wpm
Memorizing	Essay Exam	75–100 wpm	150 wpm

Reading rate should never be stressed at the expense of comprehension. Repeated readings of textual material; the previewing of important concepts, vocabulary, and ideas of text to be read; and the use of study skills (see Chapter 7) will help to improve reading rates. The present authors are not recommending "speed reading courses" for students with dyslexia as we are not convinced by supportive research that speed reading approaches are beneficial for this population.

Automaticity and Cognition

Speed in word recognition is a major factor when constructing text meaning. If too many cognitive resources are spent on decoding, there can be a concomitant loss of meaning (LaBerge & Samuels, 1974; Gough, 1983; Perfetti, 1985). " . . . automaticity in decoding is a necessary, but not sufficient, component of the meaning-making process; a decoding program can be considered only one part of a total program to improve the reading of poor readers . . ." (Gaskins, Downer, Anderson,

Cunningham, Gaskins, Schommer, & the Teachers at Benchmark School, 1988, p. 37). Certainly the repeated practice afforded by phonics programs enhances automaticity in word recognition. This is only one piece to a comprehensive reading program which should include literature offerings, sight-word recognition exercises, vocabulary skills development, whole-language activities, comprehension development, and so forth (see the sections that follow and Chapter 5). Certainly all students are in need of such well-rounded reading programs. The student with dyslexia should be able to participate in such programming efforts and not be limited to remedial worksheet skills work and the like.

Sight Word Recognition and Automaticity

The student with dyslexia must not only be able to decode but will need to have a repertoire of sight words which do not require sounding out phoneme by phoneme. Admittedly, the following approaches do require some decoding on the part of the reader. However, the main thrust of these sight word methods is to develop as many sight words as possible to improve speed and accuracy of word recognition. Although decoding is a prerequisite to reading success, it slows down the reading process when it impedes the acquisition of automatic word recognition.

Sight-Word Approaches

A sight-word approach involves having students memorize certain words by sight without sounding out the word parts. It is estimated that from 200 to 300 sight words (e.g., *was, about, the*) comprise up to 80–90% of the reading material in the elementary grades. Bender (1985) has found that students with reading disabilities have more limited sight vocabularies than non-disabled peers. Sight word approaches stress the use of configuration (word shape) cues with little emphasis on decoding letter sounds. One's sight vocabulary (i.e., words that are recognized instantly and have meaning) needs to include high frequency words found in literature and content area subjects. The *Dolch Basic Sight Word List* (Dolch, 1942), and the *New Instant Word List* (Fry, 1980) provide excellent resource listings of commonly used sight words.

Instructional Strategies to Remediate Deficient Sight Vocabularies

Word Vocabularies

Several teacher-directed activities can be used to teach sight words to students with dyslexia. These include:

1. Modeling, in which the teacher presents a sight word in an oral context and then in written form (e.g., labels placed on objects around the room). The teacher should point to initial, medial, and final letters.

2. Word bank cards—students can be paired to quiz each other on sight word identification with the teacher serving as a consultant when needed.

3. Copying—students create and read sentences with new sight words with immediate feedback for incorrect answers; rereadings may be necessary.

4. Reading in context—students read stories under the direction of the teacher with the new sight words to be learned; the teacher can point out or ask the students about new words in the story.

5. Games—students can use word games (e.g., acrostics and picture-word matches, see Table 4-6, p. 88) bingo games, etc., to reinforce new sight words; these activities should be structured with the goal of 90% success for sight word identification.

Multiple re-readings, language experience approaches, and word banks also provide good sight word recognition practice.

As can be seen (in Figure 4-6), teachers can use clip art from computer programs to create pictorial representations of words. Activities can change in which students have to fill in a name, draw a picture, and create special words to accompany pictures which are very subjectively interpreted. Chaining or sequencing word vocabularies is especially important to the writing process.

Students with dyslexia can list a "chain of events" in an outline format before writing. The following example demonstrates how "chaining" helps connect sequences of discrete thought elements as well as establish cause-and-effect relationships.

Topic: How to Scramble Eggs
Chain of Events:

> get ingredients
> turn on stove
> preheat pan with a little margarine or butter
> crack open eggs
> stir in milk
> stir ingredients in pan
> cook until liquid is gone
> flavor
> serve with toast
> eat

How to Cook Scrambled Eggs

by Kenny Spafford

To make the best scrambled eggs, gather two eggs and a half cup of milk. Then preheat the stove to medium with a pan on top of it. Add enough butter or margarine to the pan and heat until melted. Next, crack the two eggs in the pan and add a half cup of milk. Later, stir the eggs until well cooked and very soft. If the eggs are still like a liquid, cook for a few more minutes until the liquid is gone. Finally, put the eggs on a plate and add pepper with onions on top for flavor. This makes two servings. Serve with toast. Eat and enjoy.

FIGURE 4-6　Word Fun

Source: ClickArt™

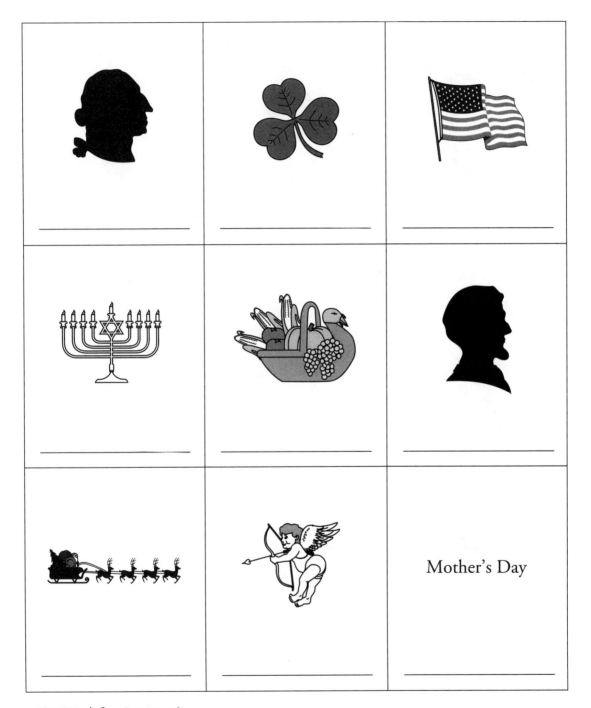

FIGURE 4-6 *Continued*

Source: Christmas 2, ClickArt™ Holidays

FIGURE 4-6 *Continued*

TABLE 4-6   Acrostic

Recycle
Everything like
Cans and
You'll even save trees
Collecting newspapers and please
Leave plastic bottles
Each week to be recycled

Multiple Re-readings or Repeated Readings.   Samuels (1979) suggested the method of multiple re-readings for fluency improvement. Samuels believed that this method could be reliably assessed under timed conditions as long as baseline data on reading rates was established. Goals are established which address reading rate with class readings repeated until the goal is achieved (this is usually done in a one-on-one tutorial type of setting). Research has shown that such an approach can increase reading rate, accuracy in word recognition, and comprehension in poor readers and students with learning disabilities (Dahl, 1979; Mathes & Fuchs, 1993). With instructional or leisure reading material, the child selects favorite segments of text for reading aloud. A tape recording of early and subsequent readings can be used to highlight the gains in fluency and accuracy. Difficult material should always be read aloud by the teacher first so that the child hears the language.

Predictable Books.   Predictable books can be found in local libraries and these utilize an easy-to-read format that is composed of repetitive words, phrases, and sentences. The repetitive structures and predictable text promote accuracy and fluency as the reader engages in multiple readings of the text. An example of such a predictable book on a multicultural topic is *The Adventures of Dr. McKite* (a pilot project) by Carol S. Spafford. The text of the first page of this book for children reads as follows:

> *In happy happy land of our dreams*
> *Was really really born it really seems*
> *Two very very special colored friendship kites*
> *A traveling traveling to wonderful sky-blue heights.*
>
> *(Spafford, 1992)*

It is recommended that the teacher first read the story aloud to the child as he/she follows the print. As familiar words and phrases are encountered, the student is encouraged to take over segments of the reading, eventually assuming the full role. In this manner, the child learns to read by reading.

Language Experience Approach.   The language experience approach is another effective whole word approach for beginning readers or the student with dyslexia. This technique utilizes the child's natural (conversational) language and

FIGURE 4-7   The Kinera for Kwanzaa

real experiences to create text for reading. The child dictates a story about a recent event or topic of interest (e.g., see Figure 4-7) while the teacher records the
sentences. The completed language story is used for reading and various exten-
sion activities. For example, sentence strips can be printed from the story and used
to reconstruct the story, first by visual matching with the original story, and then
from memory. Similarly, sentence-building tasks can be conducted using cut up
words from a single sentence. A window card can by used to isolate words within
the story for practice in word recognition. Alternatively, word-finding tasks require
the child to scan the story locating the target word. Word-slotting tasks involve the
manipulation of single words within a sentence to change meaning and expand
vocabulary, such as, "Sam wanted to ride/fix/clean his bike." The variety of practice that extends from the language experience story provides considerable re-

Directions: Name and color your kites. Write friendship adjectives in the clouds to describe your kites.

FIGURE 4-8   Friendship Kites

Source: by Kathy Sullivan

dundancy for developing automatic word recognition and fluency in connected print (Dautrich, 1994). Words that have been mastered can be used for word bank activities and bulletin boards (see Figure 4-8, p. 90).

Word Banks. Word banks are useful for collecting mastered sight words and building word families. As words from reading are mastered as sight words, they can be printed on note cards and stored for periodic review and practice. The collection of words can be used in classifying activities in which words are grouped or sorted according to similar phonetic or visual properties. For example, the student might assemble a word family utilizing the silent e pattern or a common structural ending (e.g., *tion, ed, ful*). Visual (non-phonetic) patterns are also studied (e.g., *bridge, fudge, badge*). As the word bank grows, the child has key measures of reading progress (Dautrich, 1994). The development of vocabulary through word banks and other instructional methods has been shown to increase both word knowledge and comprehension (Adams, 1990). Vocabulary words in word banks can be used in high-interest word games. Word games promote repetition in word presentations, critical to acquisition of word automaticity, which is lacking in many students with dyslexia.

Word Games. Words games can be created like "Rabble, Scrabble", "Lingo Bingo," and "Concentration Watch" using variations of commercially-produced products. Students can use scrabble tiles to create their own word games or slang/lingo terms to create a word bingo game. Concentration word games could involve taking vocabulary words in duplicate from one's word bank to create a concentration matching memory game on the floor. More well known word games like "Wordy Gurdy" and "Oxymoron" challenges have been suggested by Bowman (1991). The game "Wordy Gurdy" requires that the student have good rhyming abilities. Teachers or students (working in pairs or groups) create definition lists. In a game situation, students must find two rhyming words (same number of syllables in each word) which could be linked to the definition, e.g., big twig (branch), prime time (best time for something), a hip clip (good movie), merry Gerry (happy Gerard), and Flo's woes (Florence's troubles).

"Oxymoron" challenges could involve students working cooperatively to create oxymorons for current spelling lists, a science unit, and so on. To give a visual assist, the teacher could provide lists of terms students could use to create oxymorons. Remember that an oxymoron is a word pair where one word or term contradicts the other (e.g., *True Lies* [also movie title!], *illiterate writer, fast turtle, cat's bark,* etc.). These types of activities encourage dictionary usage (to find antonyms) and vocabulary development in a fun situation.

Developing Sight Vocabularies

Children with dyslexia are also often delayed in acquiring a sight vocabulary and do not pick up a working sight vocabulary based on continual exposure to high frequency words in their reading. Individuals with dyslexia require considerably more redundancy in their exposure to common sight words and require direct and repeated practice at processing whole words.

Many students with dyslexia have limited oral and written vocabularies. The word recognition difficulties experienced by these individuals inhibit, to some extent, vocabulary acquisition. Reading in content area subjects can be especially problematic for students with dyslexia, as content textbooks are typically more difficult in terms of vocabulary, structure, and familiarity than basal readers or library books. Skilled readers typically have expansive vocabularies. Nagy and Anderson (1984) estimate that good readers add up to 3,000 words every year to their reading vocabularies between the third and twelfth grades. This is because proficient readers encounter an average of 1,000,000 words per year on the printed page while the poorest readers are exposed to only approximately 100,000 words per year (Nagy & Anderson, 1984). Because vocabulary acquisition is strongly tied to the development of comprehension abilities (Farr, 1969) and writing quality (Duin & Graves, 1987), effective vocabulary instruction is needed for individuals with dyslexia (Beck, McKeown & Omanson, 1987). Carlisle (1993) stresses considering ". . . such problems as which words to select, how many words to teach in a unit, how much practice to give, and how much exposure to different meanings and different contexts to include . . ." (p. 100).

The Cloze Procedure—Developing an Expanded Vocabulary

Taylor (1953) first introduced the term "cloze" in reference to the Gestalt principle of "closure" or the ability to complete an incomplete stimulus. It is assumed that readers "fill-in" the gaps when needed because of prior experiences with text and background knowledge. For the student with dyslexia, the knowledge "background gaps" must be filled in with the assistance of the teacher, parent, or peer tutor. Although most professionals use the "exact word must be inserted" method of assessment, the present authors would recommend accepting synonyms for the student with dyslexia. If students with dyslexia can fill in the gaps for at least 40% of the material presented, an instructional level can be established, meaning the student is comfortable with that particular grade level textual material.

Summary of Cloze for Students with Dyslexia

1. Select a passage of 200–250 words.
2. Leave a few key sententences intact (especially main idea sentences) to provide context/meaning cues for the student.
3. Delete every fifth word and make a key of exact missing words and/or corresponding synonyms for the key words.
4. Accept synonyms or words that make sense in the blanks provided.
5. Students with dyslexia may need a "read through." That is, the teacher and student can read the selection orally with the student filling in the blanks during the oral reading. The teacher can provide clues or cues when the student is

"stuck." Repeated readings will help with fluency and content. Then the student is ready to read and write independently.

6. In order to determine a student's proficiency in completing the cloze exercise (which helps to assess vocabulary and comprehension proficiency), the teacher need only to double the number of correct responses and divide the number of correct responses by the number of errors or blanks and multiply by 100 (for a proficiency percentage). Richardson and Morgan (1994) suggest that students who score below 40% on instructional/diagnostic cloze exercises reach a frustration level where the material is inappropriate and too difficult for the student.

Using Context Clues

Students can bridge the gap between word recognition and comprehension of text by developing strategies which allow discerning word meaning from context clues. The SCANR acronym developed by Jenkins, Matlock, and Slocum (1989) instructs students to *s*ubstitute a word (*s*) for the problem word, *c*heck the surrounding context to confirm the reasonableness of the substitution(s), *a*sk or self-monitor to see if the new word actually fits, readjust if a *n*ew word(s) is *n*eeded, and *r*evise if necessary. This type of technique encourages flexibility on the part of the reader and self-monitoring and checking of ideas. Carlisle (1993) points out that given the problems experienced by students with reading disabilities, techniques like SCANR "may not be enough to teach the students the kind of mnemonic strategy for deriving meaning of unfamiliar words from context" (p. 103). Teachers will need to try a variety of approaches and techniques to enhance vocabulary acquisition such as the ones to follow.

Vocabulary Maps/Word Maps

Semantic Mapping also known as **List-Group-Label (LGL)** was developed by Taba in 1967. Taba developed this method of categorizing vocabulary terms in order to assist students with technical vocabulary in science and social studies texts. Students use three basic strategies: 1) listing stimulus words from the lesson, 2) making group/label lists, with a main topic as well as various subtopics, and 3) doing a follow-up, with reinforcement and checking. Students must have prior knowledge of the words to be classified for these techniques to be successful. LGL can be used to review material for tests and can assist a teacher in a pre-reading situation in determining where further instruction is needed. In a post-reading situation, LGL can help a teacher assess what learning has taken place.

Word analysis skills training needs to be continued at the college and university levels for students with learning disabilities. Figure 4-9 depicts how teachers of students with dyslexia at the college level can use vocabulary maps for higher level concepts. Another approach developed for the college-age student is Haggard's (1986a, 1986b) **Vocabulary Self-Collection Strategy.**

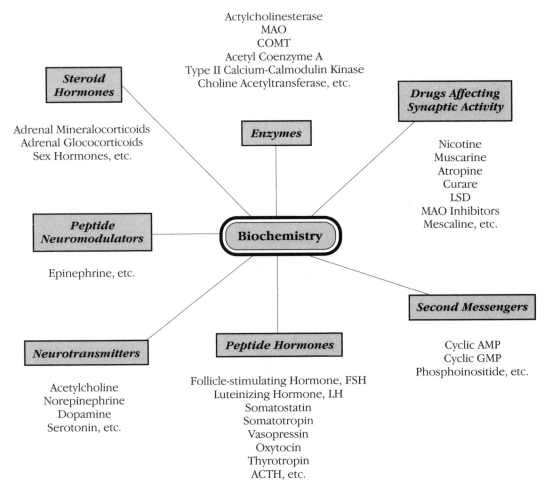

FIGURE 4-9   Illustration of a Higher Level Vocabulary Map of Nervous System Biochemistry (See also Table 4-5, page 100.)

Vocabulary Self-Collection Strategy (VSS)

This approach was developed by Haggard (1986a, 1986b) for students at all levels in helping students to create vocabulary lists that need to be learned based on the student's interest levels and prior schema. The four steps are as follows: (1) select words to be learned, (2) define words, (3) finalize word list(s), and (4) extend word knowledge. Students survey material and select words to be learned. (This can be a team effort.) In a class situation, students can nominate words to be learned, with students contributing in a discussion format as to the meaning(s) of the word(s) presented. Follow-up activities include using the chosen words in other activities, such as in composition writing with review providing opportunities for reinforcement. According to Haggard (1986b), the VSS approach, provides ". . . an internal motivation . . . [for] vocabulary acquisition and development . . . allows one to develop systematic, personalized strategies for word learning . . . [and] increases sensitivity to new words and enjoyment in word learning . . ."(p. 640). The use of interrogative reading lessons can enhance this process.

Interrogative Reading—Enhancing Vocabulary Acquisition

The student with dyslexia needs to have experiences with various types of questions during sustained silent reading. Self-questioning while reading enhances comprehension. Models and samples provide concrete feedback and assists especially if they relate to the task at hand.

Question Category	Sample Question
Background Knowledge	How can characters be used as **images** for other concepts?
Main Idea	How does the use of the three witches in the play *Macbeth* set an evil tone, a tone of suspense, and a tone of prophecy?
Character Related	What does the "hell-broth" of the three witches tell you about their characters? Remember the "toes of the frog" and the "eyes of the newt."
Recall	When do the three witches appear throughout the play?
Prediction	Can you predict the answer to the witches question in Act I, Scene I: "When shall we three meet again? In thunder, lightning, or rain?"
Inferential	Why is the vision of a child crowned holding a tree in his hand in Act IV of *Macbeth* an apparition about Macbeth becoming the King of Scotland?
Personal Feelings	What do you think about Macbeth's means of becoming King of Scotland?
Related to Other Works	Name on other Shakespearean play that uses a character as an **image.** What is the name of the character and what is the **image**?
Related to Life Experiences	Who have you read about that murdered someone else to achieve a goal? What was your reaction?
Personal Response	Who would you rather have for a friend, Macbeth or Duncan? Why?

Assignment: Describe how William Shakespeare used the three witches as **images** in his play Macbeth. Focus on what an **image** is.

Vocabulary Overview Guide

There is another approach available for the improvement of word-analysis skills among college-age individuals. Carr (1985) has offered three steps to improve vocabulary understanding, interest, and involvement in learning:

Vocabulary Overview Guide (Adapted from Carr, 1985)

1. Before Reading—(a) Define vocabulary by using familiar context after surveying material titles and headings. (b) Underline unknown words. (c) Try to help students use context first in determining meaning. (d) Use the dictionary to help with meaning. (e) Write definitions to reinforce concepts and usage.
2. During reading—Reinforce vocabulary comprehension by keying in on prereading words.
3. After reading—Complete a vocabulary overview guide by having students write (a) titles and category titles, (b) vocabulary terms, (c) definitions along with synonyms and antonyms, and (d) clues to meaning.
4. Study—Have students read titles and categories. Have students use clues and predict words in pairs. Continually review learned terms. Add synonyms and antonyms to previously-learned terms.

Vocabulary/Concept Circles

One practice format for vocabulary involves development of categorization skills through the use of vocabulary circles divided in fourths. This technique allows students with dyslexia to receive visual assists when trying to determine essential features or relationships among vocabulary terms especially in the science area. There are a variety of ways in which vocabulary circles can be used (see Figures 4-10 and 4-11).

Feature Analysis

Similar to vocabulary/concept circles are feature analysis grids which allow students to methodically display relationships according to commonalities/characteristics/differences. Feature analysis is particularly helpful when confronted with technical science jargon. (see Table 4-5, p. 100.)

Keyword Strategies

Keyword strategies are essentially memory strategies which combine familiar concepts with unfamiliar terms by some unusual but memorable linkage(s). For example, one could try to remember the meaning of the term, *radiant* by picturing radii extending from the center of an animated and smiling circle. For younger children, memory for the word meaning of, *"loud,"* could involve picturing someone holding their ears while saying *"ou[ch]."* However, we would agree with Manzo and Manzo (1993) that the memory demands of this method on students preclude its use to any great extent with children under the age of 11. These authors do stress a few potential pluses of the keyword method with adolescents: (1) the uniqueness of the key-word method provides a high-interest challenge to the learner and (2) the use of particular keyword allows teachers to obtain another look at a student's thought processes. Pressley, Levin, and Miller (1981); Mastropieri, Scruggs, and Levin (1985); and Konopak and Williams (1988) have successfully used keyword strategies for teaching vocabulary to students with dyslexia

Add Another Name to Finish Each Circle, Then Label Circle Number 2

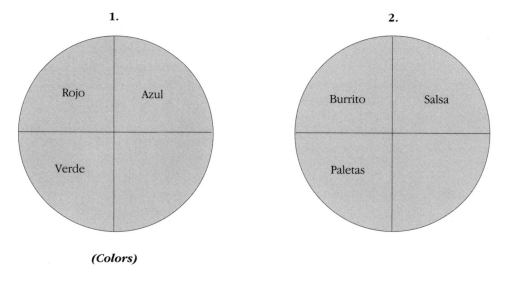

1.

Rojo   Azul

Verde

(Colors)

2.

Burrito   Salsa

Paletas

Cross out the term that does not belong

3.

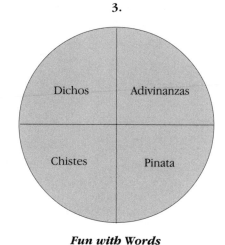

Dichos   Adivinanzas

Chistes   Pinata

Fun with Words

FIGURE 4-10   Vocabulary Circles in Spanish

and other learning disabilities. Essentially, students use a keyword mediator to represent information to be learned. (See Chapter 7 for study skills applications.)

Using the Dictionary as a Learning Aid

Manzo and Manzo (1993) suggest that dictionary usage is a necessary component to remedial programs as word prounications, meaning vocabulary, allusions, etymologies, facts, word structures, and word spellings gleaned from dictionaries can

Name the Concept That Labels the Terms in Each Circle

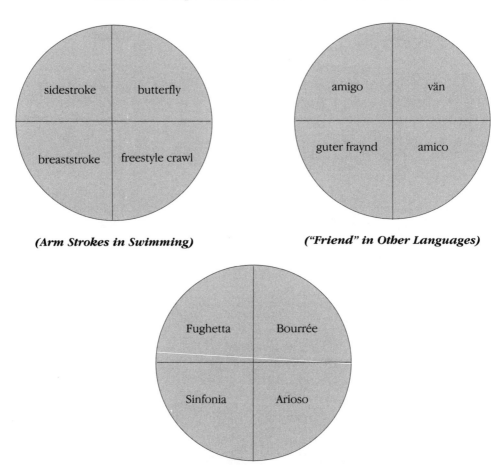

(Arm Strokes in Swimming)

("Friend" in Other Languages)

(Johann Sebastian Bach Compositions)

FIGURE 4-11   Vocabulary Circles

support vital word-literacy development. There are various types of dictionaries available to the student with dyslexia. There are *poor-spellers'* dictionaries which allow students to find entry words first by a phonetic pronunciation with correct spellings to follow; *picture dictionaries* for nonreaders; and *computer-driven dictionaries* on many word-processing programs to include spell checks, the finding of synonyms and antonyms, and multiple word meanings. Computer technology goes beyond word-processing programs to facilitate the reading process. For example, *Multimedia World* has designated Microsoft's® (available in most computer stores) Encarta® CD-ROM program as the 1994 Reader's Choice Awards favorite encyclopedic/dictionary type of program as historical sound clips, photographs, and animated sequences enhance word/topic meanings.

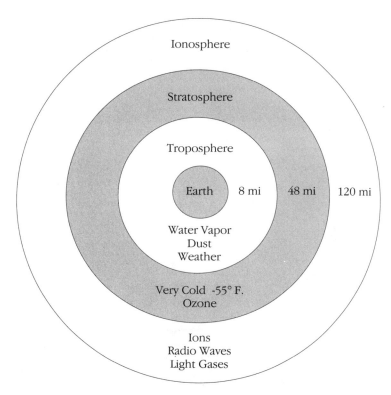

Ionosphere

Stratosphere

Troposphere

Earth   8 mi   48 mi   120 mi

Water Vapor
Dust
Weather

Very Cold -55° F.
Ozone

Ions
Radio Waves
Light Gases

**FIGURE 4-12   Concept Map (Diagram) Layers of the
Atmosphere**

Special Technology Usage

"Of all the areas in reading, the collection of readiness software is one of the richest. It is designed for both home and school markets" (Lewis, 1993, p. 223). There are several reading programs available on computer software which can help improve word recognition proficiency. As an example, there is a talking version of *Talking Reading and Me* for Apple™ IIGS computers with speech synthesizers. Word recognition practice (with vision/sound components) activities include sound matching, discrimination, and categorization skills; phonics tasks; and whole word identification (Davidson and Associates, 19840 Pioneer Ave., Torrance, CA 90503). Using words in context and spelling improvement can be done with Living Books' (available in most computer stores) popular *Arthur's Teacher Trouble* and *Just Grandma and Me Sight* programs which *Multimedia World* has cited for the 1994 Reader's Choice Awards. Sight word recognition programs are also available and include Edmark's® sight word reading program (Edmark Corporation, P.O. Box 3218, Redmond, WA 98073) (includes speech component and TouchWindow™) and the Stickybear™ talking program which is available in Spanish or English (Weekly Reader Software, Optimum Resource Inc., 10 Station Place, Norfolk, Conn 06058).

TABLE 4-5   Brain Variations Among Different Species—Higher Level Vocabulary Charting and Feature Analysis

Secondary Level

Species of Animal	Very Large Auditory **Cortex**	**Cortex** Has Very Large Touch Area for Skin of Snout	**Cortex** Has Very Large Touch Area for Whiskers	Neo**cortex** Large and Wrinkled	Sensory Activity of **Cortex** Limited to Olfactory
Mouse	No	No	Yes	No	No
Bat	Yes	No	No	No	No
Elephant	No	Yes	No	Yes	No
Human	No	No	No	Yes	No
Pig	No	Yes	No	Yes	No
Fish	No	No	No	No	Yes

Elementary Level

Species of Animal	Number of **Feet**	**Whiskers**	**Swims**
Mouse	4	Yes	No
Bat	2	No	No
Elephant	4	No	No
Human	2	No	No
Pig	4	No	No
Fish	No	No	Yes

Conclusions

Some linguistic concepts that underlie reading success at the word level include print awareness or understanding that print conveys meaning; graphic awareness or knowing that words are composed of certain letters; phonemic awareness or the ability to discriminate and recognize sound units; and the understanding and application of grapheme/phoneme correspondences. Students with dyslexia often lack basic phonological awareness or phonological processing ability (Bradley & Bryant, 1983; Perfetti, 1985; Stanovich, 1986a, 1986b). That is, these individuals are not able to use effectively basic sound units (phonemes) to access the sound sequence of words.

The complexity of the reading task itself requires that the more basic reading processes involved in word identification, such as letter and word identification, occur with little effort and with little strain on short-term memory capacity. Research has shown that when word identification is not automatic and requires slow and laborious processing, comprehension suffers. This is because cognitive efforts are spent on word identification leaving fewer resources available for comprehension. Several word identification techniques that impact automaticity and the development of comprehension strategies were mentioned in this chapter.

Effective word identification requires that the student with dyslexia develop a combination of strategies that include: using phonemic-grapheme correspondences/rules; focusing on syntactic structures/syllables/sentence patterns; and determining meaning through context/analogy/picture clues/text gist. The assessment of word recognition skills and other academic/social areas should involve gathering data from multiple sources to include parents, interviews, observations, behavior ratings, and so on. It is critical to provide intervention strategies [that] target behaviors that are valued in the child's environment (Spinelli-Nannen, 1995, p. 14).

An effective remedial program for individuals with dyslexia would also require a basic philosophy which embraces a "helping ethic" (Berenson, 1994). The classroom atmosphere should allow for the development of each student's awareness of his/her own thoughts and needs when reading so that a purpose can be set for the reading task itself along with strategies to achieve that purpose.

Suggestions were made based on a careful review of the literature, keeping in mind that some techniques will work better with some individuals than with others. Many of the techniques mentioned would be useful with any type of student. However, adaptations are usually required for the student with dyslexia and other forms of learning disabilities; these have been carefully noted. Such factors as the nature or cause of the reading problem, background knowledge, motivation, attention capacity, and intelligence are especially relevant when deciding which technique to use. The key is to be flexible (i.e., eclectic and variable) in program planning. Technological assists should be used to supplement teaching efforts. Both the diagnosis of reading problems and the identification of strengths allow for the flexibility necessary in appropriate programming. Chapter 5 deals with specific programs which focus on phonemic awareness, which is lacking in most cases of students with dyslexia.

Just to think about — [Reading Purposes]

". . . Always have at least one iron in the fire (book) and kindle the fire at least once every day . . ."

". . . The more distinctly we are aware of our own wants and desires in reading, the more definite and permanent will be our acquisitions . . ."

". . . We do well to propose definite ends and purposes . . ."

". . . Hence it is a good rule to ask ourselves frequently, 'Why am I reading this book, essay or poem?' "

FIGURE 4-13   Wise Tidbits from Yesteryear

Source: Noah Porter, *McGuffey's Sixth Eclectic Reader,* NY: American Book Co. (1896) (pp. 8–20).

Chapter 5

Word Recognition Programs That Develop Phonemic Awareness

. . . Reading . . . depends on an interrupted and protracted recall of sounds by sights which have always been coupled with them in the past . . .—(JAMES, 1893, P. 557).

Certainly an initial milestone in the development of word recognition abilities is reached when students can successfully decode or use phonetic cues. Phonetic decoding (recognizing sound/symbol correspondences as meaningful units for use in speech, listening, writing, and reading) requires mastery of 40 phonemes (phoneme = smallest unit of sound in the English language *ea,* for example) or sound units to several letters and letter combinations. By themselves, phonemes have little meaning, and must be combined to form morphemes (morpheme = smallest meaningful unit in the English language—*ful,* for example) and words. The decoding problems of many students with dyslexia stem from poor phonemic awareness.

Developing Decoding Proficiency— Phonemic Awareness

Phonemic awareness involves the ability to isolate the different sound elements in a word and then analyze and interpret these sounds (e.g., look = /l/u/k/) and is a problem area for children and adults with dyslexia (Liberman, Rubin, Duques, & Carlisle, 1985).

Young children with deficient phonics skills need reinforcement; teaching such skills is commonly referred to as a *skills perspective*. The skills perspective typically follows a sequential scope-and-sequence type of format. Rubin (1991a, 1991b) offers a developmental-diagnostic and correction sequence of phonics (developing phonetic awareness)—keying students in to auditory and visual discrimination of individual sounds are the initial foci. Consonants are usually taught first in the initial positions of words (*k* as in *kite*) and then in the final positions of words (*t* as *bat*). Consonant clusters or blends (e.g., *pl* as in *play*, *spr* as in *spring*) are introduced next. Finally, consonant digraphs are shown in the initial (*th* as in *thanks*) and final (*sh* as in *splash*) final positions of words followed by silent consonants (*k* in *knee*).

Poor Phonemic Awareness in Students with Dyslexia

Many students with dyslexia also have trouble with phoneme discrimination or the ability to differentiate one phoneme from another (e.g., /g/ in gem is different from the /g/ in goat). Young children with dyslexia may even lack the basic phonetic skill of naming the letters of the alphabet (phonetic skill = naming; *phonetic* awareness = identifying/isolating phonemes). Phonetic and phonemic awareness terms are frequently used interchangeably.

Phonetic Awareness Programs

The Lindamood Auditory Discrimination In-Depth Program (ADD)

At the elementary level, The Auditory Discrimination In-Depth Program (ADD) (Lindamood & Lindamood, 1975) has been used. Kennedy and Backman (1993) have noted that with 10 students they studied with severe learning disabilities who received the ADD program on an intensive basis, significant gains were achieved in phonological awareness and phonetic spelling strategies. More research is needed to provide conclusive evidence of the program's effectiveness.

The ADD program is intended to develop the student's abilities to read, spell, and speak through a training plan that integrates spoken sounds with stimuli from the ear, eye, and mouth that are associated with the production of those sounds. When this integration has been accomplished, the program authors assume that the student will be able to perform automatically, with self-correction, the targeted functions of reading, spelling, and speaking. The training proceeds in small steps, involving both discovery and manipulation activities, until the student becomes able to discriminate among speech sounds, perceive transitions between successive syllables, associate spoken sounds with their alphabetic symbols, use the learned sound-to-symbol associations in learning to spell (as well as to use symbol-to-sound associations in learning to read), and generalize this training to the reading of prose passages. The ADD program has several applications, depending on the type of students with whom it is used: (1) Kindergarten pupils can be given a basic set of skills; (2) Beginning readers or students of English as a second language can be given the chance to experience the sound and syllable patterns of the English language; and (3) Students with learning disabilities can be given remedial instruction in very small, easy to handle steps, with the opportunity to experience frequent reinforcement.

At the secondary level, one relatively new program which is strongly phonetically based is the *Reading from Scratch (RfS)* by D. van den Honert (1985).

Reading from Scratch

Reading from Scratch (Honert, 1985) was developed specifically for adolescents and adults with learning disabilities who need to begin phonics training from "scratch." It is essentially a two-year program for students with dyslexia, concentrating on providing assistance in three basic areas: (1) impaired ability to analyze a sequence of sounds and match it to a sequence of written symbols; (2) impaired ability to process written language through auditory channels; and (3) impaired sense of syntax and grammar which produces reading without comprehension as well as spelling problems" (Honert, 1985, p. 7). The Reading from Scratch program is essentially a series of two books (RfS Phonics and RfS Spelling) which provide phonics facts and consistent spelling rules. In regard to reading, words are to be sounded out so that the reader does not rely on context cues or visual assists (i.e., configuration clues). A column format for practice exercises assists in setting up word families and word groupings (e.g., by similar prefixes). Words are presented in the context of practice sentences and are constructed so that context cues do not provide much word predictability. The teacher must check pronunciations by listening to the student pronounce all words aloud. A companion spelling book presents phonics facts and generalizations in the same order as the reading book so as to maintain consistency between theory and practice.

Note that in RfS Phonics, the student receives a visual sequence and has to produce an auditory sequence, whereas, in RfS Spelling, the student receives an auditory sequence and produces a matching visual one (Honert, 1985, p. 9). The Reading from Scratch program is very suitable for older students (grade seven to adult). Drill and practice exercises are emphasized to develop automaticity of reading. This approach, as well as the methods listed under techniques for students with severe dyslexia, are generally synthetic ways to reinforce decoding skills as opposed to analytic techniques.

Analytic Phonics Approaches

Analytic phonics approaches (also called implicit phonics approaches) introduce students first to a number of sight words or easily learned words. Then phonics instruction begins. For example, students might be introduced to the words *cake, lake, rake,* and *bake.* The student is then asked to discover what sound the *a* makes in these words. Letter sounds are not learned in isolation, and phonics rules and generalizations are discovered through inductive reasoning. These approaches are generally useful for beginning readers and those readers who experience little difficulty with word identification skills acquisition.

Harnois and Furdyna (1994) strongly suggest reading and reviewing vowel sounds and rules in the context of different sounds and spellings. These authors have found that an analytic phonetic approach is most useful with students who are dyslexic. Harnois and Furdyna (1994) recommend first breaking words down into sound components for vowel and sound analysis of two basic rules, followed by the blending of letter combinations and then structural analysis. Phonemic tasks are done in the context of stories or meaning-based written material.

The Writing Road to Reading/Spalding Method

Romalda Spalding (1957, 1962, 1969, 1986 1990), a teacher and associate of Dr. Samuel T. Orton, developed a phonetic approach to alleviate reading/language difficulties. According to Spalding (1990), the writing road to reading involves using, "only paper and pencil, and their [the students'] minds" (p. 29). Phonics instruction involves teaching first-grade or disabled students the first 54 phonograms. As these phonograms are learned, students immediately transfer this knowledge to written vocabulary terms in "language" notebooks. Approximately 1500 of the most commonly used spelling/reading words are taught in the order of frequency used as they present all variations of spelling problems. Daily practice (three hours per day) consists of spelling/reading previously learned phonograms in isolation and in words. As students become proficient, they are expected to write sentences, followed by paragraphs and stories in their language notebooks. This notebook is the student's personalized reading-writing connection to the world of phonics/word knowledge/new vocabulary.

The reading of [reading to non-readers] quality Newbery and Caldecott award-winning literature books should accompany phonics instruction after 150 of the most used words are studied first in written spelling lessons. The reading of connected text usually begins around the end of October or November. The teacher always serves as a coach and role model for students by demonstrating his/her own analytical processes while reading/writing. Farnham-Diggory (1987) describes the interactive process between teacher and student as one "giant scaffold" as the teacher must become well versed in and use scaffolding techniques. Aukerman (1984) cites positive reading/language gains for students with dyslexia after use of this approach. These authors believe that the Spalding method (see Table 5-1) stresses skills parallel to important prerequisites to skilled reading: decoding proficiency, vocabulary development, and syntactic/grammatical knowledge.

Synthetic Phonics Approaches

According to Walker (1992), synthetic phonics activities can teach "sound-symbol relationships to facilitate word identification. The student is systematically instructed to say letter sounds in words and then blend the sounds together to

TABLE 5-1   Spalding Method—The Writing Road to Reading

	Method	Speech Spelling	Writing Reading
Objective:	To use phonogram learning, sequential word analysis and graphic markers in order to acquire necessary phonics skills for decoding proficiency		
Time Frame:	3 hours per day		
Approach:	(1) Present detailed techniques for lower-case manuscript letters using a clock face		
	(2) Teach pronunciation of most commonly used phonograms by saying them aloud as a class (26 letters in 54 [two, three, four] letter combinations)		
	(3) Teach spelling of 1,700 words in order of frequency usage		
	(4) Teach marking system or underlining of phonograms studied (i.e., *th*)		
	(5) Twenty-nine spelling rules are mastered and practiced through written exercises to include dictation in spelling notebooks		
	(6) Reading begins with stories (especially classics) after 150 spelling words have been entered in notebooks		
Follow-up Activities:	(1) Emphasis on comprehension		
	(2) Written stories, plays, poems, and research		

Source: Spalding, R.B. with Spalding, W.T. (1957, 1962, 1969, 1986, 1990). *The writing road to reading.*

decode the unknown word. Rules for the phonic relationships are presented with examples" (p. 243). Essentially the teacher selects a phonic rule to be taught [short *i* in the middle of a short word or consonant-vowel-consonant (C-V-C) combination], selects text and words to illustrate the rule, and then directly teaches the letter sound(s). For example, the letter *s* sounds like /s-s-s/; the letter *t* sounds like /t-t-t/; the letter *i* in the middle of a short word with two consonants sounds like /i-i-i/. S-i-t sounds like sit. Look at the word *sit* in the sentence, "I sit". Students then read short sentences about different people and animals sitting and perhaps a story about a cat sitting on a fence. Synthetic phonic approaches (also called explicit phonics approaches) are not useful if students cannot segment (i.e., separate out) the sound segments that comprise the words or hold a sequence of letter sounds in memory long enough to then blend them together. However, the Monroe, Fernald, and Gillingham-Stillman synthetic phonics methods (in part) have been shown to be successful with some students with more severe disabilities (Pesce, 1995). Berger (1994) found in her study that students with dyslexia who received specific training in phonological awareness tasks made progress in word recognition performance. Berger's study suggests that the impact of phonetic training can be positive if given in conjunction with other word attack training, regardless of whether or not the program is synthetic or analytic in focus.

Decoding—One Key to Future Reading Successes

In summary, ". . . while acquiring and applying decoding strategies appear to be painlessly easy for many children, the inability to break the code becomes a serious roadblock to fluent reading and good comprehension for others . . ." (Gaskins, Downer, Anderson, Cunningham, Gaskins, Schommer, & the Teachers of Benchmark School, 1988, p. 36). Gaskins (1984) points out that poor readers (i.e., individuals with dyslexia) often do experience more than one roadblock to success. We can see evidence of that in the study skills acquisition, writing skills, and comprehension development of poor readers. The next chapter deals with these issues in depth. Beginning readers need to progress to a level of rapid automaticity in decoding and accurate recognition of common sight words. However, overreliance on phonics and word recognition could interfere with comprehension.

At-Risk Preschoolers for Dyslexia—What to Look For?

Children with speech-language impairments are at risk early on for dyslexia. Catts, Hu, Larrivee, and Swank (1994) suggest that children with semantic (e.g., knowing multiple meanings of the word "run"; filling in the blank with a reasonable word choice)—syntactic (e.g., ability to imitate sentences; grammar understanding) deficits or specific language impairments are at higher risk than those students with speech articulation impairments. These authors believe that the mean length of utterances (e.g., average length of sentences or responses to sentence prompts) and preschool school measures of receptive semantic-syntactic abilities (e.g., use a picture-vocabulary test) are good predictors of future reading problems. The best predictors of future reading successes and dyslexia are the *rapid naming* of objects, colors, letters, and words and **phonological awareness** at the pre-school level. We have suggested the use of several phonological awareness tasks in the glossary to assess this important area. Deficits in phonological awareness observed should provide an impetus for further testing or a referral.

Subtyping Schemes Confound Remedial Efforts

There is some research to show that analytic phonics methods should be used with individuals who are of an auditory-linguistic type (see Lyon, 1988) because synthetic methods (studying phoneme-grapheme relationships before combining to form words) can be ineffective. Very simply, if a student has difficulty with isolated phoneme-grapheme correspondences, and the blending of those into words, analytic (studying sound-symbol correspondences within the context of words) phonics approaches should be used.

Word Recognition Procedures for Severe Cases of Dyslexia

For the severe case of dyslexia, traditional vocabulary approaches might not be sufficient (Pesce, 1995). Certainly, all reading interventions are best implemented at the earliest stages possible. It will be apparent to educators and parents when young children are considered to have severe reading disabilities or to be severely dyslexic. The following is a selection of multisensory approaches which have been developed over the past 70 years and have been proven to be effective by some researchers. There is no consensus as to what would be the best approach.

Reading Interventions for Individuals with Severe Dyslexia

Multi-sensory techniques are best implemented in the early elementary years (Pesce, 1995). These include the Monroe approach, the Fernald-Keller Kinesthetic Method, the Gillingham-Stillman Approach, the Reading Recovery Approach, the Traub Recipe for Reading program, and the Slingerland system. These approaches can be viewed at least in part as synthetic methods. They are best used when traditional methods have not been successful and are most effective in a one-to-one setting. These differ from analytic phonics methods or sight-word approaches.

Multisensory approaches and methods that are discussed include VAK (visual-auditory-kinesthetic), VAKT (visual-auditory-kinesthetic-tactile), and VA (visual-auditory).

Monroe Approach

The Monroe Method was developed in 1932 as a way to reduce oral reading errors by eliminating incorrect pronunciations of vowels and consonants and such miscues as sound and word omissions, substitutions, reversals, and repetitions. Synthetic phonics teaching is used with correct motoric response training. The Monroe Method (Monroe, 1932) employs a three-step approach which involves (1) developing the student's ability to discriminate various speech sounds by presenting various pictures of objects, (2) forming associations between letters and their most commonly used sounds, and (3) presenting stories with phonetically controlled language.

As an example, a student might be presented with a picture of a bag (for the *b* sound) and a picture of a dog (for the *d* sound). The student has to articulate the correct sound that the picture represents. Both cards might be shown so that the student can discriminate between the *b* and *d* sounds. The student is then asked to generate words with similar initial sounds. The teacher then can proceed to write the letters *b* and *d* with the student tracing over each letter while simultaneously articulating the sound. Then the consonants are blended with vowels to form words. Students continue to articulate and trace words (e.g., say *bag* slowly, b-a-g while you trace the word). Word families are presented and recall is frequently checked with word flashcards. Sound-dictation can be used to replace the tracing method. This involves having the student write words as the teacher dictates each sound and then reading the list aloud.

The Monroe approach is a synthetic type of reading method which emphasizes word recognition in isolation. Goodman (1976) and others caution teachers who present letters and words in isolation. It is to the student's best advantage to present learned sounds and words in a reading context as soon as possible. If the Monroe method is used, application to actual reading material is recommended. Fernald (1943) and Gillinghan and Stillman (1966) have offered similar approaches to Monroe (Pesce, 1995).

Fernald-Keller Kinesthetic (VAKT) Approach

Over 70 years ago (1921), Drs. Grace M. Fernald and Helen B. Keller (cited in Gillingham & Stillman, 1966) created what has become known as the VAKT approach for readers with severe disabilities. This method utilizes four sense modalities in the process of teaching word recognition and reading skills. For example, the child will see (visual) the word, *bell,* will hear the word said aloud (auditory) and perhaps even hear a bell ringing, will trace (kinesthetic) the word bell with a finger, and will feel the word as it is traced (tactile). Fernald (1943) extensively outlined a four-stage process from which Fernald and Keller developed their system.

Fernald (1943) believed that a multisensory approach was helpful for severely impaired readers with four stages necessary to the development of adequate word identification skills. Stage One involves students selecting words they wish to learn, with each word being written on a paper strip. Students trace each word to be learned with a finger while pronouncing each sound or word part as it is being traced. This procedure is repeated until the student can write the word from memory. After several words are learned, students are introduced to story-writing activities with the learned words. The teacher then types the student's work and the student maintains a word file of all the learned words. This stage involves about two months of instruction.

The student is ready to enter Stage Two when he/she can master words by saying the word(s) repeatedly without tracing. Words are then presented to students in list or flashcard form. Students memorize words to be learned by orally repeating each word over and over until a word can be written from memory.

During Stage Three the student glances at a word, says it once, and then writes it from memory. Stage Three also involves having the student read text of his/her choice; when an unknown word is encountered, it is pronounced for the student. Students can learn the unknown words by looking at the words and saying them aloud several times. Then the student writes the words from memory. Again, learned words are filed in a word box.

Stage Four involves having the student attempt to pronounce unknown words by looking at word parts or any resemblance to words already mastered. It is during this stage that the child is expected to generalize; that is, to be able to read new words based upon his/her knowledge of words previously learned.

The Fernald-Keller Method has been criticized for placing too much emphasis on whole word identification at the expense of meaning. This method does reinforce word recognition. However, it is noteworthy that meaning cannot be

abstracted when word identification skills are poor. For those students with severe reading disabilities, who need an alternative to traditional teaching methods,
Rupley and Blair (1989) suggest selecting words from a child's speaking vocabulary when using this approach to ensure the child has a referent for the words
used. Connected text (e.g., stories) should be paired with the learned words as
soon as possible.

Gillingham-Stillman (VAK) Approach

Gillingham and Stillman (1966) offer a type of phonetic method which they believe
is consistent with the evolution of language abilities. This method teaches the child
both the names and the sounds of letters; the names for spelling and the sounds
for reading. Visual, auditory, and kinesthetic reinforcements are used. The method
is intended for children at the middle elementary level but can be adapted for older
students. Gillingham and Stillman (1966) suggest four levels of phonetic training
which are intended to develop word identification proficiency.

This method begins with Level One, the presentation of sounds which are represented by letters. The teacher shows a students a letter and then says the name
of the letter. The student models this behavior. Then the teacher identifies a common sound represented by the letter and the student again models the teacher. Following this step, the teacher writes the letter with the student tracing the teacher's
lines until he/she can copy the letter from memory. The same key word is always
associated with a letter (e.g., z = zoo).

Level Two involves blending letters into words after 10 letters have been mastered (e.g., h-a-t, h-a-d, h-a-m). After the student is able to blend sounds into
words, he/she must then analyze words into sounds. As an example, the teacher
might say the word, h-a-t slowly and the students must then find the appropriate
letter cards for each sound. Word families are drilled and words are sometimes
traced and written after dictation.

Level Three involves writing sentences and stories after students can read and
write three-letter words which can be easily identified phonetically. Students prepare for sentence and story reading silently and are encouraged to avoid guessing.

Level Four includes reinforcement types of activities which address phonetically irregular words, dictionary usage, and structural analysis (looking at prefixes,
suffixes, and root words). This type of sequential study carries over into how these
authors believe spelling should be taught.

Gillingham-Stillman System of Spelling. This method of teaching spelling is
similar to reading in that it is based on a systematic training of sound to symbol
correspondence using both oral and written spelling formats (Pesce, 1995). Supplementary dictionary work and handwriting practice round out this total language
arts program.

The Gillingham and Stillman approach as well as the Fernald method stress
a multisensory perspective by emphasizing letter and word repetition through visual, auditory, and kinesthetic modalities. Gillingham and Stillman place more
stress on using a highly structured phonetic letter-by-letter approach, while Fernald has the students selecting whole words to be learned and then proceeding

to learn specific letter-sound correspondences. Both approaches do place more emphasis on word identification than on reading for understanding, which can be considered a major criticism. On the positive side, both approaches reinforce the acquisition of sound-symbol correspondences and their application to words and word parts. Regardless, either approach in conjunction with other literature-based and phonics programs (Pesce, 1995) might be necessary for the reader with a severe form of reading disability or dyslexia.

Reading Recovery (VA) Approach

The Reading Recovery Method was designed by Marie Clay of New Zealand in the late 1970s for first graders at risk for reading failure (see Table 5-2). This approach particularly emphasizes the importance of listening to the sound sequences in words and seems to blend sight word and analytic/synthetic phonics principles into one approach. According to Clay, the teacher has to work with children individually and act as an analyzer of words into sounds. The teacher must articulate words very slowly and gradually develop the same skill in her/his pupil (Clay, 1979, p. 5).

TABLE 5-2   Reading Recovery

Staff:

1. Two full-time teachers for grade 1 = 1 or both become "Reading Recovery" teachers two hours per day

2. Chapter I teacher becomes a "Read Recovery" teacher = two hours per day devoted to Reading Recovery

3. Reading Recovering Team = Chapter I teacher and at least one classroom teacher

Approach:

1. First ten lessons = "Roaming in the Known"; reading/writing emphases—children . . .
   a. Write books in own language
   b. Write down known sounds
   c. Apply problem-solving strategies
   d. Practice reading with books they wrote
   e. Use sentence structure to predict meaning
   f. Use picture clues
   g. Relate sounds to symbols

2. Follow-up Lessons to Develop Reading Independence
   a. Reread several small books to develop fluency and automaticity
   b. Teacher records oral reading progress
   c. Write self-created sentences in stories in writing—listen to the sounds of words and write the sounds
   d. Cut up a copy of a story that was self-written, rearrange sentences and self-correct using the original to self-check
   e. Read a new book and focus on meaning—the teacher can help make predictions which can be confirmed or disconfirmed
   f. Read a new book independently

Source: Marie Clay (1988). *The early detection of reading difficulties.* Auckland, NZ: Heineman Educational Books.

The Reading Recovery method (see Clay, 1988) is essentially an intense tutorial method of reading instruction for first graders and involves (1) ongoing diagnoses of reading problems, (2) an initial screening, (3) lesson frameworks, (4) intense reading instruction for 12–14 weeks (usually in 30-minute sessions), (5) placement in a regular reading class after "reading recovery" of important reading skills, and (6) teacher training.

The initial Reading Recovery screening is done using a ranking system by the classroom teacher on six basic measures: (1) Dolch sight word list; 2) upper and lower case letter identification; (3) Clay's concepts about print (e.g., how to hold a book, reading from left to right and so on); (4) Writing samples of a child's known words; (5) dictation sample of 37 phonemes presented in a sentence; and 6) Text reading to identify level at which 90% accuracy is achieved. These data are used to establish a baseline by which reading growth can be measured and as a starting point for remedial efforts. Tierney, Readence, and Dishner (1990) describe a typical tutoring session as involving, " . . . rereading two or more familiar books, writing messages and stories, then rereading them, hearing sounds, cutting up stories, and introducing, then attempting, new books . . ." (pp. 373–374).

The Reading Recovery Program typically lasts 12–14 weeks. Teacher leaders are required to undertake an intensive training program so that they can work with Reading Recovery teachers within a school. Although this method has been reported to be successful with some groups of first-grade students with reading disabilities (Lyons, Pinnell, McCarrier, Young, & DeFord, 1988), there needs to be more extensive study with this method, as it can be considered a relatively new approach; it was not formally introduced to the United States until 1984.

Recipe for Reading (VAK) Approach

This is a structured VAK (visual, auditory, and kinesthetic) approach to remedial reading developed by Nina Traub in 1972 (latest revision, 1992). In essence, a reading text guides the teacher to introduce phonetic sounds and principles sequentially from lessons on specific letter sounds to more complex vowel digraphs, consonant blends, spelling rules, and word families. According to Traub (1992), in order to use any recipe, one must ". . . (1) know what ingredients are needed, (2) understand how they are to be combined, and (3) [be] . . . able to adapt the recipe to individual needs . . ." (preface). The first nine letters taught in this approach are c, o, a, d, g, m, l, h, and t. The child learns to use these nine letters to make, spell, and read words by reading, hearing, and feeling (tracing) letters/sound correspondences. Required materials to reinforce mastery include phonetic sound cards, word cards, phrase cards, sentence cards, storybooks, word games, sequence charts, and writing paper.

Slingerland (VAK) Approach

The Slingerland Approach was developed by B.H. Slingerland in 1971 as a daily remedial procedure for children with severe written language problems so as to provide a daily approach to spelling and reading lessons in the primary and intermediate grades (Slingerland, 1976). There is a set of ninety-four 8 × 10 inch photographs with games and exercises which give young children practice in speech; visual, kinesthetic, and auditory recall; and left-right orientation. *Learning to read* involves both auditory and visual components. The auditory component (e.g., the auditory perception of a vowel position) and visual perception (e.g. pronouncing words on word lists from pocket charts) and discrimination (e.g., different letter/sound combinations) tasks. The sequence in *learning to write* is (1) teaching new letters of the alphabet with lower case preceding upper case, (2) practicing new letters as presented, (3) reviewing letters taught on a daily basis, and (4) learning how to connect cursive letter forms. The ultimate goal of independent reading and writing is facilitated by both encoding (auditory blending) and decoding (unlocking new words) exercises. Guidance charts provide students with hand-held learning assists. As an example, to reinforce word discrimination skills, the Slingerland Guidance Chart reads: ". . . (1) You will identify which letters and sounds are the same and different in these words; (2) Read each word as I point to it; (3) What letters are the same in these words? (4) What sounds are the same in these words? (5) What letters are different in these words? (6) What sounds are different in these words? (7) Spell and read each word as I point to it. (8) Read each word as I point to it . . . " (as cited in White, 1989, p. 67). This is a rote type of task which needs to be supplemented with connected reading material.

General Reading Suggestions for Troubled Readers

All reading guidelines and approaches need to reinforce the conceptualization that reading is an interactive, constructive, strategic, and analytic process (*Reading Report Card*, 1985). Certainly reading must also be purposeful especially for the student with dyslexia and other reading problems as reading tends to be tedious, hard work for these individuals.

Teachers who work with students with disabilities, reading difficulties, or dyslexia, should consider the following suggestions before determining specific techniques, study skills programs, and materials. (We hope that our Top 20 list makes at least part of your own Top 20 best reading tips!)

1. Develop a personal philosophy for students with special needs (including dyslexia) that looks to desired academic/social/emotional outcomes. How can you provide instruction which will lead to building a positive self-concept, a positive social life, positive school experiences, and positive career directions?

   The Junior Achievement Project Business Student Manual (1992) provides tips for those students looking toward their futures and job interviews. As early as the elementary level, Junior Achievement organizations prepare students before and during the interview process. These suggestions need to be emphasized to all students and might require additional reinforcement, restatement, role-playing, and even rehearsing for students with dyslexia. Sample tips for interviewing beforehand: ". . . use your best penmanship [on the job application form]. Neatness counts!! Learn about the company in advance. Think how you will fit into the job. List the skills you have to offer the company. Be prepared to ask any questions you might have [anticipate questions and rehearse answers] . . . dress up! Be sure you are on time for the interview . . . have confidence . . . put your best foot forward . . . [at the interview] SMILE! . . . shake hands . . . don't criticize a former employer . . . use eye contact . . . answer questions completely; do not give just "yes" or "no" answers . . . show enthusiasm . . . sell yourself . . . shake hands when leaving . . . thank . . . " (p. 28). Parents and professionals can contact local Junior Achievement organizations in order to involve students in basic business planning programs.

2. Provide daily reading activities (at least an hour a day if possible) in a warm and nurturing environment with much positive reinforcement and praise for accomplishments and progress (the more time spent the better, inasmuch as more exposure to reading generally results in greater reading gains and achievement).

3. Communicate with the student's home to offer praise when things are going well (and especially if they are not) and offer suggestions for family reading activities; try to call during the first month of school with some good news so that your initial contact is a positive one. Provide immediate feedback and constructive suggestions in class which will keep students on task and interested in their work.

4. Don't suggest remedial reading activities to parents as their most important role comes in providing leisure types of reading and assisting with homework assignments. After all, too much remediation is a turn-off; suggest to parents that trips to the local library, bookstore, or mall to borrow or purchase a desired book or magazine will help generate interest in reading activities. Allow the child great freedom in choosing a book. If he/she chooses material that's too difficult, that's OK. Talk about it and choose something less challenging next time. Put the book aside for reading in the future.

5. Incorporate a rich selection of multicultural offerings within any program as well as materials which are sensitive to current environmental topics and issues (e.g., pollution, recycling, etc.). The following lesson format is one example of how teachers can infuse multicultural themes throughout the curriculum. (Refer to following box.)

6. Start a drama club, play group, poetry reading group, book club, class newspaper, or some other after-school activity that would provide an inviting social context for shared language/reading activities.

7. Provide a balance between oral and silent reading activities with more stress on silent reading at the upper levels. Also provide a balance between direct instruction and constructive learning on the part of the student, with more emphasis on direct instruction at the early grades.

8. Decrease waiting times between activities by having students work in individual folders, picking up a book in the library corner, finishing a writing activity, and so on.

9. Provide study skills training. This would include planning schedules, alternatives, appropriate work loads, locales, and support systems (see next chapter).

10. Model cognitive monitoring techniques and encourage their use.

Structured Multicultural Presentations for Dyslexic Readers

We have adapted a presentation by Casper (1994) which follows a structured format to introduce the wonderful heritage of the Navajo people.

Book Used:

Knots on a Counting Rope by Bill Martin and John Archambault, Holt and Company, New York, 1987.

I. **Pre-Summarize** the story content in one paragraph

A Navajo grandfather tells his son of his roots and a story of when he was born. Grandfather's story is meant to give his young grandson the courage to go through life blind. Each time grandfather tells his story they both record the telling by tieing a knot on their "counting rope."

II. **Review** important **vocabulary**

Navajo, native Americans, knots, counting rope, family, blindness, disabilities, courage

III. **Main ideas** or Story Themes

Families telling stories about the past can help pass important traditions from one generation to another.

People who are blind or have other disabilities experience life in different ways and rely on family for strength and assistance.

IV. **Extended Multicultural Activities**

Using the writing process (see Chapter 7) or an interview, have the dyslexic student write a letter or tape record an interview with a grandparent or other relative which asks them to tell a story about their early childhood. After the student receives the letter or listens to the tape, he or she could tie a knot on a home-made counting rope each time the story is told.

Students could share in a "grandparents" or "family day" in which their stories are told or shared. Family trees, self-portraits, edited autobiographies, portraits of families, and so on could decorate the room.

V. **New Books** to Read on the Subject

The student with dyslexia will require repeated presentations to reinforce desired learning outcomes.

The Navajo by Virginia Driving Hawk Sneve, Holiday House, New York, 1993.

Lightning Inside You and Other Native American Riddles by Bierhorst, Morrow Pub., New York, 1992.

Children of the Earth and Sky by Krensky, Scholastic Pub., New York, 1991.

---

11. Tie in reading strategies and study skills to content area reading and other subject areas—show students how to adapt to various types of textual material (e.g., pace, vocabulary, pre-reading exercises, and etc.). Students with dyslexia who have math problems might require special instruction in concepts, facts, algorithms, or problem solving (see related chapters).

12. Pace instruction and reading activities according to each individual's ability to assimilate the material whenever possible—keep in mind that students with dyslexia have slower reading rates.

13. Encourage, foster, and nurture cooperative reading activities. Peer tutoring, peer coaching, adult tutoring, adult coaching, and mentoring are various cooperative learning approaches.

14. Social skills training might be in order (see related chapter) in areas such as using appropriate language, behaving appropriately, using body gestures, reciprocity, and listening.

15. Focus on a total language arts perspective; that is, the integration of spelling, writing, vocabulary, and reading development. Balance whole-language activities with phonics/structural analysis work; remember that many students with dyslexia have word-identification problems and require intense instruction in this area. A total language focus would necessarily involve pragmatics and communication skills work. The use of literature and discourse can help make important speech and language connections for the student with dyslexia. Moreau and Fidrych-Puzzo (1994) recommend concrete hand-holds which utilize symbols that portray such story grammar highlights as characterizations, setting, initiating events, internal responses, attempts at solutions, direct consequences, and story resolutions.

16. Be sure that other factors aren't adversely affecting reading progress (e.g., eyesight, hunger, etc.)—physical and psychological needs must be satisfactorily met in order for optimal learning to transpire. Physical examinations are always a must along with eye/ear and dental exams. Some type of visual or auditory training might be in order (only after a complete work-up by a qualified practitioner in the field).

17. Model good reading behaviors; complete the same projects as your students; if they must read and report on a person they admire, you do the same. Use media/technology to reinforce reading materials.

18. Don't point out all errors in reading and writing as you might discourage the student with severe reading disabilities. Try to focus on particularly important problem areas; be quick to point out good points.

19. Provide college-bound students with dyslexia assistance with note-taking skills, organizational skills, time-management skills, and test-taking strategies.

20. Continually assess progress, teach diagnostically, and adjust teaching strategies and materials accordingly. Attend workshops and presentations which will update, refresh, and refine.

If any one theme emerges from our Top 20, it is the need for balance and eclectism. After developing our goals and general overview of reading programming for individuals with dyslexia, we can now delve into specific comprehension and study strategies which can really assist all readers in actively constructing text meaning and understanding. Noticeably absent from the Top 20 listing are suggestions regarding remediation by subtype of disability.

Conclusions

The issue of how to proceed in developing a program for the student with dyslexia is confounded by the numerous subtyping schemes offered. There is no consensus in the field as to what or how many subtypes exist and therefore remediation efforts based on subtypes are a question mark at best.

Regardless of subtype, research efforts have shown that for individuals with dyslexia, a combined bottom-up/top-down approach should be used (Anderson,

1977; Posner, 1979) with VAKT methods recommended for those with severe disabilities. The Monroe, Fernald-Keller, Gillingham-Stillman, Reading Recovery, Traub, Slingerland, RfS (Reading from Scratch), and Writing to Read (Spalding) methods are tried and proven methods for those individuals with poor phonemic awareness which inhibits rapid and accurate word-identification abilities. Caution has to be exercised if undue stress is placed on letter and word identification at the expense of meaning. Whether analytic or synthetic approaches are used, application of phonetic understandings must be extended to reading text itself. We learn best to read by reading, and reading should be a meaningful process for everyone.

As in the previous chapter, we would emphasize to establish a good working relationship and rapport with the student. Whether in the classroom or in a testing situation, a professional can put a student at ease with an informal interview that conveys a warm, and supportive environment. Continued support and encouragement is a must (Lezak, 1995)!

We would agree with Brennan (1995) that the use of ". . . language is something to be treasured, caressed, nurtured, above all used . . ." For the student with dyslexia, repeated exposures to interactive language activities (e.g., choral readings, dialogue journals) and usage (e.g., the writing process, portfolio presentations) provide opportunities for phonetic, syntactic, and semantic development as conceptual and schematic knowledge in these areas can be gleaned from feedback received, role modeling, and metacognitive reflections.

The following chapter involves the actual application of word recognition skills when developing reading fluency. For the individuals with dyslexia, development of writing skills goes hand-in-hand with reading proficiency. Additionally, good study habits are a must, as disorganization and time management problems sometimes defeat the reader's best efforts (as with all of us!).

Chapter 6

Comprehension and Text Strategies

> . . . this [general] ability to recall appropriate
> facts [situations, people, and schemata] in
> given contexts is dependent primarily on three
> factors: power of retention, number of associa-
> tions, [and] organization of associations. . . .
> —(STRAYER & NORSWORTHY, 1917, P. 74).

> . . . the precise use of the term reading
> means comprehending *words, sentences,
> paragraphs, and/or entire texts*
> —(WIEDERHOLT & BRYANT, 1987, P. 37).

Diagnosing and remediating comprehension difficulties remains one of the most challenging aspects of the reading process. Because the teacher cannot enter the mind of the reader, there is no access to the cognitive processes or strategies used by the learner. Typically, it is not until students answer comprehension questions after reading that problems are revealed and suggestions made. Experienced teachers have learned that the best opportunities for successful intervention occur *before* reading actually takes place. Instructional procedures that set a purpose for reading and activate background knowledge have been shown to enhance reading comprehension by actively engaging learners in the reading process. Purpose setting for this chapter can be seen in the following chart (Table 6-1) which is one way to summarize or outline key concepts in for example, a report, article, or book. The stated characteristics of individuals with dyslexia are compared to those of proficient readers by means of remedial strategies/assistive techniques discussed throughout the chapter.

TABLE 6-1   Comprehensive Characteristics

Dyslexics	Proficient Readers	Remedial Strategies Activities/Assists
Lack Clear Purpose for Reading—Motivation a Challenge	Clear Purpose for Reading Clearly Motivated	High Interest/Motivating/ Culturally Relevant Materials Integrating Across the Curriculum Whole Language Activities
Require Explicit Comprehension Instruction	Flexible Use of Comprehension Skills	Story Maps, Story Grammar Graphic Organizers Text Structure Guides, Skimming and Scanning, Paraphrasing
Experience Difficulty Comprehending Basal and Content Texts	Adjust to Basal and Content Text Requirements	Guide-O-Ramas, Material Previews, Reading Road Maps, Anticipation Guides, Marginal Glosses
Exhibit Poor Oral Reading Skills	Good Oral Readers	Choral Repeated Readings, Radio Reading, Paired Reading, Echo Reading
Lack Efficient Metacognitive Strategies	Good Metacognitive Awareness	Self Monitoring Cognitive Apprenticeships Coaching, Scaffolding, Framing Questions, Reciprocal Teaching
Are Unable to Correct Comprehension Problems	Can Correct Comprehension Problems	Use of Technology Developing Specific Skills and Questioning Strategies
Write Relatively Poorly Tend to Focus on Mechanics	Good Writers—Focus on Ideas	Process Writing, Using Literature Semantic Organizers, Writing Across the Curriculum, Story Prompts, Journal Writing, Portfolio Projects, Writing Workshops
Evidence Poor Study Skills	Good Study Skills	Guided Notes, Time Management Skills, "Detective Q Squirt" Test-Taking Strategies, SQ3R, PORE, PQ4R
Display Problems with Information Recall	Good Memory Skills	Verbal Mediation, Mnemonics, Keyboard Technique, KWL, MAD

Setting a Purpose for Reading

Students need to know that they can read for different purposes as this helps to create "a flexible reader." If students read for pleasure, they can skim the text or read slowly depending how they feel or what assignments they receive. If students are reading content area subjects such as science or social studies, they will probably want to read slowly. With library books and literature offerings, reading rate can be accelerated. More difficult reading materials require a focused attention and concentrated cognitive efforts on the task at hand. The classroom atmosphere must provide an environment that will allow and encourage students to exert sustained attention on difficult reading tasks. For the student with dyslexia, sustained attention is a must. More cognitive attention and resources must be expended by students with dyslexia than by proficient readers to achieve and sustain satisfactory reading behaviors.

Student interest and affective dimensions impact the level of "text coherence and background knowledge" (Wade, Schraw, Buxton, & Hayes, 1993, p. 108) acquired by the reader. Just what is considered interesting information? According to Anderson, Shirey, Wilson & Fielding (1984) and Schank (1979), interesting material is usually emotionally involving for the reader, suspenseful and/or personalized. Certainly providing multicultural materials taps into the large diversity and interest levels of our students.

Wade and Adams (1990) have shown that textual material that was considered interesting but unimportant was recalled best and that details supporting main ideas were also remembered better when the material was considered interesting. In fact, Wade, Schraw, Buxton, and Hayes (1993) present evidence for improved long-term and short-term memory recall of information that is highly interesting to the reader. These authors also add that ". . . background knowledge clearly affects whether readers find a text segment interesting, easy to read, and memorable . . ." (Wade, Schraw, Buxton, and Hayes p. 110).

Activities that set up real purposes for reading and model explicit strategies for managing the text can be expected to enhance the reading-learning process. For example, if complete understanding of material is needed, students might ". . . preview it, take notes, and question themselves about it . . ." (Moore, Moore, Cunningham, & Cunningham, 1994, p. 89). The example shown in Figure 6-1 demonstrates how teachers can set a purpose for reading. If mastery of specific facts is the goal, learners might decide on a specific mnemonic device to use.

Prior to actual reading, it is important to establish a framework of prior knowledge by activating concepts, ideas, or feelings related to the topic. Once background knowledge is activated, learning takes place as new concepts are associated with and integrated into existing knowledge.

Before a reading on "Saving the Ozone Layer," background knowledge is activated by the teacher's questions and classroom discussion.

1. Do you know what the ozone hole is and what causes it?

2. In what way does the layer of gas called ozone block the sun?

3. Why do you think CFC gases and halon hurt the ozone layer?

4. Can CFC gases in aerosol cans hurt the ozone layer?

5. Why is styrofoam dangerous to the ozone layer?

6. Poll your classmates. How can you help prevent the ozone hole from getting bigger?

FIGURE 6-1 Setting a Purpose for Reading: Activating Background Knowledge

Readers must also be able to differentiate between being able to abstract the gist from the entire selection at hand (Kintsch & VanDijk, 1978), or "... reading to locate information [as this] requires selective sampling of text ..." (Symons & Pressley, 1993, p. 251). The reading process does require an interaction between the learner and text as part of this process (Vygotsky, 1962). Because some students with dyslexia and other reading disabilities may not achieve independence in "reading to learn," they cannot independently make these fine distinctions. It is all the more essential that avenues be established to create and maintain an active connection between the text and the learner. This connection should be firmly based on the background knowledge the reader brings to the written page. There are several techniques in this chapter which prepare the reader for this complex and often perplexing task. Students with dyslexia need to have adequate background knowledge of textual material before silent and oral readings and written expressive language exercises. Adequate background knowledge sets the stage for the reading task itself and the subsequent connection between the printed page and understanding. Integrating reading content across the curriculum enhances meaning and purpose setting. The history example in Figure 6-2 serves to integrate curriculum using both community resources and classroom activities.

The perspective of the teacher in program planning is important and there have generally been two distinct schools of thought regarding how to best approach

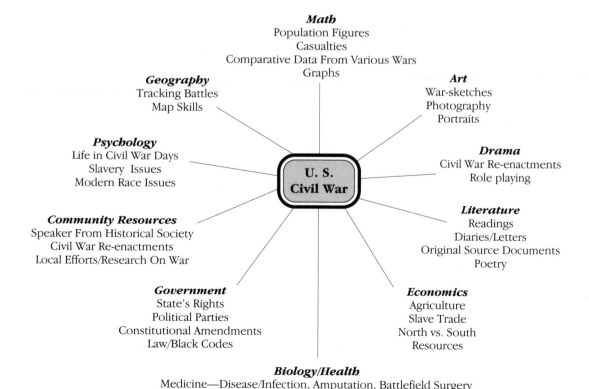

FIGURE 6-2   Integrating Across the Curriculum

teaching comprehension activities—the skills approach (bottom-up) and the whole language perspective (top-down) (see Chapter 4 for a thorough discussion of both approaches). We would suggest that both perspectives (interactive model) are necessary to a well-rounded program. Interactive models of reading are well accepted.

The Skills Perspective

The skills perspective described by Cheek, Flippo, and Lindsey (1989) considers reading acquisition to be a sequential collection of skills and subskills that culminate in designated reading levels based on grade-by-grade scope and sequence data. This approach has become known as a bottom-up theoretical perspective in that we start from the bottom with sounds/letters and work up to the top (comprehension). Guthrie (1973) and Samuels (1979) are just two of those researchers associated with this type of perspective. Typically students are taught how to recognize letters and words before they read sentences, paragraphs, and stories. Becoming skilled at decoding is necessary before comprehension skills can be learned. The previous chapter taps into several approaches (e.g., Fernald-Keller, Gillingham-Stillman) which focus on the basic skills that so many students with dyslexia lack.

The Whole Language Approach

The whole language thrust is really a philosophical position or view as to how reading should be taught. The 1970s brought several research practitioners (e.g., Goodman, 1976; Levin & Kaplan, 1970; and Smith & Goodman, 1971) to this position because they believed reading to be ". . . a natural process and as part of the other language processes, and within these contexts there was considerable interest in students' psycholinguistic experiences . . . [reading] begins with the reader's experience and predictions about meaning . . ." (Cheek, Flippo, & Lindsey, 1989). This approach is known as a top-down theory in that the highest level of cognition (e.g., schema-based comprehension) is stressed more than lower level skills (e.g., decoding). Those who adhere to this perspective believe that children learn best to read by reading and should be (1) given many opportunities for reading stories or in context, (2) involved in a learning environment which encourages risk taking, and (3) focused on a meaning-based curriculum as opposed to a skills approach (Goodman, Bird, & Goodman, 1992; Goodman & Goodman, 1982).

For students who are skilled, expert, or proficient readers, the whole language approach offers an inductive and challenging way to discover phonics rules and generalizations. As we saw in the previous chapter, many students with dyslexia are not independent, reflective, and self-monitoring. They will need instruction in skills acquisition or bottom-up processing. Several recommendations were offered in the previous chapter. This chapter will emphasize more top-down abilities whereby decoding and other word recognition skills are taught in the context of the printed page itself, especially with high-interest, motivating stories, novels, magazines, newspaper articles, and so on.

Whole language activities include sustained silent reading, the writing process, and guided study skills approaches. We would hope that practitioners would try to merge the skills and whole language perspectives into a program which emphasizes the development of word recognition abilities, comprehension skills work, and writing and study skills acquisition, or a total language arts perspective. Although much of the research regarding the reading problems of individuals with dyslexia has focused on word identification problems, it can be assumed that [some] students with such problems also experience comprehension difficulties (Stanovich, 1986b). It should, however, be emphasized that not all individuals with dyslexia have comprehension problems. The interactive perspective incorporates whole language activities with skills work.

Interactive Models

Interactive models of reading are reading perspectives which stress the interactive nature of the reading process itself. That is, we use several sources of information when reading in both word recognition and comprehension activities. We rely on the phonology of words or the letter-sound correspondences, the structure of words or structural analysis of word features (e.g., root words), and the semantics or meaning of what is read. Interactive proponents believe that students should be exposed to both skills work and whole language activities and that reading will be improved just by increasing one's general knowledge base (Kintsch, 1980; Pearson & Fielding, 1991). Manzo and Manzo (1993) astutely point to an important implication of this model—the necessity to monitor and compensate or correct deficit areas. The Interactive-Compensatory Model described by Manzo and Manzo (1993) is based, in part, on the premise that poor readers tend to use context, prior knowledge, visual cues, and prediction to *compensate* for poor word recognition ability. Those with comprehension problems tend to compensate by overanalyzing or overinterpreting words, phrases, and sentences.

Compensatory Strategies

The development of compensatory strategies is no longer viewed in terms of watered-down curriculum, alternative curriculum, typed reports, or providing listening tapes to reduce the demands of the reading task. More recent foci have stressed considering *compensatory strategies* as *thinking strategies* which *empower* the reader to have a *reflective cognitive learning style* which renders an *interactive* and *meaningful* dialogue between the reader and the printed page.

Individuals with dyslexia and other learning disabilities tend to have an impulsive cognitive style (Walker, 1985) which refers to learning/thinking styles which are reactive (and reactions are too quick) as opposed to interactive. Adequate considerations are not given to hypothesis testing, weighing alternatives, and strategic planning. A reflective cognitive learning style is one which is paced to the requirements of a reading task with metacognitive (thinking) skills and monitoring in place. Having a reflective cognitive learning style allows the reader to respond purposively and meaningfully to the printed page. In other words, readers who are empowered to interact with the printed page in a meaningful manner have developed reflective cognitive learning styles. Compensatory strategies are those activities which promote the acquisition of reflective cognitive learning styles. A cognitive strategy-instruction approach is one way to develop reflective cognitive learning styles.

Swanson's Cognitive Strategy Instruction

This strategy, Swanson (1989, 1993) proposes three principles of effective cognitive strategy instruction for individuals who are dyslexic: (1) Always keep in mind that there is no one best strategy to use—different strategies can effect different cognitive outcomes; (2) Consider the individual—what works for one individual may not work for another; and (3) Be parsimonious—use the strategies necessary to accomplish your goal and that's all!

Deshler's Strategies Intervention Model

One cognitive strategies model that has been used successfully with adolescents with dyslexia is that of Deshler and his colleagues developed at the University of Kansas Institute for Research in Learning Disabilities (KU-IRLD) (Deshler, Alley, & Carlson, 1980; Deshler, Schumaker, Lenz, & Ellis, 1984; Deshler & Schumaker, 1986; Schumaker, Deshler, Alley, Warner, & Denton, 1982). Deshler and his associates propose that the teacher or appropriate professional establish a student's current level of reading/language functioning through testing. The teacher would then model appropriate cognitive learning strategies with verbal rehearsal/practice. Positive and corrective feedback is used when the teacher monitors the student implementing a strategy. Posttesting assesses growth in learning and effectiveness of strategies usage.

An example of an elementary cognitive strategies approach would be Spafford's (1994) Detective Q. Squirt method which promises to be a challenging and fun learning tool. Some examples of specific cognitive strategies or compensatory activities are included in the comprehension and study skills strategies discussed in this chapter. Remember that cognitive strategies can be compensatory strategies which promote reflective cognitive learning styles. Any of the approaches mentioned (especially interrogative reading) which assist in the development of or require a reflective cognitive learning style, are cognitive strategies/approaches.

Cooperative Learning Activities

Strategic interventions can be accomplished individually and in a group format. Troutman and Lichtenberg (1995) recommend first deciding as a group on the learning objectives, to be followed by the teacher: modeling appropriate behaviors, checking for goal understanding, explaining appropriate goal-directed behaviors, clarifying of learning outcome expectations, and presenting how the group's progress will be assessed. Troutman and Lichtenberg (1995) also carefully note that the teacher should watch each group as the students work the problems encountered, and especially observe students with learning problems. The groups should each try to work through difficulties with closure on an assignment happening with group assessments, peer evaluations, and individual assessments.

Comprehension Activities

Typically teachers are required to follow certain curriculum guidelines in program planning. Many reading programs stress either a skills approach or a whole language perspective or a combination of both (see previous discussion). We recommend that teachers carefully select from among the reading activities and strategies provided in texts and curriculum guides and prioritize them in terms of usefulness and perceived effectiveness. Modifications can be made for students with dyslexia by using some of the techniques/assists listed later in the chapter with selected activities. Teachers have to carefully match the individual needs and interests of all learners with comprehension activities.

Consideration of Special Language Requirements

Special Subject Areas
Teachers need to be aware of the language demands required in specific academic tasks. There are several curriculum areas that have unique language demands (see music example, Table 6-2, p. 126). The following lesson ideas present a few strategies for teachers in music and Spanish, areas which have unique language requirements.

Ambiguous Sentences
Examination of ambiguous sentences embedded in text should also be undertaken especially at the upper grade levels. Teachers need to clarify and discuss these types of sentences. Modeling correct interpretations can help clarify language confusions that can interfere with problem-solving abilities (see examples in Figure 6-4, p. 127). Comparison/Contrast charts, as shown in Figure 6-5 (p. 128), can be used to help clarify confusing subject matter. Differences in *background knowledge* and *culture* need to be considered with any reading program. Mason and Au (1990) point to four general guidelines to help teachers and students get off to a good start: (1) Consider cultural differences with children who are learning how to read and consult with other professionals, parents, and community members to discover any possible source of difficulty that can be remediated; (2) Adjust teaching style/materials/methods to your population in bridging any communication gaps; (3) Assist students with conventional school styles and language usage; and (4) Always build on strengths and interest areas to build a personalized reading foundation. A careful review of the research has given the authors some specific tried

TABLE 6-2   Teaching Music to Children with Specific Learning Disabilities

Learning Challenge For:

Students with a special need for kinesthetic and tactile learning strategies

Music Strategies:
Trace the left to right note patterns on the board as the teacher and/or students play or sing the music.
Play or pantomine an ostinato (repeating melody) pattern on bells.
Identify high or low bells by feel. Arrange high and low bells by size determined by feel.
Respond to auditory discrimination tasks though physical activity.

Learning Challenge For:

Students who are poor visual learners

Music Strategies:
Use a variety of visual aids, such as the following: pictures, videos, objects, teacher movements, visual representations of music.
Observe learners while they interact with the music. Be aware of responses.
Begin with a visual example followed by an auditory example.
Use a visual aid as the music is played as a visual representation becomes an interpretation of the sound.
Model all activities using instruments to provide the visual cues needed.

Learning Challenge For:

Students who are learning disabled

Music Strategies:
Music is a primary means of success for this type of learner. Employ the use of music whenever possible. Example: In math students can learn to count by singing to "one, two buckle my shoe," etc.
Provide many opportunities which enable the learner to translate the sound to music symbols.
Give instructions orally.
Provide the opportunity for learners to use sounds to accompany all their learning experiences, ie., sound representation of math concepts, music to accompany oral literature.
Learners should be encouraged to associate music symbols with sounds from records, cassettes, instruments, etc.

Learning Challenge For:

Problems with motor coordination

Music Strategies:
Design activities which require a variety of motor activities such as clapping, whistling, dancing, etc.
Provide an adequate amount of time for students to perform on instruments.

Learning Challenge For:

Students who have difficulty learning to generalize and make learning connections

Music Strategies:
Give students varying activities practicing soft and loud phrasing or singing.
Provide varying representation to sounds, e.g., staff, letter names, shapes, colors.
Give students an opportunity to verbalize or write the concept learned.

Source: Mary Beth Will

Make connections to what students already know.

Explore Spanish Cognates

familia	requestar
vacacion	inteligente
problema	rapido
liquido	ridiculo
autobus	visitar
calendario	estudiante
planta	silencio
idea	centrio
hamburgesa	delicioso

La profesora requesta silencio imediante. La *problema* es *ridiculo*.
La *familia* van a la *vacacion* en el *autobus.*

FIGURE 6-3   Activating Existing Knowledge

Teachers report early confusion with words like "MORE." Students typically understand MORE as an additive concept:

Three apples plus two MORE = five

Then they enounter the word "MORE" within a subtraction context.

How many more apples are needed to fill the box?

The language can confound the math concept.

Think of the language POSSIBILITIES for a single time:

Three forty-five
Quarter of four
Forty-five minutes past/after three
Fifteen minutes before/of four

FIGURE 6-4   Language Confusion in Math

and proven methods to be used with dyslexic students which are readily adaptable to any reading program. However, it is the authors' contention that the techniques/assists provided could be adapted for use with all learners.

Comprehension of text requires strategic reading or the purposeful and flexible thinking person who is engaged in the task itself (Searfoss & Readance, 1994; Ruddell, 1993; Palinscar & David, 1992; Pressley, Johnson, Symons, McGoldrick, & Kurita, 1989). The comprehension of subject matter material in science, social studies, or other content areas, in large measure rests on the student's ability to perceive the organization of ideas and utilize text structure to facilitate comprehension. Determining deficit areas for the student with dyslexia would be a priority as the methods/techniques chosen should be matched accordingly. Assessment Chart 6-1 (pp. 129–130) serves as a guide for teachers in determining the strengths and reading weaknesses for the student with dyslexia. The chart introduced at the

	Mixtures	*Solutions*	*Suspensions*	*Collidal Dispersions*
Definition	Make up of two or more substances. Each substance keeps it own chemical identity.	One substance is dissolved in another substance.	A mixture that separates on standing.	Contains particles that are larger than the molecules in a solution, but smaller than the particles in a suspension.
Homogeneous or Heterogeneous	**Homogeneous** Mixture—every part of mixture looks the same, i.e., salt and water **Heterogeneous** Mixture—Some sections of mixture look different, i.e., concrete	Homogeneous Mixture	Heterogeneous Mixture	Homogeneous Mixture
Filtration	Can be separated through filtration or evaporation.	Both **solute** (substance that is dissolved) & **solvent** (substance that does the dissolving) can pass through filter.	If filtered "water part" or solvent, will pass through but the solute will not, i.e., clay.	
Examples	Salt and Water	Sugar and Water Plasma	Clay and Water RBC & WBC Form a Suspension in Plasma	Cytoplasm Smoke (Carbon Particles in Air)

FIGURE 6-5   Comparison-Contrast Chart Clarifies Confusing Language Concepts

Source: Maryfrances Peters

beginning of the chapter (see Table 6-1, p. 119) shows specific methods/techniques/assists which can address certain problem areas.

Think-Alouds—A Diagnostic/Teaching Tool

A general rule of thumb would be to present any technique first through modeling. Davey (1983) believes that modeling behaviors allow teachers (who are good readers) to demonstrate how comprehension problems can be overcome. Davey (1983) recommends using predictions and hypothesis testing, visual imagery (let's picture . . .), analogies (like a . . .), verbalizing problem areas and how to correct (fix by . . .) by various strategies. Think-alouds begin at the level of the emerging reader.

ASSESSMENT CHART 6-1   Comprehension Diagnostic Checklist

Write "Yes" or "No" to Indicate Mastery

Affective Dimensions

_____ Sets a reading purpose

_____ Motivated to read/learn

_____ Good attitude

_____ Self-confident

_____ Good attention

_____ Able to focus on task at hand

_____ Good listening skills

_____ Can follow directions

Comprehension Accuracy

Compute by counting the:

$$\frac{\text{Number of Correct Answers}}{\text{total number of questions asked}} = \text{answer}$$

Answer ($\times$) 100 = % correct
               (comprehension level)

_____ Independent Comprehension Level (90% and above)

_____ Instruction Comprehension Level (70–75% and above)

_____ Frustration Comprehension Level (below 70%)

READING RATE (Automaticity/Fluency)

Compute by:

$$\frac{\text{Number of words in selection } (\times 60)}{\text{number of seconds}} = \frac{\text{words per}}{\text{minute}}$$

Determine Reading Rate (based on work of Taylor, Frankenpohl, Pettee, 1960)

_____ Below average for grade

_____ Average

_____ Above

Grades (average reading rates according to WPM)

1	2	3	4	5	6	7	8	9	10	11	12	Col
80	115	138	158	173	185	195	204	214	224	227	250	280

Writing/Reading Connection

_____ Legible handwriting

_____ Can copy accurately

_____ Pre-writing activities include careful topic selection, brainstorming and organizing ideas, locating necessary references and materials, and organizing time frames

_____ Writing activities include enough drafts and revisions for a quality product

_____ Post-writing activities include self editing, editing from teachers/guardians/peers

Reference Usage

_____ Uses library to obtain books and references

_____ Can use a dictionary for pronunciations and word meanings

_____ Can use a map and atlas

_____ Can use a thesaurus

_____ Can use a library card catalog system

_____ Can use an encyclopedia

_____ Knows where to find resources

Story Grammar Knowledge

_____ Follows character development

_____ Identifies setting—time/place

_____ Identifies major problem(s) or plots

_____ Identifies minor problem(s) or subplots

_____ Identifies story resolution

_____ Identifies themes/morals/purposes

Metacognitive Awareness

_____ Understands the gist of a selection

_____ Can make predictions/confirm/revise

_____ Can summarize

_____ Can make cause-and-effect relations

_____ Can draw conclusions

_____ Can make generalizations

_____ Problem solves while reading

_____ Self-monitors comprehension

_____ Self-monitors reading rate

_____ Adjusts (flexibility) to task at hand

Continued

ASSESSMENT CHART 6-1   *Continued*

Study Skills

_____ Completes school assignments
_____ Completes homework assignments
_____ Has daily study time
_____ Plans ahead of time to complete large assignments/projects/reports
_____ Can take notes from oral presentations
_____ Can take notes from text presentations
_____ Can summarize oral presentations
_____ Can summarize written presentations

_____ Can outline/use graphic organizers
_____ Can use visual aids
_____ Studies appropriate exam material
_____ Organizes and reviews notes for exams
_____ Self-questions/monitors learning
_____ Can take objective T/F and multiple choice exams
_____ Can take short essay, fill-in the blank, and long essay exams

Emergent Readers

Print Awareness

The emergent reader or young reader needs to use text at the basic levels of print concepts and story sense. Print concepts help students make vital connections between language and the printed page. Print concepts students need to know include:

- how to hold a book
- how and what letters, words, and sentences represent
- the beginning, end, and middle of a story
- how to match the spoken word to the printed word
- when to use pictures to help understanding
- basic story sense (the who, what, why, where, when of a story)
- the different purposes for reading
- why reading is important
- sequencing skills (from letters to sentences)
- how to make reading-writing connections

Assessing the language readiness skills at the preschool is a must for early literacy interventions to be of optimal benefit (Bousquet, 1993; Garbett, 1993).

Yetta Goodman's Literacy Activities to Promote Print Awareness

Yetta Goodman (1980) offers four types of literacy activities which help develop print awareness:

1. *environmental reading*—children can become scouts or detectives in their environment by identifying road signs, names on mailboxes, logos of restaurants, warning words on household cleaners, their names and addresses on mail envelopes, etc.

2. *informational reading*—parents or guardians can encourage children to seek information needed through reading by posting dates on a refrigerator, checking the TV guide for a time and listing, reviewing a restaurant take-out menu, etc.

3. *occupation reading*—children can be encouraged to look at job-related information by observing people in various professions, looking at want ads, etc.

4. *leisure reading*—children can develop readiness skills by looking over comics in the daily paper, reviewing the sports section of the newspaper, listening to nursery rhymes with books in hand, playing a computer-generated game, etc.

Repeated readings of words, phrases and sentences can be helpful to the emerging reader.

Repeated Readings

Samuels (1979) describes the use of repeated readings for students with dyslexia in order to improve reading fluency and accuracy which are critical to comprehension proficiency. As noted in the previous chapter, if too much cognitive efforts are expended on word identification, fewer resources are available for comprehension. Samuels (1979) suggests first reading passages with the student with dyslexia (with or to them) and then have the student reread until word identification is automatic. Samuels suggests providing a tape recording of the teacher's reading if necessary for the student to follow until independence is achieved. It is important to begin with short passages (up to 50 words) and to *gradually* increase length with experience. After each rereading, discussions can be held regarding various aspects of the text as well as retellings of what was read. According to Lauritzen (1982), the emerging reader would need some passages that rhyme and follow oral literature patterns (e.g., "Henny Penny"). The rereadings can be done in small groups or a group type of echo reading (echoing the teacher's reading after a few words or sentences). Mason and Au (1990) encourage the use of text to develop word identification skills by putting words, sentences, or verses on paper strips of oaktag. Certainly words used could enter a student's word bank.

Literacy connections made through the introduction of stories can be enriched early on with the use of story books, nursery rhymes, predictable books, wordless books, placing words in a,b,c order, language games, singing songs, reciting short poems, telling and retelling stories to each other, having puppet shows, using repeated readings, labeling objects around a classroom with words and phrases, and reading aloud to children (see Trelease, 1982). The use of storybooks and predictable books is particularly beneficial for ESL (English as a Second Language) students (Hough, Nurss, & Enright, 1986).

Reading-Aloud

Teale (1984) stresses that reading aloud to children is probably the most significant way others can convince emerging readers that print is important. Reading aloud to emerging readers can be a receptive and expressive language opportunity where student's questions and comments generate interactive discussions (Hendrick, 1990) before, during, and after the reading. Mason and Au (1990) recommend reading aloud to ESL students a few times a day in small groups of 5–7 children. Small group settings allow for more discussion and question asking with ESL students as some may be hesitant to speak up in front of an entire class. In fact, some schools have Read-Aloud Programs with volunteers from the community reading books to children during specified times (including readings in various languages). Figures 6-6 and 6-7 show how puppets can be made following the completion of a story simply by using popsicle sticks and cut-outs. Students can decorate or create multiculturally diverse characters, and create dialogue in an interactive, socially positive manner.

Retellings Promote Emerging Reading Skills

The reading of stories aloud to children does promote comprehension and emerging reading skills because children now have to now use concepts about print in an organized manner in order to derive meaning from the printed page. Kapinus, Gambrell, and Koskinen (1988) have found that children who are poor readers gain strategic comprehension skills by retelling stories. These authors believe that teachers must first establish a purpose for the retelling and why retelling helps understanding. Kapinus, Gambrell, and Koskinen (1988) recommend the use of short passages at first of 50–100 words which can be retold in just a paragraph or less. The teacher should model some retellings of various stories or text material before students are required to do so.

When teachers witness the struggle of students with learning disabilities in the content-area classroom, their well-intentioned response may be to abandon the text altogether. Long-standing problems ranging from students' weak background knowledge and vocabulary to lack of metacognitive strategies combine to threaten the already fragile connections between the text and the learner. In this regard, the practices of the content-area teacher may well become the critical, final link between reluctant learners and literate activity (Dautrich, 1994). Reutzel (1985) suggests using story maps to help students understand the story grammar highlights, integrate events and concepts within a story, understand the relationship(s) between characters, and to summarize key concepts.

Story Maps

The example in Figure 6-8 (p. 135) shows how a **story map** can be used with non-fiction material to improve comprehension.

Reutzel's technique involves placing the main idea of a story in a center circle of a story map. Extensions from the circle are drawn to other main ideas, events, concepts, and characters in the story (which, too, are placed in circles). Subevents are also placed in circles which extend from the main ideas and characters. Story maps can be used by students in report writing and as notes for tests and quizzes. Rupley and Blair (1989) caution that "story grammar research does not generalize directly to a variety of stories and readers" (p. 210). These

Example

FIGURE 6-6 Boy Kite Puppet

Example

FIGURE 6-7   Girl Kite Puppet

authors suggest using story grammar to identify questions that help students to understand important relationships, to organize information read, and to diagnose students' comprehension abilities when readily applicable. Certainly story maps and the study of story grammar would be useful with basal readers which are

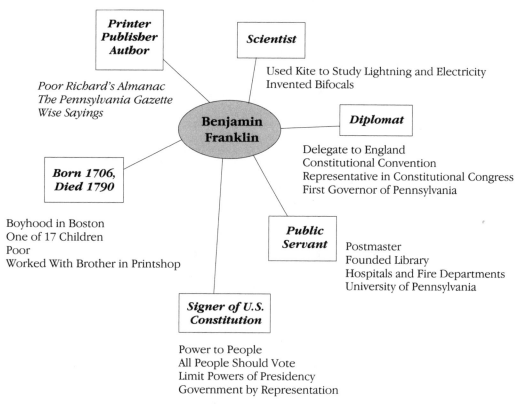

FIGURE 6-8   Story Map

used in many school systems. However, different methods may be required that assist students in handling a basal curriculum.

Story Grammar

Story grammar is a structural system of procedures/rules which describe consistent text features (Mandler, 1984; Moreau & Puzzo, 1994). At the elementary level, story grammar can focus on the basic setting, story plot, and story resolution, inasmuch as these are basic to many stories (Schmidt & O'Brien, 1986). Stein and Trabasso (1981) offer a comprehensive story grammar structure which can be used at the upper elementary and high school levels. Their story grammar identifies specific components of narrative structure, such as, a setting or time frame for the story, an episode which has an initiating event to begin the episode, an internal response by the main characters which initiates actions, an attempt to carry out those actions to reach a goal(s), a consequence(s) of actions taken, and a reaction(s) of the main character(s), including their feelings, either about successfully reaching a goal(s) or failing to attain the goal(s). The student is taught to utilize story grammar by following teacher modeling in which story elements are identified and recorded (see Tables 6-3 and 6-4, p. 136).

TABLE 6-3 Story Grammar (Secondary)

Story Analysis:

Narrative text generally follows a chain of events that are familiar and identifiable. Working with students to identify the pattern of story events develops their awareness of narrative structure and provides a scaffold for improved comprehension.

Short Story:	"The Chrysanthemums" by John Steinbeck
Setting:	A cattle ranch in the Midwest
Time:	The Great Depression
Characters:	Elisa, her husband Henry, and the tinsmith
Theme:	Economic and social injustice of the 1930s

Chain of Events

Initiating Event: While gardening her chrysanthemums, Elisa is approached by an aged tinsmith traveling in a covered wagon. He is looking to repair any pots or pans.

Internal Response: Elisa feels compassion for the weathered traveler. Noting his itinerant, impoverished life, she feels shamed by the contrast in their lives.

Attempt: Although she declines his offer to repair pots, she prepares a planting of chrysanthemums for him to take to a favorite customer of his.

Consequence: The old man is pleased but talks about his poverty and need for work.

Attempt: Elisa recovers some discarded pans for the tinsmith to repair. He completes the task at the end of his wagon with great skill and pride.

Resolution: Elisa pays the man fifty cents and he rides off. Elisa feels relieved and prepares for the evening out with her husband.

Reaction: On the way into town, Elisa and her husband pass the traveling tinsmith and his wagon. She avoids looking at the man or mentioning the encounter to her husband.

TABLE 6-4 Story Grammar (Elementary)

An episode from: *Ramona and Her Father*
by Beverly Cleary

Initiating Event	Ramona wants to get her father to stop smoking.
Internal Response	She feels excited and eager to start her plan.
1st Attempt	Ramona tapes a large poster of a cigarette with the word BAD onto the refrigerator.
Consequence	Dad ignores the poster.
2nd Attempt	Ramona posts small notices throughout the house about not smoking.
Consequence	Dad ignores the notices.
3rd Attempt	Ramona replaces real cigarettes with rolled papers containing warning messages.
Consequence	Dad has had enough. He scolds Ramona and continues to smoke.
Internal Response	Ramona feels defeated and thinks it isn't fair to be a second grader who has so little influence.

Graphic Organizers

Graphic organizers are diagrams or outlines that depict the main structure of the material to be read. Key terms and concepts are used to create a "skeleton" that depicts the order and organization of the textual material. Graphic organizers assist students in making those cause-and-effect relationships relevant to reading comprehension. Through the visual format, they are able to see the relationship between ideas and concepts. Traditional outlining procedures might not be sufficient for the student with dyslexia as organizational/study skills are frequently lacking. Varnhagen and Goldman (1986) conclude from their research that individuals who experience comprehension problems benefit from instructional techniques that focus on the causal connections/events/relationships in stories. The use of story grammar via story maps (Reutzel, 1985) and other such techniques seems to help students with comprehension difficulties (Tierney & Cunningham, 1984).

In a discussion, students' attention is drawn to the organizational format of the chapter by examining headings, bold face type, diagrams, and other visual features. This allows students to develop a framework before reading. The following figure (6-9) compares traditional outlining characteristics to that of graphic organizers.

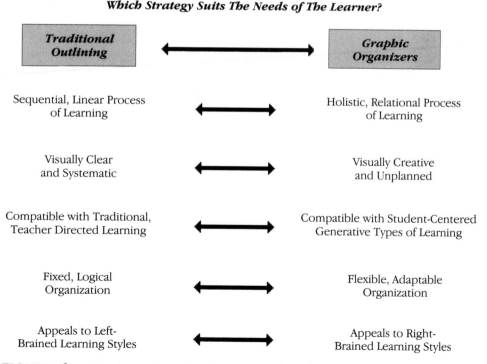

FIGURE 6-9 Traditional Outlining versus Graphic Organizers

Text Structure Guides

Questions and predictions about the reading can be developed from text structure guides which in essence outline key concepts and points to focus in on. Outlining textual material can also be done with graphic organizers. The teacher may provide instruction on specific text structures by selecting certain paragraphs or segments that illustrate five common text patterns:

Descriptive or Enumerative.   This text pattern is designed to inform the reader about particular attributes or features of the topic.

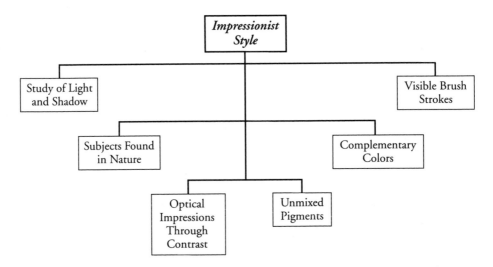

FIGURE 6-10   Descriptive

Based on: *Understanding Art,* 2nd ed., Lois Fichner-Rathus (1989) Prentice Hall, Englewood Cliffs, N.J.

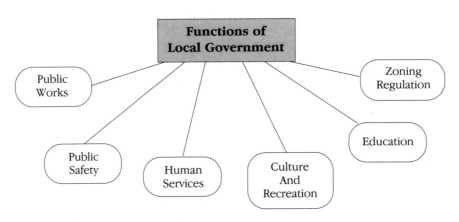

FIGURE 6-11   Enumerative

Sequential. This text pattern designates the time-order of events.

Compare and Contrast. This text pattern is constructed to illustrate similarities and differences between two concepts.

Cause and Effect. This text pattern is organized around relating the causes of certain events or conditions to their outcomes or consequences.

Problem-Solution. This text pattern presents the factors associated with a particular problem and links them to possible solutions.

Text Structure Guides

Formation of a Glacial Lake

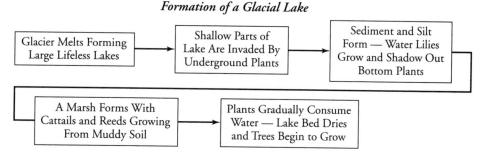

FIGURE 6-12 Sequential

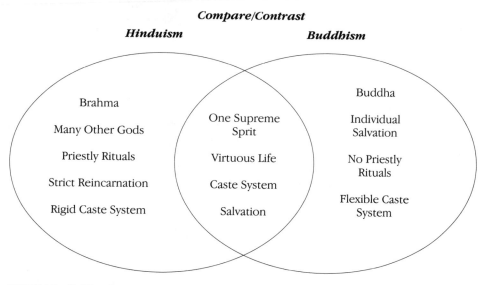

FIGURE 6-13 Compare and Contrast

Source: *The New Work Past and Present*, HBJ Land Mark Edition, 1988, Chicago.

Text Structure Guides (con't.)
Cause and Effect

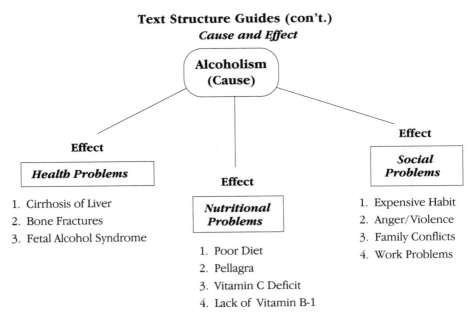

FIGURE 6-14   Cause and Effect

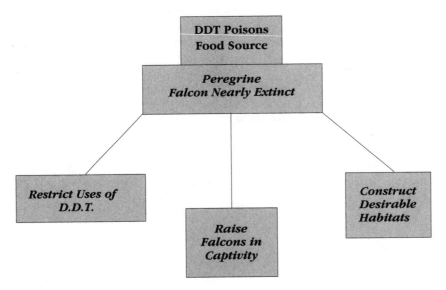

FIGURE 6-15   Problem—Solution

Created by: Dr. Barbara Dautrich (Text Structure Guides)

While proficient readers often acquire comprehension skills automatically through growing exposure to subject area texts, the student with dyslexia may require explicit instruction and practice to develop the awareness and strategies that support effective comprehension of expository text. Skimming, scanning, surveying, and paraphrasing are also popular methods aimed at this level of skill development.

Skimming

Skimming is the rapid reading of text in order to get a sense of text structure, organization, and gist. Chapter titles, bolded type, marginal glosses, chapter previews and chapter conclusions give the reader a cursory understanding of what the reading content involves. Teachers can instruct students with dyslexia to look for specific text components (e.g., chapter titles and headings, introduction and conclusion sections, pictures and graphics) when skimming so that the student gets a global picture of the reading at hand. Although skimming is part of the SQ3R study method mentioned in Chapter 7, Rubin (1991a) cautions that students be aware that skimming behaviors are not the same as studying which requires "much slower and more concentrated reading" (p. 394). If students learn to paraphrase or summarize this information as they adjust their reading rates, comprehension can be enhanced.

Scanning

Scanning is the rapid reading of text in order to locate needed information after a reading purpose has been established. Students who need to find information quickly, such as a phone number, an author in an index, a topic in a newspaper, and so on, can be trained to look for the key word(s) wanted. Teachers need to point out that once the information is located, students can read more slowly.

Paraphrasing

In studying the reading behaviors of poor readers, Winograd (1984) has found that these readers have difficulty abstracting key ideas and summarizing or paraphrasing key concepts and information. Similarly, Taylor (1984) states that individuals who are poor readers will not actively think to paraphrase information before writing about what they read. Maggart and Zintz (1990) suggest that with poor readers, teachers first concentrate on having students paraphrase their ideas orally before written expressive tasks are assigned. These authors also indicate that discussions should follow reading assignments where students can brainstorm and share ideas regarding the summary of contextual material. Teachers can assist students with dyslexia in paraphrasing what they read by alternating with students as to who will paraphrase a paragraph, page, or story.

Immediate and positive feedback should be given to the student. The teacher should be quick to point out why the summary statement(s) are good and then add/delete obviously incorrect/irrelevant information. In this way, teachers actively model good paraphrasing or summary skills behaviors as seen in the following example in Table 6-5 (p. 142).

Surveying

Surveying is the guided exploration of the structure and content of the text material which is well suited to instructional strategies with basal readers.

TABLE 6-5 Paraphrasing

Following a segment of text reading on, "The Diary of Anne Frank" by Frances Goodrich and Albert Hackett the teacher models the process of paraphrasing by writing student contributions on chart paper.

"The Diary of Anne Frank" is based on the diary of young Anne Frank during World War II. Anne was a normal happy child until Adolf Hitler and the Nazis gained control of Germany in 1933. To avoid being imprisoned or killed because they were Jewish, the Franks hid in the attic of a warehouse where Anne wrote her diary.

Working with Basal Readers

Schwartz and Sheff (1975) specify a directed teaching format when guiding students with comprehension problems through basal readers. The Schwartz-Sheff approach involves having the teacher pose questions based on the story title and predictions made by the students. The students use critical thinking skills while reading and actively seek to confirm or revise text predictions.

Prediction is one activity which lends itself to establishing fluency, confidence in reading, critical thinking skills, discovering patterns and relationships, and relating prior knowledge to new learning across the curriculum.

When using basal readers, the teacher should assume the role of a coach. S/he needs to focus students on important cues in the story for information recall, reinforces the generation of original ideas and interpretations, and guides students toward a conceptual integration of story ideas, character, and plot development. During stages two and three, students are asked literal and inferential comprehension questions in order to stimulate their reasoning skills and establish a mind-set for a basal questioning format. Teachers can also set up "comprehension assists" such as "Guide-O-Ramas," "Material Previews," "Prediction Guides," and "Marginal Glosses" when using basal readers and other content area texts.

Adjusting to Basal and Content Text Requirements

Guide-O-Ramas/Reading Road Maps. Guide-O-Ramas (Cunningham & Shablack, 1975) are reading guides teachers develop that *guide* the reader to note certain information while reading. The teacher can create personal messages for the student which will even refer the student to certain key pages while reading. A variation of the Guide-O-Rama idea is the reading road map. The following social studies example in Figure 6-16 (p. 143) highlights various reading/writing rates required for different task requirements.

Material Previews/Anticipation Guides. One way to improve motivation for reading and comprehension skills is to set up movie-like capsule previews (**material previews**) or preview checks of material to be read. Anticipation guides can involve short reviews (in the style of movie reviews) of books in a "book

Topic: Community Services

Location	Speed	Mission

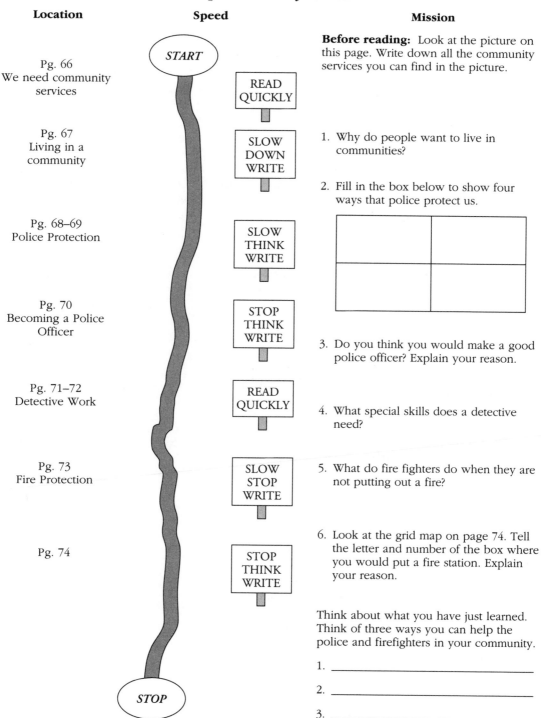

Location

Pg. 66
We need community services

Pg. 67
Living in a community

Pg. 68–69
Police Protection

Pg. 70
Becoming a Police Officer

Pg. 71–72
Detective Work

Pg. 73
Fire Protection

Pg. 74

Speed

START

READ QUICKLY

SLOW DOWN WRITE

SLOW THINK WRITE

STOP THINK WRITE

READ QUICKLY

SLOW STOP WRITE

STOP THINK WRITE

STOP

Mission

Before reading: Look at the picture on this page. Write down all the community services you can find in the picture.

1. Why do people want to live in communities?

2. Fill in the box below to show four ways that police protect us.

3. Do you think you would make a good police officer? Explain your reason.

4. What special skills does a detective need?

5. What do fire fighters do when they are not putting out a fire?

6. Look at the grid map on page 74. Tell the letter and number of the box where you would put a fire station. Explain your reason.

Think about what you have just learned. Think of three ways you can help the police and firefighters in your community.

1. _____

2. _____

3. _____

FIGURE 6-16   Reading Road Map

Created by: Dr. Barbara Dautrich

chat" type of format. Another type of previewing method is to look at certain parts of the book in order to generate anticipation on the part of the reader. The use of an anticipation guide can introduce students to the chapter concepts by having them respond to statements prior to reading. Following the reading, students review their earlier responses to revise or support prior views. Tables 6-6 and 6-7 serve as examples at both the elementary and secondary levels. Valeri-Gold (1987) suggests assisting students in estimating how long it will take to read a book and then to break the time required for the reading into manageable chunks. Students can read the book title, subheadings, pre- and post-chapter questions, chapter introductions and conclusions, graphs, charts, and pictures in order to make guesses or predictions about story content which can be confirmed or disconfirmed after the reading. We would suggest a written checklist for the student with dyslexia.

Marginal Glosses.   **Marginal Glosses** are comments authors make in margins to readers as asides, notes of clarification, vocabulary highlights, interpretations, trivia notes, and so on. These marginal glosses are sometimes printed. Teachers can also create marginal glosses with personalized notes for the student with

TABLE 6-6   Anticipation Guide (Elementary)

A pre-reading strategy that sets a purpose for reading.

Directions: Before you read "Gentleman of Río en Medio" by Juan A. A. Sedillo, think about what you already know. Read each statement and write YES or NO on the line to show what you believe. After your reading go back to each statement and decide if you still want the same answer. Be ready to tell why you changed your mind in some cases.

Before		After
_____	1. The main character is a gentleman.	_____
_____	2. Land near a river (río) must be valuable.	_____
_____	3. Sobrinos and nietos can be descendants.	_____
_____	4. A faded coat can look princely.	_____
_____	5. Something gnarled is ugly.	_____
_____	6. Trees can be expensive gifts.	_____
_____	7. When one signs a deed one sells everything that grows on the land.	_____

TABLE 6-7 Anticipation Guide for Experiment on Solutions and Sus

Using your knowledge of solutions and suspensions please predict before the experimen following are mixtures, solutions, suspensions and/or colloids. Write your predictions in tl ⌐pace provided. After performing the experiment please write down whether the following are mixtures, solutions, suspensions and/or colloids. Have your responses changed? Why or why not? Write the answers in your notebook.

Before Experiment	After Experiment	
_____	_____	Unflavored Gelatin with water
_____	_____	Food coloring with water
_____	_____	Cornstarch with water
_____	_____	Garden soil with water

Follow-up:

Experiment—Mixture, Solutions, Suspensions and Colloidal Dispersions

Gather four clear glass jars and the following substances: one packet of unflavored gelatin; one-half teaspoon food coloring; one tablespoon cornstarch; and one tablespoon garden soil. To each jar, add one-half cup of warm water and one of these substances (for the gelatin, use hot water). Mix each thoroughly, and observe for ten minutes without touching. Decide in each case whether you have created a mixture, a solution, a suspension, or a colloidal dispersion.

Source: Maryfrances Peters

dyslexia who might benefit from additional comments and interpretations. Marginal glosses can be used in any content area as seen in the health example in Table 6-8 (p. 146).

There are several other activities which can enhance academic success for individuals with dyslexia and other reading problems. For example, curriculum telescoping or compacting and content area acceleration can be used when planning academic programs for dyslexic students who are gifted. Additionally, Smith, Polloway, Patton, and Dowdy (1995) recommend with all gifted populations the use of adult mentors, higher-order thinking skills lessons, the formal teaching of research skills, exposure to interactive technologies (e.g., CD-ROM), and a balanced coverage of basic disciplines and the arts.

Working with Gifted Dyslexic Students

Curriculum Telescoping

Hunt and Marshall (1994) recommend **curriculum telescoping** or compacting for students who are gifted. This involves analyzing some subject matter (i.e., math) and eliminating or condensing curriculum requirements because the student has mastered such content. Students could then be given independent study projects, enrichment, or cooperative learning activities. Cooperative learning activities could involve learning teams with children at different learning levels coaching, assisting,

TABLE 6-8   Marginal Gloss Regarding the Topic of Alcoholism

Using a sheet that slides under the page of print, the teacher provides supporting comments and questions in the margin.

People who drink excessive amounts of alcohol are called alcoholics. Some researchers say that it is a behavior disorder like a bad habit. Others feel it is a disease that is passed on genetically within a family. Some scientists report a chemical dependency that is much like a physical addiction.	Paragraph 1 There is no simple explanation for alcoholism. Which theory would you support?
Alchohol causes many health problems in the human body. A disease of the liver, called *cirrhosis,* results when liver tissue breaks down. Over time, cirrhosis can lead to death. Bone fractures are more common in alcoholics; it has been shown that alcohol interferes with the chemicals that regulate bone growth. Pregnant women who consume alcohol endager their baby's health. *Fetal alcohol syndrome* is characterized by babies who, born undersized, show damage to the central nervous system, and develop lifelong disturbances in behavior and learning.	Paragraph 2 Alcoholics abuse their bodies. What damage occurs? Think of how a F.A.S. child might behave.
Nutritional problems result from alcoholism too. The poor diets of many alcoholics result in deficiencies in essential nutrients. For example, a loss of vitamin B-1 results in *pellagra,* a disease of the skin, mouth, and digestive tract. The toxic effects of alcohol use up the body's store of vitamin C. Vitamin B-6 is also destroyed by the toxic effects of alcohol.	Paragraph 3 Alcohol is a poor substitute for food. Which vitamins are lost?
The social dangers of alcohol are as bad as the medical problems. A drinking habit can drain the family's money supply. Alcoholics are often unable to hold a job. Excessive drinking can cause angry violent behaviors that harm others. Turmoil in the family causes emotional problems for other family members. Because of these growing problems, alcoholism has become a national concern.	Paragraph 4 Imagine the problems of an alcoholic family. Think of how the family would cope.

Created by: Dr. Barbara Dautrich

and problem solving together. Meade (1994) cites research which supports such programming efforts with gifted populations.

Content Acceleration

Content acceleration involves moving a student to a curriculum level above his/her current grade placement. This can be easily accomplished in a school with multiple grades. If a student with dyslexia is gifted in mathematics, perhaps he/she could participate in an upper level math course. The challenge and opportunities to build self-esteem could result in positive learning/social gains. Hunt and Marshall (1994) say that content acceleration can "occur within regular classes at virtually every grade level . . . everytime a teacher allows students to 'jump ahead' at a faster pace" (p. 540). It would be expected that dyslexic students would not be accelerated in subjects with heavy language demands which relate to the disability. Just how effective is content acceleration for students who are learning disabled? Research isn't available to confirm or disconfirm our hunch that it can be very effective in the right setting with accommodating teachers. One author has worked with several dyslexic students who were gifted and has found content acceleration to be most effective especially in the math and science areas. The following mini-study provides a great example of how important it is to meet the special learning challenges and cognitive learning style of dyslexic students who are gifted (see also Chapter 1).

CASE STUDY

Gifted Dyslexic: Billy, Age 17

Characteristics/Correlating Data to Support a Gifted/Dyslexic Diagnosis

- Full-Scale IQ. of 129 (Verbal IQ = 128; Performance IQ = 122) Information Subtest = 63rd percentile
- Boston Naming Task = Score was 2 Standard Deviations below the mean
- WIAT (Wechsler Individual Achievement Test), Writing Skills = 16th percentile (WAIS-R predicted percentile = 90), Reading Skills = 75th percentile (WAIS-R predicted percentile = 92)
- Frustration/anxiety exhibited during reading/language tasks
- Woodcock Reading Mastery Test (Revised Form 6), Word identification = 91st percentile, passage comprehension = 82 percentile
- Choppy oral reading skills
- Gray Oral Reading = 63rd percentile (fluency)
- Based on incomplete Sentence Blank Test, Personal Problem Checklist, and Test of Emotional Development—Feelings of sadness, worrying, isolation, and being different
- Word finding difficulties and weak expressive language skills
- Difficulties learning to read and write since the onset of schooling; learning was always a struggle
- Special education programs/placements since the onset of school with poor academic/social performance reported throughout elementary/junior high schools
- Displays excellent learning aptitude in chemistry and math
- Accepted at Ivy League College—Chemical engineering program
- Enjoys interpreting Shakespeare, memorizing history dates, and doing calculus problems
- Excellent compensatory strategies in reading/studying at age 17
- Excellent memory skills (California Verbal Learning Test; WAIS-R, Digit Span Subtest; observations)
- Inordinate amounts of time, energy and effort and required in order to read, remember, comprehend, and interpret text

Billy didn't have significant educational accommodations that tapped into his special strengths and talents until high school. Educational programming stressed reading/language remediation the first ten years of his schooling. Then Billy participated in some accelerated math/English classes with grades jumping from the Cs, Ds, and Es in grade school, junior high school, and beginning high school, to all As and Bs his junior and senior high school years. After tapping into his math strengths and interests in Shakespeare and poetry, learning became meaningful, motivating, and fun. We're pleased to say that Billy will be attending an Ivy League College soon and will be majoring in chemical engineering.

In all education programs, reading-writing connections need to be made, as most individuals with dyslexia frequently experience written expressive language difficulties which parallel their reading problems.

Oral and Silent Reading

The Importance of Oral Reading Activities

According to Harris and Sipay (1990), oral reading activities are necessary components to a remedial program. For the student with reading problems, these authors recommend taking turns in small groups during oral reading, to the extent that the oral reading activities allow: (1) the teacher to assess reading skills such as word identification, phrasing, and self-monitoring/correction strategies, (2) the students to engage in character portrayal and story dramatization, and (3) the teacher to provide social reinforcement and encouragement.

Oral reading activities can be motivating, fun, self-reflective, and educational. Activities could include poetry readings, daily newspaper article readings, choral reading, producing plays or other dramatizations, creating commercials, staging debates, providing reinforcement for silent reading activities, and so on. Individuals with dyslexia require extra time to become familiar with text before oral reading. Additionally, "on-the-spot" oral readings can be frustrating and anxiety-provoking for many students. Volunteers should be solicited if at all possible. There are structured oral reading activities which can be used to aid students with dyslexia in gaining reading skills and confidence if done in a non-threatening atmosphere. It should be noted that we are *not* encouraging "round-robin" or "circle" reading which involves each student taking a turn in order to read a small portion of text to a group while the others in the class follow silently. There is a body of research which negates the instructional usefulness of round-robin exercises (see Allington, 1984; Brulnsma, 1981). The following four oral reading methods can be useful in a well-rounded program for students with dyslexia.

Oral Reading Activities

Choral and Choral Repeated Reading

These are whole-class reading activities which involve active student participation and comprehension of text. The teacher models good oral reading behaviors by phrasing properly, changing tempos, and changing voice intonation and expression. There are different methods of casting oral reading parts from scripts: assigning dialogue parts for high and low voices, designating students to recite the refrain of a poem or narrative, having line-by-line choral readings consisting of three or more students, and so on. We recommend practicing choral reading parts with students with dyslexia before the class reading. More able readers could also be paired with reading-impaired children in a helping role.

Radio Reading

Radio reading (Searfoss, 1975) focuses on radioing or communicating a message. Essentially a script is given to (a) designated radio announcer(s) who deliver(s) a script to an audience of listeners who respond by discussing the program. The teacher can help clarify unclear messages. There is no correction of oral reading errors during the broadcast, although opportunities for prior rehearsal and practice should be provided. It is up to the listener to fill-in when errors are made. Again, the student with dyslexia will need to read, rehearse, and review reading material before a broadcast. Discussions should follow each broadcast in order to ensure comprehension.

Paired Reading

Paired reading (Greene, 1970) simply involves placing students together in pairs to read side by side. The teacher could pair the student with dyslexia with a more proficient reader who could assist with the pronunciations of difficult words. It is recommended that students try to self-monitor comprehension by asking themselves, "Does this make sense?" as they read. As each reader finishes a part, s/he should retell what was read to the listener. Then both readers can engage in a dialogue about what was read and ask each other questions. Although suggested times for paired reading activities vary from 10–15 minutes in the primary grades and 20–30 minutes in the intermediate grades, we would recommend 10-minute turns for the student with dyslexia. This could help reduce any frustration associated with the oral reading exercise.

Echo Reading

Heckelman (1969) developed the neurological impress method or what has become known as **echo reading.** Heckelman believed that traditional oral reading methods allow students to make too many errors which become deeply imprinted and difficult to correct. His method relies on high-interest material which is at a level slightly easier that what can be adequately handled by the individual with dyslexia. The teacher and student in essence read together side-by-side and in unison. The teacher does not correct oral reading errors. In the beginning, the teacher reads more loudly and slightly faster than the student. Once the student masters the material, the teacher can lag behind the student in a softer voice. The teacher's finger follows the line of print during the reading in beginning sessions with the student taking over this function as s/he becomes comfortable with the print. Comprehension checks can follow the complete readings. This method has been criticized for placing too much emphasis on word identification and not enough on critical thinking. Certainly, this method can be adapted to include comprehension checks after each page of print with varying types of question asked (e.g., alternate between literal and inferential types of questions).

Until recently, it has been assumed by many reading professionals that comprehension is lost with oral reading exercises and more emphasis should be placed on sustained silent reading. Wilkinson, Wordrop, and Anderson (1988) found that silent reading does not always result in better comprehension than oral reading. These researchers found that children at the early childhood level (K–3) actually comprehended text better in oral reading activities. For Grade 3, the comprehension levels for oral reading were about the same as those for silent reading. Above Grade 3, silent reading produced a comprehension advantage. As in all reading programs, there has to be a balance between oral and silent reading activities with more emphasis on silent activities at the upper school levels.

Silent Reading Comprehension

Sustained Silent Reading (SSR)

Sustained silent reading activities (SSR) are meant to foster/reinforce literate behavior and to encourage reading for enjoyment. These are independent reading activities which utilize literature and leisure types of reading materials. The independent reading level of the student with dyslexia needs to be identified so that sustained silent reading times can be relatively fluent and enjoyable. As an example, the DEAR (Drop Everything and Read) programs have become common SSR experiences in many schools. Teachers, principals, and students literally "drop everything and read" at specified times during the school day (usually 15 minutes). Tierney, Readence, and Dishner (1990) give three suggestions for SSR activities: (1) everyone reads, (2) there are no interruptions, and (3) no one will be asked to report on readings.

Students with dyslexia should be able to manage SSR reading material without instruction or support. Support could be provided by the type of materials used: listening tapes of books with headsets; high-interest low-vocabulary library books; leisure-type activities with high-interest low-vocabulary content such as newspapers, National Geographic books for children, wordless books, comic books (remember SSR is suppose to be enjoyable), sports magazines; hobby books; and even books with accompanying tapes. Students who also experience attention problems will need to be accommodated during SSR times.

Students with Attention Problems.   Students with attention problems may find SSR times difficult at best. Students who are highly distractible need to be strategically seated during SSR times so that interruptions to other students are kept at a minimum. Certainly giving students with attention problems a job or special duty during SSR times can help channel energies constructively. As examples, the classroom teachers could (1) appoint such students to be timekeepers during SSR times providing a stopwatch or clock—very simply a student could give the teacher a silent hand signal at each 5-minute interval (the student is alternating reading behaviors with keeping track of the time); and (2) inattentive students could shift gears every so often by changing reading materials (allowing the student to move about by selecting a new book, magazine, or other reading material).

Even more useful would be the use of self-monitoring training before and after SSR times so that inattentive students "are taught to effectively self-monitor their on-task behavior, the chances are good that their academic productivity [reading behaviors] will increase" (deBettencourt, 1990, p. 462).

Hallahan's Self-Monitoring of Inattentive Behavior.   Hallahan and his associates (see: Hallahan, Kauffman, & Lloyd, 1985) have developed a self-monitoring procedure for dyslexic students (and those with other learning disabilities) who have attention problems. The procedure is as follows: (1) the teacher operationally defines desired on-task behaviors for the student (SSR as an example) and then gives the student examples; (2) The teacher models the desired behaviors (SSR) along with the student who must self-check if he/she is on-task; (3) The student periodically receives a cue from the teacher (or a tape recorder) and at that very moment must self-record whether or no he/she was on task; (4) The cueing and self-recording behaviors are diminished until the desired behaviors become somewhat acquired. Notice we say somewhat. One can't expect perfect on-task behavior for students with attention difficulties. That is why it would be important to establish baseline behaviors and reasonable objectives before self-monitoring occurs. If a student is able to attend to SSR for only 2 minutes before the training, a 5–6 minute attention span might be extremely favorable following training. The key is to establish reasonable expectations based on the nature of the problem and the perceived stamina of the individual.

The quality of comprehension during silent reading depends on one's metacognitive awareness or knowledge of one's own cognitive processes (Flavell, 1976). Flavell (1987) proposes that readers must be aware of self (e.g., an individual's assessment of cognitive strengths and weaknesses), task (e.g., different tasks require different kinds of information processing), and strategy (e.g., self-monitoring and self- evaluation) variables related to knowledge of cognition.

Self-Monitoring During Reading

Children need to learn at an early age that they need to keep track of the reasons why (purpose) they are reading as well as their understanding of the material read. Young children can be trained early on to look at picture cues, context clues, initial word sounds, titles, and predictable words, to assist in the comprehension of reading materials. Older students can be assisted with specific questioning techniques and study skills strategies discussed later in this chapter. Individuals with dyslexia and other learning disabilities do not have as sophisticated self-monitoring abilities and other metacognitive strategies as good readers do and there is a ". . . need to teach them metacognitive skills in reading in addition to decoding and comprehension skills . . ." (Wong, 1991). All students need to be encouraged to ask questions when they do not understand what is presented. One of the best ways to develop metacognitive skills is to teach via an interrogative reading format.

Interrogative Reading

There is an old saying to the effect that our knowledge is better measured by the questions we raise as opposed to the answers we give. It has been shown that students who develop their own questions about textual material better comprehend what is read than those who do not (Palinscar & Brown, 1984). Students with dyslexia typically approach text in a passive manner, and may need direct modeling and practice to develop interrogative strategies. Certainly activities which involve students as active participants and encourage learning by the inquiry-based approach (e.g., hands-on learning in science during such science units as magnetism, electricity, exploring the characteristics of rocks and minerals, etc.) can result in improved comprehension gains (Scruggs, Mastropieri, Bakken, and Brigham, 1993). "Because most students with LD have difficulty learning from reading and workbook assignments, and benefit from concrete examples, activity-based science instruction may be preferable to textbook-based instruction" (Scruggs, Mastropieri, Bakken, and Brigham, p. 3). The questioning generated from such endeavors encourages students to self-monitor while reading and to develop better metacognitive awareness. The example in Table 6-9 emphasizes the active role the reader must assume when interacting with the printed page.

Self-Monitoring During Reading

Questioning strategies provide the individual with dyslexia opportunities for critical thinking, summarizing major portions of text, predictions for later reading which will be confirmed or nonconfirmed, filling in the blanks for unknown words and concepts, and strategies that must be taken to better understand the selection at hand (e.g., re-reading). Additionally, questioning/self-questioning strategies allow the teacher/student to assess critical deficit areas along with other assessment measures (Wallace, Cohen, & Polloway, 1987; Wallace, Larsen, & Elksnin, 1992). There are specific questioning strategies one can use even in the content area subjects in order to facilitate learning for the student with dyslexia. *Cognitive apprenticeships* and *framing questions* are two such methods. Table 6-9 (p. 153) shows how students must assume a greater role in the comprehension process if self-monitoring procedures are to be effective.

Cognitive Apprenticeships

"The central focus of much recent research in reading instruction is on the teacher's explanations to students of the cognitive activities engaged in by good readers" (Ross, Bondy, & Kyle, 1993, p. 89). Cognitive apprenticeships are one way to provide models for good reading behaviors (Collins, Brown, & Newman, 1989) in an interactive questioning type of format. The student with reading disabilities is coached by the teacher who provides suggestions, feedback, appropriate reading materials, and scaffolding. Scaffolding is the way in which the teacher implements support or specific helpful hints. The student with reading disabilities is gradually withdrawn from assistance as s/he becomes more proficient.

TABLE 6-9 Self-Monitoring During Reading

Teachers need to model the strategies that govern skilled reading. Gradually students take on a greater role in developing their own inner dialogue.

Self-Questioning Procedure		Inner Dialogue
1. Why am I reading this?	[Purpose]	To learn about the Japanese culture.
2. What will I be learning?	[Skim]	The pictures show all different parts of the Japanese culture.
3. How is this organized?	[Preview]	Each letter of the alphabet tells me about Japan.
4. What do I already know about this?	[Background Knowledge]	I remember that my uncle told me about "Aikido." I saw "Sushi" in a restaurant once.
5. Does this make sense as I read? Do I understand?	[Active Reading]	Yes. The pictures help me understand.
6. Is there new information here? Should I slow down? Reread?	[Metacognitive Strategy]	Yes. The pronunciations in italics help me pronounce the words. I should read this part again.
7. How am I doing? Am I learning as I read?	[Metacognitive Monitoring]	Yes. These words make sense because the picture images make Japan real. I'll keep a word list.

Source: A to Zen by Ruth Wells; Illustrator, Yoshi. (1992). Saxonville, MA.

Coaching and Scaffolding

Scaffolds in the construction sense are building materials used by workers to hold up structures and provide access as construction occurs. ". . . In education scaffolds are the supports teachers and students [e.g., word bank cards] use to construct new knowledge . . ." (Moore, Moore, Cunningham, & Cunningham, 1994, p. 95). Paris and Winograd (1990) emphasize that dialoguing must be the most critical component to any scaffolding approach (see Appendix II).

Collins, Brown, and Newman (1989) describe several coaching/scaffolding components one can use with all readers: initially one can formulate questions about each page—first by the teacher and then by the student; articulate how one can summarize, outline, draw conclusions and make inferences about what is read while reading; engage in reflective practices while reading, such as evaluating whether or not reading goals, mini-goals, and subskills have been achieved; provide continual feedback; and explore the use of new strategies without teacher support. Framing questions throughout this entire process is key to understanding. Table 6-10 demonstrates how teachers can implement interrogative reading strategies (p. 154).

TABLE 6-10 Interrogative Reading—Constructivism and Scaffolding at its Best

A questioning strategy is an important component of "active" reading. The inner dialogue that accompanies skilled reading needs to be modeled and practiced for passive readers. See Appendix II.

Meteoroids Meteors and Meteorites	(Teacher models inner dialogue)
Have you ever seen a falling star? Did you know that a falling star is not really a star at all? It is a meteoroid that is passing through the earth's atmosphere at great speed. As the friction from the surrounding air heats the *meteoroid,* it begins to glow and shower off sparks in a long tail.	I wonder what the difference is between these 3 words. I always thought a falling star really was a star. That's why we can see it all lit up at night.
Once it begins to glow, it is called a *meteor.* Most meteors never reach earth because their intense heat causes them to burn up in the atmosphere.	I wonder where the meteors go?
When a meteor does reach earth, it may hit with great impact and cause damage. Huge meteors fell in ancient Africa and in Arizona and caused huge craters in the earth. Once a meteor has landed it is called a *meteorite.* Many meteorites land with such force that they shatter into pieces. It is very rare that we encounter meteors striking earth.	What happens when they hit the earth? I wonder if I should be worried?
The last major occurrence was in 1877 in Iowa. The main problems that we have to worry about are meteoroid showers that may be hazardous to space craft.	I guess most meteoroids stay in space.

Created by Dr. Barbara Dautrich

Framing Questions

Framing Questions in Social Studies

Framing questions (or interactive frames) involves pre-planned question formats for a particular subject. For example, when reading social studies material which involves conflict/cooperative interactions, Jones (1985) has suggested the following types of questions: What are the people involved or groups involved? What were their goals? What was the nature of their interaction: conflict or cooperation? How did they act and react? What was the group or personal outcome?

Another topic suitable to framing questions is the issue of problems and solutions. For example, one could address the problem of government spending and how to propose solutions to reduce the government deficit. It might be necessary to frame questions for the individual with reading disabilities, for example: What was the problem? Who had the problem? Why was it a problem? What attempts are being made to solve the problem? What has been done so far to solve the problem? Have attempts worked to solve any part of the problem? (adapted from Jones, 1985).

Framing Questions in Science

Markle (1975) has suggested question frames for science concepts. For example, when conducting experiments with objects, the following could be used: What is the thing? What category does it belong to and why? What are the characteristics or critical attributes studied? How does it work? What does it do? What are its functions? What are some other examples of it? What are some nonexamples of it? Prediction strategies enable students to bridge new knowledge and learning with previous schemas or knowledge bases. Palinscar and Brown (1984) offer "Reciprocal Teaching" to increase dialogue activities between teachers and students regarding text content and cognitive processing.

Questioning Skills at the Secondary Level

Masters, Mori, and Mori (1993) also suggest providing simple questioning checklists at the secondary level which can be used in a number of content area subjects. These types of lists encourage better comprehension and critical thinking. Some sample questions are: "Do I have the main idea? Do I know what happened? Is what I know based on fact? Do I know the important people? Do I know the important places? Do I know why things happened the way they did? Is this tied to other things I have learned? Do I have feelings about this? What could happen from this event or situations? Do I know what it might do to other people or things?" (p. 116). It would also be critical for teachers of students with learning disabilities (and in general) to also partake in questioning strategies, especially in regard to self-evaluation.

Questioning Skills for Teacher Self-Evaluation

A questioning format for teachers can be used as a way of self-reflecting and self-monitoring effectiveness in the classroom. Sample questions are as follows:

- How does the classroom look?
- Will it be attractive for students?
- Are the heat, light, and ventilation in the room adequate?
- Are my goals and objectives clear to me?
- Why am I teaching this content?
- What do I need to teach this lesson?
- How can I help students see the relevance of what I am teaching?
- Is it a life skill? How can I check for understanding?
- What kinds of reinforcers can I use?
- Have I planned a success-oriented lesson that will generate student feedback?
- Who needs more teaching and/or reinforcement?
- Were the students attentive?
- Was I in control?
- How would I do things differently? How did I relate to the students?
- Did I evidence a sense of humor?
- How did students interact with each other?
- How were critical thinking skills encouraged?
- How did I assess the learning needs of my students with special needs?

- Have I identified all of my students who might need extra considerations?
- What adaptations can I make for my students with learning disabilities and other learning problems?
- Should I provide after-school assistance or extra homework assignments for reinforcement?
- Will media presentations enhance my lesson?
- Should I type my worksheets?
- Do my students need help with study skills?
- How can I help my students take good notes?
- Am I finding something positive with a poor performance?
- Should I brainstorm with a reading specialist or other school professional for lesson ideas and behavior management?

Reciprocal Teaching

Reciprocal teaching is a method where students take turns with the teacher, reading segments and formulating questions about the reading. They switch roles during some or all parts of the reading. Reciprocal Teaching has been offered by Palinscar and Brown (1984) and is particularly useful with students with learning disabilities in providing an understanding of difficult text, new or unfamiliar vocabulary terms, difficult concepts, and unclear referent words. Reciprocal teaching involves four types of cognitive strategies:

1. Summarizing—Students learn to summarize in small steps by first beginning with sentence summaries followed by paragraphs, pages, and stories.
2. Question Generating—Students identify information that is needed for a particular task as well as the type of information to use in questioning.
3. Clarifying—Teachers and students work together in clarifying difficult concepts, words, and text. Strategies are identified which can enhance understanding (e.g. rereading, cue words, etc.).
4. Predicting—Students hypothesize about meaning by using such cues as heading and subheadings in text. Teachers also provide appropriate background material before predictions are made.

Students can practice prediction strategies and certain comprehension skills such as finding the main idea, details to support the main idea, drawing conclusions, and making inferences on some computer software programs now available to most school systems.

Technology in Teaching Reading Comprehension

Lewis (1993) has reviewed many comprehension software programs in the reading area for students with special needs and disabilities and has found that most key in on literal and inferential information recall. Typically, programs that involve literal information probing measure one's memory for facts, details, and sequence of events. Inferential questioning many times involves finding the main idea of a selection along with supporting details, conclusions, and judgments relating to material read.

Sample Software

Sample software programs at various education levels include some of the following:

> Discis Books Programs by Discis Knowledge Research Inc. (NYCCPO Box 45099, 5150 Yonge Street, Toronto, Ontario, Canada M2N 6N2). This series is geared for young emerging readers and must be used with Macintosh computers. Programs consist of books with color illustrations/graphics. Students can follow stories read by a digitized voice with music and sound effects.

> The Comprehension Reading Series (for Grades 1–3) by Harley Software, Inc. (Box 419, 133 Bridge Street, Dimondale, MI 48821). Teachers are able to modify the stories and comprehension questions to the individual needs of the students.

> Living Book Series (lower elementary level) by Broderbund Software, (P.O. Box 6121, Novato, Ca. 94948). This reading series is available on CD-ROM programs in Spanish, English, and Japanese for IBM and MacIntosh computers. Color illustrated books are presented with music and sound effects.

> Read 'N Roll (upper elementary/middle school levels) by Davidson and Associates (19840 Pioneer Ave., Torrance, CA 90503). This program has 320 short passages which look at main idea, sequence, details, and inferential reasoning abilities. Instructional reading levels range from Grades 3–6.

> The Twistaplot Reading Adventures (all levels) by Scholastic Inc. (2931 East McCarty Street, P.O. Box 7502, Jefferson City, MO 65102). This series has students making decisions about story plot and subplots resulting in different story outcomes. Students need to read several pages of text on some programs so that teachers would need to preview for students who are moderate to severely reading disabled.

> Speed Reader II (secondary level only) by Davidson and Associates (see address listed previously) is geared to those independent readers above Grade 5 to improve reading speed and comprehension.

CD-ROM Multimedia Presentations

CD-ROMs are compact discs which are silver in color and are approximately five inches in diameter. CD discs store graphics, book texts, and audio components. Salpeter (1988) estimates that one CD-ROM can hold 250,000 pages of a book with 15 hours of sound. One needs a computer, CD-ROM reader, and computer add-ons to make the discs compatible with the computer (see a local computer dealer).

Complete encyclopedia sets are available on CD-ROM discs which allow students to more fully explore topics of interest through sights and sounds. Grolier, Compton, Microsoft, World Book, and InterActive Publishing offer encyclopedia references on CD-ROMs. Other series are offered on CD-ROM such as Will and Ariel Durants' 11-volume *The Story of Civilization* (includes maps and photographs). *Shark Alert* provides an animated shark game, discussions on sharks as resources, and the ability to manipulate various parts of the food chain. There are also CD-ROM games which stimulate thinking and require strategic planning efforts (e.g., *Good Buddy*—a cross between *Star Wars* and *Smokey and the Bandit*; *Re-elect JFK*—a simulated game which challenges you to be the president after the assassination of John F. Kennedy by considering the Vietnam War, civil rights issues, etc.; *Gettysburg*—an interactive U.S. History game on the civil war which allows the reader to control the troops, battle options, etc.). Computer magazines will publish current offerings and top choices for a particular month to their readers.

Conclusions

Comprehension of text necessarily entails making author-reader associations and developing interactive practices that will support long-term literacy and learning. The interest level of a student has been linked closely to text coherence and background knowledge. This is also true for the student with dyslexia. Tapping into student interests and talents creates better opportunities for long-term and short-term memory recall. It would appear that the primary components of a successful remedial reading program for students with dyslexia would include setting a purpose for the reading situation; activating background knowledge for the reader; focusing on main ideas, characters and details; formulating predictions and inferences about the material read; developing successful metacognitive strategies and study skills habits, and emphasizing the reading-writing connection. We recommend using a comprehension checklist to determine reading strengths and weaknesses, and have provided one for your use. Deficit areas can be assessed and the comprehension chart in the beginning of the chapter can be consulted for remediation ideas and strategies. Technology tools can also assist students in acquiring necessary comprehension skills. Some computer software programs and CD-ROM programs were discussed.

The preceding chapter taps into several *bottom-up* approaches (e.g., Fernald, Gillingham-Stillman) which focus skills that so many students with dyslexia are lacking. This chapter focuses on such *top-down* processes as text comprehension, the development of study skills, and forming the reading-writing connection. In developing a well-rounded reading program, the authors suggest combining both *bottom-up* and *top-down* perspectives so that the reader develops into an active constructive, invested, reflective reader and questioner.

It should be apparent that for students who are skilled, expert, or proficient readers, the *whole language* approach offers an inductive and challenging way to discover phonics rules and generalizations. As we could see in the previous chapter, many students with dyslexia are not independent, reflective, and self-monitoring. They will need instruction in skills acquisition or bottom-up processing.

Compensatory strategies or *thinking strategies* which *empower* readers to have *reflective cognitive learning styles* which render *interactive* and *meaningful* dialogue between the reader and printed page were discussed via several general and specific principles and approaches. The impulsive cognitive learning style was addressed as well as the inattentive learner. Interrogative reading is one of the most important ways to develop good thinking strategies and it has been shown that students who develop their own questions about textual material better comprehend what is read than those who do not. Students with dyslexia typically approach text in a passive manner, and may need explicit modeling and practice to develop memory and questioning strategies.

Questioning strategies provide the individual with dyslexia opportunities for critical thinking, for summarizing major portions of text, for predicting later reading (which will be confirmed or nonconfirmed), and for filling in the blanks for unknown words and concepts. Some of these will provide a better understanding of the selection at hand. Reciprocal teaching is one way to develop questioning strategies and usage. Questioning strategies can be applied in reading and also writing activities. The following chapter specifically targets that important reading-writing connection as well as how to develop efficient study skills.

Chapter 7

Developing Reading-Writing Connections and Study Skills

The dyslexic is in many ways an alien in a world where the written language is quite foreign to him[her]. Although the vernacular is familiar, the environment is strange, almost hostile. Symbols surround him[her], but to him[her] are non-symbolic, for they are devoid of reference, function or meaning. And yet, they have menacing overtones. In his (the dyslexic's view), they are angry hieroglyphs.
—(CRITCHLEY, 1975, P. 270).

Teaching efforts regarding language literacy and understanding must focus not only on word recognition development and comprehension activities but also on such meaning-based areas as writing and study skills.

Introduction

As we have seen in the previous chapters, proficient readers actively seek cognitive access to strategies which are self-monitoring and enhance learning. In other words, proficient readers are flexible in that they can adjust their reading rates and study skills according to the type of textual material presented. Individuals with dyslexia are many times passive learners and do not seek to create strategies which might assist the learning process. In the reading-writing area, students with dyslexia frequently lack the writing skills needed to become efficient and successful authors, reporters, note-takers, and organizers of study material.

In other words, written expressive language abilities are frequently unsatisfactory or impede learning in general.

Reading-Writing Connections

Writing activities are involved in many specific comprehension activities (e.g., prediction) and questioning methods as one must take notes or record answers, write reports, and so on. There are a number of techniques which would assist the student with dyslexia in acquiring necessary writing skills while constructing knowledge and interacting with the printed page. In any case, writing activities need to be integrated across the curriculum as seen in the following example. Students with dyslexia and other learning disabilities have been found to be deficient in such written expressive areas as handwriting, spelling, and thematic maturity (Hallahan, Kauffman, & Lloyd, 1985).

Good writers pay attention to the communicative aspects of writing such as expressing one's thoughts in a clear, logical, and organized manner. Good writers can also focus on the *ideas* expressed in writing because the *mechanics* (e.g., punctuation, grammar, spelling, capitalization) are automatic. As good role models, adults can communicate to less able writers by written correspondence in forms such as letters, notes, and diaries. The letter to a student (see Figure 7-1, p. 162) is a good example of how the art of writing can go beyond written communication aspects to a level of personalization and socialization enhancement.

Spelling Accommodations

Less skilled writers pay more attention to the mechanics of writing and less to the communication of ideas both at the elementary (Birnbaum, 1982) and secondary (Pianko, 1979) levels. Spelling in particular can be problematic as the task itself requires visualization of a correct word form with no visual cues present. Additionally, English irregularities present a special problem for the student with dyslexia. A limerick from the Simplified Spelling Society which was quoted by S.J. Harris in the Chicago Daily News on July 27, 1966 illustrates how phonemic irregularities can interfere with correct spelling (see Table 7-1, p. 163).

Students with dyslexia should be allowed to use *spelling crutches* when necessary such as poor spellers' dictionaries, spelling computers, glossaries, and computer spell checks. Spelling games can make the learning of spelling words fun as this can be a very rote, dry task. Cued spelling can be used in a more structured format.

Cued Spelling for Parent/Peer Tutoring

Schunk (1987) first introduced a structured format for the "Cued Spelling" technique. Students work in pairs with an individual designated as the tutor and the learner as the tutee. There are ten basic steps: (adapted from Topping, 1995)

Graduation Wishes

Dear Greg,

On your high school Graduation Day, congratulations on your accomplishment. An accomplishment is an achievement, by definition a quality or ability that equips you for society. Your greatest achievement is that you found inner resources to enable you to, when necessary, persevere and withstand the moment and cope with the potential challenges school often presents. By so doing, you have developed inner resources and a core of faith in your own ability that is your hidden wealth.

You told me what a difference teachers make in developing a sound foundation from which you learn to act and react. When they help you develop confidence in your ability to learn, set goals, choose values and contribute positively, they are enhancing your self-esteem for life. One consistently essential ingredient for encouraging a student to seek the best of what is within him is to nurture these abilities until the traits become as expansive as they can be.

If a teacher wishes to oppress a student, he or she would be hard put to come up with a more effective plan than to have one standard, the traditional learning approach, that all students must measure up to. As you so aptly stated, "that's too much pressure on a little kid!" We know that the unique nature of being human means that we all have differences in character and attitude, and that many people learn most effectively by alternate methods; not traditional approaches. And some of those people are among the most accomplished—once they are viewed from the perspective that we are all as learning different as our fingerprint. In the end, a learning pattern, no matter how it differs from the ideal, is not the only factor in deciding what we'll be able to do or to be. It is our intelligence that shapes our world and is our most powerful edge. When you give your best effort in applying your individual skills, you show that it isn't really how smart you are that makes you accomplished, it's *how* you are smart!

Mimi

FIGURE 7-1 A Graduation Letter of Accomplishments

Source: Mary Saltus

**TABLE 7-1 Phonetic Spelling Can
Be Reading Confusion**

A king, on assuming his reign,
Exclaimed with a feeling of peign:
"Tho I'm legally heir
No one here seems to ceir
That I haven't been born with a breign."

A merchant addressing a debtor,
Remarked in the course of his lebtor
That he chose to suppose
A man knose what he ose
And the sooner he pays it, the bedtor!

A young lady crossing the ocean
Grew ill from the ship's dizzy mocean,
She called with a sigh,
And a tear in her eigh,
For the doctor to give her a pocean.

And now our brief lesson is through—
I trust you'll agree it was trough;
For it's chiefly designed
To impress on your migned
What wonders our spelling can dough!

1. Student with dyslexia chooses a word to spell.
2. Both students check the spelling of the word by using a dictionary, poor speller's dictionary, or spell check. Then each student places the word in a "spelling diary" or log.
3. Both students read the word together and then the dyslexic student reads alone.
4. The dyslexic student then chooses spelling cues/assists/rules from a list provided by the teacher, which would be appropriate to the age and developmental level of the student (e.g., look at the base word and then see what prefixes or suffixes have been added; "i" before "e" except after "c")
5. Both students say the cues aloud.
6. The dyslexic student says the cue and the tutor then writes the word (e.g., use the chalkboard, a separate paper, the computer, and so on).
7. The tutor says the cue and the dyslexic student writes the word.
8. The dyslexic student says the cue and then writes the word independently.

Prepare paper for students by having it cut in squares. (A paper cutter makes this preparation quick.)

1. Fold the square of paper into a triangle. Then fold it once again into a smaller triangle so that when the square is opened again, there is an "X" folded across it to mark "dead - center" on the paper.

reopen

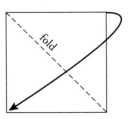 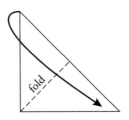  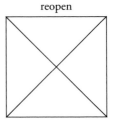

2. Fold each corner of the square into the "dead - center" as exactly as you can. This will make a smaller square.

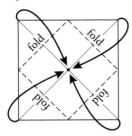 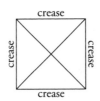

3. Turn the folded paper over so that the flaps are on the bottom, and the plain side faces upward. Again, fold the corners of the square into "dead - center."

 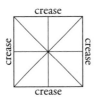

This side gives you 8 spaces on which to write spelling words.

Vary the word lengths that are next to each other on the flaps.

Turn the Fortune Teller over and you have 4 more flaps to put words on.

4. Slide your index fingers and thumbs into the 4 square flaps to make a 3-dimensional figure.

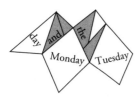

5. Alternately pinch your fingers and spread your 2 hands, and then bring 2 hands together and spread finger and thumb. Make one move for each letter of the word as you spell it aloud. One student chooses the word, the other spells it out. 1x on outer flap, 3x's on inner flaps.

FIGURE 7-2   Spelling Fortune Tellers

164

9. The dyslexic students tries to write the word quickly and then says the word aloud.

10. Repeat any steps as necessary so that cues and spellings are correct.

Topping (1995) emphasizes the essential training component for the tutor who must be able to demonstrate and provide praise for the student with dyslexia. The use of videotaping in this regard would be helpful as well as a "steps" chart for use during the "cued spelling" activity. Parent workshops or mini-lessons could be provided by the PTA, an interested teacher, and so on. In the classroom, the present authors suggest using this technique for up to 15 minutes per day, three days per week. The selection of spelling words should be monitored so that "challenging" words are included. Spelling "cues" could be derived from the student's spelling or language book, teacher input, and so on. It is also recommended that this technique be considered supplementary to the regular classroom language/spelling program.

"Poor writers can possibly be helped to become better writers through the automatization of the mechanical aspects of writing [like spelling]" (Ormrod, 1990, p. 281). Such activities would need to be structured and there are several approaches one can take when teaching writing skills. Wolfe and Reising (1983) (see next section on process writing) offer a 10-step approach that can be used to guide students with dyslexia through the writing process. Spelling activities like "Spelling Fortune Tellers" (Figure 7-2, p. 164) can make this rote subject fun for the troubled learner.

Process Writing

Richardson and Morgan (1990) believe that process writing should involve several steps and ". . . the most important factor in motivating the writing of slow learners, perhaps, is making certain we don't emphasize mechanics too early in learning the writing process . . ." (p. 436). Teaching the writing process to students with dyslexia and other learning disabilities is key to future writing successes (Kerchner & Kistinger, 1984; Radencich, 1985). The individual with dyslexia might need some organization assistance regarding key concepts/ideas surrounding a writing topic. Wolfe and Reising's (1983) teaching steps for the writing process which can be used with students with dyslexia are as follows:

1. Initial brainstorming—teachers and students can use previous experiences to brainstorm writing topics

2. Reflection—think about the topic

3. Selection—of a topic

4. Zero draft—through free writing, games, discussions, etc., data are generated and gathered for a bank of ideas

5. First draft—little editing is done

6. Peer inquiry—groups of 2–5 students exchange ideas

7. Second revision—here revision and editing is done after peer exchanges

8. Teacher review—teacher reviews and gives feedback (no grade at this point)

9. Third revision—based on teacher feedback
10. Teacher evaluation and publication (in a class newspaper, as a book, etc.)

Zaragoza (1987) points out that frequent and productive teacher conferences are critical with students with LD in developing writing skills. Zaragoza (1987) suggests teacher input on the first draft (step 5) with students with LD. We would also suggest reinforced practice in the *mechanics* of writing throughout all 10 steps. Teachers can emphasize the importance of creativity and expressive thought while at the same time teaching capitalization, punctuation, and grammar rules. The key would be to teach mechanics rules in the context of sentences, paragraphs, and stories. Word processors can be used through all phases of writing. Authentic assessment writing checks can be implemented when written assignments are given (see Table 7-2).

The following examples depict important primary, middle, and secondary writing considerations for the student with dyslexia. (Refer to following boxes on pages 167, 168.)

One of the first tools a teacher can use to assess reading proficiency and problems with students who experience dyslexia is a reading autobiography.

TABLE 7-2   Authentic Assessment Writing

Mechanics √ = Good quality * = Problem area	Writing Process √ = Can do * = Problem area
____ Spelling	____ Can set a purpose
____ Punctuation	____ Can select a topic
____ Capitalization	____ Can seek assistance when needed
____ Handwriting legibility	____ Can work cooperatively with peers
____ Grammar	____ Can proofread and revise work
____ Spacing between letters	____ Can share work
____ Spacing between words, paragraphs	____ Can adjust style to task
____ College level: can use APA style	
____ High school level: report format	Qualitative Components
____ Typewriter or word processor	
____ Spell checking or proofreading	√ = Good quality use of * = Problem area
	____ Effective dialogue
	____ Character development
	____ Plot development
	____ Logical story sequence
	____ Complex sentences
	____ Use of emotionally charged vocabulary
	____ Use of qualitatively relevant verbs, nouns, and adjectives
	____ Use of author's voice
	____ Coherent presentation

Primary Considerations for Young Authors with Dyslexia

Stice, Bertrand, and Bertrand (1995) describe how teachers can create an environment for young authors by gently guiding preschool and primary level students through the writing process. Their approach would be appealing for those who work with students with dyslexia and is modified as follows:

Level I

"Write Alouds"—the teacher scribes what the students dictate. LD teachers could accept tape recorded versions. The teacher models good writing behaviors.

Level II

"Guided Writing"—the teacher provides for group-dictated or created stories whereby vocabulary usage, syntax, and sentence structure are negotiated by the group. An overheard, chart paper, or chalkboard should provide feedback every step of the way. The teacher should provide everyone with a printed story the next day and solicit constructive feedback. The student with dyslexia (and all others for that matter!!) could use the following writer's editing guide.

Guided writing could be complemented by expressive forms of the printed page. For example, Purves, Rogers, and Soter (1995) suggest the use of drama and dramatic activities to "expand the forms and functions of language in the classroom" and to nurture enthusiasm and style in writing. We would suggest puppetry and casting students in different roles in order to appreciate and empathize with characters. Purves, Rogers, and Soter (1995) suggest first placing the teacher in a role, interviewing characters in pairs, and interrogative questioning about the events in a work.

Level III

"Independent Writing" (SSW or Sustained Silent Writing)—the teacher provides time for students to create and explore different writing options on their own; Stice, Bertrand, and Bertrand (1995) recommend writing letters (e.g., penpals); maintaining dialogue journals and observation logs; creating writing projects from thematic units covered in class; creating original works (e.g., stories, poems).

Reading Autobiographies

Reading autobiographies are histories or stories about a student's own reading experiences. Students write a chronological sequence of reading experiences which date back as far as they can remember. Students try to recall the first types of books they read, who read to them, what they liked to read, and who helped them learn how to read. For students with dyslexia, writing prompts can be used in the form of questions. It would be helpful for the teacher to write a reading autobiography to use as a model for all students. Students can work in pairs or share experiences to help generate ideas for writing. Grammar and spelling errors should not impact the student's grade if this type of assignment is to be graded. Additionally, the student with dyslexia should be allowed to write several drafts or tape the autobiography. The following format can be reworked into a checklist format if necessary. The student's insights into his/her reading problems can assist in the diagnostic-prescriptive process as well as provide metacognitive awareness/insights for the dyslexic reader.

Middle/Secondary Level Writing Guide for Dyslexics

Things I Need to Check	*Did I Check With or On? Yes or No*	
Handwriting	Neatness	_____
	Letter Formation	_____
Spacing	Between Letters	_____
	Between Words	_____
Spelling	The Dictionary	_____
	A Thesaurus	_____
	Computer Spell Check	_____
	A Proofreader	_____
Ending Punctuation	Periods	_____
	Question Marks	_____
	Exclamation Marks	_____
Other Punctuation	Commas	_____
	Quotation Marks	_____
	Apostrophes	_____
	Math Symbols	_____
Grammar	Complete Subject(s)	_____
	Complete Sentences	_____
	Sentence Sense	_____
Quality of my Work	Vocabulary	_____
	Paragraphing	_____
	Topic Sentences	_____
	Supporting Details	_____
	Interest to Others	_____
	My Own Work	_____
	Does My Work Flow?	_____
	Feedback From Others	_____
	My Best Efforts	_____

Other: _____   _____
_____   _____
_____   _____

Using Literature

One popular model for written language experiences involves the use of literature. The use of learning webs can assist the student in making important literature-writing connections as seen in the following (see figures 7-3, 7-4, and 7-5).

TABLE 7-3A   Preliminary Brainstorming Activity

After brainstorming about whales, the students will come up with some questions about the whales that they would like to learn more about. Next students will form jigsaw groups (about six students in each group) where each student in the group will become an expert about a topic pertaining to whales. There are several books and magazines in the classroom that students can use (see reference list on page 180). Some questions students might generate are as follows (the questions would vary each time you do this):

1. What types of whales are there and where are they found?

2. What do whales eat? How do they eat? How do they find food?

3. How do whales know where they are going when they migrate?

4. What is a whale song? Why do whales sing? What other types of habits do whales have?

5. What was/is the purpose of hunting whales (what products do we obtain from a whale)? What is the current status of whaling?

6. Are whales in danger of extinction? Why should we be concerned? Are whales intelligent?

Students from groups with the same topic will conference about what they have learned and share what they have researched (they will be using learning logs or double entry journals). The class as a whole will collectively share their findings, via learning web activities.

Source: Maryfrances Peters

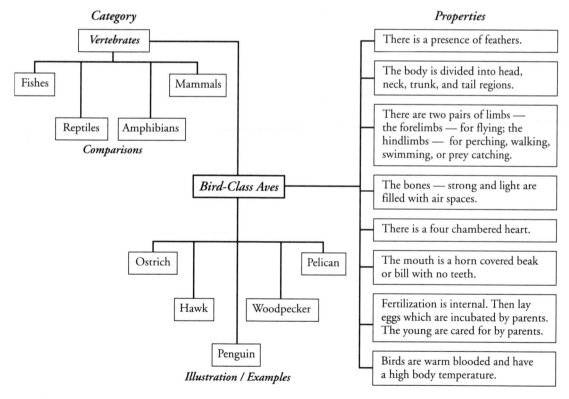

FIGURE 7-3B   Categorizing Language Concepts: Concept Definition Web—Vertebrates

Source: Maryfrances Peters

The use of literature and other whole language activities should be presented in small chunks (see Chapters 4 and 5 for more details). Theme concept webbing and concept definition maps can help in this regard (see Figure 7-5).

Journal Writing

Using Dialogue Journals to Improve Reading/Writing Skills

Recently, dialogue journals have become popular in English and reading classrooms. Students write to one another dialoguing what they are reading in a sort of book-chat format (Atwell, 1987). Learning logs and response journals are types of dialogue journals teachers can use with students with dyslexia.

Learning Logs

Learning logs can be kept by students with dyslexia as a measure of growth, performance, and learning. Glaze (1987) suggests four key questions: (1) What am I going to predict will happen in this activity, book, exercise? (2) What have I

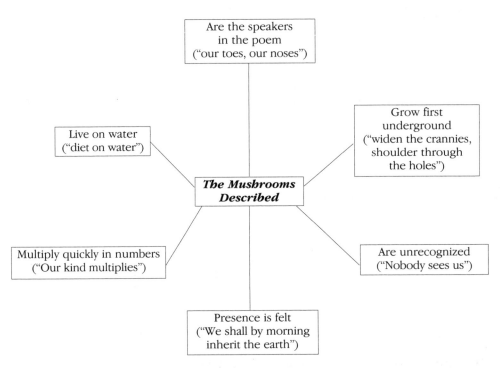

FIGURE 7-4 Categorizing Language Concepts: Poetry Example/Learning Web

Source: "Mushrooms" by Sylvia Plath

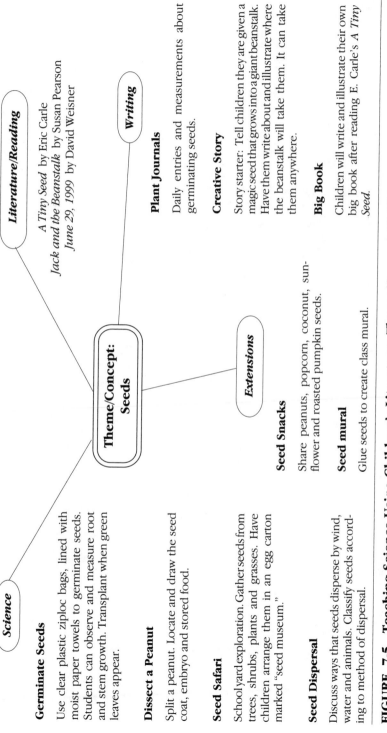

Science

Germinate Seeds

Use clear plastic ziploc bags, lined with moist paper towels to germinate seeds. Students can observe and measure root and stem growth. Transplant when green leaves appear.

Dissect a Peanut

Split a peanut. Locate and draw the seed coat, embryo and stored food.

Seed Safari

Schoolyard exploration. Gather seeds from trees, shrubs, plants and grasses. Have children arrange them in an egg carton marked "seed museum."

Seed Dispersal

Discuss ways that seeds disperse by wind, water and animals. Classify seeds according to method of dispersal.

Literature/Reading

A Tiny Seed by Eric Carle
Jack and the Beanstalk by Susan Pearson
June 29, 1999 by David Weisner

Theme/Concept: Seeds

Writing

Plant Journals

Daily entries and measurements about germinating seeds.

Creative Story

Story starter: Tell children they are given a magic seed that grows into a giant beanstalk. Have them write about and illustrate where the beanstalk will take them. It can take them anywhere.

Big Book

Children will write and illustrate their own big book after reading E. Carle's *A Tiny Seed.*

Extensions

Seed Snacks

Share peanuts, popcorn, coconut, sunflower and roasted pumpkin seeds.

Seed mural

Glue seeds to create class mural.

FIGURE 7-5   Teaching Science Using Children's Literature: Theme/Concept Webbing

Created by: Linda Rozolsky

learned? (3) What do I need to learn? and (4) How do I feel about what I have learned? Students can raise these questions consistently before writing learning log entries. The individual with dyslexia may require a typewriter or tape recorder. Vygotsky (1962) would be quick to point out that the more use and development of language leads to improved communication and thinking ability.

Using Response Journals in Content Area Subjects

Crawford (1993) suggests that students can use response journals to express how they feel about content or ideas stated by relating " . . . what the information means to them, what they think about the information, and their reactions as they studied the information . . ." (p. 268). The role of the teacher is to respond to student questions without keying in on spelling or structural details. The teacher should also raise questions and give personal reactions. The focus of journal responses is on questioning, the sharing of ideas, and exploring different ways to think about the material read. Certain accommodations can be made for the student with dyslexia as seen in double entry journal writing. The example in Figure 7-6 illustrates how teacher prompts can be useful.

Journal Writing Adaptations

We would suggest that some adaptations might need to be made for individuals with dyslexia with severe writing/spelling difficulties: (1) The teacher can be his/her secretary on occasion. (2) Encourage the use of a word processor with a spell check. (3) Arrange journal partners so that one partner has more proficient writing skills. (4) Provide writing prompts and assists, or a structured format to begin with. and (5) Tape record or videotape the journal pieces.

Combining a focus on both content and process, students can develop a *Double Entry Journal* for recording learning in the content areas. The journal can be set up in a spiral notebook in which the right-hand page is used for note-taking, problem-solving, or research. Following the "content" entry, students then reflect on the learning by writing observations, new understandings, or reviewing goals on the left hand page. Teacher prompts can be used to facilitate the "process" component. For example:

Process	*Content*
Prompt: What are some ways that you show new independence as you get older?	• Leaders met in Philadelphia. • The Declaration of Independence. • To declare freedom from England rules and taxes.
-I ride my bike to school. -I can stay up until 9 o'clock. -I clean my room and rake the yard.	• Thomas Jefferson wrote the document. • July 4, 1776 is when they read the Declaration of Independence. Now it's an important holiday.
It is nice to do things by myself and feel grown up.	• America became a free nation with its own government.

FIGURE 7-6 Response Journals

Portfolio Projects

Portfolios—Authentic Assessment Tools
A portfolio is a type of authentic assessment device (i.e., it relates assessment practices to real-life situations or authentic tasks) which consists of individual collections of academic and social accomplishments. Portfolios are essentially collections of one's work which provide documentation of accomplishments and an assessment of personal growth and development in a number of areas.

Looking at the "What" and "Why" of Journal Entries
Portfolio projects allow students to evaluate their own subject area reading/language knowledge as well as writing, reading, listening, and discussion abilities. As students select new portfolio entries, they are able to identify areas of growth while they review their earlier submissions. Reif (1991) looks at internal (the *why*) and external (the *what*) criteria for journal selections. Cordeiro (1993) stresses looking at such internal criteria as growth, risk-taking, "using only the best" and viewing a "variety of genres" as ways to encourage and inspire learners; to evaluate teaching/programs; and to communicate with parents. Possible specifics (the *whats*) for portfolio entries should consider the developmental level/abilities of the student. In Figure 7-7, Courtney (1995) offers possible specifics for portfolio collections in terms of specific suggestions for products (external criteria); as diagnostic/reflective tools; and as self-reflective instruments (pp. 174–175).

After a student has selected a portfolio entry, there should be some brief reflection as to why the entry was chosen. Hand-written or typed notes could accompany entries explaining why entries were chosen for the portfolio. For the student with dyslexia, portfolio assists can be used.

Portfolio Assists for Students with Dyslexia
Portfolio assists in the form of sentence starters can provide needed structure to the elementary-aged student with dyslexia. Secondary-level students need to engage in more complex and thoughtful reflections. The secondary-level student with dyslexia can be given concrete assists and guidance for portfolio selections, reflections, and self-evaluation (e.g., ROPE).

Travers, Elliot, and Kratochwill (1993) cite eight portfolio requirements included in the **ROPE**, or "Rite of Passage Experience," for high school students (especially those students who experience dyslexia).

Developing Portfolios at the Secondary Level—ROPE
These requirements are intended to encourage graduating seniors to reflect on their schooling, progress, and life experiences:

1. a written autobiography
2. a reflection on schoolwork
3. two letters of recommendation from anyone of the student's choosing
4. a reading record (e.g., book reports, reading test scores, reading bibliographies, etc.)

Collections

Projects
Surveys
Reports

*Finished Samples that Illustrate
Wide Writing:*
    Persuasive Pieces
    Letters
    Poetry
    Stories: mystery, realistic, fantasy, science
        fiction, biography,
    Historical fiction, non-fiction,
        personal narrative

*Examples of Writing Across
the Curriculum:*
    Reports
    Journals—science, social studies, math
    Literature logs

Literature Extensions
    Script for drama
    Visual arts
    Webs
    Charts
    Mural
    Mobiles
    Videos
    Time lines
    Topic posters
    Dioramas
    Written forms
    Pictures of projects
    Response journals

*Book Logs: Records of Books Read
and Attempted*

*Audio Tape and Video Tape
of Student Readings*

Writing Responses to Literary Components:
    Plot
    Setting
    Point of view
    Character development: profiles,
        inside/outside piece
    Theme
    Links to life
    Literary links and criticism
    Beginnings
    Endings
    Figurative language
    Venn diagrams
    Book comparisons
    Literary passports

FIGURE 7-7A Portfolios: Specific Suggestions for Products—External Criteria

Created by Dr. Ann Courtney

    5. an essay on ethics
    6. an art project or written report on some artistic endeavor
    7. a written evaluation of the mass media
    8. a written report on the student's participation in science/technology works
        (e.g., how one can use computers in the workplace or in college)

This approach avoids the unfortunate possibility of the portfolio becoming a mere depository of finished work. Research in portfolio development, use, and effectiveness is relatively new. However, preliminary findings clearly illustrate how portfolios can represent and evaluate the "literacy events that a child has experienced—especially in those classrooms that emphasize literature, writing, free-choice reading, thematic units, cooperative learning, and other experiences that encourage communications" (May, 1994, p. 395).

Possible Inclusions—Using Portfolios as Diagnostic Tools:

Reading Interviews
Reading Attitude Inventory
Miscue Analysis, or
Running Records
Spelling Analysis
Check-off Lists
Holistic and Analytical Scoring of Writing
Anecdotal Records Kept by Teacher on Computer Labels
Journal Entry Comparisons
Audio Tape of Student Reading and Teacher and Student Assessment of the Reading
Video Tape of Student Reading and Teacher and Student Assessment of the Reading
Writing Interviews
Parent-Teacher-Student Assessment of Student as Learner
Teacher Assessment of Writing Conference
Assessment of Use of Time During Writing Workshop
Assessment of Student Performance During Writing Workshop
Monthly Check of Writing Child's Name—Assessment of Letter Formation
Silent Reading and Retelling Guide Assessment
Child as a Reader/writer Survey: Parent, Teacher, Child

FIGURE 7-7B Portfolios Collections—Diagnostic and Reflective

Reader self-analysis of running records

Questionnaire of metacognitive strategy use
Assess best writing piece and why
Assess writing piece which demonstrates the most growth

Analyzing book logs:
Most challenging book, why/how did you handle the reading
Easiest book to read and why
The book you enjoyed the most and why

Writing that illustrates critical thinking about reading:

Notes from individual reading and writing conferences (anecdotal records used to develop final reflective statement on records created by teacher)

Writings that are evident of development of style:
Organization
Voice
Sense of audience
Choice of words
Clarity

Writing that shows growth in usage traits:
Growing ability in self-correction
Growing ability in use of punctuation
Growing ability in use of correct spelling
Growing ability in use of proper grammar
Growing ability in appropriate form
Growing ability in legibility

Samples in which ideas are modified from first draft to final product:
Unedited first draft
Revised first draft, and subsequent drafts
Edited final draft
Final copy

Evidence of effort:
Improvement noted on pieces
Completed assignments
Personal involvement noted

Self-evaluations

FIGURE 7-7C Using Portfolios as Self-Reflection Instruments

Created by Dr. Ann Courtney

Students unacquainted with the portfolio process may require considerable direction and support in developing their portfolios into authentic, personalized vehicles of growth. Sentence starters, reflective guides, or notecard comments can be modeled and developed by direct instruction.

Reflecting

1. Explain what your entry is: _____
   _____
   _____

2. I chose this entry because _____
   _____
   _____

3. The best part of doing this project was _____
   _____
   _____

4. This entry is an example of my growth because _____
   _____
   _____

5. When I think back on earlier work like this, I realize _____
   _____
   _____

6. Next time I do a similar project, I _____
   _____

FIGURE 7-7D Portfolios—"A Format for Reflection"

Research Findings on Portfolio Use

Tierney, Carter, and Desai (1991) believe that portfolios are a more "rich source of information about a student's literacy achievement, progress, and ongoing development than other, more formal sources" (p. 51). These authors have found that the use of portfolios has guided many *teachers and children* into considerable awareness of their own goals, growth, and accomplishments. Additionally, reports from teachers and administrators after portfolio use point to a clearer understanding of where each child is at (with an emphasis on strengths). Tierney and his associates (1991) find that portfolio evaluation procedures generally rely on a collaboration between teachers and administrators, teachers and students, and students and peers, which enhance ongoing processes involved in self-evaluation and growth.

Portfolio projects require adequate to good writing skills. Students with dyslexia may need to have someone to proof their work, consult a dictionary, and/or use a typewriter or word-processor. Participation in writing activities such as writing workshops provide practice and skills reinforcement. Teachers of students with dyslexia would need to facilitate such writing support and provide consistent guidance in the portfolio processes of selection, revision, and reflection.

Writing Workshops

Writing workshops involve setting aside a period of time in which everyone present in the classroom must write. Times are set consistently each day (10–20 minutes, depending on the level of complexity of the material) for this writing activity. Writing activities should be done across the curriculum (see Figure 7-8 below) with frequent opportunities for students to "learn through writing." Interrogative questioning and probing can help generate ideas for writing.

The role of the teacher during the writing workshop is to provide writing prompts or ideas for writing, teach mini-lessons, and provide feedback which will improve or enhance the writer's product (Calkins, 1986). The use of semantic

Writing prompts for different subject areas provide students with opportunities to "Learn Through Writing."

Science: Describe a game of baseball on the moon. What changes would be needed due to so little gravity?

Explain what might happen in the ecosystem if we eliminated all mosquitos.

Explain the special skills needed to a laboratory researcher. Do you think you would make a good researcher?

Math: Use writing to explain what an exponent is. Why is exponential notation important?

Explain some problems that would occur if our rulers were not all the same.

Choose one example in division that you solved incorrectly. Can you explain in writing what went wrong?

Social Studies: Imagine you were a Native American during the time of westward expansion. Write a paragraph that tells how you feel.

Think of some reasons that maps are changed. What kinds of things might change the map of your community?

Discrimination is still an issue in our modern society. Can you tell about a time where you felt discriminated against?

Physical Education: Think of two ways you could change the game of basketball to make it more fun or difficult. What new rules would be needed?

Health: Write a letter to a "pretend" friend that will help them to not start smoking.

Music: Pick a song you like and compare it with a song you don't like. Give many examples of how they are different.

Art: Imagine a world with no color. Describe how it would feel to have all your food, clothes, and belongings be without color.

FIGURE 7-8   Writing Across the Curriculum

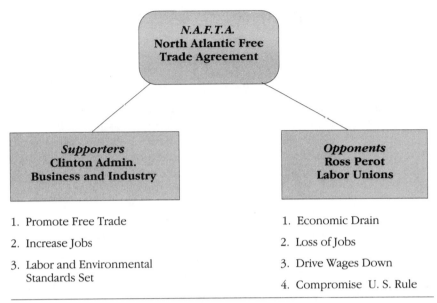

FIGURE 7-9 Semantic Organizer for Writing Current Events

organizers (see Figure 7-9 above) and graphic organizers (see Figure 7-10, p. 179) for outlining purposes before writing reports, stories, and so on, can help facilitate the writing process.

Literature Conferences

Many reading and English associations sponsor conferences which encourage professionals and other interested parties to come in contact with literature through books, authors, visuals, and workshops. Literature-writing connections can be made especially when students are allowed to pursue areas of interest. The example in Figure 7-11 (p. 180) illustrates how a high-interest topic like whaling allows students to become "science writers."

The International Reading Association (IRA) and the Assembly on Literature for Adolescents (ALAN) frequently present conferences with workshop presentations on literature materials and methods which could assist students with dyslexia. As with any teaching method or material, the individual must be kept in mind as well as any adaptations necessary to provide an optimal learning experience (e.g., taping).

Literature Festivals and Author's Receptions

These types of events put the reader in contact with authors and literature. Frequently, workshop sessions or informal meetings are held which allow for interactions between those interested in the literature and, at times, with the author himself/herself.

(a) Diagram for the Organization of the Main Part of the Nervous System

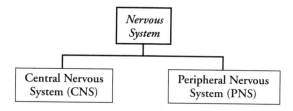

(b) Diagram for a Different Lesson

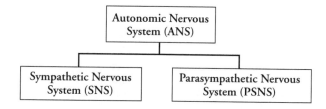

(c) The Combined Diagram, Linking the Two Above

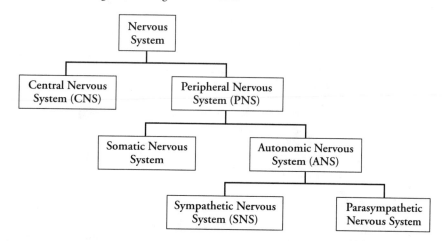

FIGURE 7-10 Illustration of Linking Two Graphic Organizers—One of Which Is for a Higher-Level Concept

Study Skills Acquisition

Many students with dyslexia have difficulty achieving independence in "reading to learn" because of poorly developed memory and study skills habits. Young adults and adults with dyslexia, in particular, have difficulty managing time and being organized. Development of effective study habits would entail note-taking skills, organizational skills, time-management, and test-taking strategies. We will begin

Moving from Science Class to Literature

Now that the students have a basic understanding about whales they will read about whales in literature. The class will read part of a chapter called, *A Certain Danger* taken from *Tales of Whales* written by Tim Dietz. This is a vivid account of the life of a whaler. The second book is a novel by Hank Searls entitled, *Sounding*. This book takes us into the mind and emotions of a sperm whale. The sperm whale is trying to understand why people can be both vicious killers and frolicking playmates. Because of time constraints the teacher will photocopy excerpts from the book for the students to read (or it can be read in class).

The two different books point out the differences in perspective, the first of the whaler (hunter) and his industry and the second of the sperm whale (hunted). The students are to do a reader response in their journals about the different perspectives (the teacher will model a reader response for the students). As a follow up, the teacher could show prepared slides of whales and whale research. Some slides could demonstrate how scientists study whales in pursuit of understanding them in greater depth.

Reference Books/Magazines

Bonner, W.N. (1980). *Whales*. Dorset: Blandford Press.
Burton, R. (1983). *The Life and Death of Whales*. New Jersey: Helix Book.
Dietz, T., (1982). *Tales of Whales*. Portland: Guy Gannett Publishing Co.
Dow, L. (1990). *Whales, Great Creatures of the World*. New York: Facts on File.
Leatherwood, S., & Reeves, R. (1983). *The Sierra Club Handbook of Whales and Dolphins*. San Francisco: Sierra Club Books.
Minasian, S.M., Bolcomb, III, K.C., & Foster, L. (1984). *The World's Whales, The Complete Illustrated Guide*. Washington, DC: Smithsonian Books.
Pich, W.C., (1985). The Whale's Pearl. The Story of Ambergris. *Oceans, 3,* 23-25.
Searls, H. (1982). *Sounding*. New York: West Southwest Corporation.

FIGURE 7-11 Making Literature/Writing Connections

this section by offering study tips developed by a college student with dyslexia and her tutor (see Table 7-3, p. 181).

Certainly study skills acquisition can begin with developing note-taking skills and *guided notes*.

Note Taking

Many students with dyslexia are overwhelmed with the task of taking notes. ". . . this is not surprising since note taking requires simultaneously listening, comprehending, synthesizing, and/or extracting main ideas, while retaining them long enough to formulate and write a synopsis . . ." (Vogel, 1987, p. 253). Notetaking can be facilitated by having good students in the same classes photocopy and share their notes. Tape-recorded lectures (with the permission of the instructor) allow students to listen to the cues that teachers provide that might signal main ideas, important information, and summary statements. Teachers can word-process their notes in a *guided* format for students to use if and when appropriate (time permitting).

Guided Notes

Lazarus (1988) developed a study skills approach named, "Guided Notes" which involves an incomplete outline of material to be studied. Teachers create a skeleton outline of material from lectures and reading assignments. Space is allowed

TABLE 7-3   Study Skills for the Individual with Dyslexia

1. Be a time manager by organizing
   -Study schedules
   -Planning calendars

2. Develop appropriate accommodations by using:
   -Pass/fail grades
   -Untimed testing
   -Word processing/spell checking
   -Tutoring
   -Taped text notes

3. Form study groups which provide:
   -Repetition and review

4. Establish a rapport with teachers and professors:
   -Request clarification when needed
   -Request additional assistance for tests, papers, and research assignments

5. Always do repeated reading of assignments by:
   -First time looking for main ideas
   -Second time looking for subtopics
   -Third time looking for essential details

6. Always thank those who assist you!

Source: Susan Guay, Tutor, and Joann McClain, Student

for students to fill in an outline as the teacher speaks or to fill in an outline after reading textual material. The easiest way for teachers to accomplish this is to highlight the material first (main ideas and terms) with transparency markers so that work-study students, secretaries, or other paraprofessionals (or the teacher herself/himself!) can type or word process for student copies. Figure 7-12 (p. 182) provides some ideas as to how students can organize key concepts abstracted from lecture notes. Guided notes can be used to prepare for tests and quizzes. Even test taking skills need to be addressed with the student with dyslexia. The use of guided notes should include the main ideas of presented material and key terms on student copies; a consistent format that parallels lecture/text material; and a review tally (Lazarus, 1988). A review tally could consist of a small box in the right hand corner of the first page of a student's guided notes which is divided into several squares. Students can check and date review dates or tally key concepts reviewed/mastered. Lazarus and McKenna (1991) have found that the use of guided notes along with a subsequent review of the material produce best learning results. McKenna and Robinson (1993) believe that this format is especially useful for the problem reader. In fact, providing the entire class with guided notes should enhance the learning experience for all.

Test Taking Strategies

First and foremost, students need to sleep well before an exam. Cramming all night at the last minute does not serve to benefit any student. Certain pretesting

Many students have trouble perceiving the organization of a verbal lecture. A listening guide provides a traditional outline or a graphic display to help students follow the content of the lecture. Notes can be filled in as the lecture proceeds.

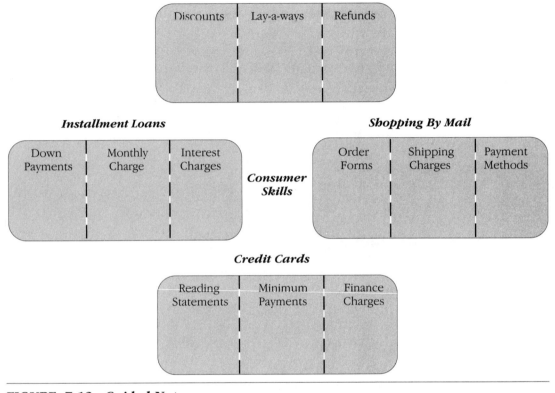

FIGURE 7-12   Guided Notes

strategies can increase the likelihood of successful performance for students with dyslexia:

1. Determine the type of test a particular teacher will give by asking the teacher for the test format (e.g., multiple choice versus essay).
2. Be certain of the material to be covered on an exam—check with other students and the teacher just to be sure.
3. Ask students who have had a particular course about the nature of the teacher's expectations for exams.
4. Students and parents or tutors can anticipate essays to be asked and practice.
5. Multiple choice exams will require recognition abilities and therefore close attention to details when studying.
6. Essay exams require more emphases on main ideas with supporting details.
7. Review material for an exam every day for 10–30 minute time segments as opposed to lengthy study just before the exam.

8. Ask someone who is in a position to assist to anticipate various ways a teacher could question a student based on the material presented.
9. Form study groups with other students.
10. If language demands are heavy, test adaptations could include a reader or an oral presentation.
11. Extra time might be needed—time considerations need to be discussed with teachers *before* exams are taken.
12. An alternate test location might be acceptable if arrangements are made beforehand and the test taking is supervised.
13. Be certain to read test directions—do you need to use a pen or pencil? need to write in a blue book? use a calculator? have a time constraint?
14. If writing presents a problem, ask the teacher *beforehand* if a word processor can be used or essay answers be dictated into a tape recorder (outside of the class setting).
15. Determine how much time you have to take the test and estimate how much time you can spend on each answer.
16. Always answer questions that you know first and save the "thinkers" for last.
17. *Always* go over an exam with someone who can help critique and plan future strategies—self-evaluation of performance requires knowledge of progress and proficiency.

Organizational and Time-Management Skills

Keeping an appointment calendar of activities and commitments (social and otherwise) is a must. Deadlines and due dates need to be noted. Students with organizational and time-management problems need to set up time-tables for work completion. There has to be a balance with one's social life. Students might need help breaking down assignments and tasks into components so that realistic expectations in regard to time expenditures can be made. The *Detective Q. SQUIRT method* (Spafford, 1993) is a fun way for students to develop an organized study-skills reading management system by using metacognitive checks.

Detective Q. SQUIRT

Spafford (1993) developed the SQUIRT mnemonic (Figure 7-13) to assist elementary-middle school students with dyslexia and other learning disabilities with a study-skills reading management system. Many students with learning disabilities have organizational problems and do not have adequate language skills (i.e., spelling and writing) to facilitate this process.

The SQUIRT technique provides a student-controlled management system with self-questioning, self-monitoring, and self-evaluating training activities reinforcing the development of metacognitive awareness skills necessary for efficient learning.

Test Taking Techniques

Students with dyslexia need to practice the "hows" of taking multiple-choice, true-false, and essay exams. Essay exams present a special problem as students with

Elementary Level Metacognitive Technique

The student assumes the role of Detective Q. (as in questioning) and must proceed to solve whatever case the teacher presents.

S   Survey the scene of the assignment. What am I suppose to do? What is the teacher assigning us? How much time do I have to solve this assignment? How can I break this case and finish on time?

Q   Question. Do I understand the assignment? If not, I must ask my classmates or teacher for important clues or information.

U   Understand. I must understand my reading material. I need to check my understanding by answering the Who? What? Why? When? Where? and How? over and over as I travel the scene of the assignment.

I   Interrogate. I must interrogate others to see if they understand the assignment. I must form good questions to show I understand the material.

R   Read and then re-read. I must re-read the topic sentences to make sure I know the main ideas.

T   Tackle the assignment. What does the teacher want me to do? After I finish I need to check my work. Should someone else check my work? After I solve this assignment I get to make a drawing of the Detective Q. Squirt Cap and spy glass on my paper.

FIGURE 7-13   Detective Q. Squirt

Created by: Dr. Carol Spafford

dyslexia often have difficulty coming to the point by not focusing on essential information regarding the question at hand. Vogel (1987) reports that it is helpful to focus students with learning disabilities on key principles, key words, and key verbs useful in a particular essay question (e.g., analyze and apply). The use of mnemonic devices, associations, rhymes, and acronyms can be helpful when trying to remember key concepts and ideas for an essay exam. Anxiety in test taking situations can be reduced by breathing exercises and biofeedback training if excessive anxiety exists.

Study Skills Training

The SQ3R method of study was developed by Robinson in 1946 and is one systematic approach to studying textual material. The purpose of this study method is to guide students through content area subjects by using the text format. This technique is more suited for secondary level students. The SQ3R format is actually five steps: (1) surveying the chapter content by reading and thinking about chapter headings, topic sentences and headings, the concluding paragraph, and end-of-chapter questions; (2) questioning by restating chapter headings in the form of a question; (3) reading the material after each topic and formulating answers to questions along the way; (4) reciting answers to questions in one's own words (repeat steps 2–4 throughout the chapter reading); and (5) reviewing notes and trying to recall main points after each main heading in the chapter. Adams, Carnine and Gersten (1982) caution against using this technique if it becomes a tedious procedure

Homework

Homework adaptations need to be in place for students with dyslexia with one hour recommended for students at the elementary level and two hours at the secondary level. The following suggestions should also take into consideration the individual learning styles and needs of each student.

Homework Adaptations for Students with Dyslexia

FOR TEACHERS:

1. Present materials in a *typed* format whenever possible.
2. *Directions* should be *clear* and *succinct* and limited to a *few steps* at the elementary level and less than five instructions at the secondary level. Review and re-word directions beforehand. Ask the student to tell you what the assignment is.
3. Ask the student to keep an *assignment pad*. Have the student *log* any homework *assignments*. Ask parents to initial the homework assignment pad if the student has difficulty in completing assigned tasks. Otherwise, try to encourage the student to take responsibility for his/her homework assignments.
4. *Adjust the submission format*. Accept typed or computer-driven products. **Allow tape recordings for students with severe written expression problems.**
5. Provide *immediate, continuous, and corrective feedback*. ALWAYS give some *positive feedback* for poor submissions if it is evident that the student put forth his/her best efforts (e.g., "nice penmanship," "I can see you really tried," "I like the way you worded this answer," and so on).
6. *Reduce the assignment load* or expectations whenever possible. Fewer examples could be given, a shorter assignment length, and so on.
7. *Record homework performance* on a chart, record book, journal, grade book, and so on. Give the child access to this record keeping as students should be given feed-

back on their progress in any learning situation.

8. *Keep parents informed* of progress especially GOOD NEWS.
9. *Provide rewards* for completed/acceptable homework. As an example, a student could be given a "free homework" pass every so often that could be turned in when the student wants a night off from homework. Other incentives could include exemption from an assignment in school, the assignment of a special responsibility (e.g., teacher's helper), and so on.
10. Work with the student on *time allocation*. Periodically check in with the student for long-term assignments and reports. Perhaps a draft submission or outline could be suggested for particularly long assignments.
11. Encourage the *study of exams and quizzes in "small chunks."* Reinforce the concept of "distributed" practice versus "cramming" for exams. Provide a peer tutor if necessary to ask questions and rehearse important concepts/materials. This could be done before school, during recess, or study hall.

FOR PARENTS:

1. Set aside a *homework time* each evening in a quiet place in the home. Try to *keep distractions to a minimum*.
2. Ask your child what the homework assignments are and *be certain* that *he/she understands when assignments are due*.
3. *Check assignment pads* and initial if there is a problem in homework completion.
4. *Let the teacher know if your child is experiencing "homework problems"*, and in particular, frustration with the format of a submission. If written expressive exercises become very tedious, brainstorm with the teacher on an acceptable format. The teacher might consider allowing you to be the "secretary" when extensive reports or assignments need to be completed.
5. Provide *immediate and continuous feedback*. ALWAYS give some *positive feedback* for poor submissions if it is evident that

Continued

your child put forth his/her best efforts (e.g., "nice penmanship," "I can see you really tried," "I like the way you worded this answer," and so on).

6. Ask the teacher to *reduce the assignment load* or expectations if you see that your child is spending more than one hour per night at the elementary level or two hours at the secondary level. Fewer examples could be given, a shorter assignment length could be expected, and so on. However, there will be some nights that your child should spend extra time on homework especially before exams, an oral presentation, to complete a written report, and so on. If you use your common sense, you'll know what to do. Parents can be fine judges of their child's learning needs at home.

7. *Ask to see* your child's *homework papers* after they have been returned from the teacher. Post them on the refrigerator or bulletin board whenever a good performance can be seen.

8. Keep in close contact with the school and periodically ask for progress reports whether they be oral or written. Call the school IMMEDIATELY if you suspect a problem. The guidance counselor in a school can be particularly helpful in bridging communications between the school and home.

9. *Provide rewards* for completed/acceptable homework over time if you deem such rewards necessary and possible to administer. As an example every so often you could give your child a special treat (e.g., a night off from a household chore, staying up an extra half-hour at night, and so on). Praise alone would also be a reward unto itself.

10. Work with the student on *time allocation*. Periodically check in with the student for long-term assignments and reports. Perhaps a draft submission or outline could be suggested for particularly long assignments.

11. *Encourage* the *study of exams and quizzes in "small chunks."* Reinforce the concept of "distributed" practice versus "cramming" for exams. Study together and ask possible questions that might come up on an exam. If necessary, seek tutorial assistance. Guidance in this area should be obtained through the school, and in particular, the guidance counselor and teacher(s).

for the student. Certainly, interrogative reading is critical to the acquisition and retention of knowledge for all students.

There have been some adaptations to the SQ3R method which have been used to enhance study skills acquisition. Simpson, Hayes, Stahl, Connor, and Weaver (1988) offered the PORPE method which focuses students on predicting, organizing, rehearsing, practicing, and evaluating study material. Similarly, Thomas and Robinson (1972) discuss the PQ4R method which involves previewing, questioning, reading, reflecting, reciting, and reviewing textual material. It would be particularly important for the teacher at the secondary level to model good time management skills by practicing those behaviors which demonstrate good time management (i.e., maintaining a calendar, referring to a watch, etc.) (Manganello, 1994) as part of study skills training.

Homework Adaptations

Homework adaptations are an important component to the study skills process. Teachers and parents can work together to facilitate successes in this area. (Refer to previous box, pp. 185–186).

There are other questioning and memory strategies which individuals with dyslexia can use to enhance learning and reading in general.

Enhancing Information Recall

". . . Because it depends on use of world and linguistic knowledge, reading also is an act of memory . . ." (Glover, Ronning, & Bruning, 1990, p. 222). Constructing knowledge in content areas subjects requires interactive processing between the learner and text. There are several memory techniques which can supplement comprehension and study skills work (see Table 7-4 below).

Verbal Mediation

One of the easiest ways to improve acquisition of information is verbal mediation. Verbal mediation refers to connecting difficult-to-remember words or phrases to something (a verbal mediator) more meaningful (Montague, Adams, & Kiess, 1966). Ormrod (1990) suggests using verbal mediation to teach mastery of foreign languages and gives the following examples to illustrate the effectiveness of such an approach (p. 286):

German Word	*English Meaning*	*Mediator*
der Hund	dog	hound
das Schwein	pig	swine
die Gans	goose	gander

Verbal mediators can also be used in spelling such as, "the princi*pal* is my pal" (not princi*ple*!). The use of mnemonic devices is similar to verbal mediation in that

TABLE 7-4   Enhancing Information Recall

Verbal Mediation

Mnemonics
> Acronyms
> Acrostics
> Imagery
> Keyword Method
> Linking Chain
> Method of Loci
> Phrases
> Rhyming Phrases

Recitation

Rehearsal

Careful Selection of Material

Focus on Middle Positions In a List

Overlearning

Spaced Practice

Review

Sleep

paired-association learning is required. Mnemonics are highly specific memory strategies that enhance memory retrieval and typically involve pairing of information to be learned with well-learned information. Good readers frequently use mnemonics without being instructed to do so (Morris & Cook, 1978; Nickerson, Perkins, & Smith, 1986). On the other hand, students with dyslexia will need to be taught certain common mnemonic devices or ways to remember and recall difficult concepts or material.

Mnemonics

Scruggs, Mastropieri and their associates (e.g., Mastropieri, Scruggs, & Levin, 1985; Veit, Scruggs, & Mastropieri, 1986; Scruggs, Mastropieri, McLoone, Levin, & Morrison, 1987) have studied mnemonic facilitation in depth with students who experience learning disabilities. Generally the findings of these researchers support the supplemental use of mnemonic techniques for improving the learning and memory performance of students with learning disabilities.

Richardson and Morgan (1990) point out the mnemonic learning techniques (see Table 7-5 below) can be welcome learning aids for poor readers. They sug-

TABLE 7-6   K - W - L

The K-W-L strategy facilitates comprehension by establishing background knowledge prior to reading and setting purposes for reading through the formation of questions. New knowledge is linked with background knowledge as reading takes place. The following example depicts a K-W-L procedure as it might be developed in a social studies class on immigration.
[(Based on Silver Burdett & Ginn - Social Studies - (1990) Morriston, N.J. and The U.S. Yesterday and Today Gr. 5)]

Immigrants In A New World

K (What I already know)	W (What I want to know or learn)	L (What I Learned)
Early Immigrants came from Europe.	How many immigrants came to the U.S.?	U.S. was "land of opportunity."
They were seeking freedom and opportunity.	Did the government limit the numbers?	Between 1840–1900, 17 million arrivals.
Life was difficult for immigrants.	What was life like for immigrants?	Between 1900–1920, 15 million arrivals.
They settled in ethnic neighborhoods.	What problems arose for them?	Laws in 1882 restricted criminals, insane, sick, and then the illiterate in 1917.
They helped one another.	Why did immigrants leave their countries?	Ghettos were the first urban settlements—Chicago, N.Y.
	Was anyone in my family an immigrant?	Tenements had poor sanitation and conditions.

gest the MAD technique to familiarize elementary students with mnemonics. MAD is simply presenting a *m*nemonic *a d*ay for thirty days. Students work in groups and must choose a different content area than the previous day. MAD logs are kept and periodically reviewed in order to reinforce the various mnemonics. There are several specific mnemonic devices which can be used to enhance memory and recall.

Specific Mnemonics Devices

Letters.   Some more frequently cited mnemonic devises include: ROY G. BIV (colors of the visual spectrum—red, orange, yellow, green, blue, indigo, and violet); HOMES (the Great Lakes—Huron, Ontario, Michigan, Erie, and Superior). Keep in mind that each letter in the mnemonic is a cue for a word to be recalled. Such mnemonics are also referred to as acronyms.

Phrases.   Mnemonic phrases are also helpful: I before E, except after C (i/e vowel rule); *e*very *g*ood *b*oy *d*oes *f*ine (the lines on the treble clef; E G B D F); when the "mites" go up, the "tites" go down (directional differences between stalagmites and stalactites); thirty days hath September, April, June, and November—all the rest have 31 except February which has 28 (the number of days in each month); "On old Olympus' towering top, a Finn and German viewed some hops" (first letter of each word cues the twelve cranial nerves—olfactory, optic, oculomotor, trochlear, trigeminal, abducens, facial, auditory, glossopharyngeal, vagus, spinal, accessory, and hypoglossal).

  "*M*y *v*ery *e*ducated *m*other *j*ust *s*erved *u*s *n*ine *p*izzas" is an example of a sentence which can be used to remember the 9 planets (in sequence from nearest the sun to outermost: Mercury, Venus, Earth, Mars, Jupiter, Saturn, Uranus, Neptune, and Pluto). The sentence, "*A*ll *e*ager children *m*ust *p*lay *y*et *a*lways *b*e *h*appy" can assist memory of the nine standard United States time zones: Atlantic, Eastern, Central, Mountain, Pacific, Yukon, Alaska, Bering, and Hawaii. In mathematics, "*P*lease *e*xcuse *m*y *d*ear *A*unt *S*ally," can be used to explain the order of operations in solving equations: p = parentheses; e = exponent; m = multiplication; d = division; a = addition; and s = subtraction. "Acrostics" is also the term used when the first letter of each word in the mnemonic represents an item to mastered.

  Sometimes a short phrase can be used to trigger more lengthy information. For example, the "right hand" rule in physics for determining the flow of a magnetic field around an electrical current can be remembered as follows: ". . . place the thumb of the right hand in the direction of the current—the curl of the fingers around the conductor will show the direction of the magnetic field . . ." (Glover, Ronning, & Bruning, 1990, p. 118). Rhyming phrases also enhance memory such as "In 1492 Columbus sailed the ocean blue," and "one, two, buckle my shoe; three, four, shut the door; five, six, pick up sticks; seven, eight, lay them straight; nine, ten, a big fat hen."

Mnemonics based on Imagery.   Some mnemonic devices involve visual imagery. Visual imagery is ". . . a powerful storage code that can be formed quickly and retained for a relatively long period of time . . ." (Ormrod, 1990, p. 286). Picturing the shape (on a map) of Italy as that of a boot, and France, a bearskin rug, visually enhances the retention of these countries' shapes. Coon (1994) suggests adding action to the visual image to enhance memory. He gives the example of picturing Van Gogh in a van (automobile) going through the middle of each of his paintings running over things and knocking things over. One can associate Van Gogh paintings with the items knocked over. Mnemonics can also be created to help explain certain visual images of experiences. The mnemonic HUVS (*horizontal-u*tricle; *v*ertical-*s*accule) can be used to account for those awful feelings when riding a fast elevator in a skyscraper office building (your stomach feels like its coming up to your head when the elevator goes down and like its falling down to your feet when the elevator goes up). This phenomenon can be explained by tiny sense organs in the inner ear: the vertical acceleration of the saccule in the ear accounts for these experiences. When you are driving a fast automobile and suddenly have to step on the brake pedal, you can experience the horizontal acceleration of the utricle. There is a mnemonic technique called the keyword method (Atkinson, 1975) which combines imagery and word associations to enhance recall.

Keyword Method.   Atkinson's (1975) *keyword method* has been shown to be effective with students with learning disabilities in mastering science facts (Mastropieri, Scruggs, & Levin, 1985; Scruggs, Mastropieri, McLoone, Levin, & Morrison, 1987), foreign langauage vocabulary (Veit, Scruggs, & Mastrpieri, 1986), and other content area learning concepts and vocabulary. Essentially this method involves taking an unfamiliar term such as *dahlia* (a flower) and recode this term to an acoustically similar KEYWORD such as *doll* (Scruggs, Mastropieri, McLoone, Levin, & Morrison, 1987). Students can later retrieve the term *dahlia* by picturing a doll smelling a flower. According to Levin (1983), students are recoding, relating, and retrieving the information needed.

Method of Loci.   The method of loci is used by memory experts and allows for retention of long lists of information (Snowman, 1986). According to Yates (1966) the method of loci dates back to the ancient Greek poet Simonides who had attended a large banquet and had to excuse himself. While he was gone, the roof collapsed and killed everyone present. Because everyone was unrecognizable, Simonides had to remember who sat where in the banquet hall in order to identify the bodies. Simonides used a method of location or loci to recall the names.

In order to use the method of loci, one has to remember a location (e.g., classroom, living room, garden path, etc.) with great detail. Once the location has been overlearned, it can be used as a mnemonic. Let's use this method (with loci = various places in a kitchen) to remember the contributions of the following five African-American individuals for a test in which we have to list their contributions from memory: Charles Drew (invented a method for storing blood plasma); George Washington Carver (developed 300 different products from peanuts and new ways of farming); Mary Bethune (started Bethune-Cookman College with $1.50); Harriet Tubman (a leader in the underground railroad movement which supplied hiding places for African-Americans during the Civil War); and Matthew Henson (the first person to place the American Flag on the North Pole). We can imagine five individuals in a kitchen: George Washington Carver is making a peanut butter sandwich (peanuts) at the table while Mary Bethune is cooking (Bethune-Cookman College). Mary had just cooked a hen for Matthew Henson who is placing Fourth of July flags (flag on the North Pole) on the table for a Fourth of July dinner. Harriet Tubman was hiding in the corner eating candy before dinner (hid slaves). Charles Drew was at the door because he had to go to the store to get soda (stored blood plasma) for everyone to drink. There are subtle cue words which should trigger memory for retrieval purposes.

Linking Chain.   These are exaggerated associations which are linked together by a common theme. The following "linking chain" can be used to remember some tips on how to improve memory!

Memory Tips

Memory can be enhanced by verbally RECITING information to be learned (many highly successful college students engage in this practice); REHEARSING or mentally repeating information to be learned; giving careful attention to important SELECTIONs or information to remember; focusing on the middle items or most easily forgotten items on a list because of the SERIAL POSITION effect (beginning and ending items are remembered best); using visual, olfactory, or auditory CUES; OVERLEARNING the material; engaging in SPACED PRACTICE (e.g., studying information on a daily basis several days before an exam) as opposed to "cramming information"; REVIEWING the material from time to time; and SLEEPING at least 6–8 hours per night as sleep deprivation interferes with recall. A mnemonic devise that can be used to remember our memory tips is as follows:

"Juana (want to remember?) RECITED to her family that she had REHEARSED a Bach SELECTION with an orchestra organized by strings and percussion in SERIAL POSITIONS with no CUES for the players who have OVERLEARNED the piece by such strategies as SPACED PRACTICE, REVIEW, and then SLEEP!"

Coon (1994) cautions that mnemonics cannot replace such memory tips but can only be supplements. There are other specific individual and group reading strategies teachers can use with students with dyslexia which will enhance information recall and understanding. One group instructional technique is offered by Ogle (1986) and is entitled K-W-L.

K-W-L

K-W-L is basically an active constructive reading method which can be used in group situations. The K represents knowing or recalling what a student already knows; W represents what one wants to learn; and L represents what one learns as one reads. The teacher determines appropriate and important content to learn and study following these steps:

Step 1   Preparation—the teacher determines the content.

Step 2   Group Instruction—Pre-reading Activities

K   a. The group brainstorms to determine what they already know about the topic.

b. After discussions, the group categorizes information and might develop semantic maps.

Step 3   Individual Reflection

W   a. Students develop questions about what they want to know (or learn) and set a purpose for reading.

b. Students predict what they might learn to answer their generated questions.

Step 4   Reading

The actual reading of text can be broken into sections or read as a whole.

Step 5   After-Reading—Learning Assessment

L   Students identify new information they have learned. They can add this information to their semantic maps to illustrate how the new information fits into existing knowledge.

The sample in Table 7-6 (p. 193) depicts a K-W-L procedure in the area of social studies.

Conclusions

Research supports the idea that combining instruction in reading and writing in the classroom enhances children's literacy learning. Many students with dyslexia have less than adequate study skills habits. Young adults and adults with dyslexia, in particular, have difficulty managing time and being organized. This is due to remnants of dyslexia still apparent in adulthood. Several ideas and strategies were discussed which focus on the development of effective study habits such as note-taking skills, organizational skills, time-management, and test-taking strategies.

Memory enhancement techniques were presented such as recitation, rehearsal, selection, giving extra attention to middle items on a list, overlearning, spaced or distributed practice, review, and sleep. Mnemonics are highly specific memory strategies that can enhance memory retrieval and typically involve pairing of information to be learned with well-learned information. Good readers

TABLE 7-6   K - W - L

The K-W-L strategy facilitates comprehension by establishing background knowledge prior to reading and setting purposes for reading through the formation of questions. New knowledge is linked with background knowledge as reading takes place. The following example depicts a K-W-L procedure as it might be developed in a social studies class on immigration.
[(Based on Silver Burdett & Ginn - Social Studies - (1990) Morriston, N.J. and The U.S. Yesterday and Today Gr. 5)]

Immigrants In A New World

K (What I already know)	W (What I want to know or learn)	L (What I Learned)
Early Immigrants came from Europe.	How many immigrants came to the U.S.?	U.S. was "land of opportunity."
They were seeking freedom and opportunity.	Did the government limit the numbers?	Between 1840–1900, 17 million arrivals.
Life was difficult for immigrants.	What was life like for immigrants?	Between 1900–1920, 15 million arrivals.
They settled in ethnic neighborhoods.	What problems arose for them?	Laws in 1882 restricted criminals, insane, sick, and then the illiterate in 1917.
They helped one another.	Why did immigrants leave their countries?	Ghettos were the first urban settlements—Chicago, N.Y.
	Was anyone in my family an immigrant?	Tenements had poor sanitation and conditions.
		Zoning and safety laws were developed.
		Settlement houses provided services.
		Growth of labor and factories.

frequently use mnemonics without being instructed to do so and students with dyslexia will need to be taught certain common mnemonic devices.

Research and theory support the notion that combining instruction in reading and writing in the classroom enhances children's literacy learning. That important reading-writing connection was discussed with several writing ideas offered for students with learning disabilities. Good writers can focus on the ideas expressed in writing because the mechanics (e.g., punctuation, grammar, spelling, capitalization) are automatic. Less skilled writers can probably become better writers through the automatization of the mechanical aspects of writing while at the same time being taught creative expression (e.g., writing process ideas).

As with all recommended treatments, we will state the obvious—in the words of Weiten (1995), "getting adequate sleep, consuming a nutritionally sound diet, and controlling overeating . . . (along with) regular exercise can lead to improved physical and mental health" (p. 555). The physical and mental well-being of the individual should always precede academic recommendations with continuous monitoring and assessment present.

The first seven chapters provided the foundation for determining the nature and characteristics of the condition of dyslexia. The following checklist can be used as a guide when making that final diagnosis. A trained professional will need to determine

1. if the individual falls two years behind age level expectations in reading accomplishment,
2. if an individual displays at least 5 of the characteristics on the Spafford-Grosser dyslexia checklist, and
3. if an IQ-reading achievement discrepancy of 1.5 standard deviation units exist.

Spafford and Grosser's Dyslexia Checklist

If you find that an individual exhibits some type of reading problem or deficit at least two years behind age level expectations and more than five of the following characteristics, you need to refer this individual for further academic/psychological evaluation. In particular, an individual well versed in testing would need to determine the discrepancy between the individual's innate intelligence (via an I.Q. measure) and reading achievement (via a reading measure). In Chapter 2, we detail step-by-step how to determine a discrepancy using 1.5 standard deviations as the final determinant of a dyslexia diagnosis.

_____ Difficulties in Acquiring Phonic Skills/Knowledge
_____ A Word-for-Word Reader
_____ Miscues or Errors in Oral Reading
_____ Relatively Slow Recognition Rates of Letters and Words
_____ Relatively Slow Naming Rates for Colors, Numbers, and Objects
_____ Delayed Language Development
_____ Below Grade Level Reading Skills
_____ Below Grade Level Language Skills
_____ Relatively Good Math Grades
_____ Reversals in Reading and Writing that Persist
_____ Perseverates on a Topic or Idea
_____ Late Talker
_____ Time and Directional Confusions
_____ Problems with Time Concepts
_____ Disorganized
_____ Confusion Between Right and Left
_____ Attention Difficulties
_____ Lack of Concentration
_____ Easily Distracted
_____ Hyperactivity
_____ Impulsive
_____ Unsatisfactory Metacognitive Awareness
_____ Inability to Follow-Through with a Task

_____ Lack of Problem-Solving Strategies
_____ Memory Deficits
_____ Serial Order or Sequencing Problems
_____ Family History of Reading Problems
_____ Motor Sequencing Problems
_____ Written Language Deficits
_____ Spelling Difficulties
_____ Mathematics Difficulties
_____ More Negative Peer Interactions
_____ Inappropriate or Excessive Displays of Affection
_____ Inappropriate Facial Gestures or Body Language
_____ An External Locus of Control (i.e., attributing one's problems to the environment or external forces)
_____ Unawareness of Social Conventions
_____ Lower Social Standing
_____ Follows the Crowd as Opposed to Being a Leader
_____ Moody
_____ Depressed
_____ Low Frustration Tolerance
_____ Diminished Self Concept
_____ Learned Helplessness Attitude
_____ Poor Decision-Making Ability
_____ Lack of Reflective Thought
_____ Inadequate Self-Assessments of Successes/Failures
_____ Reduced Reading Rates as Adults
_____ Poor Study Skills
_____ Verbal-Performance Discrepancy of at Least 15 on the Wechsler Scales
_____ ACID or AVID Profiles on the Wechsler Scales (Low Arithmetic, Comprehension/Vocabulary, Information, Digit Span Scaled Scores)

IQ-Achievement Test Performance Discrepancy of 1.5 standard deviations or more must be present to confirm a dyslexia diagnosis. See Chapter 2 for instructions as to how to compute this discrepancy.

Just to think about . . . [Standard Instructions for Reading]

". . . Always throw yourself into the spirit of what you read, and try to do your best . . ."

". . . Choose reading books carefully for the reading book teaches the reader the art of written and oral expression . . . gives . . . gems of thought and sentiment . . . holds up for admiration and imitation examples . . . there must be certain vitality to the selections to make them enjoyable and therefore profitable to the learner . . ."

FIGURE 7-14 Wise Tidbits from Yesteryear

Chapter 8

Math Disabilities and Remediation

*Not to begin the study of the subject when the child enters
school, however, is to say that the child's natural tastes
should not be fostered; what we need is to introduce, in an
informal and attractive fashion, such number work as is
within his [her] grasp at this time*
—*(WENTWORTH & SMITH, 1912, PREFACE).*

Introduction

Two important issues have been raised by Wentworth and Smith, the need to mo-
tivate the math learner, and the need to present math material within the grasp
of the learner. Math problems and disabilities are sometimes intensified in the
learning disabled population due to the complex nature of their learning problems (Myers & Hammill, 1982). Being dyslexic (i.e., having a reading disability)
does not predispose one to math problems in particular. In fact, some individuals with dyslexia perform well in mathematics. Although some individuals with
dyslexia have a mathematics disability, many others are not math-disabled. In this
regard, Gardner (1983) postulates that we actually possess a logical-mathematical
type of intelligence which is one of six types of intelligence or broad competency areas we develop. "Because many students are exhibiting difficulties in
learning mathematics at all levels of American education" (Ariel, 1992, p. 476),
we have decided to devote an entire chapter to the discussion of math disabili-
ties/problems and remedial procedures separately from the problem of dyslexia.
It would be especially critical to discuss math remediation since, "compared with
disorders of language, reading, and writing, those of mathematics have received
relatively scant attention from the theorists and practitioners of education" (Myers
& Hammill, 1990, p. 285).

Some authors describe mathematics disabilities as a type of nonverbal learning disability because verbal skills tend to be adequate. Typically these individuals have a higher verbal than performance IQ (Denckla (1991); poor visual memories and organization skills (Bley & Thornton, 1995); and a general lack of conceptual understanding in mathematics (Foss, 1991).

Historical Antecedents

Math disabilities were first described in terms of neurological deficits with researchers discussing the math behaviors of brain-injured adults in comparison to children with aberrant math behaviors (Henschen, 1919; Krapf, 1937). Gerstmann (1940) documented correlating symptoms of math disabilities in adults who experienced cerebral damage due to accidents and/or brain tumors. Gerstmann found math problems with four primary symptoms evident: finger agnosia (which is the inability to report correctly which finger has been touched), disorientation for left and right, agraphia, and dyscalculia. Gerstmann's subjects appeared to have average cognitive functioning in conjunction with the brain trauma(s).

The Gerstmann Syndrome

Strauss and Werner's work (1938) followed that of Gerstmann and they also found a relationship between finger agnosia and math disabilities. However, their 1938 study in the American Journal of Orthopsychiatry reported an average IQ of 68 for a group of 14 males between the ages of 9–15 suggesting that intellectual factors alone may have influenced math performance. Kinsbourne and Warrington (1966) studied seven cases of children who displayed what became known as the Gerstmann Syndrome (relating math disabilities to finger agnosia). These researchers found that the children with Gerstmann's Syndrome also displayed severe reading disabilities. These children evinced problems with left/right directionality, dyscalculia, dysgraphia, constructional apraxia, and dyslexia (see Chapter 1 for a detailed description of these disorders). Keogh and Babbitt (1986) suggest problems in the Gerstmann research relating to "the range of subject characteristics . . . [confounding] what may be the defining, critical attributes of the condition under consideration" (p. 16).

Math Subtypes

Although different subtypes of these disorders have been mentioned in the literature (see Chapter 1), little research has been done regarding identification and remediation by type. For that reason, issues related to diagnosis and remediation of math disabilities in this chapter will reflect a global approach to the problem. In general, there appear to be two major types of math disabilities proposed by advocates of the neurophysiological school of thought: acalculia and dyscalculia

(Keller & Sutton, 1991). (See Chapter 1 for detailed overview.) Badian (1983) has proposed a different math classification system of developmental math problems which he refers to as dyscalculic. The four types he proposes are: (1) alexia and agraphia for numbers, (2) spatial dyscalculia, (3) anarithmetria (combining addition, subtraction, and/or multiplication operations in a single calculation), and (4) attentional-sequential dyscalculia.

No Consensus on Valid Math Subtyping Scheme

We believe that (1) a visual mathematics disability type (similar to Gerstmann's acalculia), (2) a verbal mathematics disability type which would involve oral and/or written-language deficits, and (3) a mixed mathematics disability type involving visual and linguistic deficits, probably account for most math disabilities. Much research needs to be done to confirm this or any other subtyping scheme. Thus, various types of math disabilities have emerged with little consensus in the field regarding the validity of such schemata.

Math Performances—A Growing Concern

There is a consensus in the field regarding the math performances of our children and youth as these are a growing cause for concern (Lapointe, Mead, & Phillips, 1988; National Research Council, 1990). Norman & Zigmond (1980) found that only 8% of students with learning disabilities studied displayed learning difficulties in math alone while 13% had learning difficulties in both reading and math. Additionally, Carpenter (1985) has found that one-third of the elementary and secondary students who receive academic support in resource rooms are there for math help in addition to other academic support.

Causation

Causation is difficult to pinpoint therefore remedial efforts should focus on the math problem itself rather than trying to fix some "innate mechanism." "An individual faced with analysis and remediation of a child's mathematical difficulties is confronted with a myriad of possible causes" (Nunes, 1991, p. 23). Difficulties in math have been attributed to:

Faulty Metacognition

- The metacognitive view that LD-like problems in thinking and reasoning are probably due to the inability to call forth problem-solving strategies under appropriate conditions especially effective strategies for memorizing consequential math knowledge (Allardice & Ginsburg, 1983)

Processing Speed

- Slow rates in computation (Kirby & Becker, 1988; Lovitt, 1989)

Memory Problems

- Disorders in memory and abstraction (Bley & Thornton, 1995)
- Specifically, impaired short-term memory (STM) capacity (Cohn, 1961; Webster, 1979)

Motivation Problems

- A "lack of student readiness for the type of task required" (Miller & Milam, 1987, p. 121) or a feeling of frustration and helplessness when "confronted with a torrent of meaningless words and written symbols" (Baroody, 1991, p. 385)

Perceptual Processing Difficulties

- Difficulties in processing visual-spatial relationships (Landsdown, 1978; Kirk & Chalfant, 1984)

School Related Problems

- Shortcomings in traditional instructional methods (Cawley, Miller & School, 1987; Hammill & Bartel, 1990)

Developmental Delays

- A lack of maturation of math abilities (Kosc, 1974; Lawless, 1995)

Neurophysiological Reasons

- In some cases "right hemispheric dysfunctioning . . . [involving] . . . the manipulation of imagery, visuoperception, and spatial processing" (Semrud-Clikeman & Hynd, 1991, p. 616)
- Generalized language disorders related to left-hemispheric dysfunctioning (Guttmann, 1937)
- Several neuropsychological factors which include deficits in attention, verbal, and nonverbal processes (Keller & Sutton, 1991)

The variability of learning characteristics within a disabled population illustrates the heterogeneity of this group (Dautrich, 1993) such that various etiologies could reflect varying subtypes (Spafford, Pesce, & Grosser, in press). Researchers have looked for years at the variables that affect the learning process (e.g., Ammons, 1947) and have yet to come to a consensus in the LD field regarding causation (Grosser & Spafford, 1989, 1990).

Cognitive Factors

Bartel (1990) describes several cognitive factors which are necessary prerequisites for learning math. These include the abilities to form and remember associations, understand relationships, and make simple generalizations at the elementary level. As the student progresses to a secondary level, these basic skills amount to a foundation for the higher-order algorithmic procedures involved in algebra and geometry, necessary gateways for the college-bound student. Because many current math programs emphasize computation proficiency (Fair, 1988), the acquisition of higher-order math skills is impeded. Therefore, it is essential to focus on solid development of conceptual understandings that underlie mathematical procedures.

Redefining the Math Teacher's Mission

The National Council of Teachers of Mathematics (1989) proposes that twelve math areas be incorporated in the math curriculum for students at all levels. These twelve areas are problem solving, communicating mathematical ideas, mathematical reasoning, applying mathematics to everyday situations, alertness to the reasonableness of the results of analyses, practicing estimation, developing appropriate computational skills, thinking algebraically, understanding measurement, understanding geometry, understanding statistics, and understanding probability. The standards proposed for the teaching/learning of these areas include solving problems by systematic investigation, hypothesis testing, estimation, checking obtained answers, and developing communication skills. According to Hatfield, Edwards, and Bitter (1993), "This is a constructivist view of learning . . . a redefined role for the teacher, from a dispensor of knowledge to a facilitator of learning" (p. 4). In essence, teachers have to be problem-solvers with consideration given to the uniqueness of each situation presented (Cooper, 1995).

Constructivist Math Teaching

The effort of cognitive psychologists to have learners generate their own conceptual understandings is reflected in the **constructivist approach** popular in modern educational thinking. This approach advocates direct experiences with learning materials and concepts that lead students through a process of forming the generalizations and principles that govern mathematical processes. It is believed that when children form their own understandings through authentic experiences, the learning is more meaningful and the memory more enduring. Additionally, students who construct their own knowledge in this way are able to utilize these strategies in all areas of learning.

"Mathematical instruction of youth with LD [including dyslexia] . . . call for: (a) mastery learning, which builds on prerequisite skills and understandings, rather than spiral learning; (b) learning that involves *active construction of meaning;* (c) verbal teacher interactions with the child to assess and stimulate problem-solution strategies; (d) increased emphasis on assessment and teaching of mathematical concepts; (e) use of strategies, where appropriate, related to the requirements for reading comprehension and for memory in problem solving; (f) attentional cues to help students prepare for changes in problem action, operation and order of operation; and (g) novel instructional activities to facilitate overlearning basic calculations . . ." (p. 16).

Constructivist Math Builds on "Old Math Ideas"

Davis, Maher, and Noddings (1990) affirm the math teacher's role by emphasizing "guiding student activity, modeling mathematical behavior, and providing the examples and counterexamples that will turn student talk into useful communication about mathematics" (p. 3). The constructivist approach sees both the teacher and student as active learners in their investigation and pursuit of math knowledge and concepts. Constructivist math teaching is not new. Some educators have advocated this interactive teaching style dating back to the 1800s as seen in the following: ". . . Never give a pupil a direct answer to any question he [she] may propose respecting the operation of any problem, nor perform the labor for him, but suggest such principles as will enable him[her]to perform the question himself/[herself] . . ." (Greenleaf, 1846, p.3).

Constructivists Support NCTM Recommendations

Constructivists frequently cite curriculum changes cited by the National Council of Teachers of Mathematics in the March 1991(a, b), Professional Standards for

---

Through inquiry and exploration of mathematical concepts, children are able to construct new meanings based on their concrete experiences.

Using various sized discs and lengths of string, students are asked to examine the relationship between a circle's edge (circumference) and its diameter. The discovery of the constant relationship leads to the concept of π (pi).

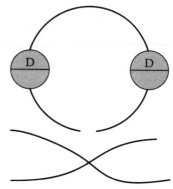

Students are asked to develop a number system based on units of six rather than on our familiar base-ten system. Beans, cups, and chart paper provide the elements for constructing new meaning.

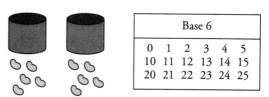

Base 6					
0	1	2	3	4	5
10	11	12	13	14	15
20	21	22	23	24	25

FIGURE 8-1 Constructivist Approach to Math

Teaching Mathematics. These teaching standards should be embraced by those who work with students who have math disabilities. Essentially consideration is given to: (1) moving the curriculum away from a classroom of individuals to a mathematics community where mathematics learning is an interactive reflective process; (2) moving toward an emphasis on logic and mathematical evidence deriving from the students in the classroom as well as from the teacher; (3) moving away from pure memorization of math procedures to more math reasoning and communicating; (4) moving more toward conjecturing, problem-solving, and inventing as opposed to mechanical problem solving; and (5) moving toward connecting the ideas in math and applying math to everyday life, as opposed to treating mathematics as an isolated subject.

NCTM Professional Standards in Math—The Professional Standards for Teaching Mathematics (NCTM, 1991b)—consist of six standards which are intended to guide teachers of mathematics so that the math needs of all students can be met. Hatfield, Edwards, and Bitter (1993) have suggested how teachers should organize a math curriculum and teach the skills required for math literacy, using the Professional Standards for Teaching Mathematics of the NCTM (1991b). Table 8-1 below lists some of the principal points related to each of the six standards.

Standard 6 emphasizes the importance of strategic planning which diagnostic [math] teaching can offer. Essentially during diagnostic teaching, the instructor

TABLE 8-1 Professional Standards for Teaching Mathematics of the National Council of Teachers of Mathematics (NCTM)—1991

Standard 1: Worthwhile Math Tasks

Curriculum Focus:
- Significant Mathematics
- Knowledge of Student Interests and Experiences
- Knowledge of Diverse Learning Styles
- Communicating Math Concepts and Making Math Connections

Standard 2: The Teacher's Role in Discourse

Teachers Should:
- Promote Questioning
- Promote Critical Thinking and Student Ideas
- Promote Clarification and Justification of Ideas
- Monitor and Model Discussions

Standard 3: The Student's Role in Discourse

Teachers Should Encourage Students to:
- Listen, Question, and Respond to Classmates and Teacher
- Hypothesize and Propose Solutions
- Rely on Math Evidence and Arguments in Determining the Validity of a Statement

Standard 4: Tools for Enhancing Discourse

Teachers Should Encourage Students to Use:
- Computers, Calculators, and Other Technology
- Graphs, Charts, Models, Pictures, and Diagrams
- Dramatizations and Oral Presentations
- The Language of Math

Standard 5: The Learning Environment

Teachers Need to Create an Environment Which:
- Uses Physical Space and Materials to Facilitate Learning
- Respect and Value the Ideas of Students
- Encourages Independence and Collaboration in Math Learning

Standard 6: Analysis of Teaching and Learning

Teachers Need to:
- Observe and Assess Student Growth and Learning
- Gather More Important Information about Math Learning
- Examine the Impact of the Learning Environment, Materials, and Pedagogy on the Student's Math Learning

(1) assesses student strengths and weaknesses, (2) develops and implements an effective plan to remediate weaknesses, and (3) continually monitors the plan to determine which portions are most beneficial—ensuring that skills at which students need work are developed at his/her pace/learning style (Enright, 1989). A well-thought out scope-and-sequence format based upon diagnostic information should be incorporated in all math classes so that subject matter presented follows a logical and sequential process whereby concrete foundations lead to acquisition of higher-order math skills. Teaching specifics needs to be individualized to each member of the population served.

Thornton, Tucker, Dossey, and Bazik (1983) emphasize a well-balanced math curriculum should include: (1) the teaching of the fundamental operations and computation skills, (2) the teaching of math concepts and integration of these concepts within the regular subject curriculum, and (3) the teaching of math application skills by building a solid foundation of problem-solving strategies and approaches. In all instances, cooperative learning activities can be used to foster math learning. The specific NCTM (1989) curriculum standards are listed at the end of this chapter.

Cooperative Activities Enhance Constructivist Approach

Peterson and Knapp (1993) suggest that cooperative math learning can involve group sharing, debating, constructing, modifying, and strategies for problem solving. Knowledge of the developmental stages of learners is critical to the planning and implementation of appropriate math programs and curriculum materials for individuals with math disabilities. Peer tutoring and cooperative math exercises provide opportunities for math learning when the teacher's efforts might be limited by time constraints and sheer numbers of students. For example, a student having difficulty acquiring math facts might play before-school flash card drills with a proficient math student for reinforcement. Students with higher level math skills might provide tutoring and receive some type of extra credit or reward for this help. Post (1992) suggests that the role of the teacher is important in facilitating cooperative learning activities in math and one must be flexible, serve as a coordinator and collaborator, involve the students in activity selections, be patient, provide frequent opportunities for group reports, ask higher-level questions, choose groups with caution, and define success in terms of both the process and product. Finally, the constructivist approach needs to key in on specific developmental learning characteristics. As an example, the middle school child has a unique learning style requiring that important math language-communication connection be reinforced.

Let's Not Forget the Middle School Child

Farrell (1994) emphasizes the importance of providing many opportunities to middle school students which allow for the communication of math ideas. Farrell points out that the communication process at this level requires students to reach agreement about the meanings of math vocabulary terms; to recognize the importance of related terminology; to be able to defend one's math ideas orally and in writing; to anchor math concepts with related vocabulary; and to discuss connections between said concepts and symbols.

Assessment

Resource room teachers typically are given achievement test scores and insufficient error pattern information which impedes successful diagnosis and program planning for each individual learner (Thomas, 1985). Evaluation of the learning problems of students with LD is frequently limited to an intelligence test, comprehensive reading test, and a relatively quick measure of achievement (Bateman, 1992). Teachers must have information regarding a general math skills assessment, specific skills assessment, problem-solving assessment, and math attitude (Mercer, 1991) in order to effectively evaluate and service the learning needs of students.

Consideration of NCTM Standards

The NCTM (National Council of Teachers of Mathematics) (1989) lists 5 general goals for all students . . . "(1) that they learn to value mathematics, (2) that they become confident in their ability to do mathematics, (3) that they become mathematical problem solvers, (4) that they learn to communicate mathematically, and (5) that they learn to reason mathematically" (NCTM, 1989, p. 5). It would be critical for teachers to assess student performance in all of five areas. The NCTM has provided these standards for all teachers of mathematics to implement during the decade of the 90's in order to raise the math proficiency level of the students we serve. These standards need careful consideration when selecting assessment instruments in math and subsequent remedial and non-remedial materials.

Well-Rounded Math Assessments—
Formal/Informal Measures

It would be important to assess several areas important to math success in the classroom when determining the math competence of individuals with dyslexia. The practitioner must be able to analyze the student's factual knowledge, ability to perform the basic operations, ability to apply the basic operations when problem solving, and ability to apply mathematics knowledge to life situations. Formal and informal assessments can be used by the classroom teacher which relate to the curriculum in use. Particularly helpful would be informal criterion-referenced inventories which are based on the scope-and-sequence of skills covered within the classroom texts, basals, or programs. Teachers can use such inventories in developing objectives checklists which can assist in lesson planning. Survey tests found in many math texts are particulary useful when identifying specific math strengths and weaknesses related to specific math curricula.

There are a myriad of invented and faulty algorithms displayed by individuals with math disabilities stemming from their different conceptualizations and interpretations of their mathematical experiences (Ashlock, 1994; Baroody, 1984; Cox,

1975a). Therefore, they tend to process such experiences in different ways. It would be critical to analyze such errors for remedial purposes. Error pattern analysis is considered to be one of the most important tools for diagnosing and remediating math disabilities (Ackerman, Anhalt, Dykman, 1986; Borasi, 1987; Nesher, 1987; Cox, 1975a; White, 1995).

Error Pattern Analysis

Earlier Studies of Error-Pattern Analysis

Error pattern analysis was utilized by Myers in 1924 and Brueckner and Elwell in 1932 as a reliable diagnostic tool. Grossnickle (1935) discussed two mathematics error types, constant errors (recurring incorrect responses related to specific number combinations) and careless errors. Roberts (1968) as cited by Cox (1975a,b) refined and expanded Grossnickle's work to four categories: (1) use of wrong operations, (2) computational errors, (3) defective algorithms or procedures, and (4) random errors. Since these initial works, several error pattern classification types have been offered (Cox, 1975a, 1975b).

Error Pattern Analysis—An Efficient Diagnostic Tool

Error pattern analysis is considered "the most efficient tool for diagnosing [mathematics] learning difficulties (Nunes, 1991, p. 26) and as such provides constructive remedial directions (Ackerman, Anhalt, & Dykman, 1986; Borasi, 1987; Humphery, 1981; McEntire, 1981). There are various error pattern classification systems. Tatsuoka (1984) points to some two hundred "erroneous rules of operation" (p. 120) relating to faulty math algorithms. It would be prudent for the special educator to designate an error pattern system which closely coincides with the school curriculum and the needs of the children served. Error pattern analysis can become very detailed and irrelevant to the practitioner if applications are not readily made in remedial programming.

Error Patterns Experienced by Children with Learning Disabilities

Bley and Thornton (1989) and others have found that students with dyslexia and other learning disabilities may experience problems in writing numbers, recognizing number patterns, understanding the concepts of greater than and less than, and understanding the language of math. Enright (1983) has identified seven error patterns which frequently emerge with students who have learning problems in math: regrouping, process substitution, omission, directionality, placement, attention to sign, and guessing. Samples of each error pattern can be seen in the following examples:

1. Regrouping Errors:

$$
\begin{array}{r}
880 \\
-\,229 \\
\hline
660
\end{array}
$$

The student failed to regroup the tens and ones columns. The improper use of 0's is frequently seen in students with math problems.

2. Process Substitution Errors:

$$\begin{array}{r} 134 \\ \times\ 12 \\ \hline 268 \end{array}$$

The student failed to complete the process by multiplying the 1 times 134 for the second step. This type of error could involve omitting steps or substituting incorrect steps or algorithms.

3. Omissions:

$$\begin{array}{r} 21 \\ 6\ \overline{|1206} \end{array}$$

The student failed to add a 0 in the quotient. Omissions include leaving out parts of answers or a step in completing a problem.

4. Directional Errors:

$$\begin{array}{r} 129 \\ +\ 678 \\ \hline 7917 \end{array}$$

The student completed the problem from left to right instead of right to left. Directional errors involve the wrong direction or order when problem solving.

5. Placement Errors:

$$\begin{array}{r} 35 \\ +\ 17 \\ \hline 412 \end{array}$$

The student doesn't regroup the ones into tens.

6. Attention to Sign:

$$\begin{array}{r} 9 \\ \times\ 3 \\ \hline 12 \end{array}$$

The student used the wrong operation and did not follow the multiplication sign. Sign errors involve calculating an incorrect answer because the correct sign was not used.

7. Guessing:

$$2 + 4 + 5 = 1000$$

The student randomly gave an answer. This kind of error is merely a wild guess, in which the reasonableness of the answer is overlooked.

Error analyses can be done formally (i.e., testing) or informally by using the student's work (see Figure 8-2, p. 207). However there are times when, . . . "it is necessary to conduct a more formal diagnosis using tests . . . in aiding the teacher in assisting pupils to overcome their handicaps" (D'Augustine & Smith, 1992, p. 21).

Error analysis can be conducted on the student's finished product to determine the source of confusion.

$$\begin{array}{r} \$\ 2.74 \\ -\ 1.37 \\ \hline \$\ 1.47 \end{array}$$

$$\begin{array}{r} 2\ \text{ft.}\ 7\ \text{in} \\ +\ 1\ \text{ft.}\ 8\ \text{in} \\ \hline 4\ \text{ft.}\ 5\ \text{in} \end{array}$$

Child A has forgotten that in borrowing from the tens column, the 7 is changed to a 6.

Child B is applying a base-ten addition algorithm to measurement units based on 12.

Sometimes error analysis requires direct observation of the learning event itself as when the error pattern is not apparent.

9:40

Only by observation will the teacher learn that child C begins counting by fives from zero point at the top of the clock.

FIGURE 8-2   Error Analysis

Focusing Remedial Efforts After Testing

Cruikshank and Sheffield (1992) list observations, questioning, performance-based assessments, diagnostic interviews, teacher-designed tests, writing activities and group problem solving as important to the diagnostic process. Remedial efforts need to focus on:

a. task-analyzing the skills necessary to performing a particular math problem
b. providing concrete representations to provide a conceptual base
c. applying sound principles of learning and behavior management
d. considering the individual's math strengths and weaknesses with work on both
e. assessing ongoing math proficiency for program planning
f. relating math to everyday life situations
g. building self-esteem and confidence in math
h. providing high-interest challenging problems of the day in order to stimulate problem solving abilities
i. providing many opportunities for problem solving frequently re-working and re-wording the problems
j. building math vocabulary through reading and other content area subjects
k. providing immediate feedback and reinforcement procedures
l. analyzing errors on math work

m. varying teaching approaches, instructional materials and teaching assists

n. continually monitoring student progress

o. continually reviewing previous work

Validation of such data through the diagnostic teaching process would provide a high measure of concurrent validity which is a critical first-step to elevating math proficiency levels in the students we serve. This diagnostic process is a first step to fine-tuning our professional evaluative math procedures so that instruction is relevant, interesting, inclusive and research-based.

Remediation

Reliance on Teacher Input

Teachers are also recognized as the major source of information about student performance (Sharpley & Edgar, 1986) with Gresham, Rechly, and Carey (1987) citing teacher estimates of student performances as valid measures of psychoeducational test scores. It is critical that teachers conduct error analyses of student work in order to provide optimal intervention. This would include immediate and positive feedback regarding areas of strength and areas of math deficiencies. These points would necessarily lead to the implementation of diagnostic teaching within the math classroom setting. Many children with math disabilities encounter difficulties related to comprehending text (Troutman & Lichtenberg 1987) and specific problems with computation, number concepts, and problem solving (Novick & Arnold 1988). This pattern is due in large part to the technical and unfamiliar math vocabulary encountered. Culture and gender issues need to be addressed as part of this process.

Culture and Gender Issues

Stanley and Spafford (1995) and Spafford and Stanley (1995) analyzed the results of 1200 achievement tests of urban eighth-grade students who ranged in age from 12.17 to 17.08 with a mean age of 14.19. Significant differences were observed between minority and non-minority groups in terms of mathematics grade equivalent scores, national percentile rankings, and normal curve equivalent scores. Additionally, negligible gender differences in mathematics proficiency were found in the population studied, which was contrary to the more common finding that males exceed females in math performance. Stanley and Spafford (1995) and Spafford and Stanley (1995) suggest that mathematics language as a highly "specialized literacy form" must be merged with the "cultural literacy" of the learner. Cultural integration of the learner's values, beliefs, ethnic heritage, and so on should be done in such a way so as to empower the math learner. Dagostino and Carifio (1994) suggest that using the native language of a student as a standard in conjunction with cultural information are important components to mathematics instructional planning efforts. In regard to gender, a "gender-fair" classroom environment requires the teacher to consciously provide equal time and opportunities for males and females to interact and respond to questions. In all cases, the classroom teacher needs to promote and nurture math learning for all students that will impact occupational and life situations.

The Language of Math

Math terminology is not easily understood as it does not appear in a conversational context nor in most other subject area text books or library readings (with the exception of counting numbers). Mathematics skills acquisition is unique in that the language of math is typically removed from conversational and reading contexts (Spafford, 1994 submission). Rittner (1982) emphasizes how problems in language can seriously impact math learning. Certainly the language problems of dyslexics could impact math performance but this is not always the case. Many math programs heavily emphasize computation proficiency allowing dyslexics to excel in minimal language-cue types of environments.

Teaching Mathematical Vocabulary Comprehension

Cangelosi (1992) suggests that math communication involves the use of general, special, and technical vocabulary terms. The special-usage and technical-usage terms present special learning problems and Cangelosi suggests identifying and presenting these terms before using them in problem-solving situations. General-usage terms consist of math vocabulary generally known to everyone (e.g., red, circle, add, and so on). Special-usage terms involve words and symbols whose meaning can change depending on the context used in (e.g., power, union, remainder, associate, and so on). Technical-usage terms involve words and symbols that have meaning only in mathematics (e.g., quadrilateral, sine, and vector space). The examples in Figures 8-3; 8-4A,B show several ways to develop important math vocabulary knowledge.

Teachers also need to spend time with math symbols, an important part of mathematics vocabulary. The presentation of symbols and formulas can be teacher-directed or a cooperative interactive investigative format can be used. Math applications depend not only mastering math vocabulary, but also on estimating the reasonableness of an answer.

Developmentally Appropriate Practices

Concrete Curriculum Materials Should Precede Abstract Learning

Math materials should be first presented on a concrete level if at all possible. Many researchers believe that math concepts should be developmentally presented, and

Note Cards can be used to collect and practice the relevant terms in a particular area of math. Students are instructed to:

1. Put the term on the front of the card.

2. Put an example on the back.

3. Write a definition on the back to help you remember what the term means.

4. Practice working front to back and back to front.

Fractions
(Student Responses On Reverse Side of Note Cards)

like fractions	$\dfrac{1}{4} + \dfrac{2}{4} = \dfrac{3}{4}$
lowest terms	$\dfrac{3}{6} = \dfrac{1}{2}$
improper fraction	$\dfrac{16}{9}$

FIGURE 8-3   Math Vocabulary

Using toothpick models, students investigate various configurations and try to develop a formula to calculate the total number of toothpicks in any given pattern.

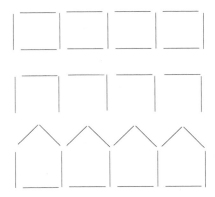

A variety of formulas and explanations should be generated. Through discussion and demonstration students should determine the preferred formula.

Students discuss known formulas for their utility:

$$D = R \times T \qquad A = 1/2\ BH$$

$$C = \pi d \qquad A = \pi r^2$$

FIGURE 8-4A   Fostering Mathematical Discourse

FIGURE 8-4B Spending Time with Symbols

The symbols used in algebra require thorough introduction and understanding in order to serve as a working foundation for higher level skills.

For example:

Parentheses tell us that everything inside is to be treated like one number. The parentheses below show how to begin with working parenthetical terms first.

$8 + (4 \times 3) = 8 + 12$

$(7 - 4) + 6 = 3 + 6$

$8 + (x + x) = 8 + 2x$

$(3y - y) + 4 = 2y + 4$

$(3x)^3 = 3x \cdot 3x \cdot 3x$

Incremental practice with much review may be needed to set this vital foundation.

Instruction should be arranged so that experiences are provided at the Concrete, Graphic, and then Symbolic levels as students indicate readiness.

Concrete Level	***Example***	
Students use real objects to represent concepts 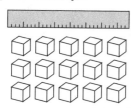	$3 \times 5 = 15$ $5 \times 3 = 15$ $15 \div 5 = 3$ $15 \div 3 = 5$	Students work with small cubes and a ruler to practice combinations of multiplication and division using arrays.
Graphic Level Students use pictures of objects or graphics to represent concepts. Name Date 	$4 \times 8 = 32$ $8 \times 4 = 32$ $20 \div 4 = 5$ $20 \div 5 = 4$	Students draw arrays or work from drawings to illustrate multiplication and division.
Symbolic level Students work from symbols alone to represent concepts. $8 \times \underline{} = 32$	$4 \times 8 = 32$ $8 \times 4 = 32$ $32 \div 8 = 4$ $32 \div 4 = 8$	

FIGURE 8-5 Developmental Sequence of Activities

It is important to understand the complex cognitive demands made on beginning learners in something as simple as acquiring counting skills. The coordination of visual, auditory, language, motor, and conceptual processes is required:

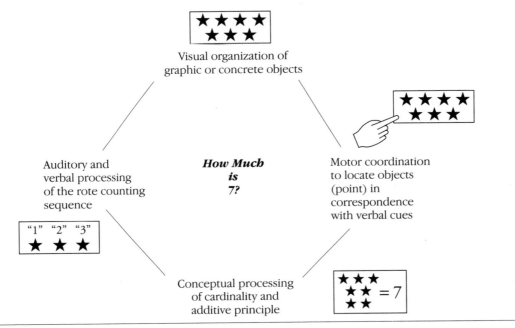

FIGURE 8-6   Demonstrating One-To-One Correspondence

initially with concrete math manipulatives. Pictorial representations are then introduced with purely abstract modes presented last (Baroody, 1991; Mercer & Mercer, 1989, 1991). For example, if one is teaching classification or sorting skills, students should be given math manipulatives (e.g., M&M candies; Pattern Blocks) to classify or sort by attributes (i.e., by shape, color). Pictures of objects could then be given for students to abstract common qualities or characteristics. Finally, students could be asked to give examples of categories which could be used to classify certain objects (with the objects not present). It is especially important to teach students with math disabilities strategies for estimating the reasonableness of an answer. Whenever possible, concrete manipulative materials should be utilized so that conceptualizations of math material can assist in making those important abstractions so often required in mathematics both at the elementary and secondary levels (see Figures 8-5, 8-6).

Secondary Level Topics Need Special Consideration

A major topic of remedial focus at the secondary level needs to be the study of fractions. "Perceptual and language requirements for learning fractions may prove troublesome to many learning-disabled children" (Myers & Hammill, 1990, p. 318).

Bley and Thornton (1989) recommend a scope-and-sequence of activities for teaching fractions: (1) reading, writing, and interpreting fractional numbers and concepts (especially emphasizing vocabulary knowledge of key terms); (2) copying fraction problems from the board, text, and so on; (3) using the ruler as a number-line assist; (4) using fraction number lines; (5) understanding improper fractions and mixed numbers; (6) using equivalent fractions; (7) reducing fractions; (8) finding the least common demoninator (LCD) and then adding/subtracting fractions with unlike denominators; (9) borrowing or regrouping in subtraction problems; (10) multiplying proper and then improper fractions; and (11) dividing fractions.

Remedial mathematics class projects will "enable students to apply their skills in a variety of interesting and motivating ways" (Posamentier & Stepelman, 1990, p. 101). Having students select their own topics (especially at the secondary level) allows students to construct knowledge, plan long-range activities as a group, acquire math knowledge and skills, and relate math knowledge across the curriculum. At the secondary level, Posamentier and Stepelman (1990) offer some appropriate topics for students with math problems: the abacus, angles, the calendar, computers, the history of mathematics, magic squares, the Mobius strip, parabolas, prime numbers, and square roots. For younger students, topics could include: the number line, important people in math, math patterns, how the Egyptians wrote numbers, number tricks, and so on.

Math Manipulatives

Math manipulatives (see Table 8-2, below) have been found to be effective with students with dyslexia and other disabilities as long as they are meaningful to the student and can tie in important math concepts to be learned (Dunlap & Brennan, 1979). Some of the more common math manipulatives used are

> **Attribute Blocks**—These are sets of blocks or objects (e.g., animals) which have different characteristics (e.g., as in color, size, texture, shape, and thick-

TABLE 8-2 Math Manipulative Tools

Abacus	Factor Cards	Number Trays
Arrays (Egg Carton)	Flash Cards	Place-Value Charts
Balance Scales	Fraction Kits	Probability Spinners
Base Ten Blocks	Fraction Pieces	Roman Numeral Cards
Blocks (Legos)	Geo Boards	Rounding Verifiers
Charts (Facts)	Graph Paper	Show-Me-the-Answer Cards (Group Activity)
Checkers	Holey Cards	
Chips	Interlocking Blocks	Sorting Devices or Attribute Devices (Blocks, Animals)
Clothespins	Number Lines	
Counters (Macaroni, Beads)	Number Rods	Tangrams
Decimal Cards		Toy or Play Money

ness). Students can use these attribute blocks and objects when learning about such math concepts as 1 to 1 correspondence (one number per object), classification (e.g., by color or shape), and seriation (placing things in order).

Cuisenaire Rods—These are sets of 10 colored rods which range in length from 1 to 10 centimeters and are 1 centimeter in width. The rods 1 cubic centimeter in cross-section are: white (1 centimeter); red (2 centimeters), light green (3 centimeters), purple (4 centimeters), yellow (5 centimeters), dark green (6 centimeters), black (7 centimeters), brown (8 centimeters), blue (9 centimeters), and orange (10 centimeters). Cuisenaire rods can be used to help children master sorting and classification concepts, patterning, developing numeration and number sense, fraction concepts (e.g., finding the least common multiple), and place value.

Base Ten Blocks—These are metric blocks that are different sizes. The largest block is made up of 10 flat blocks. A flat block is made of 10 long blocks (longs) and a long is made up of 10 units.

Geoboards—Geoboards are wooden or plastic squares which are covered with pegs or nails at regular intervals. Rubber bands or cloth bands are stretched in order to form geometric shapes (e.g., squares for younger children; congruent nonconvex decagons for older students).

Number Line—The number line can be considered a math manipulative and be used with older students to help master and visualize such math activities as the addition and subtraction processes of rational numbers. Rewriting the number line in "terms of fractional parts" will allow students to locate fractional distances when confronted with fractions problems (Sgroi & Sgroi, 1993, p. 244).

Homemade Counting Objects—Teachers and parents can be resourceful and use manipulatives right out of the kitchen! Noodles, shells, buttons (careful with young children), and star cookies, can be used when teaching children how to count, sort, and so on. Using these concrete materials can reinforce rote counting skills before rational number concepts are more fully developed. That is, rational counting involves knowledge of "number sense" or "numeration" so that children understand that numbers represent quantity regardless of size, shape, color, and spacing.

The use of manipulatives would also assist secondary level students. The aforementioned materials could be adapted and used to reinforce important math concepts at all levels. Figure 8-7 (p. 215) illustrates manipulatives used at the secondary level. The question now arises, "Should students with math disabilities have to learn math facts by rote?"

Rote Drill and Practice

Math facts should be memorized *if at all possible*. The mastery of basic math facts is a prerequisite for performing all operations. If students lack knowledge of basic facts or the automaticity required for classroom success, specific assists can be

Older students can benefit just as well from using concrete materials to demonstrate concepts:

 Calculating the surface area of solids can involve students in "breaking down" soap boxes, cereal boxes, etc. to determine surface area on a flat plane.

 The area of a circle can be illustrated by seeing its relationship to a square. Have students fit cut-out circles into their corresponding squares and discuss the constant nature of the relationship. Move to the diagramatical concept of $A = \pi r^2$

 Concepts of exponential notation can be initiated with methods of square and cubic forms.

FIGURE 8-7 Manipulatives In Higher Math

One technique for quick assessment in the classroom or with individual students is the one-minute probe. Without over-emphasizing speed, teachers ask students to complete as much as they can of a particular skill within a timed one-minute interval. Daily or weekly comparisons on progress are useful guides to instruction. Students can record their own growth as well.

At the elementary level:

6	9	8	9	6
+1	+6	+4	+2	+8
4	8	2	6	9
+8	+2	+7	+5	+3
6	7	5	6	7
+6	+4	+2	+8	+7

At higher levels: $26.6 \overline{)84.2369}$

Students work for one-minute. **All** correct digits generated in the problem are counted in a correct "score."

FIGURE 8-8 The Mad Minute

used. Math charts, number lines, and calculators can provide the reinforcement a student with math disabilities may need. The use of these assists should be accompanied by continued reinforcement and work on deficient facts while instruction continues in the areas of problem-solving heuristics, concepts, and specific algorithms. The answer to the question is, "Yes, students with math disabilities should try to memorize basic math facts." "The Mad Minute" (see Figure 8-8, p. 215) is one way to make rote learning fun.

Automaticity in facts recall allows students to focus more on the algorithms and problem-solving efforts. However, some students may never master their math facts and unreasonable stress on fact mastery can be counterproductive. It has been reported that many mathematics applications in real life depend more on estimated answers as opposed to exact counting skills or computations. Some rote drill and practice ideas are illustrated in Figure 8-9 (see below).

Teaching Estimation Strategies

Math reasoning requires students to ask the question, "Does my answer make sense?" The discussion sequence in Table 8-3 could be modeled in developing important math reasoning sense when teaching estimation strategies (see p. 217).

The repetitious practice of certain facts and skills may be the only way for some students to acquire the fluency required for higher order applications. Finding new and novel approaches to the "same old stuff: requires multiple variations using manipulatives and verbal or written responses."

Addition and Subtraction Facts:

Number Families: Students write the four number facts on the back that correspond with each number family. Families can be grouped according to common sums.

Using beans and green paper lily pads, students drop the "frogs" on the pad. They write number stories to show addition and subtraction combinations.

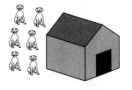

Using ten to twenty markers as "puppies," students collect random amounts under a cardboard box. Number facts are used to describe the puppies inside and outside the box.

Tossing dice, students can fill out a probability chart showing the number of times various combinations occur.

FIGURE 8-9   Rote Drill and Practice

TABLE 8-3   Math Reasoning

Does My Answer Make Sense?

Students discuss possible operations to correspond with a word problem. If eight children are sharing a package of 32 cookies, how many cookies will each child get?

Will it make sense to A D D the numbers?
32 + 8 =
Why not?

Will it make sense to S U B S T R A C T the numbers?
32 – 8 =
Why not?

Will it make sense to M U L T I P L Y the numbers?
32 × 8 =
Why not?

Why does D I V I D I N G the numbers make sense?
32 ÷ 8 =

Certainly an easy estimation strategy would be to round up or down and "guestimate" an answer. The focus should be on good "ball park" answers as opposed to exactness. For example, when teaching students how to compute a 5% sales tax, one could estimate a reasonable answer by figuring 5 cents to a dollar for money spent to the nearest dollar. Reyes (1986) has also suggested more sophisticated strategies be taught even to young students. Some of these include the front-end approach, clustering, and compatible numbers.

Front-End Approach

This estimation strategy focuses on the front-end or leftmost digits as these are the most significant to the problem. Then adjustments are made to the remaining digits with the "amount of adjustment encouraged . . . [dependent] on the level of the student" (Post, 1992, p. 293). Example: George purchased a physiology dictionary for $9.95, a pen for $2.95 and a computer disk for $2.50. How much did he spend? The front-end approach would estimate $13.00 based on the leftmost digits. Adjustments could focus on rounding the rest of the change to the nearest dollar—.95 to 1.00 and .50 to 1.00. These roundoffs add up to $3.00. Now, add the $3.00 to our previously found $13.00. A reasonable estimated answer would be $16.00. We're in the ballpark.

Clustering Strategy

A clustering strategy can be used with certain problems which contain numbers which tend to cluster or hover around a certain range of numbers. Clustering would involve eyeballing the average of the group and then performing the appropriate operation. Example: Attendance at a large regional fair, The Big E, for each of six days was 50,000, 45,000, 53,000, 58,000, 52,000, and 51,000. Scores tend to cluster in the 50,000 range. One could multiply 50,000 times 6 and divide by 6 (average = 50,000) for an estimated average attendance.

Compatible Numbers

This is an advanced type of rounding strategy. Compatible numbers are identified and manipulated by rounding. For example: 19 + 86 + 18 + 89 =? One could round 19 and 18 to 20, and 86 and 89 to 90, and figure 20 + 20 + 90 + 90 = 220 for an estimated answer.

It is certainly critical that all students including those with learning disabilities have opportunities to learn mathematics from rote factual knowledge, through conceptual formation, to the fine-tuning demanded by algorithms. Estimation skills allow one to examine the reasonableness of answers so that errors can be immediately corrected. The complexity of our technological society demands math proficiency at a rather sophisticated level to include strategies involved in problem-solving. Remedial efforts would necessarily focus heavily on problem solving efforts.

Problem Solving

Developing Problem Solving Strategies

Students with math disabilities must not only learn problem-solving strategies but strategies which focus on taking notes from class presentations, using the library, using reference books, using visual aids, writing research papers, taking tests, and managing time (Strichart & Mangrum, 1993). The National Council of Supervisors of Mathematics (1989) recommends that good math instruction place more emphasis on problem-solving and technology as opposed to paper-and-pencil computation tasks (see Figure 8-10, pp. 220–224).

Polya's Model

Polya (1945) devised a simple but strategically sound problem-solving method students can use and at all levels. One need only to follow Polya's four steps: (1) Understand the problem—Emphasize that students must clarify ambigous language by using a dictionary, talking out the problem, asking for help, and so on. Students must be able to restate the problem by listing what is known and what is unknown. Figures, graphs, charts, and lists might be helpful. (2) Devise a plan—Students must be able to determine appropriate operations to use in problem-solving, steps to follow, and estimation checks. Students need to learn that they are hypothesis testing and need to confirm or disconfirm their "hunches." (3) Carry out the plan—Students should follow a step-by-step approach so that accuracy checks can be made along the way. Estimation strategies are essential and time savers. Students must be able to confirm or disconfirm hypotheses as well as be able to devise new plans and strategies. (4) Look back—Students need to be able to look at a math answer and then determine the reasonableness of that answer. Is the answer in a form that can be used?

SQRQCQ is a more sophisticated problem-solving approach which has provided students with "an effective way to approach two of the most important requirements they face in school: reading textbooks and solving math word problems" (Strichart & Mangrum, 1993, p.72).

SQRQCQ

SQRQCQ was developed by Leo Fay (Forgan & Mangrum, 1989) and involves six steps of (1) *S*urvey, (2) *Q*uestion, (3) *R*ead, (4) *Q*uestion, (5) *C*ompute, and (6) *Q*uestion. Students must carefully survey word problems for an understanding of the language and what the problem is looking for. Questioning at every step provides time for self-reflection, assessment, and re-thinking new strategies. The final question must reflect on the answer at hand—does it make sense and is it reasonable?

Enright's Problem-Solving Model

The authors offer a mnemonic (RODEO) (see Table 8-4, below) to help students remember a five-step problem-solving model identified by Enright (1992). Enright (1992) offers a five-step problem-solving model which clearly and succinctly provides a how-to step-by-step format for the student with disabilities when problem solving. With assistance wherever needed, students must 1) *r*ead and *u*nderstand the problem, (2) *o*rganize the information, (3) *d*evelop a plan of action, (4) *e*agerly compute the answer, and (5) *o*nce finished, evaluate the answer.

"Students with LD (learning disabilities) should be given opportunities to explore a variety of strategies to assist them in learning how to solve problems. Some might learn best through the discovery approach, others might profit more through peer tutoring, and others might find teacher-directed instruction more efficient" (Smith & Rivera, 1991, p. 348). Holistic scoring of math problem-solving ability can be used to assess effective strategy implementation (see Table 8-5, p. 225).

TABLE 8-4   Enright's Rodeo

R = Read and Understand

O = Organize

D = Develop Plan

E = Eagerly Compute

O = Once Done, Check

Ten More Assists in Problem Solving

Mnemonic—*T* (Tally) *E* (Estimate) *N* (Number Line) *M* (Manipulatives—Use and Act with) *O* (Over Simplify) *R* (3 R's) (Reorganize, Remove Excess, Reinterpret) *E* (Easily Separate the Parts) and Always Guess and Test if you don't know.

Important: Label As Much Information as Possible—Encourage Students to Communicate Mathematically!!!

1. Tally and Solve (T)

   Skills Covered: Organization and tabulating data, categorizing information, counting up, reasoning, patterns and functions, and problem solving.

   Problem: Students are given 3 coupons for every year of perfect attendance to Abdow's Restaurant. If a sixth grader had perfect attendance except in Grade 4, how many coupons did she/he receive at the end of sixth grade?

   Solution: Set up a table and tally.

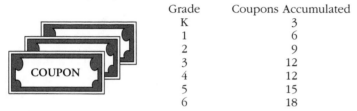

Grade	Coupons Accumulated
K	3
1	6
2	9
3	12
4	12
5	15
6	18

   Answer: 18 coupons for Abdow's Restaurant

2. Estimate Based on Prior Experience and Background Knowledge (E)

   Skills Covered: Communicating mathematically, number sense, reasoning, estimation, determining relevant versus irrelevant information (e.g., the size of the items versus the color), and problem solving.

   Problem: Students must estimate the number of items in an estimation jar which is kept in the classroom. Items (e.g., coins, paper clips, candy, toothpicks, pencils, plastic bears, marbles, and so on) will change every month. Students can collaborate to *come up with quantity estimates or work independently*.

3. Use a Number Line (N)

   Skills Covered: Sequencing, logic, making a visual representation of a problem, patterns and functions, problem solving.

   Problem: There are 5 vehicles parked in the first aisle at Valleys C's. Rita's black car is in front of Ed's yellow car which is behind Eileen's white car. Eileen's white car is in front of Sr. Mary's red truck. The yellow car is in front of the red truck. Caitlyn's blue mini-bus is in front of Rita's *black car. What is the order of the vehicles?*

   Solution: Use a number line.

   Number Line

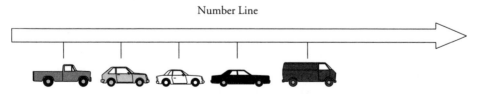

   Answer: First—the blue mini-bus, the black car, the white car, the yellow car, and then the red truck.

FIGURE 8-10 Helping Students with Disabilities to Problem Solve

4. Use and Act Out with Math Manipulatives (M)

Part I: Use a Math Manipulative

Skills Covered: Using math manipulatives, forming hypotheses, reasoning, verifying hypotheses, estimating reasonable answers, and problem solving.

Problem: Jose walked 1 block east from his home and then walked 2 blocks north. He then walked 1 block south to see Michele and Danielle. What is his shortest route home?

Solution: Use a geoboard or draw a geoboard to map out the problem.

Geoboard

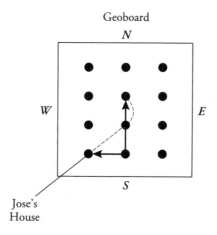

Jose's
House

Answer: 1 block heading SW (southwest)

Part II: Act Out with a Math Manipulative
Place 10 play dollars on your desk. Replace every other dollar with a quarter. Replace the 5th dollar with a dime. How much money is on the table now?

Solution: Actually act out the problem and replace the money.

Using Play Money

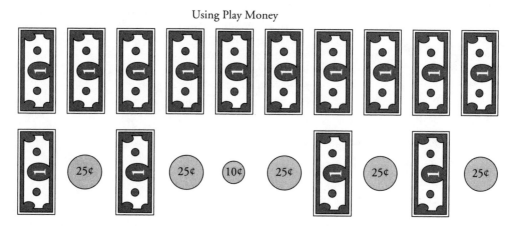

Then Tally: $1.00 × 4 = $4.00
              $.25 × 5 = $1.25
              .10 × 1 = $ .10
Total $5.35

Answer: There is now $5.35 on the table.

FIGURE 8-10 *Continued*

5. Oversimplify or Reduce Problem to an Easier Problem (O)

Skills Covered: Using a table to summarize information, restating information in another format, reasoning, patterns and functions, problem solving.

Problem: Sidney has a sore throat and has to take medicine every 4 hours. She started taking her medicine at 9:00 A.M. She is suppose to take 4 doses by the end of the day. Will Sidney have taken what she needs for medicine for the day by 9:00 p.m. bedtime?

Solution: Create a time table

Time	Dose
9:00 a.m.	1
1:00 p.m.	2
5:00 p.m.	3
9:00 p.m.	4

Answer: Yes

6. Reorganize the Information (R)

Skills Covered: Analyzing and synthesizing information, sequencing, reasoning, patterns and functions, using tables to summarize data, problem solving.

Problem: Richard and Kenny emptied out their coin jar. They counted out 5 quarters, 2 dimes, 10 pennies, 6 nickels, 4 half-dollars, 2 quarters, 3 nickels, 11 pennies, 2 dimes, and finally 3 quarters. How much money did they have?

Solution: Set up a table and total columns to solve.

	Half-Dollars	Quarters	Dimes	Nickels	Pennies
	4	5	2	6	10
		2	2	3	11
		3			
Totals	4	10	4	9	21

Tabulate:
$.50 × 4 = $2.00 in half-dollars
$.25 × 10 = $2.50 in quarters
$.10 × 4 = $ .40 in dimes
$.05 × 9 = $ .45 in nickels
$.01 × 21 = $ .21 in pennies
$5.56 Answer/Total Amount of Money in Jar

7. Remove Excess Information (R)

Skills Covered: Using the language of math, communicating mathematically, sorting irrelevant from relevant data, reasoning, analyzing and synthesizing information, problem solving.

Problem: Mary read the Big Y shopping circular which offered dog food at a special sale price of 3 cans for $1.00 instead of the usual $.45 per can. Thanksgiving greeting cards were reduced 20%, and school supplies by 10%. There was also a 2 for 1 sale on bacon, eggs, and Big Y bread. Mary decided to buy her dog Bobbins 24 cans of dog food so as to save as much money as she could that week. How much money did Mary save by buying Bobbin's dog food on sale at the Big Y ?

Solution: Find information to answer the question and write that down first. Label all information!!!!

FIGURE 8-10 *Continued*

Dog Food—Regular Price: $.45 per can
Sale Price: 3 cans for $1.00
Purchased: 24 cans of dog food

Solve: 24 × $.45 = $10.80 Regular Price for 24 cans
24 divided by 3 = 8; 8 X $1.00 = $8.00 Sale Price for 24 cans
$10.80 (regular price) - $8.00 (sale price) = $2.80 savings

8. Reinterpret the Language of the Problem or Simplify the Language (R)

Skills Covered: Using the language of math, communicating mathematically, analyzing and synthesizing information, reasoning, problem solving.

Problem: Grandma has 15 grandchildren. Her friend Edna has 7 grandchildren and her friend Jorge has 3 grandchildren. How many MORE grandchildren does Grandma have than Edna and Jorge put together?

Solution: Students can make a visual presentation of the information by showing a one-to-one correspondence. Note that the term "more" frequently signals one "to add." The language of this problem can be confusing. A visual picture can help clarify the solution. The teacher can point out that when making a comparison between two things or people, you can be looking at how they DIFFER.

Grandma's Grandchildren

Edna's Grandchildren   Jorge's Grandchildren

Set-Up the Equation After Looking at the Visual

We can add Edna's number of grandchildren (7) to Jorge's number of grandchildren (3) for a total of 10. Then subtract 10 from Grandma's number of grandchildren or 15–10 = 5 for the answer.

Answer: Grandma has 5 more grandchildren that Dottie and Jorge.

9. Easily Separate Problem into Manageable Parts and Solve Each Part Separately (E)

Skills Covered: Communicating mathematically, organizing information, analyzing and synthesizing information, reasoning, and problem solving.

Problem: Padre, Lizvette, Erica, and Andrew bought 6 cans of tunafish for $1.29 per can; 6 cartons of milk which cost $.60 each; 2 apple pies for a total of $1.99; and 3 loaves of bread at a cost of $1.49 each. How much change did they receive from a $20.00 bill?

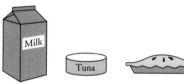

Solution:

Determine the total cost for each food item:

tunafish = 6 × $1.29 = $7.74   apple pies = $1.99 (remember that total was given)
milk = 6 × $.60 = $3.60   bread = $1.49 × 3 = $ 4.47

Total food items = $7.74 + $3.60 + $1.99 + 4.47 = $17.80
Change from $20.00 = $20.00 – $17.80 = $2.20.

FIGURE 8-10 *Continued*

10. Guess and Test

Skills Covered: Estimation, logic, communicating mathematically, reasoning, formulating and verifying hypotheses, and problem solving.

Problem: What 2 numbers could I be thinking of? They are different and both add up to 21. Each number is greater than 7 but less than 15. The difference between both numbers is greater than 3. What are my two secret numbers?

Solution: List numbers greater than 7 but less than 15

8, 9, 10, 11, 12, 13, 14

guess and test which of these two numbers combined can add up to 21

12 and 9; 13 and 8; 11 and 10

now look at each pair to determine which pair has a difference greater than 3

13 and 8

Answer: Your secret numbers are 13 and 8.

FIGURE 8-10 *Continued*

By Dr. Carol Spafford. *TEN MORE Assists when Problem Solving.*

Language Problems

Research has shown that students with learning disabilities have deficient word-problem solving skills (Englert, Culatta, & Horn, 1987; Montague & Bos, 1986) because of problems with syntax and vocabulary (Cawley, Fitzmaurice, Shaw, Kahn, & Bates, 1979). Math and reading both are dependent on good language skills and students "cannot be expected to solve word problems without having adequate vocabulary and comprehension skills." The overall population mean of 29.76 (SD = 23.63) on the TOMA5 (story problems) in Spafford's 1995 research would indicate that the total 8th grade population studied is deficient in math vocabulary and comprehension skills necessary for average math proficiency. This information could provide valuable insights for the regular classroom teacher since they, as adolescents with LD in particular, "require programming much different from elementary students" (Weiderholt, 1978).

Clarifying Directions

Students with dyslexia and other learning disabilities may have difficulty following multi-step problems and directions when a teacher is presenting a new skill or concept. It is incumbent upon the teacher to (1) be clear and concise about directions and procedures, (2) check for understanding of directions, and (3) continually assess progress and monitor performance. Remediation of math problems for the dyslexic or individual with math problems or disabilities requires ingenuity on the part of the teacher and an eclectic approach. Problems may have to be broken into

TABLE 8-5   Holistic Scoring Example—Problem Solving

Point Scale

0 Points
- Incorrect answers with no work shown
- No attempt to complete assignment
- Simply recopying problem or data with no work done

1 Point
- Started an algorithm or approach to the work with some understanding—However, approaches will not lead to successful completion of work
- One approach is tried that does not work and the student gives up
- The student does not achieve a subgoal

2 Points
- An appropriate problem-solving strategy is used but not completed
- The student reached a subgoal and then stopped
- A correct answer is recorded with no work shown or the work is not understandable

Point Scale

3 Points
- An appropriate problem-solving strategy is used but part of the problem was not understood or ignored
- An appropriate strategy was used but part of the problem was answered incorrectly or was mislabeled
- A correct answer is given but not labeled or labeled incorrectly
- Implementation of problem-solving strategies is confusing or unclear

4 Points
- Appropriate algorithms or strategies are implemented and the correct answer is given
- Appropriate algorithms or strategies are selected and implemented but an error is made in carrying out the problem steps—This error(s) does not reflect misinterpretations about the problem or steps to solve the problem

Charles, Lester, and O'Daffer, 1987

smaller steps or directions presented step-by-step to ensure understanding. Task analysis is one way to accomplish this end (see Figure 8-11, p. 226).

Enhancing Problem Solving Abilities

One way to build in flexible approaches to remediation is to present operation models in different ways. For example, subtraction can be presented several ways. Using different models to present problems provides the students for opportunities to (a) expand their vocabulary base in mathematics, (b) be flexible in looking at problems, and (c) consider alternatives or different ways to solve problems. Note that some of the following problems could also be solved by adding on or using the process of addition.

Take-away model: Jeanne had five pieces of gum and gave three to Betty. How many pieces of gum did Jeanne have left?

Comparative model: Miriam had seven pairs of pierced earrings and Leticia had four pairs of pierced earrings. How many more pairs of earrings did Miriam have than Leticia?

Partitive model: Dimitra had nine blue and red cars. She had five red cars. How many of Dimitra's cars were blue?

One approach to assessment and remediation in math is to break down a particular skill or set of skills into its smallest components or steps. Arranging the subskills into a hierarchy or sequence provides a format for diagnosing the specific breakdown and providing remediation. The following breakdown gives an example of task analysis applied to skills in telling time.

FIGURE 8-11 Task Analysis

Additive model: There was room for 20 books on Ms. Sullivan's bookshelf. Mr. Coleman placed five books on the shelf on Monday. How many more books can Mr. Coleman place on Ms. Sullivan's bookshelf?

Decrease model: Mamiere weighed 145 pounds but lost 40 pounds after she had a baby. How many pounds does Mamiere weigh now?

Condensing Word Problems

To ease the language demands of many word problems, teachers can condense the content for students with dyslexia and math disabilities as seen in the example in Figure 8-12 (p. 227). Eventually students are taught to condense word problems on their own.

Formatting Problems in Different Ways

Teaching problem-solving skills in math allows applications across the curriculum. "Careful selection of problems is critical to nurturing successful problem solving. Challenging students to think about mathematics can be difficult . . ." (Heddens & Speer, 1992, p. 34). Heddens and Speer suggest that teachers present problem-solving situations in such formats as follows: with pictures; without explicit reference to numbers; with manipulatives; with more than one answer; with real-life applications; with no easily identified answer; requiring the use of data collection and interpretation; requiring the use of tables, graphs, and charts; with a drawing or requiring that a drawing be made; with no solution; with insufficient information; requiring formula usage; requiring inductive thought; requiring deductive thought; and requiring that logical conclusions and inferences be made. The method in Figure 8-13 (below) is one example of presenting math problems in a unique format.

To reduce the language demands that accompany many word problems, teachers can teach their students to construct a mini-problem to identify key information.

> Every spring, the boy scouts hold a car wash to earn money for camping. With all the boys working, they can wash seven cars in one hour. If they work for five hours and earn $2.00 for each car they wash, how much money will they raise?

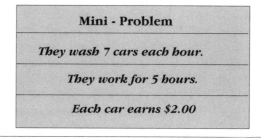

Mini - Problem
They wash 7 cars each hour.
They work for 5 hours.
Each car earns $2.00

FIGURE 8-12   Condensing Word Problems

Remove the numbers from simple word problems. First ask students to think about the operation needed to solve the numberless story. Then ask them to go back in the story and put in numbers that would make sense.

A ride on the ferris wheel costs [ ] Blain bought [ ] tickets. How much did he spend?	Tasha and her two friends have [ ] dollars. If ice cream cones cost [ ] how many cones can the girls buy?

FIGURE 8-13   Critical Thinking In Math Numberless Word Problems

Restating the Problem

Verbalizing or talking out a problem provides opportunities for insight and learning.

> **Example:** Barb told Henry and Gus that her friends, Rich and Kenny Spafford played baseball for the Sox Baseball Club. They each played for five years and had the following batting averages:
>
> Rich—.355, .379, .312, .333, and .398,
>
> Kenny—.322, .344, .323, .301, and .398.
>
> What was the average batting performance for each player?
>
> **Talking the problem out:** What is the name of each player?
>
> What is the question asking?
>
> **Average performance**—how can I figure out average performance?
>
> I can use a mean average for each player.
>
> I can add up all of the scores for each player and divide by five.

Problem-Solving Mnemonics

Mnemonic devices can be used when assisting students in learning certain procedures or algorithms. As an example, the mnemonic, FOIL, can be used when learning the procedures for multiplying two sets of variables: Example: (b + c) (d + e) = Foil; Multiply the First of each multiple (bd); then the Outer numerals (be); then the Inner numerals (cd), and then the Last numerals (ce) for bd + be + cd + ce = ?

Memorizing Steps to Problems

Students can memorize steps to an algorithm for hard-to-figure math problems. Example: $\frac{3}{4}$ divided by $\frac{1}{9}$; (1) fractions only—$\frac{3}{4}$ divided by $\frac{1}{9}$; (2) change to multiply— $\frac{3}{4}$ times . . . ; (3) flip last fraction—$\frac{3}{4}$ times $\frac{9}{1}$; (4) multiply across—$\frac{27}{4}$; (5) answer in lowest terms—$6\frac{3}{4}$.

Clumping Strategies

Clumping or clustering can be done when series of digits must be used. Students can learn to cluster digits for easy recall and improved math performance. Example: When students are learning their phone numbers, the digits can be grouped as follows:

(413)	747–	****
area code	Spfld. area	last 4 digits

Representing Math Problems Graphically

Charts, graphs, diagrams, maps, drawings, and number lines can be used to depict word problems. For example, if a student needed to compute distances between cities, maps could be used to verify answers in an estimated format. If students are to compute growth or other changes (e.g., plant growth) during science classes, graphs can be used as visual depictions.

Use of Scientific Inquiry

Allow students many opportunities to use investigative skills in mathematics where a variety of problem-solving strategies can be applied. In this way, the use of the methods of science can be enhanced. For example, ask the students to first estimate and then calculate the average height in a particular grade—this means that students must collaborate, formulate hypotheses, gather data, analyze the data, confirm or disconfirm hypotheses, and assess techniques used.

Graph Paper

Many individuals with dyslexia display spatial/orientation problems which may interfere with the computation process. Algorithms might be in place but alignment problems might cause calculation errors which result in wrong answers. Since math requires *right* not *wrong,* answers, precision is a must. The use of graph paper which allows students to record one number per box, helps eliminate alignment errors and confusion errors related to spacing. Also, helping students to organize their work on paper may require having boxes or folds to guide placement of separate problems. Using color markers to highlight columns of numbers or starting points can assist learners with spatial orientation.

Visual Imagery to Enhance Learning

Forming visual images of everyday scenes can assist math learning especially in the area of fractions.

Example: $3/4$ divided by $5 = 3/4$ multiplied by $1/5 = 3/20$

Visual Imagery: If you invited 5 individuals to a birthday party and decided to serve $3/4$ths of a 20 slice pizza from the previous evening, how many pieces could you give each person?

Patricia

Clifford

Janice

Erroll

George

Each person receives 3 pieces out of an original 20 pieces assuming ¼ of the pizza had been eaten. In other words, ¾ of the pizza divided by 5 = ³/20 of the original pizza for each person.

Certainly the frustrations experienced by students with problem solving difficulties and math language problems can lead to poor math attitudes.

Developing Positive Math Attitudes

Fostering a positive attitude toward math is critical in overcoming math problems (Lord, 1995). Students with negative attitudes about their academic failures and ability to succeed are more likely to have pessimistic expectations of future successes and are less likely to attend consistently to academic tasks (Weiner, Frieze, Kukla, Reed, Rest, & Rosenbaum, 1971; Okolo, 1992).

The classroom teacher needs to work hard on developing positive math attitudes as students with math disabilities frequently experience negative attitudes toward math. A problem of the day (e.g., What would the monthly cost be of a $9,000 car if payments were spread over three years?; or How many pennies could fit in this jar?); speed drill; math trivia (e.g., What was the cost of a house in 1979?); math bingo games on Fridays, and so on, can be utilized within a mathematics curriculum so as to foster positive feelings and attitudes toward math. The teacher can create personalized problems for students by using their names, the names of family members and pets, local addresses, favorite singers and TV personalities, and so on. "The Secret Numbers Game" is an example of a personalized number game (see Table 8-6, below). Additional motivators could include bulletin boards, math art, and games.

TABLE 8-6   Secret Numbers

Directions

The problems will be read aloud and the students will be asked to solve the problems either individually or in small groups.

1) My secret number is greater than 5. It is less than 10. It is not 6, 7, or 8. What is my secret number?

2) My secret number is the number of Kwanzaa principles and the days in a week. What is my secret number?

3) My secret number has two digits. It is less than 2 dozen. It is not 11. Both numbers are the same. What is my secret number?

4) My secret number is more than the number of feet on a puppy. It is the same as the number of your mom's toes. What is my secret number?

5) My secret number is the number of days in a school year. What is my secret number?

Source: Melanie Jennings

Bulletin Boards

Math bulletin board ideas can come from teacher magazines, students, the newspaper, books, TV, and so on. Displays of student's good math work provide reinforcement and enhance positive math attitudes. Instructional bulletin boards are especially useful in the mathematics area (see Figure 8-14 below).

Math Art

Math art activities are highly motivating and stimulating at all levels. Geometric patterns can be developed from compasses, protractors, inserts in specially made rulers, store-bought cut-outs, and geometric wheels. When designs are made (and possibly colored), instruction could then focus on the measurement of angles, segments, area, perimeter, properties of shapes, and so on. At the younger level, math art activities could include teachers creating pictures in a puzzle format with specific problems or computations to figure out. The color-by-specific-number method could be used in creating pictures.

String Math Art

String art activites could involve, for example, the use of string, copper wiring, and elastic bands. Students could create designs by connecting to numbers (younger levels) or by connecting to specific points (e.g., X1 and X2; Y1 and Y2) in forming an envelope for a parabola (for older students).

The importance of selecting appropriate curriculum materials for individuals with math disabilities cannot be overstated, as Jenkins (1992) and others have found that curriculum significantly impacts math attitude. Appropriate math cur-

It is helpful to use bulletin boards to display new concepts or areas of learning. The visual reference serves to remind students of the new skill and can be used for periodic review and practice.

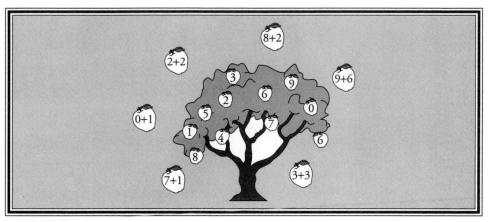

FIGURE 8-14 Instructional Bulletin Boards

riculum would be work that is within the instructional range of the learner so that new concepts can be directly linked to previous learning. Success must be built in by pacing instruction so that sufficient time is provided for practice and mastery of new concepts. Current literature recognizes the importance of the classroom teacher in developing positive attitudes toward learning. Parents can assist teachers in developing positive math attitudes and reinforce learned skills and concepts.

Games

One author is reminded of the great joy and excitement generated in her remedial math class when weekly math Bingo games occurred (see Figure 8-15).

Reducing Fractions

Students need to reduce the fraction called and match it with a Bingo fraction.

CALL = 6/8

CALL = 3/9

$\frac{1}{2}$	$\frac{2}{3}$	$\frac{3}{5}$	$\frac{1}{8}$	$\frac{2}{5}$
$\frac{3}{8}$	$\frac{3}{4}$	$\frac{1}{3}$	$\frac{1}{2}$	$\frac{1}{5}$
$\frac{1}{4}$	$\frac{2}{7}$	FREE	$\frac{3}{7}$	$\frac{1}{9}$
$\frac{2}{5}$	$\frac{2}{3}$	$\frac{1}{5}$	$\frac{1}{6}$	$\frac{2}{9}$
$\frac{1}{7}$	$\frac{3}{4}$	$\frac{4}{5}$	$\frac{5}{8}$	$\frac{2}{3}$

Equivalent Fractions

Students find fractions that are equivalent to the one called.

CALL = 1/2

CALL = 3/4

$\frac{2}{3}$	$\frac{4}{7}$	$\frac{5}{10}$	$\frac{3}{18}$	$\frac{3}{15}$
$\frac{5}{15}$	$\frac{9}{12}$	$\frac{6}{8}$	$\frac{3}{12}$	$\frac{3}{6}$
$\frac{4}{8}$	$\frac{2}{8}$	FREE	$\frac{4}{9}$	$\frac{3}{9}$
$\frac{4}{6}$	$\frac{6}{8}$	$\frac{4}{16}$	$\frac{2}{4}$	$\frac{6}{18}$
$\frac{4}{20}$	$\frac{4}{12}$	$\frac{4}{10}$	$\frac{9}{12}$	$\frac{5}{20}$

FIGURE 8-15   Fraction Bingo

Games can be highly motivating and at the same time reinforce learned concepts and problem-solving heuristics or strategies. Heimer and Trueblood (1977) postulate that the use of games can promote desirable interactions among students, provide teachers with important diagnostic information, can assist students with language deficiencies, and can be used to integrate mathematics across the curriculum. Some games which the entire family can enjoy include backgammon, chess, checkers, math bingo, fishing games with magnets and math fish, Concentration, Jeopardy, Monopoly, Treasure Hunt, and so on. Even old games like Bingo can be given a different twist when such difficult material as fractions is presented.

Positive parental involvement in math activities promotes better attitudes and reinforcement of important math vocabulary, concepts, and procedures.

Parental Involvement

Parents can take an active role in the development of mathematics skills and attitudes with their children. The following can be considered important steps for parents to take in promoting greater math successes:

Tips for Parents

1. Foster a positive math attitude (see Table 8-7 below) by using numbers in positive ways. Point out the importance of learning math material when shopping, determining an allowance, figuring out a car payment schedule, etc.
2. Show an interest in math homework assignments. Assist when possible. Solicit help from friends or family when you can't answer math questions. There are a number of math homework hotlines that can be used (e.g., Big Y su-

TABLE 8-7 **Parent Involvement in Developing Maths Skills and Attitudes**

- Point To Importance of Math When Shopping, Determining an Allowance, Determining Car Payment Schedules, etc.
- Assist With Homework Whenever Possible
- Solicit Assistance from Friends and Family When Everyone Is Stuck
- Use Math Homework Hotlines in Your Community
- Encourage After-School Participation in Help Classes
- Solicit Tutorial Assistance
- Call the Education Department of a Local College—Solicit Assistance from Students Completing Field Work Requirements in Math Methods Coursework
- Encourage Participation in Algebra and Pre-Algebra Courses for College-Bound Students
- Identify Math Weaknesses at the High School Level Via PSAT Tests
- Assist With Arranged Special Test Considerations
- Seek Specific Math Scholarships and Awards for All Students
- Seek Specific Math Awards for Minority Students
- Participate in Family Math Activities Such As Monopoly Game, Preparing Shopping Lists, Coupon Cutting, etc.

permarkets' sponsored hotline) free-of-charge. Additionally, most schools have teachers who will volunteer to stay after school or who will help during study halls with problem areas in math. It is important to connect your child to these resources when problems arise.

3. Pre-algebra and algebra courses taken at the junior high school level are a must for students who wish to pursue college careers. Science, engineering, teaching, etc. demand solid algebra backgrounds.

4. Be certain that students with learning disabilities make good decisions regarding mathematics courses if college is in sight. General mathematics and business mathematics courses do not satisfy most college admissions requirements.

5. Students with mathematics LD are not necessarily unable to pursue higher level math courses. In fact, tutorial assistance, one-to-one individualization of curriculum, and support at home can empower students with math LD to take geometry, trigonometry, statistics, calculus, functions, etc.

6. In high school, ask the guidance counselor if your adolescent can take the PSAT (Preliminary Scholastic Aptitude Test) at the beginning of the school year so that math weaknesses can be identified and addressed before SAT exams are taken. Special testing arrangements can be established for students with learning disabilities (e.g., untimed test administration rather than timed). Signed documentation must confirm the learning disabilities condition.

7. Hispanic and Black students with learning disabilities in reading and language areas (with strengths in math) may be eligible for the College Board's National Hispanic or African-American awards.

8. Participate in family math activities such as the ones sponsored by many school systems. Informal participation in family math activities can be just as useful in promoting math successes. For example, special times could be set aside for games involving math numbers and concepts (e.g., Monopoly).

9. Encourage your child to watch the public television program, "Square One." Watch it with your child the first few times and demonstrate how you can interact with the presentation.

A sample activity for parents would be how to reinforce measurement use in everyday experiences (see Figure 8-16, p. 235).

Parents could also give their children math technology tools on those special occasions such as birthdays, Hanukkah, Kwanzaa, and so on.

Using Technology in Math

Using Calculators

Calculators can be used to reinforce and teach a number of skills advocated by the National Council of Teachers of Mathematics (1989) such as numeration, counting, sequencing, estimating, and calculating statistics and probability problems. Calculators should be used as a positive instructional tool. "One of the most obvious

Because parents provide continual exposure to the daily activities of living, they engage children in all types of incidental learning. One example is the broad exposure to **UNITS** of measure.

How many **MILES** to school?

How many **WEEKS** before vacation?

How many **GALLONS** of milk this week?

How many **POUNDS** of hamburg?

How many **FEET** of rope?

How many **MINUTES** until supper?

How many **CUPS** of flour?

If parents can emphasize the language of math and give children practice in using the words and concepts, an important conceptual foundation can be established.

FIGURE 8-16   Measurement In Everyday Experiences

advantages of using the calculator in teaching learning disabled students is enabling them to compute accurately" (Post, 1992, p. 371). Instruction could then be focused on the more important aspects of problem solving, critical thinking, and mastering algorithms. Some sample activities one could use at any grade level are provided by Heddens and Speer (1992) (see pages 56–60): Calculating the number of times one's heart beats in one day (how about a week?); dramatizing problems with students using calculators to solve the problems; state mathematics problems orally and have students compute with calculators at their seats; create bank statements using the calculator; and collect and organize data into tables and graphs after calculating required information (e.g., what is the average number of questions in the class per day?).

Computer-Assisted Instruction

There are a variety of computer programs which can be used in school and at home in order to provide math reinforcement, drill, and insights. Computer programs seem to be most beneficial in drill and practice types of activities involved in skill learning, problem solving, and exploration of math concepts (Suydam, 1984). Some computer software is adaptable to students with disabilities such as "Alligator Mix," (Developmental Learning Materials) and "Soccer Math" (Compu-Tation) while other software is not well-suited to special needs populations. The math software programs listed in Table 8-8 (p. 236) were evaluated by Lewis (1993) as suitable for students with learning problems/disabilities.

Math department chairpersons or instructors in school systems and colleges could be consulted in order to obtain computer catalogue information and information regarding software quality. Computer software should be carefully evaluated before adoption. There is computer software available in the math area which

TABLE 8-8   Special Education Technology—Classroom Applications

Conquering Math Series (upper elementary to high school)—Several activities focus on students conquering such math concepts as fractions, ratios, decimals, and percentiles. Students are allowed to estimate and make more than one attempt at an answer. MECC, 6160 Summit Drive North, Minneapolis, MN 55430.

Exploring Measurement, Time, and Money (three levels: K–2; 3–4, 5–6)—Several activities (e.g., talking clock, sticker store) are presented according to level of difficulty. Students practice computation skills as well as such measurement activities as length, volume, weight, and temperature. IBM Special Needs Information Referral Center, P.O. Box 2150, Atlanta, GA 30301.

Gertrude's Secrets (nursery through Grade 3)—Problem-solving activities surround "Gertrude," the goose and her secrets. Math readiness skills and basic math concepts are presented in an entertaining format. Learning Company, 6493 Kaiser Drive, Fremont, CA 94555.

Money Box Keyboard (elementary)—Practice in actual counting of money as a plastic cover fits over a computer keyboard (Apple™ IIGS). Students count money, buy goods, and make change on both the computer and in the money box. This keyboard technology accompanies five computer programs.: KT's Special Sweet Shop, KT's Sweet Shop, KT's Corner Store, KT's Take Away, and KT's Grocery Store. Apple Computer, Inc., 20525 Mariani Ave., Cupertino, CA 95024.

New Math Blaster Plus (for all ages)—Rote drill arcade-like program for IBM™ and Macintosh computers are practiced in "space." Students can work on mastering math facts in the basic operations of addition, subtraction, multiplication, and division as well as fractions and decimals. Students blast their spaceperson, "Blasternaut," to the correct answer location after problems are presented. Davidson & Associates, 19840 Pioneer Avenue, Torrance, CA 90503.

Stickybear Math Activities (nursery through lower elementary)—Students can reinforce math readiness skills and basic math concepts. Weekly Reader Software, Optimum Resource, Inc., 10 Station Place, Norfolk, CT 06058.

Survival Math (middle school *reading* levels to high school)—four problem-solving situations (e.g., Travel Agent contest) are presented which require computation proficiency with multidigit numbers, estimation skills, and some knowledge of percents and decimals. Wings for Learning/Sunburst Communications, 1600 Green Hills Road, P.O. Box 660002, Scotts Valley, CA 95067.

Source: Rena B. Lewis (1993).

allows students to self-pace their learning or practice, receive immediate feedback on correctness of responses, log progress and exercises completed, adjust for difficulty in programming (e.g., different levels), and provide sound reinforcement.

Secondary-Level Topics Available on Disk

Posamentier and Stepelman (1990) cite several secondary-level math topics available on disk from software dealers: "logic and problem solving, how to solve linear equations-drill and practice, solving quadratic equations-drill and practice, arithmetic operations-drill and practice, algebra tutorial disks—all of first year algebra, selected areas in geometry, graphing linear equations, graphing trigonometric functions, selected topics in calculus, Scholastic Aptitude Test preparation, interpreting graphs, and selected topics in statistics" (p. 143). One need only to consult computer software publishers in your local area for specific programs. Computer programs at this level should be able identify errors for students with problem-solving options offered for response corrections. Special computer projects can be assigned to groups of students and include: generating a Fibonacci sequence on screen, determining the prime factors of a number, finding the area of a geometric shape, calculating income and sales taxes, computing car payments over 2 years, setting up a household budget, keeping a checking account, calculating probability estimates, and finding the mean, median, and mode of a given problem and then determining which measure of central tendency is most appropriate for the data.

Conclusions

We would suggest a constructivist approach to math diagnosis and remediation which would reaffirm the teacher's role as a classroom facilitator and model. The constructivist approach sees both the teacher and student as active learners in their investigation and pursuit of math knowledge and concepts. Cooperative math learning can involve group sharing, debating, constructing, modifying, and strategies for problem solving. Knowledge of the developmental stages of learners is critical to the planning and implementation of math programs for individuals with math disabilities.

Students with dyslexia who experience math disabilities can improve their math performance (Peterson, Mercer, & O'Shea, 1988; Scheid, 1990; Kirby & Becker, 1988). "Although providing children with the opportunity to learn seems to be nothing more than common sense, we shortchange many students, assuming they can't learn mathematics . . . while everyone readily accepts the idea that all children need to learn how to read, many presume these same children need to learn nothing more than the basics when it comes to mathematics . . ." (McKinney, 1993). The study of these mathematics learning problems has been an area of neglect for many years (Cawley, Miller, & School, 1987) in that researchers on LD place less emphasis on proficiency in mathematics than in other academic areas (Cohn, 1961; Kosc, 1974; Rourke & Strang, 1983; Hallahan, Kauffman, & Lloyd, 1985; Keller & Sutton, 1991). This is probably due to the fact that most LD researchers have relegated investigations of math problems to a secondary position to that of reading problems, which they consider to be of primary importance (Ackerman, Anhalt, & Dykman, 1986; Cox, 1975a). Many of the problems associated with math disabilities are associated with the individual's lack of understanding of the processes involved (Ariel, 1992).

It should be emphasized that individuals with dyslexia do *not* necessarily have problems in mathematics. In fact, many individuals with dyslexia are quite proficient in mathematics. Many mathematics programs heavily emphasize computation proficiency thereby reducing the language demands for individuals who have reading difficulties. It would be expected that students with dyslexia and other reading/language difficulties would need the same type of reading assistance mentioned in the previous two chapters with curriculum materials that have heavy reading demands.

Concrete learning experiences are necessary at both the elementary and secondary levels as ways to establish important math foundations for higher level concepts and material. Mathematics is a highly abstract subject matter which requires a unique vocabulary and the application of algorithms in a sequential manner. There are some specific math techniques teachers and parents can use with disabled and troubled math learners which consider these points. For that matter, the suggestions mentioned could be used with all learners.

The use of technology via calculators and computers is recommended to enhance the acquisition of important math facts and problem-solving abilities. Math software programs are plentiful especially in the computation area with some "tried-and-proven" programs cited in the chapter. Time, measurement, and survival skills areas are also more than adequately covered in several programs on the market. Software that emphasizes problem solving frequently uses simulations, hypothesis testing, and frequent accuracy feedback.

Cawley, Miller, & School (1987) have verified that certain strategies will assist students with learning disabilities (LD) to be successful problem solvers and these math strategies can be taught. Webster (1979) found that math disabled students recall more math information with strategic use of visual presentations. Brown (1978) has also determined that LD and LD-like children can be taught exactly those strategies they previously lacked in math and whose absence resulted in math errors. Several problem-solving ideas were presented for both teachers and parents.

Approaching the issues of diagnosis and remediation from these cognitive and empirical standpoints involves the tacit assumption that difficulties in math can be remedied to a greater extent than some of our present efforts are doing. Many of the suggestions mentioned in this chapter focus on a developmental constructivist approach to learning keeping in mind the important National Council of Teachers of Mathematics Standards for the 1990s. The next chapter details the remedial placements and related suggestions.

NCTM Curriculum Standards

Grades K-4	Grades 5-8

Mathematics Focus On:

Grades K-4	Grades 5-8
1. Problem Solving	1. Problem Solving
2. Language/Communication	2. Language/Communication
3. Reasoning	3. Reasoning
4. Connections/Links	4. Connections/Links
5. Estimation	5. Number Relationships
6. Numeration/Number Sense	6. Number Theory/Systems
7. Whole Number Operations	7. Estimation/Computation
8. Computation	8. Patterns/Functions
9. Geometry/Spatial Dimensions	9. Algebra
10. Measurements	10. Statistics
11. Statistics/Probability	11. Probability
12. Fractions/Decimals	12. Geometry
13. Patterns/Relationships	13. Measurement

Source: (NCTM, 1989)

Chapter *9*

Placement Issues

". . . to instruct others aright, the teacher's life must be a "constant progress of self-education" . . . —(DURELL, 1894).

Introduction

Durell in 1894 entitled a book *A New Life in Education,* in which he proposes to assist teachers in becoming the best they can be for all students. In dealing with students who have dyslexia and other learning disabilities, programs must involve . . . "the planning, design, and implementation of appropriate service options and instructional strategies . . . predicated upon all concerned professionals having a clear understanding of what learning disabilities are, and the manner in which these different disabilities modify how an individual learns" (NJCLD position paper of February 21, 1982b).

Children and adolescents with dyslexia do evidence several warning signs as we have learned from previous chapters. The following guide is helpful when considering special education referrals and subsequent diagnostic procedures. When looking at this checklist, it is important to keep in mind that not all individuals with dyslexia will evince these symptoms and that all of us have at least a few of these symptoms. Most individuals with dyslexia evidence several symptoms with severity based on the intensity of the individual symptom (e.g., years behind grade level in reading) as opposed to sheer numbers of symptoms.

Symptoms Prevalent in Individuals with Dyslexia

- below grade level reading skills
- below grade level language skills
- below grade level spelling skills
- poor group performance test scores

- poor grades in reading based subjects
- relatively good math grades
- reversals in reading and writing that persist past normal time frames
- poor short-term memory or long-term memory skills
- attention problems
- hyperactivity
- slowness in completing assigned tasks
- problems with time concepts
- difficulties in reproducing written material
- gross motor awkwardness
- visual anomalies
- difficulty in problem solving and looking at different alternatives when problem solving
- difficulty in sequencing
- perseverates on a topic or idea
- problems in understanding and following directions
- organizational problems
- lack of metacognitive awareness
- disorganized thinking
- low self-image
- low self-persona
- impulsivity
- easily distracted
- lack of adequate concentration
- lack of reflective thought and self-assessment
- low frustration tolerance
- depressed self-esteem
- inappropriate social behaviors
- developmental language delay
- developmental delays in motor actions
- failure to look ahead or see consequence of one's actions
- peer relation problems
- problems in adult relations
- moody
- a follower and easily led by peers
- inappropriate facial gestures and body language
- inappropriate, insufficient, or excessive displays of affection
- poor study skills
- difficulty in decision making
- poor adjustment to changes in the environment

How to use diagnostic information is as important as gathering the information. Orton and his colleagues in the early 1900s recommended that remedial techniques be based on theories of causation. However, dyslexia is "an unusual type of severe reading disorder that has puzzled the educational and medical professions for many years [regarding causation]" (Lerner, 1989, p. 349), so one can only address overt medical problems and health issues (e.g., therapies for ADD/ADHD (see

Appendix I); vision interventions if visual dysfunctioning is established) along with good solid teaching techniques. There are many techniques which have been used through the years and in recent times which have been used with "slow readers" which do not appear to be at all different from specific teaching programs for individuals with dyslexia.

Key Questions

A key component to any successful teaching program would be the ability of the teacher to tie in diagnostic information with classroom applications and student outcomes (Storey, 1995; Watson, 1994; Goodwin, 1993). Important would be the raising of such questions as: What is the extent of the cognitive learning problems of the individual with dyslexia? What is(are) the underlying cause(s) of the dyslexic condition if known? How much are secondary emotional/social problems occurring concomitantly with the dyslexic condition? And, specifically, what factors and social support systems can assist in improving the overall welfare of the student with dyslexia?

Life After Diagnoses

After a child has been diagnosed as dyslexic by a qualified professional, a report should be compiled to detail findings and recommendations. Such a report should be broken down into sections which would be meaningful and understandable to the lay person. After all, parents and teachers will be the primary facilitators and advocates of the dyslexic's educational, social and emotional well- being, so it is incumbent on diagnosticians to "pen their findings" in terms of an audience of lay persons. This would include providing clear, operational definitions of all terms and testing instruments, to include the results and the recommendations.

IFSP (Individualized Family Services Plans) are reports written for preschoolers and **IEP's** (Individual Education Plans) are reports written for school-age children in grades K–12.

Individual Family Service Plans (IFSPs)

The Individual with Disabilities Education Act (IDEA) of 1990 (see Council for Exceptional Children (CEC), Winter 1992) contains special legislation that mandates an early intervention program (Part H) for students at risk for learning disabilities and other special needs. Early intervention programs may be federally funded if states apply for grants for planning and implementing programs which are multidisciplinary (using different agencies and specialists; e.g., health care workers, social workers, teachers, and so on). A comprehensive system of personnel development (CSPD) must be in place as well as an IFSP (Individual Family Service Plan) for each child.

An IFSP has to address the developmental needs and learning styles of the preschool child in the areas of cognition, speech, psycho-motor skills, language, and self-help skills. Responsible caretakers and service providers must be named as well as a statement of the major learning and social outcomes expected to be achieved by the child and family as a cohesive unit. Transition procedures to pre-school programs must be identified. Options also need to be provided to resolve disputes between parties involved in the education process of the children involved.

Individual Educational Plans (IEP)

As you can see from the report provided beforehand, the dyslexic child (as determined through a team evaluation) is required to have what is called an IEP or Individual Education Plan. This is a requirement under Federal Public Law PL 94–142 (Education for All Handicapped Law) if special services are provided. The IEP serves a dual function, as a diagnostic/evaluation tool and as a remedial teaching plan. Diagnostic information is provided in the context of educational planning and teaching strategies. Most IEPs include the following: a description of the presenting problem and student history, the student's present levels of academic/social functioning, student strengths and weaknesses, short-term and annual goals/objectives, the names of TEAM members and affliation, projected dates for implementation and duration of special services, specific criteria and evaluation procedures to be used to assess progress in meeting goals, names of persons responsible for special services and evaluation, program descriptions, and the extent to which the student will participate in regular education programs. Parent approval must appear in the form of a signature on the educational plan. If there is disagreement with any of the contents of the IEP, the parent(s) has(have) a right to a due process hearing within the local and state system.

IEP Reviews

IEPs must be **reviewed every year and rewritten every three** years depending on the state and school system. If an IEP is not written for a child on a yearly basis, then an addendum must be attached in order to give an update of progress in relation to the goals and objectives stated on the initial plan. The type and schedule of remedial placement and instructional methods and materials are stated on the original IEP with updates again noted on subsequent addenda. One of the intents of the IEP is to place the dyslexic child in what is called the least restrictive setting. This would be the setting where the school system is removing the child for the minimal time required out of the regular classroom in order to remediate his/her disabilities. Sometimes, services can be provided in the regular classroom without any pull-out at all; such is the case in an inclusionary classroom.

Placement

Placement of the Dyslexic within the School Sector

There are general recommendations which can first be made to schools which can assist personnel in best meeting the educational needs of all students with special needs to include students with dyslexia. All of the recommendations can enhance the educational experiences of all children. Numbers 1–8 address various legal requirements; the remaining recommendations look at best meeting the needs of the whole child. The recommendations are to:

1. Provide service delivery options for students with dyslexia in the least restrictive environment.
2. Provide a variety of educational support programs to include resource rooms, inclusion programs, Chapter I programs, substantially separate classrooms for the severely impaired, tutorial assistance, after school programs, before school programs, and parent programs.
3. Provide opportunities for school-based management decisions which allow school personnel and professionals to brainstorm ideas about special education programming for students with dyslexia and other special needs.
4. Provide opportunities for multidisciplinary TEAMs to form and meet regarding the educational decisions for students with dyslexia from the assessment process to service delivery. TEAM members could include the school nurse or doctor, regular classroom teachers, special educators, the students (if appropriate), parents, speech therapists, language specialists, reading specialists, school psychologists, counselors, occupational therapists, physical therapists, vision specialists, hearing specialists, and so on.
5. Provide opportunities for staff development which incorporate curriculum adaptations and programming decisions which will impact students with dyslexia.
6. Provide opportunities for staff collaboration if only one period per week, bi-monthly, or monthly.
7. Set high standards for student and teacher performance.
8. Provide assessment information and procedures which allow for the evaluation of student progress in an IEP defined program plan, effective curricula, and behavior modification plans when appropriate.
9. Provide curriculum materials which will address the rich cultural diversity of our society for all students.
10. Provide curriculum materials which can be adapted to the individual learning styles and needs of students with dyslexia.
11. Provide curriculum materials which foster and nurture the development of productive and active citizens.
12. Provide curriculum materials which foster and nurture effective/affective teacher-learner reflective experiences in all classrooms.
13. Provide curriculum materials which foster and nurture acquisition of behaviors which key in on environmental awareness.
14. Provide curriculum materials which tie in learning to life situations, life skills, and vocational information.
15. Provide clear guidelines as to academic and social performances both in and out of the classroom.
16. Create an integrated school atmosphere which fosters collaborative relationships among students, teachers, administration, and other school personnel.

Appropriate Placements

Placement of the dyslexic child in an appropriate program is necessary to her/his social/academic/emotional/cognitive well-being. Self-contained classes (also known as pull-out models) for dyslexics and other learning disabled children were prevalent during the '60s and early '70s. The late '70s and the decade of the '80s saw resource rooms or centers (also called pull-out models because services are received outside of the regular classroom) as providing supplemental support to the regular classroom initiative. In the 1990s, several private schools have emerged that deal specifically with the needs of the learning disabled. A new programming trend has emerged in the 1990s which is most commonly called the **inclusion model.** This model is becoming a popular alternative to the resource room setting.

Flexibility in Programming

As public school systems become increasingly strapped with financial burdens as a result of the influx of bilingual and special needs students, the need to deliver services for the learning disabled will require flexibility in programming (Wieder-holt, 1989; Wiederholt, Hammill, & Brown, 1983) and a continuum of alternatives which must take into consideration the very special learning styles and needs of the students with dyslexia.

Research-Based Factors in Programming

Research regarding the effectiveness of programming for students with dyslexia and other learning disabilities has criticized pull-out models such as the popular resource rooms of the 79s and 80s because high percentages of these students have been dropping out of school despite the resource room support. Additionally, some research has shown that student outcomes have not been enhanced by the supportive services offered by pull-out models (Mass. Dept. of Ed., 1990; Walker, Singer, Palfrey, Ozra, Wenger, & Butler, 1988). There have been two initiatives taken in order to address the high drop-out problem with students who are learning disabled. (1) There is a requirement under P.L. 101–476 for IEPs beginning at age 16 to contain recorded statements of transition services and agencies responsible for monitoring special needs students at the high school level. The purpose is to promote "movement from school to postschool activities, including postsecondary education, vocational training, integrated employment (including supported employment), continuing adult education services, independent living, or community participation" (CEC, Winter 1992, p. 5). A coordinated set of activities is required under P.L. 101–476 that will consider a student's interests, ability levels, community experiences, life skills functioning, and so on. (2) The second initiative involves the above-mentioned inclusion model. In its purest form it calls for the full integration of students with dyslexia into the regular classroom regardless of the severity of the reading problem. Inclusion models usually involve having special educators working with the regular classroom teachers within the regular classroom setting with students who require additional services. The special educator in essence provides all required special services within the regular classroom setting. The inclusion model has its proponents and its skeptics and it will probably take another decade before research can either substantially validate or cast doubt upon the basic tenets of this approach. Before an inclusionary model is recommended which would involve special educators working within the regular classroom setting with the regular education teacher, an assistance option could be tried that is called Teacher Assistance Teaming.

Teacher Assistance Teaming

Teacher-Assistance Teaming very simply involves a consultation model whereby teacher assistance teams within a school building (e.g., to be made up of special educators and regular staff) are available to network with the teacher who has a student with dyslexia in dealing with any academic, social, or behavioral problems. This model has been in use for over 20 years (e.g., see Chalfant, Pysh, & Moultrie, 1979). Problem solving would center on accommodating the student with dyslexia within the mainstream setting before other program options are considered. If teacher-assisted teaming doesn't provide enough support for an optimal educational experience for all, then inclusionary models can be tried. This same teacher assisted teaming concept can be used with students.

Cooperative Learning Ventures

Slavin (1992) cites the importance of cooperative learning ventures when students with disabilities are mainstreamed. Various cooperative learning models can include the teaming of 2–3 students or slightly larger groups if necessary. Slavin (1992) suggests cooperative learning groups can be involved in partner readings, story-related writing, math activities, story retellings, spelling, and partner checking in all areas. One of the most important side effects of this approach is the development of friendships among students who can grow to respect and nurture the unique differences and similarities among them in regard to learning, race, sex, and so on.

Cooperative learning skills are not easily taught by teachers nor are the skills presented easily mastered by students. Cooperative learning will not work with just the grouping of students. Teachers must take the time to develop appropriate attitudes on the part of the students as well as the acceptance of others and an interdependent frame of reference (Ryder & Graves, 1994). It is recommended that teachers consult tried and proven cooperative learning programs (see Slavin, 1992).

Student Teams-Achievement Divisions (STAD)

Slavin offers the Student Teams-Achievement Divisions (Slavin, 1992) as a cooperative learning model. This approach uses groups of four with differing abilities, ethnicity, gender, and social class (SES) working together. After the teacher presents a lesson, students work together to ensure that each member of the group masters the material presented. Group members share answers, encourage each other, problem solve, present alternative solutions, and quiz each other. After students accomplish their learning goals they are individually quizzed and receive points based on learning gains from a previous performance. Individual points are totaled for team scores. This approach is best suited for subjects which require convergent answers such as in math/spelling where there are limited response options.

Jigsaw

Jigsaw is another cooperative learning model which was developed by Aronson, Blaney, Stephan, Sikes, and Snapp (1978). Essentially with Jigsaw, groups of six students are formed. Lesson material is broken down into sections with each student in a group mastering a section of the material being studied. For example, students might be studying the solar system. One student in each group might investigate the planets, another the sun, another the moon, and so on. Each member of the group becomes an expert on his/her topic and then must return to the group to share information about about his/her topic. Students are quizzed both on the material they learned and what they learned from the group. This approach can only be used with material that is easily broken into topics/units/areas of study (e.g., especially in science and social studies).

The Inclusion Model

Inclusionary programs are frequently referred to as models of *full inclusion, fully integrated programs, inclusive educational programs,* and *unified systems approaches*. Inclusionary models consist of the following: (1) full mainstreaming or participation of the student with dyslexia in regular classroom activities (full inclusion programming), (2) support provisions (e.g., special education initiatives) are provided within the regular classroom setting, with the service provider working with the student at his/her seat or a corner of the room, and (3) curriculum planning as a collaborative effort between the regular education staff and the special education staff.

Classroom Teachers—Key Facilitators to Inclusion

"Classroom teachers hold the keys to inclusion for an excluded student" (O'Brien & Forest, 1992, p. 29). It would appear that school systems which are committed to the inclusion model require additional staff to assist teachers in coping with and providing for the unique needs of the student with dyslexia and other disabilities. Some school systems have *integrated consultants* who maintain strong lines of communication between the home and the school. Integrated consultants "coach family members, teachers, students, and administrators to identify their capacities and develop their skills . . . [help] with problem solving. . .[instruct] faculty, staff, and students on integration and inclusion issues . . . and [stick] with people through time" (O'Brien & Forest, 1992, p. 10).

Benefits to Classmates

Proponents of inclusionary programs cite benefits to classmates with some of the following considered particularly important: (1) classmates can develop an increased sense of responsibility and self-esteem by relating to and assisting the *included classmate,* (2) classmates can gain a better understanding of the full range of human diversity and experiences, (3) classmates can use the included classmate as a role model in the sense that coping mechanisms are observed and can be emulated, and (4) classmates can be enriched by special friendships with individuals with disabilities (Rogers, 1993). However, there are some cautions which must be exercised, as not all students with dyslexia will benefit from inclusion models.

Cautions Regarding Full Inclusion

Hallahan, Keller, McKinney, Lloyd, and Bryan, (1988); Bryan, Bay, and Donahue (1988); and Sachs (1988) have stated that fully inclusionary programs such as those proposed under the Regular Classroom Initiative (RCI) are not always the optimal educational experience for those involved. Problems with full inclusion are related to the overburdening of understaffed and undertrained teachers, a lack of adequate professional development, and a lack of resources. These practical difficulties require that some students with moderate-to-severe disabilities be serviced outside of the regular classroom setting. The Learning Disabilities Association of America (LDA) would concur with these remarks.

LDA's Position on Inclusion Models

We would agree with the LDA (Learning Disabilities Association of America) position on inclusion models which in essence rejects totally inclusionary programs or policies which absolutely mandate a uniform treatment program (i.e., full inclusionary policies) for students with dyslexia. This LDA position on inclusionary models is stated in a 1993 position paper on full inclusion policies for all students with learning disabilities in the regular education classroom: "the regular education classroom is not the appropriate placement for a number of students with learning disabilities who may need alternative instructional environments, teaching strategies, and/or materials that cannot or will not be provided within the context of a regular classroom placement" (LDA, 1993, p. 1). A reaction statement to these full inclusionary models was issued in January 1993 by the National Joint Committee on Learning Disabilities (NJCLD) which strongly believes that "full inclusion . . . violates the rights of parents and students with disabilities as mandated by the Individuals with Disabilities Education Act (IDEA)" (NJCLD, 1993a). We would recommend that school systems adopt a policy of program flexibility which would allow inclusionary programs for students who would benefit from such programs as well as pull-out programs which address the needs of students who need a great deal of one-to-one attention or specialized services not optimally delivered in large group settings. Resource rooms are a type of pull-out model.

Resource Room Programs

Definition

The resource room or center in the public school system is one placement choice for a child or student with dyslexia, particularly if the child cannot be easily handled in the regular classroom. Substantially separate classrooms and programs tend to be reserved for students who have been diagnosed with other primary problems such as emotional disturbance, mental retardation, and so on. Although emotionally disturbed individuals can display learning disabilities, the primary presenting problem tends to determine the child's classification. Resource rooms are a popular component of special education programs especially for the dyslexic. A resource room is just what the name implies—a resource center. A special education or learning disabilities teacher provides remedial assistance for the dyslexic child as well as for several other children with varying special needs (i.e., gifted children, children with speech impairments, children with physical handicaps, etc. Typically, this resource teacher is supported by an auxiliary staff of specialists (e.g., speech therapists, counselors, psychologists) and teacher aides who theoretically work as a team in implementing a child's educational plan or IEP.

Role of the Resource Teacher or Resource Specialist

Typically, resource teachers and aide(s) work with small groups of students and tailor-make individual programs for all students attending this classroom. The dyslexic would, hopefully, be provided with a detailed plan specifying his/her strengths and weaknesses, interests, and preferred modes of learning. The resource teacher would essentially be a diagnostic teacher in the sense that the progress and needs of the dyslexic would need continual monitoring. Because no one technique has been found to be most effective in providing remedial support for all dyslexics, various methods and materials should be at the fingertips of the professionals involved. The resource teacher needs to give this educational support but must also provide programs which deal with non-academic areas (e.g., social skills) so as to promote independence, participation as a productive citizen in the community, and responsibilities/skills (e.g., getting along with co- workers, being on time, consulting with one's supervisor, etc.) needed in future careers.

Sasso (1988) reviewed several investigations of resource room programs with results showing that learning disabled and mildly handicapped children showed positive academic gains. However, positive effects of resource rooms in the areas of social/emotional growth have not been established (Lovitt, 1989).

Primary Advantages and Disadvantages of Resource Room Placements

Advantages.   Lovitt (1989) states that, "the primary advantage of resource room programs is that children in need of special help in a specific academic or social area will be given that help by specially trained teachers, and children might thus be able to maintain the expected academic and social pace of the regular program" (p. 104). Certainly the impact of seeing other children with similar and more handicapping conditions provides some comfort and comradery with the dyslexic.

Disadvantages.   Disadvantages cited in resource room programming include any problem associated with a pull-out model. Whenever children are pulled out of a regular classroom program, they are missing something. The increased movement of these children out of the regular classroom lessens the ability of teachers to closely monitor progress so that inconsistencies in instructional approaches can result. Perhaps of even greater importance are social considerations that would greatly impact the dyslexic's self-image and self-esteem. However, there are some children "whose behaviors limit their access to the mainstream to such an extent that they need a highly structured, special environment for most of the school day" (Blackhurst & Berdine, 1993, p. 554). Those students might benefit from what are termed *self-contained classrooms.*

Self-Contained Classrooms

Definition and Program Overview

There are some individuals with severe forms of dyslexia whose learning and behavior problems limit the extent to which they can be mainstreamed within regular classes. Many such self-contained classes exist in school systems with such teachers well-equipped and well-trained to deal with severe learning disabilities. However, most school systems have few self-contained programs that deal with severe forms of dyslexia. Teachers and other professionals must search out the particular schools which have substantially separate programs (busing is always an issue), find school systems which will collaborate (e.g., by providing collaborative classrooms) or systems which will accept students with severe learning disabilities. Many school systems participate in collaborative programs, which keeps funding within reasonable limits and allows smaller school systems with few provisions for the severely disabled freedom from having to create expensive programs for very small numbers of student users.

Collaborative Programs

Definition and Program Overview

Collaborative programs are just what the name implies—a collaboration between and among school systems in creating classroom programs which are difficult to put in place for one school system. Typically, these programs service students with severe learning problems and disabilities who require specialized services and consulting. Optimally, student-teacher ratios are low and students do have accessibility for some mainstreaming (e.g., gym, lunch). It is a typical practice for the school system to pay a tuition fee for the student who is being referred to the collaborative system. A parent or teacher could call the local SPED (special educational services) department or a state department of education to find out about regional collaborative programs. This tuition is much more cost-effective than residential or schools and allows students to interact with non-disabled peers in social situations. Additionally, there are residential and day schools for individuals with dyslexia that are relatively expensive to attend because they operate independently of the public school sector.

Special Schools for Individuals with Dyslexia

Sometimes individuals with dyslexia may benefit from participation in schools for students with dyslexia both at the K–12 levels and at the post-secondary level. Such programs can provide an education which is designed specifically to meet the needs of students with dyslexia. Programming can follow that of such programs as Landmark College in Vermont (see 1995–1997 reference) which provides: (1) one-to-one tutorial assistance daily in 55 minute blocks of time, (2) small classes with individualized attention with an emphasis on task commitment and hard work in a special environment, (3) trained faculty members including the tutors in the education of students with dyslexia, (4) the use of a diagnostic approach which follows the student from the admissions process to post-tertiary placements, (5) the teaching of reading/language strategies and study skills within an integrated curriculum, (6) a liberal arts curriculum which involves the integration of various subjects into a program which would allow the student with dyslexia to pursue a college career, and (7) classes, special lectures, meetings with advisors, and interactions with other students with dyslexia. Courses are even taken by students entitled, "Faces of Dyslexia" and "Introduction to Learning Disabilities." Social as well as academic activities round out an entire program. Counseling services are available to address the social problems and stresses which many times characterize the student with dyslexia. Special schools for dyslexics require tuition payments that generally equate to an average college tuition regardless of level. Parents are most often responsible for such payments as these schools are considered *private,* meaning that *private tuition* is required. However, many of the professional services available in private schools and clinics are also available in public schools. Another special school for individuals with dyslexia worthy of mention is the Eagle School in Greenwich, CT.

Professionals Working with Individuals Having Dyslexia

Spafford/Grosser's LD Problem Consultant

We recommend that parents and school personnel designate an LD problem consultant (and backup) who can assist the student with dyslexia when problems are encountered. This consultant could be an informed and interested friend, a teacher, a school guidance counselor, the school nurse, the school psychologist, an informed relative outside of the immediate family, and so on. The consultant could (1) brainstorm with the individual with dyslexia on the nature and cause of the problem(s) and various problem-solving strategies and alternatives; (2) role-play various ways and verbalizations to use when addressing the problem; (3) refer the individual with dyslexia to someone more able to assist with the problem (see Chapter 10 for various resources); and (4) follow up to see how the problem was handled, as well as examine the various outcomes. Followup would include reflection on how to handle similar situations in the future and perhaps a self-reflective assessment on the positives and negatives of performance. In recent times, some parents and professionals have found that substantially separate schools for students with dyslexia and other learning disabilities provide peer support in the form of comradery but also educational and social experiences which key in on the unique learning styles of the dyslexic. LaVoie (1988) also mentions other consultants available to teachers and parents who can assist in program planning regardless of the placement option.

School Consultants—Specialists to Assist Practitioners/Parents

Most school systems and communities have available:

1. School psychologists—these are psychologists who are trained to diagnose learning problems, including dyslexia and learning disabilities, and who are well versed in placement options and programs. Many times school psychologists consult with teachers and provide counseling services for students.
2. Clinical psychologists—these are psychologists available to school systems who specialize more in the social/behavioral problems of students with dyslexia when such problems severely impact school functioning and require outside consultation(s).
3. Occupational therapists (OT)—these are therapists who can assist with occupational (TO), mental, and physical well-being of the individual with dyslexia by focusing on pre-vocational and vocational skills training.
4. Physical therapists (PT)—these are therapists who are trained to deal with any physical problems that are not necessarily related to the learning disabilities, but which can impact one's overall functioning and well-being. These therapists can treat disorders involving the muscles, bones and nerves with exercises, light, etc.
5. Diagnosticians—these are individuals frequently hired by school systems from within (e.g., school psychologist) or outside the school setting (e.g., a private clinic) to diagnose or pinpoint the specific learning problems of the individual with dyslexia.
6. Psychiatrists—these are medical doctors who are generally hired on a case-by-case basis to address medical and psychological issues for individuals who can't be handled within the regular school setting. Generally, individuals with severe forms of dyslexia do experience social problems which can be

intensive and require medical and psychological interventions. Some individuals with dyslexia also have ADHD (attention deficit with hyperactivity) (see Appendix I) and require medical treatment under a doctor's supervision.

7. Social Workers—these are professionals trained to provide social guidance and services to the student which involve frequent school-home communications. If home problems are determined (or even just thought) to affect learning adversely, then social workers or home-school adjustment counselors may provide supportive services.

8. Home School Adjustment Counselors—these are professionals who serve in the role of counselors for individual students or small groups of students (i.e., group counseling). Issues related to school and outside of the school setting can be discussed. Such counselors usually make home visits as part of the therapeutic program. Home school adjustment counselors work hard on developing appropriate social skills and behaviors. Group counseling sessions many times focus on appropriate group behaviors and collaborative problem solving or developing peer power strategies.

Peer Power

Certainly developing positive peer relations with a wide range of individuals is a critical plus. The peer group greatly influences the acquisition of social status and self-esteem.

Enhancing Peer Relations and Relationships

The fostering and nurturing of positive peer relationships with individuals who are dyslexic must involve some type of understanding on the part of the peer group of the special learning problems of the dyslexic. This process can be facilitated by parents and teachers alike. We would suggest the following:

1. Encourage openness and honesty in regard to the student's learning problems. It's OK for the student who has dyslexia to say he/she receives extra help in reading or has trouble with reading.

2. Try to instill coping mechanisms that allow the student with dyslexia to handle kidding or jabbing from peers or even other adults. Comeback questions could include: "I'm not sure I understand what you are trying to say?" "Could you explain what you mean?" "I'm sorry you feel that way." "Do you want me to have someone explain what dyslexia is (or what learning disabilities are)?" "I guess you don't understand my problems—that's OK." "It must be great not to have any learning problems."

3. Tell the child with dyslexia that it might be harder for him/her to make friends, as some kids don't understand what learning problems are. Emphasize that everyone has problems and that everyone's problems are different.

4. Encourage opportunities for positive relationships by invitations to the house, a movie, a visit to a mall or video store, etc.

5. Encourage the individual with dyslexia to discuss problems, concerns, or any issue with a responsible person. If he/she doesn't want to listen, there is always someone else who will care and who will listen. It might take a few doors to knock on.

6. Teachers can assign cooperative learning activities such as book reports, science projects, social studies visits, and so on, that encourage positive networking. The activities should be structured with some type of assistance available for proofreading, typing, or editing the work of the individual with dyslexia. Other students could serve as editors.

7. Help build self-esteem by emphasizing positives. Remember individuals with dyslexia often have low self-esteems and self-images. Make it a point to comment, in a positive way, on the dress, work project, and so on, the individual with dyslexia is involved in. Teachers and other professionals can call the home to compliment the caretaker or parents regarding schoolwork on a regular basis. Then, when phone calls need to focus on a problem, much of the groundwork has been done to establish nurturing/caring relationships as opposed to adversarial confrontations.

8. Teachers who have students with learning problems should call parents to clue them into positive and healthy relationships they can foster, by invitations to the home or other after-school activities such as arts and crafts, a class newspaper, and club activities.

9. Teachers need to encourage parents to seek professional support and guidance, when needed, by giving referrals to proven programs, respected practitioners, advocacy groups, etc. (see Chapter 10 on resources).

10. Provide many and varied cooperative reading activities (see Chapters 4–7). Children learn best to read by reading. Keep leisure types of reading materials around the house and in the classroom such as rock magazines, Weekly Readers, paperback books, newspapers, movie star magazines, etc. Encourage classroom and family reading times when leisure reading would be appropriate. Also, encourage game playing that involves reading such as Trivial Pursuit, In Search of Identity, Monopoly, Word Search, etc. Make frequent group trips to the library (with friends or siblings). Allow the student with dyslexia to choose his/her own reading materials. If the material turns out to be too difficult, take it in stride, show that it's OK, and indicate that next time it might be better to get something that is a bit easier to read.

11. Teachers and parents need to place the individual with dyslexia in a helping role as opposed to always being the one who is helped. The individual with dyslexia could assist a younger child with homework; read books to preschoolers; visit a nursing home and read to senior citizens; be a friend or big brother or sister to a needy child; volunteer time in boys and girls clubs; visit a hospital or homeless shelter during the holidays; complete a chore at home, assist in after-school activities, etc. It is important to keep in mind that these activities should be structured with clear expectations and directions as well as continual feedback. The teacher or parent should ask the student exactly what he or she will do step-by-step before beginning the activity. Mock dramatizations can be done beforehand. Discussions also need to center on

---

TABLE 9-1   Developing Self Esteem with Students with Learning Disabilities

- Provide positive and constructive feedback first and foremost
- Develop strengths as well as weaknesses
- Provide opportunities for responsible actions both in the classroom (e.g., tutoring others) and at home (e.g., chores)
- Do not compare performances to others including siblings
- Keep a portfolio of achievements and social/academic growth
- Develop talents and special abilities
- Provide opportunities for positive social interaction with peers (e.g., clubs)
- Develop hobbies and collections
- Establish realistic goals and expectations—encourage the same with the student
- View mistakes and errors as opportunities for self-reflection and growth
- Point to others with similar struggles

---

what to do if the person(s) the individual with dyslexia is trying to assist doesn't want the help or is(are) very negative. At that point, it would be wise for the student with dyslexia to call or find a predesignated problem consultant to discuss what to do.

Of particular importance to the dyslexic is the need for positive interactions and reinforcement from teachers and peers, which would enhance the dyslexic's self-image and self-esteem (see Table 9-1 above) as dyslexics have been noted to have a less than positive self-worth. The root of this perception seems to lie in the complex interactive effect of the failures wrought by the disability itself and personal and environmental consequences such as negative peer and teacher perceptions (Spafford & Grosser, 1993). Activities such as those listed in Table 9-1 enhance self-esteem and need to be continually implemented.

Removal of the dyslexic from the regular classroom can intensify feelings of alienation as the dyslexic can end up not being "bonded" to a particular classroom. Teachers have to try to reinforce the concept of "belongingness" for the dyslexic, with a concerted effort made toward providing as much cohesiveness and stability in the dyslexic's schedule as possible.

The Adult with Dyslexia

Overview

After students finish school, what next? Remember that the 1988 NJLCD definition states that learning disabilities may occur across one's life span. The NJCLD (1988) addresses some basic tenets and issues related to adults with learning disabilities: (1) learning disabilities may last a life time, (2) problems associated with the learning disability may change over time, (3) current assessment procedures are geared for children and adolescents with learning disabilities (not adults), (4) adults with

dyslexia and other learning disabilities are frequently denied equal vocational opportunities and counseling, (5) most professionals in the field are trained to work
with children and young adolescents, (6) employers frequently are not prepared
to handle the very special needs of individuals with learning disabilities, (7) advocacy programs for adults with learning disabilities are not sufficient, and (8) program funding for adult programs is lacking in most states. The fact that learning
disabilities most often persist into adulthood implies that interventions, strategies,
and other coping mechanisms must be available for this population if optimal life
successes are to be achieved (Zigmond & Sansone, 1986; Zigmond & Baker, 1994).
There are no magic cures which eliminate childhood dyslexia. The problems are
still there in one form or another. Some cope better than others, with adequate
support systems a critical component to this population's future successes.

No Magic Cures

Overview

"It would be less than honest to leave the impression that magical techniques and
procedures will work wonders for the learning-disabled child" (Ekwall & Shanker,
1988, p. 365). It would appear that the personality of the teacher who is knowledgeable about dyslexia would have more of an impact than a particular technique
or approach. Balow (1971) sums up this thought quite well, "Until experimentally
proven otherwise, it may be that the simplest explanation of success obtained with
any treatment for learning disabilities is the power and skill of the teacher who believes in it" (p. 519). It is our hope to develop remedial visual accessories, approaches or strategies for those dyslexics who evidence visual-perceptual anomalies after research has verified the existence of such problems. Various
controversial approaches are also presented in Chapter 3, which carry the caveat,
"buyer beware." It is critical for all of us to be aware of unproven methods which
can sometimes be damaging.

A Reflective Process

It would be important to note that the assessment process must be an active, reflective, and ongoing process so that adaptations can be made every step of the
way. Regardless of how one applies assessments and other relevant information to
techniques and assistance for individuals with dyslexia, support systems must contain individuals who demonstrate warmth, care, and support. We would recommend designating an LD Problem Consultant(s) to assist individuals with dyslexia
to cross the hurdles in everyday school and life situations. Regardless of the
specifics used, "The greater the repertoire of interpersonal and specialty program
responses, the higher the probability that the helper can meet the helpee's unique
needs" (Carkhuff & Berenson, 1976, p. 184).

Conclusions

The planning, design, and implementation of appropriate service options and instructional strategies for students with dyslexia must also be concerned that professionals have a clear understanding of what dyslexia is and the manner in which unique learning problems of the individual with dyslexia should be addressed. After a child has been diagnosed as dyslexic, a report should be compiled to detail findings and recommendations. Dyslexic children are then required to have what is called an IEP or individual education plan (as determined by an evaluation team) which is a requirement under Federal Public Law PL 94–142 (which has since been renamed to IDEA or The Individual with Disabilities Education Act of 1990), if special services are provided.

The IEP serves a dual function, as an evaluation tool and as a teaching plan with diagnostic information provided in the context of educational planning and teaching strategies. An IEP should include a statement of the student's present levels of functioning, both short-term and annual goals, projected dates for initiation and duration of special services, specific criteria and evaluation procedures to be used to determine if goals have been achieved, the names of persons responsible for special services and evaluation, descriptions of special services to be provided, and the extent to which the student will participate in regular education programs

Placement of the dyslexic child in an appropriate program is necessary to her/his social/academic/emotional/cognitive well-being. Self-contained classes (also known as pull-out models) for dyslexics and other learning disabled children were prevalent during the '60s and early '70s. The late '70s and the decade of the '80s saw resource rooms or centers that are pull-out programs, as providing supplemental support to the regular classroom initiative. The regular education initiative (REI) which began in the mid to late 1980s began to place greater emphasis on programs which educated students with dyslexia in the regular classroom. REI trends for the 1990s have involved collaborative consultations, and the inclusion model which is becoming a popular alternative to the resource room setting.

Cooperative learning was discussed as one way to increase learning and positive social interactions in students with dyslexia and other learning disabilities. Cooperative learning activities are not easily presented or learned by students. If a teacher is willing to invest the time and effort required for successful implementation, payoffs will be seen in academic growth and social skills acquisition. Teachers must select subbjects and appropriate time frames for cooperative learning activities based upon the individual and group needs of his/her classroom.

The inclusion model involves the full participation of the student with dyslexia in regular classroom activities. We recommend a continuum of service options be available to students with dyslexia which is consistent with the LDA (Learning Disabilities Association of America) position which doesn't fully support inclusionary programs or policies which mandate uniform program treatment (i.e., inclusionary policies) for students with dyslexia. It appears that there must be a middle ground between substantially separate programs and total inclusionary models. Common sense should prevail. Certainly students with severe disabilities and/or physical/emotional problems might benefit more from special-ized programs outside the regular classroom which have the staff and low stu-dent-teacher ratios to provide the most optimal educational experience for all. Most teachers have all they can handle in coping with the everyday happenings and diversity in the classroom and are ill-equipped to deal with students who re-quire intense one-to-one instructional programming. Students with severe forms of dyslexia require substantially separate programs and many private schools now also provide wonderful services in that regard.

The next chapter deals with resources available to parents, teachers, students, and professionals who are interested in the problem of dyslexia.

Chapter 10

Resources

. . . It is good for us to be here. We stand where we have
an immense view of what is, and what is past . . .
Let us . . . reflect . . . —(BURKE, 1855, P. 373).

Professional Improvement

"There are many organizational factors that affect the direction of a learning disabilities program, including the administration of the institution, the working and personal relationship among staff members, the goals and ambitions of the organization, and the role and status of the learning disabilities specialist within the organization" (Lerner, 1971, p. 256). A key ingredient to making all of this work is professional development.

The phrase, *professional improvement,* implies an integrative professional growth and development plan. Arranging such a plan is a necessary requisite to achieving a major teaching goal; that is, we must continually advance our efforts to meet the educational, social, psychological, and medical needs of all of our learners, to include those with dyslexia and other learning problems. Educators faced with the prospect of working with increasingly large numbers of students, all with varying learning styles, needs, and problems, must be able to call on support systems to assist in the educational/social/emotional program planning of the children and adolescents served.

Professional Improvement Plans (PIPs)

Many schools now implement PIPs or Professional Improvement Plans which select goals and develop programs when planning for the educational/social/emotional needs of students with dyslexia. Through PIPs and similar strategies, educators are agreeing to upgrade curriculum-planning efforts and professional performance by

TABLE 10-1 Key Resource Components to Professional Improvement Development

PIPs—Professional Improvement Plans

Organizational Support

- Public Agencies
- Private Resources Listed by New England Index
- State Level Department of Rehabilitation
- Specific Organizations
    - NJCLD Organizations
    - National Resources Promoting Literacy
    - Professional Support for Parents and Professionals

Periodicals

Data–Based Computer Program Search Systems

- ERIC
- NICEM
- CEC
- PAIS
- PsychScan: LD/MR
- SpecialNet Communication Network

Legal Services

- LRE

Conducting Research

participating in a number of activities, to include school-wide meetings, observations of other classrooms, in-service workshops, participation in research, the reading of periodicals, education journals, and so on (see Table 10-1 above).

Professional Portfolios

The development of professional portfolios on the part of educators would be a necessary ingredient to any professional improvement efforts. A portfolio is a personalized compilation of outcomes generated from one's growth as a reflective teacher practitioner. Bozzone (1994) suggests that educators consider including the following in a professional portfolio: a summary of professional participation in workshops, classes, and related organizations; samples of students' exemplary work; class newsletters, letters to parents, and samples from student journals; photographs of classroom activities with captions; notes from colleagues, parents, and students; a statement of one's philosophy of education or education credo; journal entries which reflect how you made a difference in the lives of your students; video- and audiotapes of the class and one's teaching; records of successful strategies used with students who experience disabilities and behavior difficulties; reflections from your students about your teaching; newspaper or magazine clippings about members of your class or the class as a whole; student accomplishments; a list of "What I did that I'll never do again!" and a listing of goals and monthly self-assessment with accompanying modifications when appropriate.

Organizational Support

Program planning also involves considering and deciding to utilize any or several of the organizations which can assist in the programming/placement decisions of individuals with dyslexia; parent advisory committees for those who have children and adolescents with dyslexia; agencies which can address vocational/rehabilitation needs of individuals with learning disabilities; journals which can provide guidance as to appropriate and valid assessment tools, remedial techniques, behavior management plans, in-service plans for schools, and so on. There are a number of types of agencies which can address all of the factors mentioned. One need only to determine what is needed, whom to turn to, the monetary costs involved, the time requirements, and the intended outcomes. The list of public agencies in Table 10-2 (below) provides a general overview of service offerings which can assist professionals, parents, and individuals with dyslexia and other learning disabilities and problems.

Public Agencies

The list that follows describes how a variety of governmental agencies may be of assistance to people with disabilities and their families.

Office of State Coordinator of Vocational Education for Handicapped Students

All states receiving programs supported by Federal funds for vocational education programs must assure that funding is used in programs which include students with handicaps, including dyslexia.

TABLE 10-2 Public Agencies

- Office of State Coordinator of Vocational Education for Handicapped Students
- Protection and Advocacy Agency and Client Assistance Programs
- Programs for Children with Special Health Care Needs
- State Education Department
- State Developmental Disabilities Council
- State Developmental Disabilities Office
- State Mental Health Agencies
- State Vocational Rehabilitation Agency
- University Affiliated Programs

Protection and Advocacy Agency and Client Assistance Programs

Protection and Advocacy systems are responsible for protecting the rights of people who are developmentally disabled or mentally ill, regardless of their age. Protection and Advocacy agencies may provide information about health, residential, and social services in your area.

Programs for Children with Special Health Care Needs

The U.S. Department of Health and Human Services' Office of Maternal and Child Health and Resource Development provides grants to states for services to children with handicapping conditions. Services will vary from state to state. Additional programs may be funded for training, research, special projects, and counseling services. For additional information about current grants and programs in your state, contact the National Center for Education in Maternal and Child Health, 38th and R Streets, N.W., Washington, D.C. 20057.

State Education Department

The State Department of Education in your state can answer questions about special education and related services for dyslexics.

State Developmental Disabilities Council

State councils plan and advocate for improvement in services for individuals with developmental disabilities.

State Developmental Disabilities Office

The general purpose of this office is to plan, administer and develop standards for state/local developmental disabilities programs provided in state-operated facilities and community-based programs. This office provides information about available services to dyslexics' families, educators, and other professionals.

State Mental Health Agencies

State mental health agency functions vary from state to state, but, generally, they provide outreach programs and medical services to their clients.

State Vocational Rehabilitation Agency

Your state vocational rehabilitation agency should provide medical, therapeutic, counseling, education, training, and other services needed to prepare people with learning disabilities for work. This agency will provide you with the address of the nearest rehabilitation office where discussion of eligibility of services with a counselor can occur.

University Affiliated Programs

A national network of programs affiliated with universities provides training for professionals and offers programs and services for children with disabilities and their families. One can obtain a listing of all University Affiliated Programs by contacting The Maternal and Child Health Clearinghouse, 38th and R Streets, N.W., Washington, D.C. 20057.

American Association of University Affiliated Programs for Persons with Developmental Disabilities (AAUAP)
8605 Cameron Street
Suite 406
Silver Spring, MD 20910

Private Resources Listed by New England INDEX

The New England INDEX of the Shriver Center at Waltham, MA has listed private agencies that assist people with special needs in general and dyslexia in particular. INDEX also lists newsletters for those concerned with learning disabilities.

Agencies

Federation for Children with Special Needs
95 Berkeley Street, Suite 104
Boston, MA 02116

A parent-run child advocacy and information center, with parent training in assertiveness, communication, due process, mediation, resource identification, and maintaining positive relations with schools. Provides information on special education laws. Publishes a quarterly newsletter. A resource library and speakers bureau are available. CAPP and NEC-TAS are also housed at the Federation.

CAPP (Collaboration Among Parents & Health Professionals)
National Parent Resource Center
(see address for Federation for Children with Special Needs)

A resource for materials on family-focused practices in the areas of early childhood education, health care, and special needs.

NEC-TAS (National Early Childhood Technical Assistance System)
(see address for Federation for Children with Special Needs)

A clearinghouse for information about information, ideas, projects, literature and research on siblings, etc., family-related issues with the handicapped. Provides bibliographies, lists of audiovisual materials, resources for siblings, and assistance on researching sibling-related topics.

Siblings Information Network
Connecticut's University-Affiliated Program
991 Main Street, Suite 3A
East Hartford, CT 06108

A nation-wide parent-run resource system providing training, technical assistance, and print materials for parents of children with special needs; annotated bibliographies.

National Information System
University of South Carolina
Benson Bldg., First Floor
Columbia, SC 29208

Nation-wide, computer-based information and referral system for information about specific disabilities, medical/educational/counseling/social services for children with disabilities and their families.

Information Center for Individuals with Disabilities
Fort Point, first Floor
27–43 Wormwood Street
Boston, MA 02210–1606

A computerized database with information for disabled individuals concerning 16 major issues: architectural access, personal care, communication, transportation, travel, recreation, disabilities, housing, finances, law, education, counseling, employment, information, equipment, and medical care. Staff is bilingual. Database covers services statewide. Print library contains over 10,000 books, brochures, and catalogs. Provides access to a nation-wide network of sources of information.

Special Needs Project
1482 East Valley Rd. #A–121
Santa Barbara, CA 93108

An organization that sells books about physical and mental abilities by mail. Customized bibliographies on specific topics are available. The project consults with public and private agencies, schools, and libraries.

Newsletters

"The Exchange"
LD Network
72 Sharp St., Suite 2A
Hingham, MA 02043

A newsletter for professionals in the learning disabilities field, assisting in professional development, referrals, and information.

"Disability Issues"
Information Center
27–43 Wormwood St.
Boston, MA 02210–1606

A newsletter providing information of interest to disabled persons.

Special Needs Advocacy Network (SPAN)
259 Jackson Street
Newton Centre, MA 02159

A newsletter providing a schedule of seminars and lectures on topics of interest to those interested in the rights of people with special needs.

Support for the Adult with Dyslexia

The adult with dyslexia requires specialized vocational guidance which can be provided by direct services through state-level departments of rehabilitation including employment counseling, placement, and job retraining. For example, the state of Illinois' Department of Rehabilitation Services (DORS) provides secondary transitional experience programs (STEP) and vocational adjustment counselors for students with dyslexia at the secondary school level. Counseling, vocational evaluation, and assistance in locating employment after program completion are provided through the Illinois DORS. The Illinois DORS' "Next Steps Program" also gives "parents of children with disabilities . . . effective methods of planning for their child's education and career opportunities through a specific training course . . . a smooth transition to vocational education, community work or higher education for children with disabilities" is emphasized (Illinois Department of Rehabilitation Services, 1993, p. 8). The state listings in Table 10-3 (see pp. 265–268) provide similar information for students with dyslexia and other learning disabilities. State departments of education are included as they frequently house departments which deal directly with individuals who have dyslexia and other learning disabilities.

Specific Organizations Addressing the Problem of Dyslexia

National Joint Committee on Learning Disabilities (NJCLD)

There are specific organizations which key in on the special problems and needs of the individual with dyslexia. The National Joint Committee on Learning Disabilities (NJCLD), in particular, is a consortium of organizations concerned with learning disabled individuals and consists of several subunits. The NJCLD has the following aims: (1) facilitating communication among the member organizations; (2) providing for interdisciplinary review of issues in order to serve educational and governmental agencies and to serve as a resource committee for such agencies; (3) responding to national issues involving learning disabilities when the need arises; (4) resolving disagreements on learning disability issues; (5) preparing public statements to clarify issues related to learning disabilities; and (6) identification of needs for research and/or services in the learning disabilities area.

There are five organizations which deal exclusively with individuals who are learning disabled: Learning Disabilities Association of America **(LDA)**, Council for Learning Disabilities **(CLD)**, Division for Learning Disabilities of the Council of Exceptional Children **(DLD),** The Orton Dyslexia Society, Inc. **(ODS)**, and the National Joint Committee on Learning Disabilities **(NJCLD)**.

TABLE 10-3 State-Level Departments of Rehabilitation

Alabama State Dept. of
Education
Program for Exceptional
Children and Youth
1020 Montgomery, AL 36117

Alabama Division of
Vocational Rehabilitation
2129 E.S. Blvd.
P.O. Box 11586
Montgomery, AL 36111

Alaska Division of Vocational
Rehabilitation
801 West 10th Street
Suite 201
Juneau, AK 99801

Arizona Rehabilitation
Services Administration
1789 W. Jefferson
Phoenix, AZ 85007

Arizona Department of
Education
1535 W. Jefferson
Phoenix, AZ 85007

Arkansas Division of
Rehabilitation Services
300 Donaghey Plaza North
P.O. Box 3781
Little Rock, AR 72203

Arkansas Dept. of Ed.
Education Building
Room 105-C
54 Capital Mall
Little Rock, AR 72201

California Department of
Education
830 K Street Mall
Sacramento, CA 95814

California Department of Ed.,
Special Education Division
721 Capitol Mall
P.O. Box 944272
Sacramento, CA 95814

Colorado Dept. of Social Serv.
Rehabilitation Services, 4th
Floor, 1575 Sherman Street
Denver, CO 80203-5196

Colorado Dept. of Ed. Special
Education Serv. Unit, Works
with Service Providers
(CMIC/VH)
201 E. Colfax Avenue
Denver, CO 80220

Connecticut Bureau of
Rehabilitation Services
10 Griffin Road-North
Windsor, CT 06095

Connecticut State Board of
Education Services for the
Blind
170 Ridge Road
Wethersfield, CT 06109

Dept. of Public Instruction
Exceptional Children and
Special Programs Division
P.O. Box 1402
Dover, DE 19903

Delaware Div. of Voc. Rehab.
Department of Labor
Elwyn Building
321 East 11th Street
Wilmington, DE 19802

District of Columbia
Department of Education
Webster Admin. Building
10th & H Streets 76, NW
Washington, DC 20001

District of Columbia
Rehab. Services Admin.
605 G. Street, NW
Suite 111
Washington, DC 20001

District of Columbia
Rehabilitation Service Admin.
Commission of Social Services
Department of Human
Services
605 G Street, NW, Room 1111
Washington, DC 20001

Florida Division of Vocational
Rehabilitation
Department of Labor and
Employment Security
1709-B Mahan Drive
Tallahassee, FL 32399-0696

Florida Department of Ed.
Bureau of Education for
Exceptional Students
Knott Building
Tallahassee, FL 32399

Georgia Division of
Rehabilitation Services
2 Peachtree Street, NW
23rd Floor, Room 102
Atlanta, GA 30303

Hawaii Division of Vocational
Rehabilitation
Dept. of Human Services
Bishop Trust Building
1000 Bishop St, Room 605
Honolulu, HI 96815

Hawaii State Dept. of
Education
Special Needs Branch
3430 Leahi Avenue
Honolulu, HI 96815

Idaho Division of Vocational
Rehab.
650 W. State Street
Room 150
Boise, ID 83720

Illinois Department of
Rehabilitation Services
623 E. Adams Street
P.O. Box 19429
Springfield, IL 62794-9429

Illinois State Board of Ed.
Specialized Ed. Services
100 N. First Street
Springfield, IL 62777

Indiana Division of Disability
Vocational Rehab. Serv.
402 W. Washington Street
Government Center South
Room W453
Indianapolis, IN 46207-7083

Indiana Division of Special
Education
229 State House
Indianapolis, IN 46204

Iowa Division of Vocational
Rehabilitation Services
Department of Education
510 E. 12th Street
Des Moines, IA 50319

Continued

TABLE 10-3 *Continued*

Iowa Dept. of Public Instr.
Special Education Division
Grimes State Office Build.
Des Moines, IA 50319-0146

Kansas State Department of
Education
120 East Tenth Street
Topeka, KS 66612

Kansas Rehabilitation Serv.
Biddle Building
300 SW Oakley
Topeka, KS 66606-1995

Kentucky Office of Vocational
Rehabilitation
930 Capital Plaza Tower
Frankfort, KY 40601

Kentucky Vocational
Rehabilitation Services
Capital Plaza Tower, 9th Floor
500 Mero Street
Frankfort, KY 40601

Louisiana Division of
Rehabilitation Services
Department of Social Services
P.O. Box 94371
1755 Florida Street
Baton Rouge, LA 70804-9371

Louisiana State Department of
Education
P.O. Box 94064
Baton Rouge, LA 70804

Maine Bureau of
Rehabilitation
Dept. of Human Services
32 Winthrop Street
Augusta, ME 04330

Maine State Department of
Educational and Cultural Serv.
Division of Special Education
State House, Station 23
Augusta, ME 04333

Maryland Division of
Rehabilitation Services
2301 Argonne Drive
Baltimore, MD 21218-1696

Maryland State Dept. of Ed.
Division of Special Education
200 W. Baltimore Street
Baltimore, MD 21201

Massachusetts Rehabilitation
Commission
Fort Point Place
27-43 Wormwood Street
Boston, MA 02110-1606

Massachusetts State
Department of Education
1385 Hancock Street
Quincy, MA 02169

Michigan Rehabilitation Serv.
608 W. Allegan
P.O. Box 30010
Lansing, MI 48909

Michigan Department of Ed.
Special Education Services
P.O. Box 30008
Lansing, MI 48909

Minnesota Division of
Rehabilitation Services
Dept. of Jobs and Training
390 N. Robert Street, 5th Floor
St. Paul, MN 55101

Minnesota Department of
Education
Capitol Square Build. Rm 813
St. Paul, MN 55101

Mississippi Department of
Rehabilitation Services
P.O. Box 1698
Jackson, MS 39215-1698

Mississipi Bureau of Special
Services
State Department of
Education
P.O. Box 771
Jackson, MS 39205-0771

Division of Special Education
Department of Elementary
and Secondary Education
P.O. Box 480
Jefferson City, MO 65102

Missouri State Department of
Education
Division of Vocational Rehab.
2401 E. McCarty
Jefferson, MO 65101

Montana Department of Social
and Rehabilitation Serv.
Rehabilitative/Visual Ser. Div.
P.O. Box 4210
Helena, MT 59604

Montana Office of Public
Instruction
Educational Services
State Capitol
Helena, MT 59604

Nebraska Division of Rehab.
301 Centennial Mall
South-6th Floor
Lincoln, NE 68509-4987

Nebraska Special Ed. Branch
Box 94987
301 Centennial Mall South
Lincoln, NE 68509

Nevada Rehabilitation
Division of Human Resources
Kinkead Building, 5th Floor
5505 E. King Street
Carson City, NV 89710

Nevada Dept. of Education
Special Education Branch
400 W. King Street
Capitol Complex
Carson City, NV 89710

New Hampshire Division of
Vocational Rehabilitation
78 Regional Drive, Build 2
Concord, NH 03301

New Hampshire Department
of Education
Division of Education
101 Pleasant Street
Concord, NH 03301

New Jersey Division of
Vocational Rehab. Services
CN 398
Treton, NJ 08625-0398

New Jersey Dept of Labor
Division of Vocational
Rehabilitation
CN 398
Treton, NJ 08625-0398

TABLE 10-3 *Continued*

New Mexico Div. of Voc.
Rehabilitation
State Dept. of Ed.
435 St. Michael's Drive
Bldg. D
Santa Fe, NM 87505

New Mexico Special Ed. Unit
State Department of Ed.
Educational Building
Santa Fe, NM 87501-2786

New York State Ed. Dept.
Office of Vocational Rehab.
99 Washington Avenue
Room 1907
Albany, NY 12234

New York State Dept. of Ed.
Office for Ed. of Children with
Handicapping Conditions
Educational Building Annex
Room 1066
Albany, NY 12234

North Carolina Div. of
Vocational Rehabilitation Ser.
Department of Human Res.
State Office, P.O. Box 26053
Raleigh, NC 27611

Division for Exceptional
Children
State Dept. of Public Instr.
116 W. Edenton Street
Raleigh, NC 27603-1712

North Dakota Office of
Vocational Rehabilitation
Department of Human Serv.
400 E. Broadway Ave
Suite 303
Bismark, ND 58501-4038

North Dakota Department of
Public Instruction
State Capitol
Bismark, ND 58505

Ohio Rehabilitation Services
Commission
400 E. Campus View Boulvd.
Columbus, OH 43235-4604

Oklahoma Dept. of
Rehabilitation Services
P.O. Box 36659
Oklahoma City, OK 73136

Oregon Vocational Rehab.
Division
Dept. of Human Res.
2045 Silverton Road, N.E.
Salem, OR 97310

Oregon Dept. of Ed.
Special Ed. & Student Services
700 Pringle Parkway, SE
Salem, OR 97310

Pennsylvania Office of Voc.
Rehab
Dept. of Labor and Industry
1300 Labor & Industry Build.
7th and Forster Street
Harrisburg, PA 17120

Pennsylvania Dept. of
Special Ed.
333 Market Street, 7th Floor
P.O. Box 911
Harrisburg, PA 17126-0333

Rhode Island Office of Rehab.
Services
40 Fountain Street
Providence, RI 02908

Rhode Island Dept. Of Ed.
Roger Williams Build., Rm 102
22 Hayes Street
Providence, RI 02908

South Carolina Voc. Rehab.
Department
P.O. Box 15
1410 Boston Avenue
W. Columbia, SC 29171-0015

South Dakota Div. of
Rehabilitation Services
Richard F. Kneip Build
700 N. Governers Drive
Pierre, SD 57501-2275

South Dakota Section for
Special Ed.
900 N. Illinois
Pierre, SD 57501

Tennessee Division of
Rehabilitation Services
Citizen Plaza State Office
Build.
400 Deaderick Street, 11 Floor
Nashville, TN 37248-6000

Tennessee Dept. of Ed.
Division of Spec. Programs
132 Cordell Hull Building
Nashville, TN 37219

Texas Rehabilitation
Commission
4900 N. Lamar Blvd.
Austin, TX 78751-2399

Texas Ed. Agency
Dept. of Special Education
1701 N. Congress Ave.
Austin, TX 78701-1494

Utah State Office of
Rehabilitation
250 E. 500 South
Salt Lake City, UT 84111

Utah State Office of Education
Special Education Dept.
250 E. 500 South
Salt Lake City, UT 84111

Vermont Vocational Rehab.
Division
Agency of Human Services
Osgood Building
Waterbury Complex
103 S. Main Street
Waterbury, VT 05676

Vermont Division of Special
Education
State Office Building
120 State Street
Montpelier, VT 05601

Virginia Dept. of
Rehabilitation Services
4901 Fitzhugh Avenue
P.O. Box 11045
Richmond, VA 23230-1045

Virginia Office of Special
Compensatory Education
P.O. Box 6Q
Richmond, VA 23216-2060

Washington Division of
Vocational Rehab.
P.O. Box 45340
Olympia, WA 98504-5340

Continued

TABLE 10-3 *Continued*

Washington Office of
Superintendent Public
Instruction
Old Capitol Building, FG-11
Olympia, WA 98504

West Virginia Division of
Rehabilitation Services
P.O. Box 50890
State Capitol Complex
Charleston, WV 25305-0890

Wisconsin Dept. of Public
Instruction
125 S. Webster Street
P.O. Box 7841
Madison, WI 53707

Wisconsin Dept. of Health
and Social Services
1 W. Wilson, 8th Floor
P.O. Box 7852
Madison, WI 53702

Wyoming Division of
Vocational Rehabilitation
1100 Herschler Bldg.
Cheyenne, WY 82002

American Samoa
Office of Voc. Rehab.
Dept. of Human Resources
American Samoa Gov.
P.O. Box 3492
Pago Pago, AS 96799

Guam-Harmon Ind. Park
Dept. of Voc. Rehab.
Government of Guam
122 I T and E Plaza
Tamunin, GU 96911

Guam Dept. of Education
Special Education
P.O. Box DE
Agana, GU 96910

Federated States of Micronesia
Voc. Rehab. Services
Office of Education
Ponape, FM 96941

Puerto Rico Voc. Rehab.
Dept. of Social Services
P.O. Box 1118
Hato Rey, PR 00910

Puerto Rico Dept. of Ed.
G.P.O. Box 759
Hato Rey, PR 00910

Republic of Palau
Vocational Rehabilitation
Bureau of Education
P.O. Box 189
Koro, PW 96940

Republic of the Marhsall
Islands
Voc. Rehab. Health Services
Dept.
P.O. Box 832
Majuro, MH 96960

Commonwealth of Northern
Mariana Islands
Vocational Rehabilitation
Division-Public Schools
Lower Base
Saipan, MP 96950

TABLE 10-4 NJCLD Organizations

**American Speech-
Language-Hearing
Association (ASLHA)**
10801 Rockville Pike
Rockville, MD 20852

**Association on Higher
Education and Disability
(AHEAD)**
P.O. Box 21192
Columbus, OH 43221-0192

**Council for Learning
Disabilities**
P.O. Box 40303
Overland Park, KS 66204

**Division for Children with
Communication Disorders
(DCCD)-CEC**
1920 Association Drive
Reston, VA 22091

**Division for Learning
Disabilities (DLD)-CEC**
1920 Association Drive
Reston, VA 22091

**International Reading
Association (IRA)**
P.O. Box 8139
Newark, DE 19714-8139

**Learning Disabilities Assoc.
of America (LDA)
(Formerly ACLD, Inc.)**
4156 Library Road
Pittsburgh, PA 15234

**National Assoc. of School
Psychologists (NASP)**
808 17th Street, NW
Suite 200
Washington, DC 20006

**The Orton Dyslexia Society
(OSD)**
724 York Road
Baltimore, MD 21204

NJCLD—Political and Professional LD Arm

"These (NJCLD) organizations are the political and professional arms of the learning disabilities movement. It is through membership in these associations that parents, teachers, psychologists, researchers, and others find a professional identity with learning disabilities. The lobbying efforts of these associations protect exist-

TABLE 10-5   National Resources for the Promotion of Literacy

American Assoc. for Adult and Cont. Ed. 2101 Wilson Blvd., Suite 925 Arlington, VA 22201	**General Foundation of Women's Clubs** 1735 N. Street, NW Washington, DC 20036-2990	**National Center for Family Literacy** 401 S. 4th Avenue, Suite 610 Louisville, KY 40202
American Bar Association Special Committee on Law and Literacy 1800 M. Street, NW Washington, DC 20036	**International Reading Association** 800 Barksdale Road P.O. Box 8139 Newark, DE 19714-8139	**National Institute for Literacy** 800 Connecticut Avenue, NW Suite 200 Washington, DC 20202-7560
American Library Assoc. 50 E. Huron Chicago, IL 60611	**Laubach Literacy Action** 1320 Jamesville Ave., Box 131 Syracuse, NY 13210	**Reading is Fundamental (RIF)** 600 Maryland Avenue, SW Suite 600 Washington, DC 20024
Clearinghouse of Adult Literacy and Learning Division of Adult Ed. and Literacy U.S. Department of Ed. 400 Maryland Avenue, SW Washington, DC 20202-7240	**Literacy Volunteers of America, Inc.** 5795 Widewaters Parkway Syracuse, NY 13214	

ing funding for learning disabilities programs and garner new sources of financial support" (Hammill, 1993, pp. 297–298). The following societies or organizations comprise the NJCLD.

There are organizations other than those affiliated with the NJCLD which can provide support for parents and educators and in a number of areas; special testing considerations for dyslexics, coping strategies, technological advances in the field, fund raising, legal rights, advocacy, and so on. The following professional support groups are easily accessible and provide valuable input and support.

National Resources for the Promotion of Literacy

Some agencies have been organized that are dedicated to the stamping out of illiteracy in the United States. These agencies are listed in Table 10-5 above.

Professional Support for Parents and Educators

Several of the organizations listed in Table 10-6 provide assistance to parents and educators for individuals with learning disabilities and other co-occurring handicaps.

Organizations for Dyslexics and Other LD Individuals

Alexander Graham Bell Association for the Deaf
3417 Volta Place, NW
Washington, DC 20007

Provides assistance to individuals with hearing disabilities.

TABLE 10-6   Professional Support for Parents and Educators

- Alexander Graham Bell Association for the Deaf
- American College Testing Program
- Architectural and Transportation Barriers Compliance Board
- Association of Learning Disabled Adults (ALDA)
- Association on Handicapped Student Service Programs in Post-secondary Education
- Association for Supervision and Curriculum Development
- Center for Special Education Technology
- Closer Look
- Co-ADD (Coalition for the Education and Support of Attention Deficit Disorder)
- Council for Exceptional Children (CEC)
- Council for Learning Disabilities (CLD)
- Disability Rights Education and Defense Fund, Inc.
- Division for Learning Disabilities (DLD)
- Education Testing Services/College Board
- Equal Employment Opportunity Commission (EEOC)
- Foundation for Children with Learning Disabilities
- HEATH Resource Center (Higher Education and the Handicapped)
- House Annex #2 (House Document Room)
- International Reading Association
- Job Accommodation Network (JAN)
- Learning Disabilities Association of America (LDA)
- National Center for Learning Disabilities
- National Center for Special Education Technology Information Exchange
- National Easter Seal Society
- National Information Center for Children and Youth with Disabilities (NICHCY)
- National Institute of Dyslexic/TRI Services
- National Joint Committee on Learning Disabilities (NJCLD)
- National Network of Learning Disabled Adults (NNLDA)
- National Organization on Disability
- President's Committee on Employment of People with Disabilities
- US Department of Health and Human Services
- US Department of Transportation

American College Testing Program

ACT Test Administration
Special Testing
P.O. Box 168
Iowa City, IA 52243

Produces a Special Testing Guide for the ACT assessment program and standardized tests in the areas of English, math, social studies, and natural sciences.

Architectural and Transportation Barriers Compliance Board

1331 F. St., NW, 10th Floor
Washington, DC 20004–1111

Provides information regarding architectural requirements for those who also have physical handicaps.

Association of Learning Disabled Adults (ALDA)

P.O. Box 9722
Friendship Station
Washington, DC 20016

A support network of learning disabled adults which offers help in finding more effective ways for learning disabled individuals to cope with their disabilities.

Association on Handicapped Student Service Programs in Postsecondary Education (AHSSPPE)
P.O. Box 21192
Columbus, OH 43221

This referral network consists of members and institutions of postsecondary education. It encourages the participation of disabled individuals in mainstream campus life. Inquiries to the national office are referred to the campus network of disabled student service programs.

Association for Supervision and Curriculum Development
1250 North Pitt Street
Alexandria, VA 22314

Provides materials in the areas of supervision and curriculum for all grade levels for all students.

Center for Special Education Technology
1920 Association Drive
Reston, VA 22091

Publisher of the Resources Inventory series and Tech Use Guides for parents and teachers, the Center is a resource for computer-related materials and assistive devices for learning-disabled individuals.

Closer Look
Box 1492
Washington, D.C. 20013

A national information center for parents and professionals in the field which provides information on program planning for students with learning disabilities and other handicaps.

Co-ADD (Coalition for the Education and Support of Attention Deficit Disorder)
P.O. Box 242
Osseo, MI 55369

Provides information for individuals with attention deficit disorders.

Council for Exceptional Children (CEC)
1920 Association Drive
Reston, VA 22091–1589

The Council provides programs for special educators, education specialists, classroom teachers, researchers, and other professionals committed to educating children and young people having unusual (high or low) learning abilities. One of the subdivisions of CEC is the DLD (later in list). The Clearinghouse on Handicapped and Gifted Children, a part of the Educational Resources Information Center (ERIC) network, is administered by the Council. The Council also publishes journals, such as *Exceptional Children, Teaching Exceptional Children, Exceptional Child Education Resources, Behavioral Disorders, Career*

Development for Exceptional Individuals, Journal of Early Intervention, Education and Training in Mental Retardation, Diagnostique, Journal of Childhood Communication Disorders, and *Learning Disabilities—Research and Practice.*

Council for Learning Disabilities (CLD)

Box 40303
Overland, KS 66204

An independent organization for professionals working with the learning disabled. CLD publishes *Learning Disability Forum* and *Learning Disability Quarterly.* The Council serves the educational and general welfare needs of persons with specific learning disabilities.

Disability Rights Education and Defense Fund, Inc.

2212 6th Street
Berkeley, CA 94710

This legal resource center provides education, advocacy, research, policy analysis, and local referrals to callers.

Division for Learning Disabilities (DLD).

Council for Exceptional Children
1920 Association Drive
Reston, VA 22091

A division of the CEC (listed earlier) which is dedicated to services for those with learning disabilities.

Education Testing Services/College Board
ATP Services for Handicapped Students

P.O. Box 6226
Princeton, NJ 08541–6226

Provides assistance in accommodating learning disabled students taking standardized tests such as the Scholastic Aptitude Tests (SAT).

Equal Employment Opportunity Commission (EEOC)

1801 L St., NW
Washington, DC 20507

Provides information about the Americans with Disabilities Act, Title 1: Employment. Publishes a manual of addresses and names of agencies which assist in this regard.

Foundation for Children with Learning Disabilities

6th Floor (FCLD)
P.O. Box 3392
99 Park Ave.,
New York, New York 10063

A foundation dedicated to needs of individuals with learning disabilities.

HEATH Resource Center (Higher Education and the Handicapped)

One Dupont Circle, NW
Suite 800
Washington, DC 20036

Provides resources for disabled individuals regarding postsecondary education. The Center publishes free information sheets on various topics and offers referral on a toll-free line.

House Annex #2
House Document Room
2nd and D. St., SW
Washington, DC 20515

Provides copies of the American with Disabilities Act in regular print, large print, braille, audio-tape, and computer disk.

International Reading Association
800 Barksdale Road
P.O. Box 8139
Newark, DE 19711

Promotes literacy and suggests/promotes reading resources for all children and adults to achieve this end. Membership allows one to attend conferences which address all facets of the reading experience. This organization publishes a newsletter and supports research endeavors.

Job Accommodation Network (JAN)
West Virginia University
809 Allen Hall
Morgantown, WV 26506–6123

Provides information about job opportunities, accommodations, and employability for individuals with disabilities.

Learning Disabilities Association of America (LDA) (formerly known as the Association for Children and Adults with Learning Disabilities)
4156 Library Road
Pittsburgh, PA 15234

This organization includes parents, learning disabled adults and children, schools, camps, recreation programs, educators, and other care givers. LDA offers direct services and published information on learning disabilities. It is committed to advocacy on behalf of services for the learning disabled. Inquiries to the national office are referred to approximately 800 state and local chapters. A newletter entitled, "News Brief" is published bimonthly. State and national conferences are held. The LDA legislative services committee provides information on legislation pending which may impact individuals with learning disabilities and their families.

National Center for Learning Disabilities (formerly: Foundation for Children with Learning Disabilities)
99 Park Avenue
New York, NY 10016

The Center's fundraising efforts provide support for programs that service learning disabled persons and their families.

National Center for Special Education Technology Information Exchange Council for Exceptional Children
1920 Association Drive
Reston, VA 22091

This organization collaborates with the LINC Resources of Columbus, Ohio, and JWK International of Annandale, Virginia. This center provides a clearing-house of information about technology that can be applied to the educational programs of students with dyslexia and other learning/handicapping conditions. There are two electronic bulletin boards on the Special/Net (described later in this chapter) computer telephone program called Tech.Line and Tech.Talk. Tech.Line provides information relevant to technology in special education areas and Tech.Talk provides a forum for exchange between educators, professionals, and interested persons in the field of special education. The phone is toll-free at 1-800-345-TECH (Monday through Friday during normal business hours.)

National Easter Seal Society
2023 W. Ogden Ave.,
Chicago, Illinois 60612

Provides sources of information regarding publications addressing the child with learning disabilities. This organization also sponsors research and workshops.

National Information Center for Children and Youth with Disabilities (NICHCY)
P.O. Box 1492
Washington, DC 20013–1492
(703) 893–6061 (Local); (1–800) 999–5599 (Toll Free) (703) 893–8614 (TDD)
SpecialNet User Name: NICHCY; Scan User Name: NICHCY

This is a free information service which provides answers to questions and information relevant to the problems of individuals with dyslexia. Parents, educators, students, advocates, caretakers, colleges, etc. may utilize this service. NICHCY distributes up-to-date facts sheets and newsletters and will work with committees and task forces on problems related to learning disabilities and other handicapping conditions.

National Institute of Dyslexic/TRI Services
3200 Woodbine Street
Chevy Chase, MD 20815
State Agencies Administering Special Education and Rehabilitation Services for Learning Disabled Persons

National Joint Committee on Learning Disabilities (NJCLD)
The Orton Dyslexia Society
724 York Road
Baltimore, MD 21204

This society is dedicated to helping disabled readers become able readers and to the recognition of those individuals who have made significant contributions to that cause. This organization was formed in order to promote cooperation and networking among the various agencies and programs that service individuals with learning disabilities. There are several organizations that are represented on the NJCLD including: American Speech-Language-Hearing Association, Association on Higher Education and Disability, Council for Learning Disabilities, Division for Children with Communication Disorders, Division for Learning Disabilities, International Reading Association, Learning Disabilities Association of America, National Association of School Psychologists, and the Orton Dyslexia Society. This association disseminates policy statements, research updates, and information related to learning disabilities. Importantly, being updated on research requires the reading of periodicals and factual summaries in the field. Participating in research endeavors can also be extremely exciting, and personally and professionally rewarding!

National Network of Learning Disabled Adults (NNLDA)
808 North 82nd St., #F2
Scottsdale, AZ 85257

Provides information for adults with learning disabilities A quarterly newletter is available entitled "NNLDA Newsletter."

National Organization on Disability
910 16th St., NW
Washington, DC 20006

Provides information about disabilities and how to accept and promote positive directions for people with disabilities of all ages. There is an ADA (Americans with Disabilities Act) Watch Center where individuals with disabilities can discuss how the ADA law affects their lives.

President's Committee on Employment of People with Disabilities
1331 F. St., NW
Washington, DC 20004–1107

Provides information regarding employment opportunities and practices for individuals with disabilities. It is a public-private coalition of national and state organizations which seek to increase employment opportunities for all individuals with disabilities.

U.S. Department of Health and Human Services
Public Health Service
Division of Scientific and Public Information
5600 Fishers Lane
Rockville, Maryland 20857

Provides information regarding learning disabilities in general. Fliers are available with helpful hints and national organizations which deal with various issues impacting the individual with learning disabilities. Fliers are often reproducible without permission.

U.S. Department of Transportation
400 7th St., SW
Washington, DC 20590

Provides information on transportation requirements of the Americans with Disabilities Act (ADA).

The Importance of Reading Research

Bender (1992) in one sentence best sums it up: "Teachers of pupils with learning disabilities should read several articles monthly which come directly from the major journals in the field" (Bender, 1992, p. 358).

Periodicals that Address Dyslexia and Other Forms of LD:

Journal Reading a Must in Professional Development

The journal listing in Table 10-7 (pp. 277–279) can be overwhelming but certainly gives the reader a nice selection of materials to choose from. Periodical and research review is important in developing new and research-based (sound) teaching strategies when working with individuals with dyslexia. Because the field of learning disabilities is so new with so few definitive answers, it would be beneficial for teachers and other educators to consider participating in research projects involving dyslexia and other learning disabilities. The next questions might be, how does one locate the above journals or find articles of interest in the field of learning disabilities, or dyslexia in particular? There are several computer data-based systems in college and public libraries which allow one to search for specific topics, authors, titles, and areas of study. You can conduct a library search yourself or pay for these services if available. The data-based systems of particular interest for college students can also be accessed by the general public.

Data-Based Computer Program Search Systems

Technology use in the classroom requires a firm grounding in data-based systems, which can provide valuable information for program planning. (See box and Table 10-8, p. 280.)

Currently available are several data-based systems which allow one to search for and find written materials related to the subject matter of dyslexia. Most libraries have at least a few of these systems, and larger universities usually have several of them. There are six systems which span the human services field. These are all explained in this section. Such services are especially important for the college student who might have to write a paper on dyslexia or learning disabilities, the teacher who is looking for new study techniques, the parent who is looking for support groups, the professional who is looking for state-of-the-art assessments, and yes, the authors who are looking to keep current! The ERIC System

TABLE 10-7   Periodicals which Address Dyslexia and Other Forms of LD

Academic Therapy
PRO-ED, Inc.
8700 Shoal Creek Boulevard
Austin, TX 78758-6897

Advances in Learning and Behavioral Disabilities
JAI Press, Inc.
55 Old Post Road
No. 2, Box 1678
Greenwich, CT 06836-1678

American Journal of Occupational Therapy
American Occupational Therapy Association, Inc.
1383 Picard Dr.
Rockville, MD 20850

American Journal of Orthopsychiatry
American Orthopsychiatric Association, Inc.
19 W. 44th Street
New York, NY 10036

American Journal of Psychiatry
American Psychiatric Assoc.
1400 K Street, NW
Washington, DC 20005

American Psychologist, The
American Psychological Assoc.
1200 17th Street, NW
Washington, DC 20036

Annals of Dyslexia
Orton Dyslexic Society
724 York Road
Baltimore, MD 21204

Applied Psycholinguistics
Cambridge University Press
Edinburgh Building
Shaftesbury Road
Cambridge CB2 2RU England

ASHA
American Speech and Hearing Association
9030 Old Georgetown Road
Washington, DC 20014

Behavior Therapy
Association for Advancement of Behavior Therapy
15 W. 36th Street
New York, NY 10018

Brain and Cognition
Academic Prress, Inc.
Journal Division
1250 Sixth Avenue
San Diego, CA 92101

Brain and Language
Academic Press, Inc.
Journal Division
1250 Sixth Avenue
San Diego, CA 92101

British Journal of Disorders of Communication
Cole & Whurr, Ltd.
196 Compton Terrace
London, N1 2UN England

British Journal of Psychology
British Psychological Society
St. Andrews House
48 Princess Road
E. Leicester, LE1 7DR, England

Bulletin of the Orton Society
Orton Society
724 York Road
Baltimore, MD 21204

Career Development for Exceptional Individuals
Council for Exceptional Children
1920 Association Drive
Reston, VA 22091-1589

Child Development
University of Chicago Press
Journals Division
5720 S. Woodlawn Avenue
Chicago, IL 60637

Cognition
Elsevier Sequoia SA
P.O. Box 564, CH-1001
Lausanne 1, Switzerland

Cognition and Literacy
Ablex Publishing Corporation
35 Chestnut Street
Norwood, NJ 07648

Diagnostique
Council for Exceptional Children
1920 Association Drive
Reston, VA 22091-1589

Education and Psychological Research
University of Southern Mississipi, School of Education and Psych.
Box 5028, Southern Street
Hattiesburg, MS 39401

Education and Treatment of Children
PRO-ED Publishing, Inc.
8701 Shoal Creek Blvd.
Austin, TX 78758-9966

Educational Leadership
Association for Supervision and Curriculum Development
125 N. West Street
Alexandria, VA 22314-2798

Educational Psychologis
Lawrence Erlbaum Associates, Inc.
365 Broadway
Hillsdale, NJ 07642

Educational Research Quarterly
University of Southern California, School of Education
WPH 703D
University Park—MC0031
Los Angeles, CA 90089-0031

Educational Technology
Educational Publications, Inc.
720 Palisade Avenue
Englewood Cliffs, NJ 07632

Elementary School Journal
University of Chicago Press
Journals Division
5720 S. Woodlawn Avenue
Chicago, IL 60637

Continued

TABLE 10-7 *Continued*

**Exceptional Child
Educational Resources**
Council for Exceptional
Children
1920 Association Drive
Reston, VA 22091-1589

Exceptional Children
Council for Exceptional
Children
1920 Association Drive
Reston, VA 22091-1589

Exceptional Parent
1170 Commonwealth Avenue
Boston, MA 01234

Exceptionality
Lawrence Erlbaum Assoc., Inc.
365 Broadway
Hillsdale, NJ 07642-9969

Focus on Autistic Behavior
PRO-ED Publishing, Inc.
8700 Shoal Creek Blvd.
Austin, TX 78758-9965

**Focus on Exceptional
Children**
Love Publishing Co.
1777 S. Bellaire Street
Denver, CO 80222

Gifted Children Quarterly
National Association for Gifted
Children
1155 15th Street, NW
Suite 1002
Washington, DC 20005-2706

Gifted Children Today
GCT, Inc.
Box 6448
Mobile, AL 36660

**Harvard Educational
Review**
Harvard University, Graduate
School of Education
Longfellow Hall
13 Appian Way
Cambridge, MA 02138

**International Journal of
Mental Health**
M.E. Sharpe, Inc.
80 Business Park Drive
Armonk, NY 10504

**Intervention in School and
Clinic
(Formally Academic
Therapy)**
PRO-ED Publishing, Inc.
8700 Shoal Creek Blvd.
Austin, TX 78758-9965

**Journal of Abnormal Child
Psychology**
Plenum Press
233 Spring Street
New York, NY 10013

Journal of Abnormal Psy.
American Psychological Assoc.
1200 17th Street, NW
Washington, DC 20036

**Journal of the American
Academy of Child and
Adolescent Psychiatry**
Williams and Wilkins
428 E. Preston Street
Baltimore, MD 21202

**Journal of the American
Optometric Association**
American Optometric Assoc.
243 N. Lindbergh Blvd.
St. Louis, MO 63141

**Journal of Applied Analysis
of Behavior**
Society for the Experimental
Study of Behavior
c/o Department of Human
Dev., University of Kansas
Lawrence, KS 66045

**Journal of Applied
Developmental Psychology**
Ablex Publishing Corporation
355 Chestnut Street
Norwood, NJ 07648

**Journal of Autism and
Developmental Disorders**
Plenum Press
233 Spring Street
New York, NY 10013

**Journal of Child Psychology
and Psychiatry**
Pergamon Press, Inc.
Journals Division
Maxwell House, Fairview Park
Elmsford, NY 10523

**Journal of Childhood
Communication Disorders**
Council for Exceptional
Children
1920 Association Drive
Reston, VA 22091-1589

**Journal of Clinical and
Experimental
Neuropsychology**
Swets Publishing Service
Heereweg 347, 2161 CA Lisse
Netherlands
Distributed in USA & Canada by
Swets & Zeitlinger
Box 517, Berwyn, PA 19312

**Journal of Clinical Child
Psychology**
Lawrence Erlbaum Assoc., Inc.
365 Broadway
Hillsdale, NJ 07642

**Journal of Clinical
Psychology**
Clinical Psychology Publishing
Co., Inc.
4 Conant Square
Brandon, VT 05733

**Journal of Consulting and
Clinical Psychology**
American Psychological Assoc.
1200 17th Street, NW
Washington, DC 20005

**Journal of Early
Intervention**
Council for Exceptional
Children
1920 Association Drive
Reston, VA 22091-1589

**Journal of Educational
Psychology**
American Psychological
Association
1200 17th Street, NW
Washington, DC 20005

**Journal of Educational
Research**
Heldref Publications
4000 Albemarle Street, NW
Washington, DC 20016

TABLE 10-7 *Continued*

Journal of Experimental Child Psychology
Academic Press, Inc.
Journals Division
1250 Sixth Avenue
San Diego, CA 92101

Journal of Experimental Psychology: Human Perception and Performance
American Psychological Assoc.
1201 17th Street, NW
Washington, DC 20006

Journal of Learning Disabilities
PRO-ED Publishing, Inc.
8701 Shoal Creek Blvd.
Austin, TX 78758-9966

Journal of Pediatric Psy.
Plenum Press
233 Spring Street
New York, NY 10013

Journal of Personality and Social Psychology
American Psychological Assoc.
1200 17th Street, NW
Washington, DC 20005

Journal of Precision Teaching
Plain English Publications
P.O. Box 7224
Kansas City, MO 64113

Journal of Psycho-Educational Assessment
Clinical Psychology Publishing
Co., Inc.
4 Conant Square
Brandon, VT 05733

Journal of Reading
International Reading Assoc., Inc.
800 Barksdale Road, Box 8139
Newark, DE 19714-8139

Journal of Reading Behavior
National Reading Conference, Inc.
11 E. Hubbard Street, Ste. 200
Chicago, IL 60611

Journal of School Psychology
Pergamon Press, Inc.
Journals Division
Maxwell House, Fairview Park
Elmsford, NY 10523

Journal of Special Education
PRO-ED Publishing, Inc.
8700 Shoal Creek Blvd.
Austin, TX 78758-9965

Learning Disabilities Research and Practice
Council for Exceptional Children
1920 Association Drive
Reston, VA 22091-1589

Learning Disability Quarterly
Council for Learning Disabilities
Box 40303
Overland Park, KS 66204

Neuropsychologia
Pergamon Press, Inc.
Journals Division
Maxwell House, Fairview Park
Elmsford, NY 10523

Pediatrics
American Academy of Pediatrics
141 Northwest Point Blvd.
Box 927
Elk Grove Village, IL 60009-0927

Perceptual and Motor Skills
Box 9229
Missoula, MT 59807

Psychology in the Schools
Clinical Psychology Publishing
Co., Inc.
4 Conant Square
Brandon, VT 05733

Quarterly Journal of Experimental Psychology
Lawrence Erlbaum Assoc., Ltd.
27 Palmeira Mansions
Church Road
Hove, E. Sussex
BN3 2FA, England

Reading Improvement
Project Innovation of Mobile
Box 8508, Spring Hill
Mobile, AL 36608

Reading Research Quarterly
International Reading Assoc., Inc.
800 Barksdale Road
Box 8139
Newark, DE 19714-8139

Reading Teacher, The
International Reading Assoc., Inc.
800 Barksdale Road
Box 8139
Newark, DE 19714-8139

Remedial and Special Education
PRO-ED Publishing, Inc.
8700 Shoal Creek Blvd.
Austin, TX 78758-9965

Review of Child Development Research
University of Chicago Press
57205 S. Woodlawn Avenue
Chicago, IL 60637

Review of Educational Research
American Educational Research Assoc.
1230 17th Street, NW
Washington, DC 20036

Teaching Exceptional Children
Council for Exceptional Children
1920 Association Drive
Reston, VA 22091-1589

Topics in Early Childhood
Special Education
PRO-ED Publishing, Inc.
8700 Shoal Creek Blvd.
Austin, TX 78758-9965

scanners	printers	computers	keyboards	CD ROM
monitors	light pens	mouse inputing devices		modems
morphing tools		electronic encyclopedia		telephones faxes

Technology in the Classroom

Outcomes: Learning about learning
Reinforcement
Enrichment
Self-directed Instruction
Improved Attitude/Motivation/Interest

Camcorders	LCD Panel	Television	Laser Disks
Hard Disks	Floppy Disks	Sound Synthesizers	Graphics Tablet

TABLE 10-8   Data-Based Computer Search Systems

ERIC (Education Resources Information Center)

Provides:

CIJE—(Current Index to Journals in Education) which is a major bibliography of journals in the field

RIE—(Resources in Education) summarizes materials in ERIC Clearing Houses.

NICEM (National Information Center for Educational Media)

Provides:

NICEM Indexes for non-print materials in special education. Media materials include: videotapes, CD-ROM's, transparencies, slides, and filmstrips.

PAIS (Psychological Abstracts Information Services)

Provides five major services:

1. PAIS data base of literature summaries

2. Psychological abstracts

3. Three-year Cumulative Index to Psychological Abstracts

4. Thesaurus of Psychological Index Terms

5. PASAR (Psychological Abstracts Computer Search and Retrieval Service)

Special/NET Communication Network

A compilation of state and national services and events related to the special education field which is accessible via personal computer system controlled by NASDSE (National Association of State Directors of Special Education).

CEC (Council For Exceptional Children) Information Services

Provides three major services:

1. Computer Searches

2. Bibliographies and

3. ECER (Exceptional Children Education Reference) volume.

Psych SCAN: LD/MR

A quarterly abstract document published by the American Psychological Association which focuses on abstracts on LD, MR, and communication disorders.

(Education Resources Information Center) is probably the most widely used of the six (the others are: National Information Center for Educational Media or NICEM, Council for Exceptional Children or CEC Information Services, Psychological Abstracts Information Services or PAIS, PsychSCAN:LD/MR, and SpecialNet Communication Network) and is the most comprehensive system of its kind available.

ERIC—Data-Based Education Computer Program Search System

The ERIC system allows the user to peruse the entire education field from preschool to college levels, reading to science subject areas, mildly to severely handicapped, and so on, when looking at the problem of dyslexia. Because ERIC is a clearinghouse of 16 different types of education input, a comprehensive index is required to classify and categorize by subject area and by author. The *Current Index to Journals in Education* (CIJE) represents over 700 publications in the education field and provides a major bibliography of the current literature in the field. The CIJE publishes updates on a monthly basis. The Resources in Education (RIE) is published by the U.S. Government Printing Office and also summarizes the materials found in the 16 individual ERIC clearinghouses. Before 1975, the RIE was called Research in Education. An ERIC Document Reproduction Service (EDRS), under the directives of the National Institute of Education which oversees ERIC policy and operations, produces microfiche versions of ERIC materials for public sale.

Additional ERIC Services

Besides providing leads for articles and subject matter related to the field via a sophisticated computer network system, ERIC provides other services for the public which should be and are extensively used. These include: (1) workshop presentations for professionals regarding the use of the ERIC system, (2) search assistance for those difficult-to-find, or specialized, or extensive searches, (3) computer search reprints, (4) current bulletins on ERIC topics such as ERIC Fact Sheets, and ERIC Exceptional Child Education Reports, and (5) published brochures on how to use various aspects of the ERIC system (e.g., Directory of ERIC Microfiche Collections, ERIC Information Analysis Products, and How to Use ERIC.

National Information Center for Educational Media (NICEM)

The NICEM began in 1958 at the University of California as a center for cataloging non-print instructional materials. In 1967, the NICEM published the first bound volume of NICEM indexes. In 1984, the NICEM data base was purchased by Access Innovations, Inc., of Albuquerque, New Mexico. NICEM is a major resource for any individual interested in regular or special education non-print materials. The NICEM claims to be the world's largest computer-based index system with over 500,000 main item listings related to special and regular education students—

including the individual with dyslexia. The NICEM publishes computer-based index listings of audiovisual educational materials such as videotapes, filmstrips, slides, computer software, CD-ROMs, and transparencies available for use by school districts, universities, and libraries. Names and addresses of the producers and distributors of these materials are provided by NICEM. The address for NICEM is: P.O. Box 40130, Albuquerque, New Mexico 87196. A toll free number is 1-800-468-3453.

NICEM Catalogue of Indexes

The master catalogue of the NICEM Special Education Information System provides several indexes. Those indexes that are related to how to secure currently-marketed non-print materials for individuals with dyslexia and other learning handicaps are: Film and Video Finder, Audiocassette and CD Finder, Index to AV Producers and Distributors, and Filmstrip and Slide Set Finder. The indexes may be purchased from Plexus Publishing, Inc., 143 Old Marlton Pike, Medford, NJ 08055–8750; FAX (609) 654–4309. Some state departments of education and college libraries have these volumes. On-line files and CD-ROMs are also available (e.g., just under $100.00 per hour of on-line time and so much per unit; or starting at just under $1,000.00 for yearly subscriptions).

On-line Computer Files

The on-line print indexes of non-print materials associated with the NICEM are as follows: A-V Online, Dialog File 46 (Dialog Information Services, Inc., 3460 Hillview Ave., Palo Alto, CA); Training Media Database (National Standards Association, 1200 Quince Orchard Blvd., Gaithersburg, MD 20878).

CD-ROMs

CD-ROMs which may be obtained from NICEM are the A-V Online (Silver Platter Information, 100 River Ridge Drive, Norwood, MA 02062–5026); NICEM A-V MARC via BiblioFile (The Library Corp., Research Park, Inwood, WV 25428–9733); and Via LibraryWorks (CASPR, Inc., 635 Vaqueros Ave., Cupertino, CA 95014).

Council for Exceptional Children (CEC) Information Services

The CEC has operated under federal support since 1966 and houses an information service which continually updates comprehensive literature listings of commercial books and media journal coverage related to dyslexia and other special handicapping conditions. There are three major services provided by the CEC Information Service which would be of interest to those in the education/special education fields: (1) Computer searches on dyslexia or other specified topics. These searches involve a fee and take 2–3 weeks to complete. The ERIC Clearing House on Disabilities and Gifted Education within the CEC provides this service and the address is 1920 Association Drive, Reston, Virginia 22091–1589. (2) Bibliographies related to specific topics involving dyslexia (e.g., subtypes of dyslexia, the social misperception syndrome, etc.) can be researched with brief abstracts provided for each citation. Hard copies of articles can be secured from EDRC, 7420 Fullerton

Road, Suite 110, Springfield, Virginia 22153–2852. (3) The Exceptional Children Education Resources (ECER) reference volume (formerly Exceptional Child Education Abstracts) is available through CEC Information Services and is an annotated bibliographical reference of printed materials, AVA materials, and professional development offerings related to specific handicapping conditions and giftedness.

Psychological Abstracts Information Services (PAIS)

PAIS is a computerized library information system which is provided by the American Psychological Association (750 First Street, NE, Washington DC 20002–4242). Most college libraries employ this system as there is a heavy emphasis on psychological research and topics. There are five related services one could use in researching topics related to dyslexia: (1) **PAIS Data Base**—this computerized data base covers literature summaries (i.e., journal articles, books) in psychology and related fields published in Psychological Abstracts (from 1967 to the present). (2) **Psychological Abstracts**—This is a monthly reference volume (in journal form)of brief summaries or titles of articles related to major psychology topics. There are specific topic sections which include learning disabilities and dyslexia (although perhaps not in every monthly issue). A Volume Index is published twice a year by subject and author. (3) **Three-Year Cumulative Index to Psychological Abstracts**—this three-year summary of subject and author entries for specific topics is a time-saver when researching! (4) **Thesaurus of Psychological Index Terms**—alternative terms and topic descriptions allow one to key in on those hard-to-find research areas! (5) **Computerized Literature Search and Retrieval Services** (specifically: PASAR—Psychological Abstracts Computer Search and Retrieval Service)—this service allow one to conduct extensive literature searches in the field of dyslexia and learning disabilities.

PsychScan: LD/MR (Learning Disabilities/ Mental Retardation)

The American Psychological Association (750 First Street, NE, Washington DC 20002–4242) also publishes *PsychScan: LD/MR* which is a quarterly abstract document which focuses on abstracts of literature on learning disabilities, communication disorders, and mental retardation. The abstracts are listed in two volumes: (1) PsychINFO Retrospective: Mental Retardation—An Abstracted Bibliography, and (2) PsychINFO Retrospective: Learning and Communication Disorders An Abstracted Bibliography. These volumes list topical areas relevant to the study of dyslexia and other learning problems by subject and by author.

Special/Net Communication Network

The Special/Net Communication Network is an updated compilation of current service offerings and events related to national, state, and regional news in the special education field. One subscribes to Special/Net Computer System which falls

TABLE 10-9 **Special Technology for Those Who Work with Students with Special Learning Problems—Using Technology to Improve Oral/Written Communication Skills**

Internet—The is the largest international network of computers which Elmer-Dewitt (1994) has labeled as the "information superhighway" (p. 50) and "one giant, seamless, global computing machine" (p. 52). Internet was created by students and scientists in an effort to create a giant information trading station. There is no central locale for Internet. One would need to consult with a local computer dealer, university computing center, local library for information as to how to be connected with Internet and Internet related services. Essentially, users exchange information via electronic bulletin boards, mail, dialogue, and documents. The use of many Internet services can cost up to $30.00 per month which is reasonable according to today's computer standards. A **TCP/IP** (Transmission Control Protocol/Internet Protocol) connection is needed. Features: **E-Mail,** a computerized post office. Users can send messages and post information on electronic bulletin boards; **TALK,** a telephone interactive format between users; **WAIS** (Wide Area Information Services), which provides tools for searching the Internet libraries; **CHAT** allows Internet users to chat with others all around the world. **UseNET News** is a giant bulletin board with approximately 5,000 topics. Delphi Internet is one online service which offers full access to Internet (1-800-695-4005; E-Mail is INFO@delphi.com).

Telecommunication Phone Networks—This computer technology can be purchased through local vendors. These networks allow information to be transferred over telephone lines to computers, TV monitors, and so on. Samples: **GROUPwriter** and **Realtime Writer** which can be purchased through WINGS for learning/Sunburst Communications, 1600 Green Hills Road, P.O. Box 60002, Scotts Valley, CA 95067. These writing programs allow writers to conference interactively whereby products can be shared, edited, and revised via computer terminals.

Hyper-ABLEDATA—The CD-ROM version of AbleData technology base. This Macintosh database provides descriptions, pictures, and audio recordings of approximately 20,000 assistive devices and technology products for individuals with physical, mental, and learning disabilities. Source: Trace Research and Development Center, University of Wisconsin-Madison, S–151 Waisman Center, 1500 Highland Ave., Madison, WI 53705.

HyperCard—An interactive computer format where students can collect information and prepare reports using text, graphics, graphics with sound, animation, and special effects. Source: HyperCard, Apple Computer; Educator Advantage Program: 1-800-959-2775.

Interactive TV Videodiscs—An interactive presentation of information where students can link visual images seen on maps, pictures, and videos to textual information. Students can create their own presentations using multimedia modes. Example: National Geographic's history and social studies presentations for the Macintosh™, Apple IIg™, and MS-DOS™ computer systems. Call **National Geographic** for information at 1-800-368-2728.

SpecialNet—A database system for Apple™ and IBM™ computers consisting of an information collection for special educators involving bulletin boards, E-Mail, and conferencing. One feature is Kids.Talk, a bulletin board which links students with disabilities all over the United States and Canada. Source: GTE Education Services, GTE Place West Airfield Drive, P.O. Box 619810, Dallas/Fort Worth Airport, Texas 75261.

under the auspices of the National Association of State Directors of Special Education (NASDSE). One must own a computer equipped with a modem in order to use this service (which can also provide legal and technical special education advice). Communications can be sent to other members of this system and to member organizations. Topical bulletin boards are updated on a daily basis.

Internet

Internet Services have been accessible to the general public since about 1993; before that time the network was used primarily by university professors, scientists, and researchers (see Table 10-9, p. 284).

Legal Services Available

The National Institute of Education (NIE)-LRE (Law Related Education) Division provides legal assistance for students with dyslexia in terms of their rights and responsibilities under the law. There is a students with disabilities program which provides advice and materials not only for students but for professionals as well. The NIE-LRE offers technical assistance, teacher training, and "stimulating" curriculum materials for professionals who work with students with learning disabilities, to include dyslexia. The NIE-LRE address is: 711 G. Street SE, Washington, DC 20003.

Research Participants

Teachers and other professionals could endeavor to participate in research projects by following some of these leads:

1. Contact an area college or university which is engaged in learning-disabilities research. Ask how you could become involved: offer to test students (after securing necessary permissions from principals, parents, superintendents, school committees, students and the like); volunteer to score or correct materials; volunteer to "hunt down and locate" research articles and books at area libraries; offer to assist in writing and editing phases; offer computer and typing skills; and so on.

2. Contact the research director in a large city or community who might be able to assist with research questions, funding ideas, and so on. The Springfield, Massachusetts School System provides a research coordinator/facilitator who can be consulted on statistical designs, feasibility questions, appropriateness of research proposals, grant questions, the nature of the student population, research needs for the school system and so on. This type of resource is invaluable and can (and should!) be tapped.

3. Contact college doctoral programs that are involved in research in learning disabilities. Perhaps you could assist a doctoral student in some phase of dissertation work.

4. Contact learning disabilities organizations that are involved in research projects and ask about your involvement.

5. Inquire about grants. Most large cities and large city libraries have grant directories and sometimes grant directors. Find out about how you can obtain grant monies in dyslexia research. Perhaps you would like to try a new

teaching technique; social skills strategy plan; cognitive skills model; whole-language application; portfolio assessment adaptation; informal assessment checklist; family workshop; and so on.

6. Share a mini-research project by submitting to an educational journal an idea, lesson, unit, reflection, and so on, regarding your work with (a) student(s) with learning disabilities that worked well (remember: how did you assess effectiveness and what were the learning outcomes?). Certainly professional magazines, such as Mailbox, K–8, and so on, welcome ideas (even tidbits) from professionals. The networking of ideas is really mini-research and can only enhance the quality of teaching delivery to students with dyslexia. After all, all teachers need to have several teaching ideas and assists at their fingertips in order to adapt to the rapidly-changing learning styles, attitudes, and interests of students.

7. Conference or solicit the expertise and willing participation of colleagues in any research endeavor. Brainstorming, cooperative learning, and networking are powerful builders.

8. Participate on school-based management committees and become involved in PIPs (Professional Improvement Plans) for your school and suggest mini-research projects.

9. Solicit parent involvement and support through parent-organization groups, parent conferences, newsletters, personal phone calls, and so on. Always give parents feedback when research is completed. Their involvement can be extremely beneficial.

10. Conduct workshops within your school and for groups and individuals outside of the school which provide information for individuals working with dyslexics. The give-and-take in workshops can provide research ideas and directions.

11. Suggest after-school research groups for interested teachers and professionals. The Longmeadow Schools (of Longmeadow, Massachusetts), as an example, have offered school-wide research chats. Multiple copies of three to four research articles are provided in a relaxed setting with refreshments! Professionals choose an area of interest and join a group to discuss the article. There are no parameters set regarding rules of discussion, with the exchange of ideas determining the direction the group takes. Individuals are free to mingle, and even to leave one group to join another.

Learning Disabilities Research Institutes Affiliated with College Programs

Columbia University
Teachers College
Research Institute for the Study of Learning Disabilities
Box 118
New York, New York 10027

University of Illinois at Chicago
Chicago Institute for Learning Disabilities
Box 4348 Chicago, IL 60680

University of Kansas
Research Institute in Learning Disabilities
Room 313 Carruth-O'Leary
Lawrence, KS 66045

University of Minnesota
Institute for Research on Learning Disabilities
350 Elliot Hall
75 East River Road
Minneapolis, MN 55455

University of Virginia
Learning Disabilities Research Institute
Department of Special Education
152 Ruffner Hall
Charlottesville, VA 22903

Legal Issues for Individuals with Disabilities

There has been key legislation which has impacted significantly the lives and education of individuals with disabilities to include dyslexia. The key Public Laws which are still referred to today are: Public Law (PL) 93-112 (1973), Section 504 of the Vocational Rehabilitation Act which prohibits federally funded programs from discriminating against individuals with disabilities; PL 94-142, Part B of the Education of All Handicapped Act (1975) mandates a free and appropriate education for all individuals with disabilities and one that is recorded on an IEP (individual education plan) (see Chapters 1 and 2); PL 99–457 (1986) extends education services for students with disabilities to those children ages 3–5 or preschool intervention; PL 101–336, which is better known as the Americans with Disabilities Act (1990) ensures that individuals with disabilities are not discriminated against in such areas as public transportation and accommodations and telecommunications; and PL 101–476 (IDEA) (1990) (see page 2) which essentially renames PL 94–142 and now includes services to autistic/traumatic brain-injured individuals with educational services extended to include such areas as social work and rehabilitiation.

The National Institute for Citizen Education in the Law (NICEL) is a nonprofit institution which is committed to empowering non-lawyer individuals with and without learning disabilities with knowledge of the law. Law-related education (LRE) is a relatively new education concept which is focused on teaching non-lawyers about legal issues and the fundamentals of our system of government. Specific materials and programs are available for teachers which focus on relevant legal content using an interactive teaching style. Acquiring citizenship skills and civic literacy are focuses of these programs. NICEL programs assist public schools, juvenile justice programs, corrections departments, and state and local governmental agencies by providing teacher and professional training programs, developing curriculum materials, and providing technical assistance in pilot programs. The following LRE programs are available: Adult and Community Education Programs;

International Programs in starting Street Law Programs and Human Rights Programs; Mentor Programs; Mock Trials, Students with Disabilities Programs; School Programs for grades K–12 with LRE (law-related education) infused into history and social studies courses; Juvenile Court Alternative Programs (first-offender youngsters are taught street law); and Juvenile Corrections Education Programs (for incarcerated youngsters). Some of these programs have corresponding curriculum items.

NICEL Social Studies School Service

Books, videos, and reproducibles are available for all grade levels. As examples, "We Can Work It Out: Problem Solving Through Mediation," and "Street Law Mock Trial Manual," programs are suited for the secondary levels and concentrate on such skills as developing conflict resolution through mediation, problem-solving, and so on. *Teens, Crime, and the Community* (3rd ed., 1992), is an 11-lesson curriculum which explores the topics of drug and alcohol abuse, crime, shoplifting, vandalism, and drunk driving (suited for middle and high school levels) (West Educational Publishing, School Division, 610 Opperman Drive, P.O. Box 64833, St. Paul, MN 55164–1803). One goal of the NICEL is to reduce juvenile delinquency. Because a higher percentage of the adjudicated youth are learning-disabled than in the population at large, it would be critical to focus on prevention for those "high-risk" children. The NICEL address is: 711 G. Street, S.E., Washington, D.C. 20003; phone: (202) 546–6644.

Conclusions

The improvement of diagnosis and remediation with individuals who experience dyslexia can only be enhanced by concerted professional development efforts. Professional development would necessarily involve research efforts, workshops, readings, and exposure to AVA/computer materials shared among all who are interested in the problem of dyslexia. Professional portfolios (i.e., using a large notebook with tabs for different sections) assist educators in reflecting on goals, achievements, and student input/achievements/difficulties so that instructional strategies and student interactions continue to improve. The reflective practitioner must rely on student-generated outcomes when assessing one's growth and success as a facilitator of knowledge. Organizing student-generated and teacher-generated outcomes can be successfully done via the portfolio process.

College students and other perennial fact-finders will find the computer-based index systems discussed in this chapter useful in their research endeavors. The ERIC System (Education Resources Information Center) is probably the most widely used of the six systems discussed (also: National Information Center for Educational Media or NICEM, Council of Exceptional Children or CEC Information Services, Psychological Abstracts Information Services or PAIS, PsychSCAN:LD/MR, and SpecialNet Communication Network).

PIPs (Professional Improvement Plans) for individual schools need to address current research in the field if only to provide research journals educators can consult. Several suggestions were given for research participation and we hope we stimulated some new and exciting research endeavors beginning now!

There are many services available to those interested in the field that might be new to you. As an example, when conducting extensive library literature searches, one can rely on such resources as the *Thesaurus of Psychological Indexes,* the *Three-Year Cumulative Index to Psychological Abstracts,* and the like. The reader may not have been aware of the wealth of organizations and journals which deal with the problem of dyslexia and other handicapping conditions. Finally, state rehabilitation centers can assist individuals with dyslexia with vocational assessment and placement issues. Several of these addresses have been provided for convenience and information. Careful reference to the chapter should provide new research avenues which might well have an impact upon professional growth and development.

When we get to the bottom line of all of this, we need to follow the advice of the NJCLD: (1993a) ". . . ask people with learning disabilities about their needs; show respect and sensitivity for people with disabilities; use what works; [and] use your resources creatively and effectively" (p. 93).

Finally, we end the chapter by stressing the importance of developing civic literacy and citizenship skills. Although the acquisition of reading skills is important for individuals with dyslexia, becoming positive, collegial, and productive citizens is foremost, your authors' top priority.

FIGURE 10-1 Wise Tidbits from Yesteryear

Source: Sir Joshua Fitch, M.A., L.L.D. (1900). *Education Aims and Methods: Lectures and Addresses.*

Appendix *I*

Attention Deficit Problems

ADD and ADHD

In the literature, ADD refers to <u>a</u>ttention <u>d</u>eficit <u>d</u>isorders and ADHD, <u>a</u>ttention deficit <u>h</u>yperactivity <u>d</u>isorders. The U.S. Department of Education (1991) uses "ADD" when referring to both disorders. However, DSM III-R and DSM IV use the ADHD terminology. Previously, DSM-II and DSM-III relied on the use of "ADD."

Although C.H.A.D.D. (<u>C</u>hildren with <u>A</u>ttention <u>D</u>eficit <u>D</u>isorders organization—see page 15) (1992) cautions that medical procedures, such as blood tests, EEGs, and PET scans not be used in ADD and ADHD diagnoses, research clearly points to distinctly different brain imaging in children with these disorders (e.g., Denckla, 1991). Many individuals with dyslexia do experience ADD or ADHD (Wender, 1987).

For clarity, the DSM-IV (1994) is the fourth edition of the American Psychiatric Association's, *Diagnostic and Statistical Manual of Mental Disorders* (Washington, DC: Author). DSM-IV uses a multiaxial system (see page 300) but practitioners/clinicians may opt to list diagnoses in a nonaxial format. As an example, a student with dyslexia and ADHD might be classified as follows using DSM-IV dimensions:

Axis I (focus of clinical/education efforts)—315.00 Reading Disorder (Dyslexia); 314.01 ADHD, Combined Type

Axis II (personality disorder)—none

Axis III (medical)—Otitis media, recurrent (ear infections)

Axis IV (environmental)—Depressed school grades

Axis V (global functioning)—75 highest level* last year

(*Scale = 1 represents severe problems in psychosocial functionings; 100 represents superior life adjustments)

ADD was classified as ADD without hyperactivity in DSM-III; undifferentiated ADD in DSM-III-R; and ADHD-IA or the primarily inattentive subtype in DSM-IV. ADHD was known as ADHD in both DSM-III-R and in DSM-IV. The following table clarifies the differences between ADD and ADHD in terms of overtly observed or reported symptoms.

ADD
Attention Deficit Disorder

ADHD
Attention Deficit Hyperactivity Disorder

Similarities

Symptoms

1. Failure to attend to details in schoolwork; avoidance strategies develop
2. Listening skills are deficient; reading comprehension can be erratic
3. Easily distracted by environmental stimuli
4. Attention shifts to other activities before present task is completed
5. Disorganized in work and study habits
6. Can be socially inappropriate
7. Lowered self-esteem
8. Emotional sensitivity
9. Careless
10. Forgetful

ADD

ADHD

Differences

Symptoms

1. Excitability not a problem
2. Sporadic impulsivity
3. Attentional problems are usually not disruptive
4. Excessive physical activity not a problem
5. Can be passively defensive (e.g., tune out painful experiences)
6. Fair written work

Symptoms

1. Overly excitable
2. Chronic impulsivity
3. Disruptive behaviors (e.g., difficulty remaining seated)
4. Constant motor movements or excitement
5. Can be outwardly defensive (e.g., fighting in scuffles)
6. Poor written work

A p p e n d i x *II*

Constructivism and Scaffolding

Constructivism: Based on a work of Piaget, 1973, *To Understand is to Invent* (NY: Viking Press).

Definition: To understand or construct meaning by discovery/rediscovery. The role of the adult is to facilitate learning by interacting with the child through questioning and discussions; responding to ideas.

Scaffolding: Based on work of Vygotsky, 1978, *Mind in Society: The Development of Higher Psychological Processes* (Cambridge, MA: Harvard University Press).

Definition: to guide a child to higher learning by first determining the appropriate developmental level and then structuring activities to lead the child above this level to higher levels of understanding. The role of the adult is to facilitate learning by structured guidance (scaffolding) at first until the child reaches independent/unassisted performance/achievement. The **zone of proximal development** or the developmental area between what a child learns with assistance/guidance and what the child learns without assistance is where optimal learning takes place.

Similarities: Constructivism and scaffolding are interactive learning approaches that place the adult/teacher in the role of a facilitator. The learning process is active and reflective requiring specific role taking on the part of the teacher and student alike. The following graphic illustrates how the teacher also becomes a student/learner and the student a facilitator of knowledge. Similar learning outcomes can generate positive school experiences.

Constructivism/Scaffolding

Teacher's Role   **Student's Role**

Interchangeable

<table>
<tr><td>

1. Provide background information/knowledge
2. Facilitate conceptual links/inferences/generalizations
3. Assist in task analysis of complex learning episodes
4. Encourage positive social/listening skills
5. Provide cues/guidance for study tips/metacognitive strategies

</td><td>

1. Try to construct own reading/language/math concepts
2. Adapt and accommodate new ideas/concepts
3. Self-monitor and evaluate own learning
4. Plan, pace, and structure study times/habits
5. Seek feedback/assistance when needed

</td></tr>
</table>

Generated By

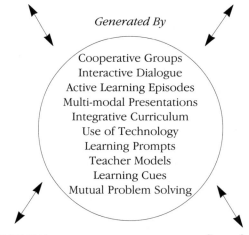

Cooperative Groups
Interactive Dialogue
Active Learning Episodes
Multi-modal Presentations
Integrative Curriculum
Use of Technology
Learning Prompts
Teacher Models
Learning Cues
Mutual Problem Solving

Learning Outcomes: **Learning Outcomes:**
Becoming a Better. . .   *Becoming a Better. . .*

<table>
<tr><td>

1. Problem Solver
2. Critical Thinker
3. Group Participant
4. Initiator
5. Reflective teacher practitioner and student learner

</td><td>

1. Problem Solver
2. Critical Thinker
3. Group Participant
4. Initiator
5. Reflective student learner and facilitator of learning

</td></tr>
</table>

Positive School Outcomes:

1. A more cooperative learning/social environment.
2. Improved learning gains reflected in test scores.
3. Reflective teacher practitioners/student learners.

Created by: Dr. Carol Spafford

Glossary

Acalculia Acalculia is an acquired math disorder resulting from brain trauma or injury after birth. It involves a failure of math ability in many areas. Four types of acalculia have been described in the literature: (1) primary acalculia, (2) secondary acalculia, (3) visual-spatial acalculia, and (4) Gerstmann's acalculia.

Acalculia with Alexia (and/or agraphia for numbers) Also called secondary acalculia, and aphasic acalculia. (See Secondary Acalculia.)

Achievement Tests Tests of acquired knowledge and ability. Achievement tests in essence measure academic accomplishments in such areas as reading, science, spelling, and so on.

ACID Profile A profile is a distribution of subtest scores for a complex test such as the Wechsler Intelligence Scales (the WAIS, the WISC or the WPPSI). Male dyslexics are said to have lower scores on four particular subtests than on any of the other six; these four are the Arithmetic, Coding, Information, and Digit Span, an acrostic for which is ACID.

Agnosia A type of aphasia involving the inability to understand or recognize certain sensory stimuli.

Agrammatism Difficulty in using proper grammar structures frequently seen in individuals with Broca's aphasia. Such patients tend to drop articles and auxiliary verbs.

Agraphia The inability to write, due to spelling difficulties. Acquired agraphia is a result of damage to a portion of the cerebral cortex.

ALAN An acronym for the Assembly on Literature for Adolescents.

Alexia The total inability to read despite having adequate vision. The individual can copy the letters of words, but cannot read or decode them as symbols for meanings. Alexia is an acquired reading problem due to a severe brain trauma or injury. The individual in essence loses a previous ability to read.

Analytic Phonics Approaches Phonics approaches which introduce students first to a number of easily learned words. Then phonics instruction begins. Letter sounds are not learned in isolation and phonics rules and generalizations are discovered through inductive reasoning. These approaches are best used with beginning readers who appear not to have reading/learning problems. (See also Synthetic Phonics Approaches.)

Anarithmetia Also called primary acalculia and true acalculia. (See Primary Acalculia.)

Anomia Word-finding difficulties frequently seen in individuals with Broca's aphasia.

Aphasia A loss of speech/language functions which are rooted in cerebral disease or damage. Aphasia can involve both expressive and receptive problems. (See Receptive Aphasia and Expressive Aphasia.)

Aphasic Acalculia Also called acalculia with alexia and/or agraphia for numbers and secondary acalculia. (See secondary acalculia.)

Apraxia A type of aphasia involving the inability to exercise learned motor movements not due to sensory or motor disturbances.

Aptitude Tests Tests of the individual's potential ability to acquire skills and/or knowledge, emphasizing what the individual starts with, before going on to acquire (i.e., to learn) skills and/or memorized factual knowledge. Intelligence tests supposedly measure one's overall ability. More specific aptitude tests focus on such areas as music, creativity, math, and so on.

Acquired Refers to the causation of a disorder, disability, or handicap. Specifically, resulting from injury to the brain, leading to the loss of an ability (antonym of *developmental*).

Assistive Technologies Technology used by students with disorders or disabilities. It can be any piece of equipment that is used to increase or improve the academic/social/emotional functioning of individuals with disabilities.

Asymmetry Any discrepancy of size (expressed as weight, volume, length, or width) between a part of the forebrain on one side and its counterpart in the opposite side of the forebrain.

Attention-Deficit/Hyperactivity Disorder (ADD-H) The inability to attend to the same stimulus or stay on task for long periods of time accompanied by overactivity (hyperactivity) during different times. This disorder can be accompanied by restlessness and impulsive actions. Formerly, attention deficit disorders were designated with hyperactivity or ADD-H, or without overt hyperactivity (ADD-WO). Not all learning disabled children have ADD-H. There are three types of attention deficit/hyperactivity disorders according to DSM-IV: (1) attention deficit/hyperactivity inattention type, (2) attention deficit/hyperactivity impulsive type, and (3) a mixed type evincing symptoms from (1) and (2). Four times as many males as females are given diagnoses of ADHD.

Attribute Blocks Math manipulative sets of blocks or objects (e.g., animals) which have different characteristics (e.g., as in color, size, texture, shape, and thickness).

Auditory Dyslexia This is a type of dyslexia first described in detail by Myklebust in 1978 which is characterized by the individual's inability to integrate auditory information or to make the connection between phonemes and graphemes.

Auditory-Linguistic Dyslexia Type A hypothetical dyslexia subtype characterized by intact visual functioning and language dysfunctioning in either the oral or written realms.

Autism Severe isolation of the individual is what the name implies. In this severe developmental disorder, the infant (and later, the child) cannot react with the appropriate emotional response to the actions of others. The autistic child will have severely restricted language abilities. As a result of these two essential features of this syndrome, autism presents great problems to special educators.

AVID Profile Female dyslexics have been hypothesized by Spafford to do more poorly on four subtests of the Wechsler Intelligence Scales (WAIS, WISC, and WPPSI) than on the six other subtests. These four subtests are Arithmetic, Vocabulary, Information, and Digit Span, for which AVID is an acrostic.

Authentic Assessments A type of assessment technique that relates the assessment activity to one used in the outside environment (e.g., work samples, exhibitions, videotapes). Students are required to demonstrate their knowledge through an outcome measure. Multiple outcome measures are encouraged (traditional tests, essays, lab reports, art project, and so on). The most commonly known authentic assessment is the portfolio assessment. (See also portfolio assessment.)

Base Ten Blocks Math manipulative metric blocks that are different sizes. The largest block is made up of ten flat blocks. A flat block is made of ten long blocks (longs) and a long is made up of ten units.

Bottom-Up Reading Models These models consider oral and written language processing to consist of a series of steps that begin with detection of auditory and visual stimuli.

Brainstorming An interactive format in which students generate a collective fund of existing knowledge. All students' ideas related to the topic are accepted and recorded.

Brain Structure Abnormalities The cerebral cortex of the human brain can vary in structure from one person to another. Sometimes the variation is so extreme that it leads to unusual brain functioning and, almost always, to a learning disability.

Broca's Aphasia An acquired language loss involving the posterior portion of the left frontal lobe which is involved in speech production (articulation). The individual with Broca's aphasia displays articulation problems and paucity of speech.

Broca's Area An area of the frontal lobe (usually in the left hemisphere) of the cerebral cortex; when it is damaged, the patient finds it nearly impossible to make intended speech sounds. Furthermore, particles and prepositions are dropped entirely. Nevertheless the speech is meaningful and consistent within those limitations.

Buros Mental Measurements Yearbook A highly

regarded test assessment review which is comprehensive, critical, and detailed. The 10th (year 1989) and 11th (1992) editions are considered addendums to the 9th (1985). One can abstract information regarding test descriptions, test administration, appropriateness for different populations, reliability and validity coefficients, and tests' effectiveness.

CAI Acronym for computer-assisted instruction.

Case Study Approach The approach to assessment which considers one person's individuality at a time. That is, tests and other assessment measures are chosen based on the individual's age, schooling, hypothesized learning and social problems, teacher's assessment of the problem, school performance, and so on. This approach would probably result in very few individuals having the same assessment battery, report style, and recommendations. Reports would differ in some way due to the individual differences exhibited during the assessment process.

CEC Council for Exceptional Children

Central Nervous System or CNS Consists of the brain and spinal cord.

Cerebellar-Vestibular Dysmetria A hypothetical malfunctioning of the neural pathway going from the vestibular sense organs through the cerebellum toward the cerebral cortex and toward the midbrain areas that control the external muscles of the eyes. As a result of this disorder, sensory messages reach the cortex much too quickly, producing a feeling much like vertigo.

Chelation Therapy A proven medical treatment which involves reduction of toxic levels of lead from the blood.

Chiropractic Intervention Therapeutic activity initiated by professional chiropractors.

Choral and Choral Repeated Reading Whole-class reading activities which involve active student participation and comprehension. The teacher models good oral reading behaviors by phrasing properly, changing tempos, voice intonation, and expression.

Classroom Observations An informal assessment tool which allow the classroom itself to provide an opportunity for the teacher to gain insights into a child's learning problems, strengths, styles, and social adjustments. The impact of the classroom environment can also be assessed.

Cloacal Another name for pelvic. The hip joints are hypothesized to take part in cloacal reflexes that control the alignment of the head.

Clustering Strategy An estimation strategy used with certain problems that contain numbers which tend to cluster or hover around a certain range of numbers. Clustering would involve eyeballing the average of the group and then performing the appropriate operation.

Coding The formation of energy and/or material patterns (in time or space) into vehicles for carrying intended meanings (e.g., framing the words of a spoken sentence).

Cognition The use of any of the higher mental process such as knowing, thinking, decision-making, judgment, deliberative memory, interpretive perception, and so on.

Cognitive Learning Style The ways in which learners internally process information. A reflective cognitive learning style allows the learner to hypothesis test, problem solve, and weigh alternatives. An impulsive cognitive learning style is one in which response rate is so quick that appropriate problem solving does not occur with the same frequency as it would using the reflective cognitive learning style.

Cognitive Mediation A technique in which the teacher models the *internal dialogue* that directs skilled reading. By thinking aloud, in response to a specific passage, the teacher makes explicit the internal cognitive process of reading. Gradually, the student is encouraged to verbalize his/her own dialogue.

Collaboration or Collaborative Consultation The concept of teachers and professionals actively networking together in order to share experiences, network, and problem solve together when trying to educate all students including those with special needs.

Collaborative Programs Substantially separate programs which frequently contain students from many communities. Typically, students in collaborative programs require exceptional special services which ordinarily cannot be provided within the regular classroom setting or a resource room type of program. Students in these programs frequently have severe disabilities and disorders and require specialized programming.

Compatible Numbers An advanced type of estimation rounding strategy. Compatible numbers are identified and manipulated by rounding. For example: 19 + 86 + 18 + 89 = ? One could round 19 and 18 to 20 and 86 and 89 to 90 and figure 20 + 20 + 90 + 90 = 220 for an estimated answer.

Competency Testing Achievement testing in a particular domain. Competency testing involves evaluating an individual in order to determine suitability for a task, job, or academic pursuit. For example, teachers are frequently required to take competency tests in the areas of reading, writing, and math before qualifying to teach in the classroom.

Comprehension The integration of the graphophonic, syntactic and semantic aspects of written language at four distinct levels of processing: (1) *literal comprehension* or understanding explicit text information; (2) *interpretation* (based on metacognitive awareness); (3) *critical reading* or making evaluative judgments; and (4) *creative reading* or applying textual knowledge and meaning beyond the scope of the text. Creative reading includes the ability to problem solve and predict story outcomes.

Comprehension Monitoring In good readers, the ability to independently assess self-understanding of printed text through self-questioning, critical analyses, and retellings. Students with dyslexia are deficient in comprehension monitoring strategies and need direct instruction therein.

Concept Maps Word diagrams that provide general and specific concepts demonstrating linkages between words which are labeled to show what connections are made. Such visual maps can be used to illustrate important material from a science text, a current issue in social studies, math terminology, and so on. Students read the material and select important ideas and concepts related to the topic. Main ideas and related details are listed in a hierarchial list to form relationships. Students with dyslexia can use these concept maps as study guides and can revise their maps as needed.

Conduction Aphasia A language deficit resulting from damage to the arcuate fasciculus, which is a bundle of axons running from Wernicke's area to Broca's area. Unlike a person with damage to Broca's area, the person with conduction aphasia articulates speech well. The person may have some problem with comprehending heard language, but not as badly as someone with Wernicke's aphasia. The patient with conduction aphasia is unable to repeat phrases correctly.

Cones One of two types of light-sensitive receptor cell in the retina. Many of them are packed into the fovea of the eye, providing visual acuity and color discrimination. Cones are responsible for photopic vision.

Construct Validity The behavior or ability being measured must be a well-established, genuine trait or behavioral tendency. Ingredients for making a favorable decision on a test's construct validity include a showing that it has high content validity, proof that it has high internal reliability, and its having significant correlations, some positive and some negative, with other tests and measurements, as appropriate.

Constructivist Math Teaching A teacher-directed math investigative approach where the teacher presents math materials and concepts in a way that leads students through a process of forming generalizations and principles that govern mathematical processes.

Content Area Acceleration A teaching technique for gifted populations which involves accelerating or moving the student on to a higher level, whether it be in more advanced curriculum materials or upper level class participation.

Content Validity A sophisticated version of face validity, in that the tasks required of the examinee should be an adequate sample of the skill or behavior that the test is meant to measure. The decision as to whether a test has high content validity must be made by someone who is an expert in that skill or activity which is being measured.

Cooperative Math Activities Math activities which are completed in pairs or groups. Cooperative math exercises provide opportunities for math learning when the teacher's efforts might be limited by time constraints and sheer numbers of students.

Correlates of Dyslexia Refers to social (e.g., social misperceptions), psychological (lowered self-esteem), academic (e.g., spelling problems), cognitive (AVID profile), and physiological (e.g., cerebral dysfunctioning) behaviors or symptoms which co-occur with the major presenting problem of the individual with dyslexia, reading impairment.

Criterion-Referenced Tests (CRTs) These tests are meant to check the extent to which a given reading program's objectives are being met. They tend to measure specific skills, unlike the norm-referenced tests, which usually score general areas of skill. CRTs are intended to be used with an absolute standard of successful achievement, while NRTs relate performance to that of the norm group.

Criterion-Referenced Validity Any measure of validity that permits the calculation of a correlation coefficient between the test score and some other measurement which represents the actual skill or behavior being measured. If that other measure is taken at the same time that the test is administered, the test's concurrent validity is being determined. If the criterion measure is made some time after the test has been administered, the test's predictive validity is being assessed.

CRT An acronym for criterion-referenced test.

CSPD A comprehensive system of personnel development (CSPD) for early childhood special needs students which is mandated under IDEA.

Cuisenaire Rods Math manipulative sets of 10 colored rods which range in length from 1 to 10 centimeters and are 1 centimeter in width. The rods (1 cubic centimeter in cross-section) are: white (1 centimeter); red (2 centimeters), light green (3 centimeters), purple (4 centimeters), yellow (5 centimeters), dark green (6 centimeters), black (7 centimeters), brown (8 centimeters), blue (9 centimeters), and orange (10 centimeters). Cuisenaire rods can be used to help children master sorting and classification concepts, patterning, developing numeration and number sense, fraction concepts (e.g., finding the least common multiple), and place value.

Cultural Bias Refers to the fact that intelligence tests and other assessment measures reflect a strong white, Anglo-Saxon, middle-class value system and bias. Minorities are thought to have somewhat depressed test scores because of cultural bias.

Cultural Loading The degree to which a test reflects a cultural background.

Culture-Fair Assessments More appropriate would be the terminology, "cultural loading."

Culture-Fair Tests Tests which are assumed to eliminate the effects of cultural bias which is usually white middle-class Anglo-Saxon value systems. Research doesn't support the use of culture-fair tests and it is improbable that any test could be.

Curriculum Telescoping Also known as compacting. This is a teaching strategy for gifted populations which involves condensing those parts of the curriculum deemed inappropriate or not challenging for the individual. Alternative curriculum materials are provided.

Decoding The "cracking" of the English language code or making sense out of the printed page. Decoding involves: (1) matching printed words to sound which in turn activates semantics or meanings in long-term memory

and (2) recording or translating printed words or word segments into sounds. Sound patterns activate meanings in long-term memory.

Deep Dyslexia Deep or phonic dyslexia is described as an inability to decode words from phonic-based principles. The dyslexic relies instead, on the whole-word approach with meaning substitutions frequently seen in oral reading miscues (e.g., "humor" is pronounced as "happy"). As in the case of surface dyslexia, deep dyslexia is thought to result from neurological damage.

Delacato System The method of treatment of learning disability devised by Delacato and Doman. A key point is the reeducation from the ground up of the individual's patterns of basic locomotion.

Developmental Approach This is an approach whereby the researcher or professional considers developmental issues for particular age ranges as important to assessment and remediation issues. Piaget is probably the best known developmental psychologist and he describes cognitive development in terms of developmental stages.

Developmental Dyslexia A developmental approach to dyslexia whereby the reading disability is unexpected. This is an exclusionary definition which rules out such causes as cultural deprivation, a brain injury, or a low intelligence level. Developmental dyslexia is thought to develop over time as opposed to constitutional causes.

Dialogue Journals Journal writing which involves students who write to one another dialoguing what they're reading in a book-chat format.

Differential Diagnosis The process of diagnosing various diseases or disorders by differentially defining symptoms particular to a problem area. For example, in order to differentially diagnose an individual as dyslexic, one would have to look at correlating behaviors and test performances.

Differential Treatment Hypothesis A theory about juvenile delinquency which focuses on the question, "Are youths with LD more likely to be arrested and adjudicated than youths without LD?"

Discrepancy Differences [1] These are differences observed when one's actual performance deviates from past performances or expected ability levels. Hence, there is a discrepancy between one's innate intellectual capacities and actual test performance. [2] It is believed by some that significant discrepancies seen in verbal-performance IQ scores (e.g., verbal IQ = 90; performance IQ = 115) are symptomatic of possible learning disabilities or learning problems.

Dolch List A popular sight word listing.

D-R-T-A or The Directed Reading-Thinking Activity A reading technique which supports the reading process by modeling active thinking strategies. Small segments of text are approached by having students make predictions about the ideas and concepts based on headings or topic sentences. With a "purpose" in place, students read the segment to confirm or amend their predictions. The cycle of predicting and proving is continued throughout the reading.

DSM-IV A multiaxial assessment system which includes five diagnostic axes: Clinical Syndromes, Personality Disorders, General Medical Conditions, Psychosocial and Environmental Problems, and Global Assessment of Functioning. This system is used to diagnose mental and behavioral disorders including learning disabilities and reading disorders in particular.

Dyscalculia A difficulty in performing arithmetic tasks so that the individual's performance is well below the standard expected of her/him on the basis of I.Q., age level, or grade level. Specific types of dyscalculia have been identified in the literature: verbal dyscalculia, practognostic dyscalculia, lexical dyscalculia, ideognostical dyscalculia, and operational dyscalculia.

Dyseidetic Dyslexia The inability to read efficiently because of visual perceptual disturbances or anomalies.

Dysgraphia The relative inability to write based on extreme spelling disability which is due not to observable brain damage but to a developmental, probably genetic, condition.

Dyslexia The inability to read which is inappropriate to the individual's level of general intelligence. There are social, psychological, academic, and physiological correlates of dyslexia which co-occur with the reading difficulties. Dyslexics appear to be a very heterogeneous group with different forms of dyslexia pointing to different kinds of language/reading/processing difficulties. There is no consensus in the field as to a specific classification system with the present authors offering a three-part typology system of dyslexia based on their research and Boder's work: (1) visual-dysphonetic dyslexia, (2) auditory-lin-

guistic dyslexia, and (3) mixed dyslexia (with both visual and language problems). Dyslexia is thought to have a consitutional origin which is neurologically based.

Dysnemkinesia The third of Christenson *et al.*'s subtypes of dyslexia, involving the combination of visual and kinesthetic inputs.

Dysphonesia The inability to learn the phonic elements for which visual symbols stand.

Dysphonetic Dyslexia The inability to read words by using appropriate grapheme-phoneme conversions.

Dysphonetic-Dyseidetic Dyslexia The combination in one person of two types of dyslexia, the dysphonetic and the dyseidetic. This is also called the "mixed" form of dyslexia.

Dysplasia An abnormality of development.

Echo Reading Also known as the "Neurological Impress" method. The teacher and student read together side-by-side and the teacher does not correct oral reading errors. At first, the teacher reads louder and slightly faster than the student with the student's reading virtually "an echo" of the teacher's reading. Eventually they read in unison.

Eclectism Refers to an educational philosophy which emphasizes incorporating many and varied learning activities, methods, and materials into the curriculum.

Ecological Assessment An observational approach which involves viewing the individual with dyslexia in a number of settings with a focus on the interactions between the individual and peers, family members, teachers, and other authority figures. Physical surroundings are considered important to the individual's overall well-being with observations made regarding physical seating arrangements, lighting, ventilation, and noise factors. Blame/causation for disorders or learning problems is not attributed to the individual but is thought to reside somewhere in the interactions between the disabled individual and significant others.

Electronic Assessment The use of electronic media such as videos and laser disks with computer technology.

Elimination Diet A diet intended to eliminate toxic chemicals from the dieter's body. The Feingold diet is intended to serve as an example, or perhaps the model, for this concept.

Encoding Framing the words of a spoken phrase or sentence (see Coding.)

Erratic Eye Movements Normal eye movements in reading, including fixations and saccades, have been observed by some researchers. Many dyslexics have different sorts of eye-movements, including regressions and reversals. These abnormal events have even been used as a basis for dyslexic subtyping by some investigators.

Ethics in Testing The consideration of those principles in testing which involve fairness, equity, honesty, and informed decision making. Several committees and organizations offer codes of ethics such as the Code of Fair Testing Practices in Education by the Joint Committee on Testing Practices.

Expressive Aphasia A type of aphasia involving impairments in oral and written language usage. Agnosia and apraxia are considered types of expressive aphasia.

Extended Scale Scores (ESSs) These allow a group's development in reading to be followed for several years on one continuous scale of measurement Like NCEs, the ESSs are arranged in equal-sized steps so that they may be added up and averaged.

External Locus of Control Some individuals with LD tend to be extrapunitive or to have an external locus of control. That is to say, whenever anything goes wrong, the individual never blames himself or herself but blames problems on other people or on some external agency.

Exclusionary Definition Defining a concept or condition by what the concept or condition isn't. For example, the term dyslexia is frequently defined by researchers as to what it isn't. It is sometimes defined by excluding individuals with below average IQ, primary emotional disturbance, primary sensory disorders, cultural disadvantage, and so on.

Eye-Patch Treatment The radical solution for dyslexia proposed by Stein and his associates. Since the dyslexic has basic problems coordinating the visual axes of the two eyes, according to these investigators, let them simply use one eye!

Face Validity The apparent appropriateness of the test items for assessing the intended behavior or ability, in the estimation of someone who knows about this behavior or ability. This is not considered to be a sound basis for evaluating the usefulness of a test, but it has great acceptance among lay people who have not been trained in the theory of testing.

Fernald-Kinesthetic Approach Fernald laid the basis for this approach in 1921 in what has become known as the VAKT approach. This method utilizes four sense modalities (i.e, visual, auditory, kinesthetic, and tactile) in the process of teaching word recognition and reading skills.

Formal Tests These tests, usually standardized, include specified tasks and procedures that must be adhered to very strictly, so that the test results can be comparable to those from other administrations of the test. Test interpretations target grade levels of functioning, percentile standings, stanine scores, NCE's, standard scores, and so on.

Framing Questions or Interactive Frames Preplanned question formats for a particular subject.

Front-End Approach An estimation strategy which focuses on the front-end or leftmost digits as these are the most significant to the problem. Then adjustments are made to the remaining digits with the amount of adjustment dependent on the level of skill of the student.

Frustration Reading Level An individual's frustration reading level implies just that—the level at which reading becomes frustrating for the reader whereby word recognition and comprehension fall below 75% accuracy.

Fry List A popular sight word listing.

Full Inclusion Refers to the policy of providing instructional materials and methods currently available to students without learning problems to students with handicapping conditions. Special education services are provided in the form of training and consulting with the regular classroom teacher.

GEs (grade equivalents) A kind of score that places a student's test performance in the grade grouping that it best matches. A GE score of 4.7 means the kind of performance expected from the average fourth-grader after seven months of the school year. GE differences do not come in equal steps and therefore they should never be averaged.

Gender Differences It has frequently been reported that males with dyslexia outnumber females in prevalence distribution ratios of 3:1 to 5:1. Reasons for this have generally centered on (1) excessive testosterone in male fetuses, (2) less well-developed left-hemispheric language functioning on the part of males, and (3) greater bihemispheric verbal and spatial processing skills on the part of females. Recent evidence would challenge these ratios and suggests prevalence rates for dyslexia are comparatively equal for both males and females.

Genetic Subtype A type of dyslexia which is marked by a strong familial link where reading problems tend to "run in families." Bannatyne suggests that this group displays a WISC-R subtest profile pattern of Spatial > Conceptual > Sequential (Spatial = Picture Completion + Block Design + Object Assembly; Conceptual = Similarities + Vocabulary + Comprehension and Sequential = Arithmetic + Coding + Digit Span). DeFries and Decker refer to a genetic subtype which is characterized by spatial representation and reasoning deficits instigated by visual-perceptual problems.

Geoboards Math manipulative wooden or plastic squares which are covered with pegs or nails at regular intervals. Rubber bands or cloth bands are stretched in order to form geometric shapes (e.g., squares for younger children; congruent nonconvex decagons for older students).

Gerstmann's Syndrome A controversial cluster of four symptoms which some consider to be a type of acalculia and some propose to be one of the subtypes of dyslexia. The four symptoms of this supposed syndrome are dyscalculia, right-left perception problems, finger agnosia (the inability to identify which finger has been stimulated), and dysgraphia.

Gifted Individuals who demonstrate high performance capability in such areas as overall intellectual functioning (IQ's over 120), creativity, the visual and fine arts, leadership, specific academic areas, and sports. These individuals require some differentiation in program planning efforts not ordinarily provided within the regular classroom setting (e.g., curriculum telescoping or compacting and content area acceleration).

Gifted Dyslexic Individuals Individuals who are gifted in some way but display the characteristics of individuals with dyslexia. Enrichment is recommended in the areas of talent or strength.

Gillingham-Stillman Approach This approach developed by Gillingham and Stillman in 1935 offers a type of synthetic phonics method which teaches both the names and sound of letters; the names for spelling and the sounds for reading.

Global Dyslexia Subtype Weller and Strawser have identified a global or mixed dyslexic subtype which they define by a dysfunctioning in all areas to include language and visual-perceptual realms. Denckla has described a global language disorder with several noted problems in language as a result of some type of right hemispheric involvement.

Grapheme The smallest written unit in the English language. Examples include individual letters of the alphabet.

Graphic Organizers Diagrams or outlines that depict the main structure of the material to be read. Key terms and concepts are used to create a "skeleton" that depicts the order and organization of the textual material.

Graphical Dyscalculia A type of math disability which involves the impaired ability to write math symbols, equations, or other relevant math terms.

Guide-O-Ramas Reading guides teachers develop that "guide" the reader to note certain information while reading.

Guided Writing Independent writing activities that are guided by the teacher who provides specific guidance in the mechanics of writing (e.g., punctuation usage), strategic planning, and the elicitation of ideas so as to promote and foster independent writers especially during SSW activities. The teacher also demonstrates good writing habits. (See Sustained Silent Writing.)

Hair Color A small number of researchers have linked melanin which is involved in determining one's hair color to the development of motor dominance. More specifically, left-handedness paired with blondness is claimed to be at greater risk for dyslexia as well as for immune disorders.

Hair Mineral Analysis A technique used to detect excess mineral traces such as lead, cadmium, aluminum, arsenic and mercury which have been linked by a few researchers to learning disabilities.

Handedness The specification of the dominant hand, as in right- handedness, left-handedness, or ambidexterity (neither hand dominating).

Hawthorne Effect, The A behavior change which is not due to the treatment given in order to effect the change, but, rather, to the individual's sense of participation in important research under the eye of prestigious supervisors, professionals, etc. Most of the time, when these other factors are controlled, the treatment in question would be ineffective.

Heterogeneity of Symptomatologies This refers to the notion that the characteristics or correlates frequently associated with dyslexics are so diverse that this population cannot be defined by one set of criteria. However, there appear to be subgroups within this diversity containing similar within group symptoms with between-group differences distinct enough to warrant categorization classifications. No one subtyping system has been consensually accepted to date.

Higher Peripheral Brightness Threshold Hypothesis, The The Spafford-Grosser hypothesis which is a component of the Grosser-Spafford peripheral cone theory. This is the prediction that dyslexics should require unusually high intensity stimulation in order to detect small test lights on the peripheral retina, compared to normal readers.

Homogeneity of Subtypes This is a concept promulgated by Ellis who believes that a multidimensional model of dyslexia should be embraced in which dyslexic characteristics are widely scattered but not clustered into groups or subtypes.

Hyperlexia A heightened ability to read (words) without concomittant understanding. Considered to be a rare disorder. There is no known cause. Also known as Williams' Syndrome.

Hypermedia A computer system which links computer programs that have text, audio, graphics, video, and word-processing abilities.

IDEA See Individual with Disabilities Education Act.

Ideognostical Dyscalculia A math disability which centers on impaired mathematical thinking or impaired conceptualizations of math processes.

IEP or Individualized Educational Plans IEPs are reports written for school-age children in grades K–12. The IEP serves a dual function, as an evaluation tool and as a teaching plan and is mandated under P.L. 94–142 since renamed IDEA. An IEP should include all of the following: a statement of present levels of functioning; short-term and annual goals; projected dates for initiation and duration of special services; criteria and evaluation procedures to be used to determine if goals have been achieved; names of persons responsible for special services and evaluation; program descriptions of special services to be provided; and the extent to which the student will participate in regular education programs.

IFSPs or Individual Family Service Plans IFSPs are reports written for pre-schoolers. An IFSP has to address the developmental needs and learning styles of the pre-school child in the areas of cognition, speech, psycho-motor skills, language, and self-help skills.

Inclusion Consultants Consultants who are committed to an inclusion model by coaching family members, school professionals, and students in identifying and developing their skills and becoming knowledgeable about inclusion models and issues.

Inclusion Programs or Models Inclusionary programs are frequently referred to as models of *full inclusion, fully integrated programs, inclusive educational programs,* and *unified systems approaches.* The basic inclusionary model consists of the following: (1) full participation of the student with dyslexia in regular classroom activities to the maximum extent possible, (2) support provisions (e.g., special education initiatives) provided within the regular classroom setting with the service provider working with the student at his/her seat or a corner of the room, and (3) curriculum planning involving collaborative effort between regular education staff and special education staff. (See also Full Inclusion.)

Independent Reading Level Generally, an individual's independent reading level is the level at which an individual can read 90–99% of textual words and a passage with 90–99% comprehension at a comfortable and at least average reading rate. Independent reading levels are just what the term implies, the levels at which individuals can read without assistance, or independently.

Individual with Disabilities Education Act (IDEA) of 1990 (under P.L. 101–476) The renaming of P.L. 94–142 of 1975 which was the Education of All Handicapped Children's Act. IDEA includes the 1983 amendment (P.L. 98–199), and the 1986 amendment (P.L. 99–457). IDEA involves legislation which mandates early intervention programs for students at-risk for learning disabilities and other special needs. A CSPD (comprehensive system of personnel development) must be in place as well as an IFSP (individual family service plan) for each child.

Informal Assessment Supplementing the standardized formal tests that can be given to a group of examinees are such other measures as observations, teacher-made classroom tests, sample behavior situations, anecdotal records, checklists, etc. Informal assessments do not rely on normative data.

Informal Reading Inventory These are reading inventories which are prepared commercially or can be teacher-made. They usually consist of graded vocabulary lists and comprehension passages which are also graded. The vocabulary lists are used to establish reading grade levels, word attack ability and the accuracy and speed of decoding. Comprehension questions tap into the individuals, literal and abstract thinking abilities as well as grade level functioning.

Information Processing Model The theoretical representation (i.e., modeling) of perception, learning, cognition, and/or reading as equivalent to the computerized handling of information, with input, data, processing, and output functions serving as models for the brain's activities.

Instructional Reading Level This is the reading level of the individual whereby a teacher can focus instruction because the student can read words accurately with at least 80–85% proficiency and with 80–90% comprehension proficiency. In other words, this would be a comfortable reading level where instruction could begin.

Interactive Reading Models These models stress the simultaneous information-processing of verbal data at high or low levels, using both bottom-up and top-down channels of information flow.

Internal Releasing Mechanism (IRM) The simultaneous triggering of a series of reflexive actions by the appropriate environmental stimuli. These stimuli are the supposed releasers, while the mechanism itself is an organization of a part of the brain. Levinson regards the brain's programming of seasickness after the rapid inflow of visual messages into the cerebral cortex as one example of an IRM.

IQ or Intelligence Quotient A standard score used to indicate the test taker's general cognitive ability. When the Stanford-Binet test was the standard for intelligence testing, the IQ was defined as the mental age of the individual divided by the true (chronological) age times 100. If the two age scores were identical, the IQ would come out at an even 100. If mental age were higher than chronological age, the IQ would be greater than 100; if lower, the IQ would be less than 100. The Wechsler Intelligence Scales are based on the normal curve, so that the average performance of a large group of persons (the standardization group)

is used to define what raw score should be set at 100, as the average IQ score. Raw scores higher than the average one would correspond to IQs higher than 100, and so on. This approach is consistent with modern standardized testing; the IQ is not a quotient but a deviation IQ.

IRA An acronym for International Reading Association.

K-P (Kaiser Permanente) A diet recommended by a few practitioners which eliminates synthetic food colors and natural salicylates in order to remedy learning disabilities and behavior problems.

Language The symbolic notation/communication system in both written and oral forms which allows one to communicate coherently concepts, thoughts, social intentions, feelings, factual material, stories, and so on. Language proficiency does depend on how well one uses the phonology, syntax, pragmatics, and semantics of language. Individuals with dyslexia have been found to be deficit in one or more areas. (See Phonology, Pragmatics, Semantics, and Syntax.)

LD or ld Acronym for learning disabled, learning disability, or learning disabilities. See also *Learning Disabled or Specific Learning Disabled*.

LD Problem Consultant Spafford's and Grosser's term for a predesignated responsible person an individual with dyslexia can consult with when life problems are encountered. The consultant can (1) brainstorm with the individual with dyslexia on various problem-solving strategies and alternatives, (2) role play various ways to handle the problem, (3) refer the individual to someone who is better able or equipped to assist, and (4) follow- up to see how the problem was handled and mutually assess outcomes and future ways to handle similar situations. It is important to follow the problem-solving process from assessment of the problem to solutions and outcomes and finally to a reflective evaluation of the entire process.

LDA Learning Disabilities Association of America.

Learned Helplessness An "I can't do this myself" attitude. This attitude is learned and is "an easy way out." The external locus of control syndrome probably initiates the learned helplessness characteristic which in turn leads to poor social relationships with peers and teachers.

Learning Disabled or Specific Learning Disabled As defined by THE NJCLD: Refers to a heterogeneous group of disorders that are characterized by difficulties in acquiring and using listening, speaking, reading, writing, reasoning, or mathematics abilities. These types of problems are presumed to result from central nervous system dysfunction (i.e., genetic, biochemical, or structural anomalies). A learning disability may occur concomitantly with other handicapping conditions (e.g., low IQ, psychogenic factors) but does not result from said factors.

Current practice points to the following characteristics:

1. average IQ
2. differing subtypes/types
3. familial patterns
4. persistence through to adulthood
5. social misperceptiveness
6. at least 50% having dyslexia or reading disabilities
7. the majority having language deficiencies
8. males/females affected in equal proportions
9. lowered self-esteem, self-images
10. require specialized assessment/remediation
11. favorable prognosis/and acquisition of compensatory strategies enhance life/school/social successes

Lexical Dyscalculia   A type of math disability involving impaired reading of math vocabulary and symbols.

LGL Approach   The List-Group-Label Approach developed by Taba in 1967 is better known as *Semantic Webbing*. (See Semantic Mapping-Webbing.)

Literature Conferences   Reading and English associations which sponsor conferences which allow professionals and other interested parties to come in contact with literature through books, authors, visuals, and workshops. The IRA and ALAN frequently sponsor such conferences.

L-Type Dyslexia   The condition of a dyslexic whose reading problems are primarily linguistic, according to Bakker and Licht. The L-type dyslexic uses the left hemisphere prematurely, never having learned to identify the shapes of letters and letter groups well enough for the reading task to be done efficiently. He/she reads quickly, but makes many word-identification errors.

Mainstreaming   Refers to the process of selectively placing students with dyslexia and other learning problems in one or more regular education classes (e.g., science, art, gym, and so on). Students are expected to keep up with their classmates with modifications made to the curriculum if necessary. Mainstreaming is associated with traditional educational service delivery models and programs.

Marginal Glosses   Comments authors or teachers make in the margins of books such as personal asides, notes of clarification, vocabulary highlights, interpretations, trivia notes, and so on.

Material Previews   Movie-like capsule previews of material to be read. Such previews can have students reading book titles, subheadings, pre- and post-questions, chapter introductions and conclusions, graphs, charts, pictures, and so on in order to make guesses or predictions about story content which can be confirmed or nonconfirmed after the reading.

Math Manipulatives   Hand-held math objects which have been found to be effective with students with dyslexia and other disabilities as long as they are meaningful to the student and can tie-in important math concepts to be learned. Examples of math manipulatives are attribute blocks, Cuisenaire Rods, base ten blocks, geoboards, and the number line.

Mathematics Disabilities   Developmental or acquired problems in one or more of the general areas of number sense or numeration, computational ability, problem-solving, symbol interpretation, algorithm application, and visual-motoric-task completion. The two major types of math disabilities found in the literature are acalculia and dyscalculia.

Megavitamins   The concept of taking vitamins in megadoses thousands of times the size of the RDA (recommended daily allowance), on the theory that most illness is due to disordered brain or body chemistry, according to the orthomolecular school.

Memory Disorders   Memory dysfunctioning which can interfere with language development and usage. Memory disorders can involve faulty short-term memory (also called working memory), long-term memory, and memory strategies, monitoring, and recall.

Metacognition   An awareness of one's thinking or cognitive processes which includes the ability to self-monitor and self-evaluate one's performance. Students with dyslexia lack as sophisticated a metacognitive awareness as non-disabled peers.

Metacognitive Awareness   Awareness or knowledge of one's own cognitive processes (e.g., ability to self-monitor, self-evaluate, and self-question).

Minimum Competency Tests (MCTs)   Tests that set a minimum for performance in various subjects. Generally, MCTs are used to determine eligibility for promotion or graduation. They are popular with state legislatures which believe that by mandating the use of such tests, schools are held accountable. Test authorities tend to agree that the standards used for MCTs are subjectively selected and that no single measurement should be decisive for the promotion or graduation of a student.

Mixed Dyslexia Subtype   A type of dyslexia whereby the individual displays symptoms in a number of areas. Typically, the individual has language and perceptual (e.g., visual) problems which interfere with the reading process.

Mixed Subtype   One of Spafford and Grosser's dyslexia subtypes, in which learning difficulties in reading and language have roots in both visual and linguistic areas of the cerebral cortex resulting in some dysfunctioning in both areas.

Monroe Approach   This synthetic phonics approach was developed in 1932 as a way to reduce oral reading errors by eliminating incorrect pronunciations of vowels and consonants and reading miscues such as omissions, substitutions, reversals, and repetitions. Synthetic phonics teaching is used with correct motoric response training.

Morpheme   The smallest meaningful unit in the English language. Examples include "pre-," "-ing," "run," etc.

Multicultural Issues   Issues regarding one's ethnicity that need to be considered when assessments are administered and subsequent educational programs are implemented. Multicultural considerations include sensitivity to one's cultural background, the provision of material in a native language if necessary, providing extra time and assistance when needed, clarifying directions or instructions when needed, providing a positive and comfortable testing or learning environment, using multiple presentations or different ways to present the same material in order to ensure understanding, and so on.

Multicultural Literacy, The Teaching of   Strategies for teaching multicultural content topics in an effort to provide opportunities for students to transact a wide range of meaningful and func-tional learning experiences.

Multimedia   The use of computer data in the forms of audio, video (visual) graphics, and computer script in order to produce a sophisticated/visually appealing instructional presentation.

NCEs Normal Curve Equivalents   These measures of performance are based on percentiles and, like percentiles, show where someone stands within the group. However, they are transformed from non-additive percentiles into a scale of units that represent equal steps of reading achievement. A difference of 6 points, e.g., is the same amount of difference whether the measures found near the middle of the scale or toward either the high or the low end of the scale. This property of the NCEs makes them suitable for averaging.

NCTM   See page 238.

Neuropsychological Measures   Measures of behavioral symptoms of damage to the central nervous system. Some of these measures (e.g., the absence of normal reflexes) are considered *hard signs* that absolutely indicate physical damage and other measures may be *soft signs* (e.g., hesitation about which side is left or right) that may be taken as contributing pointers, but not as absolute evidence.

NJCLD   Acronym for National Joint Committee for Learning Disabilities. The 1988 NJCLD definition of learning disabilities is well-regarded and appears in Chapter 1.

Normative Data   Data converted into statistical terms (e.g., standard scores and percentiles) which allow comparisons with scores derived from national or local groups of individuals at comparable age/grade levels. The determination of one's relative standing on a test is important for instructional purposes as remedial measures can build on both individual strengths and weaknesses.

Norm-Referenced Tests (NRTs)   These are formal, standardized tests whose directions for administration must be closely followed. They should include items representing all levels of difficulty. The items should not be too similar in content, style, or vocabulary to any one particular published reading program.

NRT   An acronym for norm-referenced test.

Ocular Lock   A hypothetical limitation of the eyes' range of movement which is attributed to malfunctioning cranial bones.

Ontogeny   The development of an individual living thing (an organism) from conception to old age.

Operational Dyscalculia A math disability involving an impaired ability to perform the basic math operations.

Orthomolecular The belief that producing the correct chemical condition of the brain and of the rest of the body is the major key to health. Orthomolecular doctrine holds that megavitamins, and often megaminerals, should be taken in order to restore (and maintain) the body's inner state to (or in) normal health.

P-type Dyslexia The condition of a dyslexic whose reading problems primarily involve visual perception, according to Bakker and Licht. The P-type dyslexic uses the right hemisphere primarily (a developmental fixation, because after the good reader learns the fundamentals of language, he/she uses the left hemisphere primarily). While accurate, a P-type dyslexic will read very slowly.

Paired Reading Placing students together in pairs to read side-by-side.

Peer Power A phrase used to describe ways in which students can support one another in a cooperative sense. The formation of instructional teams, peer advocates, and peer partners are examples of peer power.

Performance IQ A component of the Intelligence Quotient (IQ) on the Wechsler series of Intelligence tests. It consists of the following subtests: Object Assembly, Picture Arrangement, Picture Completion, Block Design, Digit Symbol (Coding), and, optionally, Mazes.

Pervasive Language Deficit The presence in one individual of several language-related problems, such as the combination of poor spelling, poor reading, articulation difficulty, a lack of word fluency, etc. Whether some people can have extremely severe dyslexia (which would entail such widespread language deficits) and still not be classifiable as "garden-variety poor readers" (simply poor learners in anything) is controversial.

Phoneme The smallest unit of sound in the English language. Examples would be "ea," "F," "ie," etc.

Phonemic Awareness (See Phonological Awareness.)

Phonics Specific instruction in sound-symbol relationships/rules. Words are sounded out and spelled according to specific rules.

Phonological Awareness Also known as *linguistic awareness* and *phonemic awareness*, it is a type of phonological processing ability that involves a metalinguistic awareness of

speech-sound correspondences (e.g., the *c* in cat has the *k* sound) and relationships (e.g., a vowel followed by a consonant and final silent *e* is usually long). Phonological awareness is considered an important predictor of future reading problems, with individuals who experience difficulty in this area requiring specific phonological training. Students who are dyslexic frequently experience difficulty in phonological awareness and processing abilities. (See Phonological Awareness Tasks, Phonological Processing.)

Phonological Awareness Tasks Tasks used to measure one's phonological awareness ability which is considered pivotal to reading success. Such tasks include but are not limited to the following categories. Teachers can create similar informal assessment measures.

Sound-to-Sound matching: What sounds are similar in the words *break* and *lake?*

Sound-to-Word Matching: Is there an *s* sound in the word *city?*

Word-to-Word Matching: Do *eat* and *egg* begin with the same sound?

Blending: Put the following sounds together to make a word—/h/ /a/ /t/

Deleting Phonemes: What word do you have if you left the /h/ sound off of the word hat?

Moving Phonemes: What other words can you make from the letters e-a-t besides eat? (tea, ate)

Adding Phonemes: What word would you have if you added the /h/ sound before at?

Phonemic Segmentation: What are the different sounds you hear in the word *happy?* or Break the word *smile* into its different sounds.

Phonemic Counting: How many sounds are there in the word *happy?*

Phonemic Classification: What word is different and why?—*cake, make, lake,* and *pie.*

Phonological Dyslexia This type of dyslexia is a developmental analog to Boder's dysphonetic dyslexic, Coltheart's acquired dyslexic, and Doering and Hoshko's phonological deficit type; it is marked by problems in interpretation or execution of the phoneme-grapheme correspondence match.

Phonological Processing The ability to recognize and utilize the important sound-symbol correspondences of the printed page. Such processing requires that an individual be able efficiently (1) to *encode* or represent phonological information in short-term or working memory, (2) to *retrieve* phonological information from long-term memory, and (3) to exhibit *phonemic awareness* or the metalinguistic knowledge or phonological awareness of sound-symbol relationships and correspondences. (See Phonological Awareness.)

Phonology Refers to the auditory/aural sound components to language (e.g., sound elements associated with graphemes) and is important to the decoding process.

Photopic Vision Refers to bright-light vision. The receptors are cones. Photopic visions allows color discrimination and keen acuity of detail. It is central, not peripheral, except in some dyslexics.

Phylogeny The evolutionary development, flourishing, and extinction of biological species over vast eons of time.

Percentile Ranks A percentile rank for a given raw score shows the percentage of the examinees whose raw score was the same or lower. For example, if only 14% of the group who took the test with you scored higher than you did, you would have chalked up a respectable percentile rank of 86th. If, however, 86% of the scores were better than yours, your percentile rank would be 14th.

PIP Acronym for professional improvement plan. This is an integrative professional growth and improvement plan for educators.

P.L. 98-199 An amendment to P.L. 94–142 (now called IDEA) which emphasizes parent education and preschool, secondary, and post-secondary programs for individuals with special handicapping conditions.

P.L. 99-457 An amendment to P.L. 94–142 (now called IDEA) which emphasizes pre-school programs for infants and toddlers from birth to age two.

P.L. 101-476 The legislation which renamed P.L. 94–142 to IDEA.

Portfolio A type of authentic assessment (assessments which relate testing to meaningful or significant life tasks) which represents a person's collective academic and personal accomplishments. Teachers provide guidance as to the type of content a portfolio should possess. Portfolios document progress in school as well as reflect student growth and development in a number of areas (e.g., written language skills, outlining, speech making [on audiotape], and so on). Portfolio projects allow students to evaluate their own subject area reading/language knowledge as well as writing, reading, listening, and discussion abilities.

Portfolio Assessment A type of reflective authentic assessment which is a meaningful collection of one's work over a period of time. Portfolios should demonstrate one's communication skills and language proficiency as well as competencies and growth in a number of areas. (See also Authentic Assessment.)

Postural Rehabilitation The basic aim of the Doman-Delacato approach to correcting learning disabilities. The individual restarts his/her development of crawling, walking, and running.

Practognostic Dyscalculia (gnostic=knowing; practo=doing; knowing by doing) A type of math disability involving the application of math concepts when using manipulative objects in the environment (either visual or three dimensional).

Pragmatics Refers to the social interpretations and uses of language (e.g., body cues, facial language, reasons for communication).

Prereading Activities Reading activities (e.g., brainstorming, semantic mapping/webbing, surveying, graphic organizers, cognitive mediation, and vocabulary activities). The greatest potential for prereading activities lies in their immediate usefulness within a specific reading task.

Primary Acalculia Also called anarithmetia and true acalculia. This is an acquired type of math disability which involves difficulties in applying algorithms to basic math operations although memory and language skills appear relatively intact. In other words, calculating abilities are impaired across the board.

Process Writing The actual teaching of the writing process via an initial brainstorming session(s) with reflection, three drafts, peer inquiry, and teacher feedback to follow. The teacher evaluates and publishes the final product.

Professional Standards for Teaching Mathematics (NCTM, 1991b) The six standards which are intended to guide teachers of mathematics so that the math needs of all students can be met: Standard 1: Worthwhile Math Tasks; Standard 2: The Teacher's Role in Discourse; Standard 3: Students' Role in Discourse; Standard 4: Tools for Enhancing Discourse; Standard 5. The Learning Environment; and Standard 6:

Analysis of Teaching and Learning.

Radio-Reading Script reading in the form of a radio announcement or program which is delivered to an audience.

Raw Score A simple total score such as the number of test items correctly answered. The raw score has very little meaning in the absence of any allowance for the ease or difficulty of the test items.

Reading Recovery A method of teaching reading which was developed by Clay in New Zealand in the late 1970s for high-risk (for reading failure) first graders. This approach emphasizes listening to sound sequences in words and blends analytic/synthetic phonics principles into one approach. This intense 12–14 week program is essentially tutorial and requires ongoing diagnoses and treatment.

Recapitulation Doing something over again. In the cliche, "ontogeny recapitulates phylogeny," the human embryo starts out looking fishlike, then somewhat resembles an amphibian, still later a reptile, then a smaller mammal, and looks like a recognizable human being only rather late during gestation.

Receptive Aphasia Disorders in understanding receptive language or the understanding of verbal symbols.

Receptor Hypothesis, The The hypothesis stated by Grosser and Spafford that, in the retina of dyslexics, there are relatively more cones and fewer rods than in the retinae of normal readers; this would particularly apply to the peripheral parts of the retina.

Reciprocal Teaching A method where students take turns with the teacher; reading segments and formulating questions about the reading. Teachers and students switch roles during some or all parts of the reading.

Recoding An important component of word recognition. (See Decoding.)

Referring Question This is the initial hypothesized reason for a special education referral for testing/and or placement. Referring questions can be general (e.g., Heather has been referred for overall academic failure and behavior difficulties in the classroom) or very specific (Heather has been referred for testing because of reading and written language problems across the curriculum and acting out and attention-getting behaviors in the classroom when work tasks become overwhelming).

Reliability That test is reliable which measures the same object or phenomenon consistently, even under varying conditions.

Regular Education Initiative or REI A term used to describe efforts to reform traditional educational practices which emphasize "pull-out" models for students with dyslexia and other special needs by encouraging the education of students with dyslexia in the classroom.

Reliability Measurements The test-constructor does not know what exactly are the sources of error in the test, or, obviously, she/he would never have let them enter into it. Test reliability has to be computed indirectly, by one of three different strategies: (a) Test-Retest Coefficient—Give the test to a group of subjects, wait a while (allowing enough time for normal forgetting of test items to occur) and give the same test again to these subjects. Compute the correlation coefficient between the first set of scores and the second. (b) Parallel, or Alternate, Forms—Construct a second test containing the same kind of test items as the original and based on the same theory as the original. Give both forms of the test to the same subjects. Compute the correlation coefficient for the two forms of the test. (c) Internal Reliability—If the test were to be split in half, the total score for the items in one half of the test could be correlated with the total for the items in the remaining half.

(c-i) Spearman's split-half reliability coefficient Take all the odd-numbered test items and treat them as one form of the test; do likewise for all the even-numbered test items. Compute the correlation between these two halves. Since cutting a test's length lowers its reliability, a correction factor is applied to that correlation, so that the reliability coefficient is increased appropriately.

(c-ii) Kuder-Richardson Internal Consistency coefficient Use the formula devised by Kuder and Richardson to take an average of all possible split-half coefficients the test can yield. There are more ways to divide a test in half than just to take the odd-numbered and even-numbered items. This method does not require us to know which is the best way to subdivide the test.

Resource Rooms A type of *pull-out* service model for students with dyslexia and other special needs. A resource room is just what the name implies—a resource center. A special education or learning disabilities teacher provides remedial assistance for the dyslexic child as well as for several other children with varying special needs (i.e., gifted children, children with speech impairments, children with physical handicaps, and so on). Typically, this resource teacher is supported by an auxiliary staff of specialists (e.g., speech therapists, counselors, psychologists) and teacher aides who theoretically work as a team in implementing a child's educational plan or IEP.

Response Journals   Journal writing which involves having students express how they feel about content or ideas stated in text read. The role of the teacher is to respond to student questions without keying in on spelling or structural details.

Rods   The more prevalent type of light-sensitive receptor cell in the retina. The most central part of the retina is entirely free of rods but at the extreme periphery, they are numerous enough so that their properties account for the nature and properties of peripheral vision. (See Scotopic Vision.)

Role of Cognitive Ability   A factor in determining the self-esteem in persons with LD which is frequently assessed via an IQ score. Children with LD as a whole generally fall in the "normal" range of IQ, but IQs generally fall in the low 90s.

ROPE   Acronym for *Rite of Passage Experience,* a portfolio approach which lists eight requirements for graduating high school seniors, to include reflections on schooling, progress, and life experiences.

Rote Drill and Practice   The practice of memorizing math material by repetition and practice. Little thought is given to cognitive processing. Math facts are best learned by rote drill and practice (in other words, by sheer memorization).

Scaffolding   Providing supportive teaching strategies in steps so that learners master one-step-at-a-time. Scaffolding is like helping a student climb a ladder rung-by-rung. Students hopefully develop independence in reading activities when the teacher "fades out" any active assistance thereby allowing the student to assume responsibility for the reading task.

Scotopic Sensitivity Syndrome (SSS)   This is Helen Irlen's conception of a dyslexic's underlying problem, that is, a painful sensitivity to light and difficulties perceiving certain wavelengths and black-white contrast. Prescriptive colored lenses are thought to resolve the problem.

Scotopic Vision   Refers to faint-light vision. The receptors are rods. Scotopic vision is very sensitive, capable of detecting very faint lights. It also detects motion and depth (three-dimensional distance). Usually, this kind of vision is peripheral, not central.

Secondary Acalculia   Also called aphasia acalculia, acalculia with alexia, and/or agraphia for numbers. This is an acquired type of acalculia which involves math impairments in oral and written number formation. Computational proficiency remains intact.

Self-Assessment   A type of assessment which involves reflecting on one's own learning and learning problems, growth, success or failure in different situations, social and academic strengths and weaknesses, and so on. One must be able to review and analyze growth in learning.

Self-Monitor   The metacognitive ability to plan, monitor, and evaluate one's abilities and performance.

Semantics   The meaning(s) associated with words and word elements especially as they combine to form sentences and cohesive passages of text.

Semantic Mapping-Webbing   The development of a graphic display which depicts the organization and relationship of generated ideas. As teachers and students work to cluster the ideas into a visual display, the structure of knowledge is made explicit. This is also known as the LGL or List-Group-Label Approach because through brainstorming students must generate lists of relevant stimulus words from a lesson, and then group and label lists under main topics or headings.

Sight Word Approach   A word recognition approach which involves having students memorize certain words by sight without using phonics skills. The Dolch and Fry Sight Word Lists are excellent compilations of frequently used sight words.

Short-Term Memory Deficit   There is some evidence to show that some dyslexics are slower than proficient readers in retrieving information from short-term memory and this slowness hampers comprehension of textual material.

Social Behavioral Problems of Individuals with Dyslexia   Individuals with dyslexia are known to exhibit such social behavioral problems as more negative peer interactions, lower social standing in the eyes of significant adults, diminished self-concepts, external locus of control and learned helplessness, lower levels of cognitive ability, and unawareness of social conventions.

Social Environment The social climate in the classroom which contributes to one's active and participatory role as a student/learner. Certainly the social interactions among and between students contribute to the overall social climate of the classroom. The teacher can set a negative or positive tone in regard to attitudes, beliefs, how students treat one another, and so on.

Social Misperception Impaired social awareness which is attributable to impaired communication or impaired perceptual skills.

Social-Perceptual Problems There are several researchers who have found that dyslexics lack social skills that are largely dependent on one's ability to accurately perceive and interpret social situations and contexts. For example, it has been frequently noted that some dyslexics inaccurately perceive body-language cues such as facial expressions and therefore act and react inappropriately.

Sphenoid A winged, compound bone at the base of the skull.

SQRQCQ a mathematics problem-solving method which involves the six steps of (1) Survey, (2) Question, (3) Read, (4) Question, (5) Compute, and (6) Question. Students must carefully survey word problems for an understanding of the language and what the problem is looking for. Questioning at every step provides time for self-reflection, assessment, and rethinking new strategies. The final question must reflect on the answer at hand—does it make sense and is it reasonable?

Standard Error of Estimate This is the standard deviation (square root of the variance) of the errors in predictions made from the test. It is equal to the product of the standard deviation of the criterion scores times the square root of the quantity 1 minus r^2, where r is the correlation between the test scores and the criterion measures. The lower the correlation, the greater will be the standard error of estimate. It is not advisable to make predictions from scores on a low-validity test.

Standard Error of Measurement If one examinee were to take the same test many times, the scores would yield a variance statistic, the square root of which is called the standard error of measurement. This standard error is equal to the product of the square root of the observed variance times the square root of the quantity one minus the test's reliability coefficient.

Standard Scores These are computed from raw scores by the following process. Begin with an individual's raw score, X. Let M be the arithmetic mean of all the raw scores. Subtract the mean from X; this is the right order, because if the raw score is above the mean, the difference will be positive, and, if the raw score is less than the mean score, the difference will be negative. Now divide this positive or negative difference score by s, the standard deviation of the raw scores. The results will be a conversion from X. the raw score in test points, to z, the standard score in standard deviation units. A standard score of +1, for example, is exactly 1 standard deviation higher than the mean. The process is akin to obtaining the number of feet equivalent to 72 inches, which you would divide by 12, which is the size of 1 foot in inch units. Another analogy is the conversion of 537 cents to its equivalent in dollars. The key step is dividing by the size of 1 dollar in cents, namely, 100, to obtain the answer of $5.37. An advantage to using standard scores is that results can be compared from radically dissimilar tests, once the raw scores have been converted from each test to standard scores.

Standardization Group, or Norm Group This is a large and representative sample of the population for whom the test is intended.

Standardized Tests These tests are administered to a large sample, the norm group, of those types of people for whom the test is intended. The statistical data describing the performance of the norm group, or standardization group, are known as norms.

Stanines The term comes from *standard nine* scale. The stanine scale is a modified scale of standard scores, with the mean set at 5 (instead of zero, as it is for the z-scale) and the standard deviation at nearly 2 (while the standard deviation is 1 on the z-scale). The widths of stanines 2 through 8 are equal, but, at the extremes, stanines 1 and 9 are very wide. Stanine values represent ranges rather than specific points.

Stereopsis Seeing the world stereoscopically, in three dimensions.

Story Grammar A structural system of procedures/rules which describe text features. At the elementary level, story grammar can focus on the basic setting, story plot, and story resolution.

Story Maps Circular-like drawings on one page of

key concepts related to story grammar highlights. Key concepts, characters, or main ideas appear in large circles with extensions leading to smaller circles containing other ideas, concepts, and characters in the story. These are useful study guides and enhance comprehension development.

Story Prompts Cue cards which contain such prompts as the time and place of the story, characters, problem and problem resolution, and story ending. These story elements provide stimulation and organization in writing.

Strategic Teaching Teaching based on observations of student learning, strengths, and weaknesses, that provides children with the essential information to solve problems, think critically, self-monitor, and assess their own learning. Strategic teaching could mean providing one student with multisensory phonetic materials and another with whole language activities. The teacher is aware of the unique needs and learning styles of all learners and provides instruction accordingly.

Strategy Instruction The teaching approach which focuses on the teaching of learning strategies as opposed to specific subject matter. Learning strategies could include specific memory devices, study skills, or metacognitive skills.

Strephosymbolia Twisted symbols—Orton's concept of what a dyslexic sees on the printed page. The letters, numbers, and words in print are scrambled in position, reversed, and/or upside-down.

Structural Analysis The linguistic knowledge or study of word parts or elements that have meaning in isolation, such as prefixes, suffixes, compound words, and syllables.

Subluxation A partial dislocation of a bone.

Subtyping Research has shown that dyslexics display diverse symptomatologies with possible clusters of individuals evincing enough within group homogeneity to warrant classification into subtypes. The present authors have suggested 3 dyslexic subtype groups: (1) visual-dysphonetic dyslexia, (2) auditory-linguistic dyslexia, and (3) mixed dyslexia type involving symptoms from (1) and (2). The rationale for subtyping any type of disorder involves identification for purposes of (1) conducting research, and (2) providing fine-tuned remedial efforts for specific problems.

Superior Ability to Recognize Peripheral Color Hypothesis, The A component of the Grosser-Spafford peripheral cone theory, this is the prediction that dyslexics should recognize the colors of test objects at extremely peripheral locations of the retina, compared to normal readers.

Surface Dyslexia Surface or semantic dyslexia has been described as an inability to recognize whole words rapidly and accurately, although phonetically regular words can be decoded. This suggests some phonemic synthesis ability. The misreading of irregularly spelled words has been seen to result from an overapplication of phonics principles (e.g., *precise* is pronounced *priest*). Neurological damage has been postulated to cause this problem.

Sustained Silent Reading (SSR) Activities meant to foster/reinforce literate behavior. These are independent reading activities which utilize literature and leisure types of reading materials. As an example, the DEAR (Drop Everything and Read) programs, have become common SSR experiences in many schools.

Sustained Silent Writing (SSW) Independent writing activities which are done without direct guidance or intervention from the teacher so as to promote the writing process, creativity in thinking, and exploration of novel ideas and concepts. SSW activities could include journal and dialogue writing, original story writing, letters to pen pals, and so on. SSW activities should not be done with students who are dyslexic unless some guided writing activities occurred beforehand or in conjunction with the SSW task. (See Guided Writing.)

Syntax The order and complexity of language elements (e.g., words).

Synthetic Phonics Approaches Phonics approaches which first introduce isolated letters and corresponding sound(s) which students later blend together to form words. The Monroe, Fernald Kinesthetic, and Gillingham-Stillman methods are, in part, synthetic approaches and are used with students with more severe forms of dyslexia.

Syntonics A system used for treating learning disabilities by hypothetically expanding the visual field with red and blue lights.

Task Analysis The learning process of breaking a skill (e.g., telling time) or task (e.g., reading) into several subskills or parts.

Technology in the Curriculum Using computers, calculators, multi-media and assistive technology to support and extend the curriculum.

Temporal Bone A compound bone at the side of the skull.

Tomatis Audiological-Psycho-Phonology (APP)

Method A hearing training method which involves dialoguing with the unborn fetus and playing high frequency sounds to young children via headphones. Children with learning disabilities are supposedly improved with hearing retraining. There is little research to substantiate this position.

Top-Down Reading Models These models stress the importance of scripts, inferences, and knowledge schemata that contribute to one's ability to formulate hypotheses about information processed.

Tourette's Syndrome A chronic tic disorder with uncontrollable vocal and motor tics prevalent. Coprolalia or vulgar cursing is observed in 30% of all cases. Seen in 1% of ADHD cases. Three times as many males as females are diagnosed as having Tourette's syndrome.

True Acalculia Also called primary acalculia and anarithmetia. (See Primary Acalculia.)

Unconditional Positive Regard The demonstration by a teacher or psychotherapist of absolute and unqualified respect for the student or client. One objective of requiring the helper to have this attitude is the development of unconditional positive self-regard on the part of the helpee.

VAK Approach Acronym for visual-auditory-kinesthetic approach.

VAKT Approach Acronym for visual-auditory-kinesthetic-tactile approach.

Validity This is the degree to which a test measures that which it is designed to measure. It is expressed as a correlation coefficient computed between the test and some criterion measurement of the behavior or ability that is meant to be measured. *Note: A test with low reliability can never have high validity, but a test with high reliability may or may not be valid.*

Verbal Dyscalculia A math disability type characterized by difficulties in retrieving mathematics labels, terms, and symbols (verbal aspects of math language).

Verbal IQ Half of the Wechsler Intelligence Test series is based on verbal tests whereas the other half is based on performance tests. These produce the verbal IQ and the performance IQ, respectively. The two are averaged to yield the Full Scale IQ. Subtests contributing to the verbal IQ are: information, comprehension, arithmetic, similarities, digit span, and vocabulary.

Verbal-Linguistic Subtype Spafford and Grosser's dyslexia subtype which roots learning difficulties in reading and language in traditionally believed areas of the cerebral cortex which involve language. Visual functioning is determined to be normal.

Verbal-Performance Discrepancy This refers to a statistically significant difference between one's verbal IQ score and one's performance IQ score. There has been widespread debate regarding whether or not verbal-performance discrepancy differences can differentially define dyslexic and proficient readers. One of the present authors, Spafford, has found that such differences can be of diagnostic utility.

Vergence The movement of a single eye. Convergence refers to the movement of both eyes so that the lines of sight converge, allowing the close scrutiny of a nearby object. When eye movement control has been disrupted, the separate control of each eye's movement becomes an issue, hence, *vergence.*

Vestibular Senses The senses of the inner ear other than hearing. The semicircular canals monitor rotary accelerations of the head in any directions; there are three semicircular canals, each positioned at right angles to the two others. The two otolith organs report linear accelerations, one covering vertical changes of speed and the other dealing with horizontal accelerations. They are often called, collectively, the sense of balance.

Visual Dyslexia Myklebust has provided a succinct explanation for this type of dyslexia; visual dyslexia simply stated is the inability to obtain meaning from print because of visual-perceptual deficiencies or deficits.

Visual-Dysphonetic Subtype This subtype classification suggested by Spafford and Grosser suggests that a group of dyslexics exists who display deficits in the visual-perceptual area with causation stemming from aberrant visual receptors and/or other neurons in the visual nervous pathways.

Visual-Spatial Subtype This dyslexic subtype identified by Pirozzolo and others, can be described as an impairment in visual-discrimination ability, analysis, and memory.

Vocabulary Activities Activities which focus on building active learning strategies for tackling difficult or unknown words.

Vocabulary Self-Collection Strategy (VSS) An approach developed by Haggard in 1986 to help students create vocabulary lists that need to be learned, based on the student's interests and prior schema.

Webbing A language approach which involves

brainstorming about a topic and creating a learning web of the major topic branching out to several subtopics.

Wechsler Adult Intelligence Scale-Revised-WAIS III This is the most widely accepted measure of adult (i.e., over age 16) intelligence which yields three intelligence scores: verbal IQ, performance IQ, and full-scale IQ. This test was published in 1939, and revised in 1955 and 1980.

Wechsler Intelligence Scale for Children-WISC III This is the most widely accepted measure of intelligence with children ages 5 to 15 and yields three intelligence scores: verbal IQ, performance IQ, and full-scale IQ. This test was published in 1949, and was revised in 1974 and 1991.

Wechsler Preschool and Primary Scale of Intelligence-WPPSI-R This is the most widely accepted measure of intelligence with children ages 4 to 6½. The WPPSI-R yields three intelligence scores: verbal IQ, performance IQ, and full-scale IQ. This test was published in 1967 and revised in 1989.

Wernicke's Aphasia An acquired receptive language loss which is characterized by faulty speech comprehension as seen in the nonsensical oral speech of the individual.

Wernicke's Area A subdivision of the auditory area in the temporal lobe of the cerebral cortex (usually specific to the left hemisphere) that is necessary for understanding spoken speech and for framing intelligent, meaningful conversation.

Whole Language An approach to the teaching of reading and language arts which stresses integration of reading, spelling, speaking, writing, and listening areas into a meaningful reading/language context (e.g., teaching from literature books).

Word-Analysis Skills The wide range of word recognition skills we use to read such as: phonics analysis, sight word reading, context cues, and structural analysis (e.g., looking at root words).

Word-Blindness W.P. Morgan, an ophthalmologist from England, first used the term "congenital word blindness" (which is also referred to as developmental alexia) to describe an inability to read despite apparently normal intelligence.

Working Groups (also known as Cooperative Learning Groups) Small working groups of students (2–6) whose purpose it is to collaborate during instructional activities. The authors favor the following group dynamics/structure for cooperative learning/working groups: (1) teachers/students agree on clear learning purpose(s)/goal(s), (2) specify learning outcomes/expectations/time frames for task completion at the onset, (3) carefully construct groups—the dyslexic student should be paired with at least one proficient reader if possible who can coach/mentor; groups should be as heterogenous as possible; group membership should change from assignment to assignment, (4) convey high expectations in terms of individual and group accountability, (5) provide guidance/format for role-taking; examples: checkers, evaluators, recorders, researchers, writers, spokespersons, artists, supply gatherers, product producers, report presenters, and so on. Students may assume more than one role with the teacher ensuring that the student with dyslexia has an appropriate role(s), (6) students should share in leadership responsibilities, (7) provide opportunities for positive socialization/growth, (8) students/teacher all assess learning outcomes—criterion-referenced measures (e.g., did the group accomplish specified learning objectives as demonstrated by a specific learning outcome/products?; Samples—experiment, book report, oral presentation, model, artwork, music composition, persuasive piece, and so on) are preferable in assessing group achievements; individuals may be evaluated with more traditional achievement measures, (9) teacher feedback is important; grading can reflect group performance or individual performance if great variability in achievement/effort are observed, and (10) always emphasize a team approach/spirit/benefits derived from teamwork.

Write Alouds The use of an adult such as a teacher to scribe or write down what a student dictates. This early literacy activity builds a foundation for guided writing activities. Students learn to acquire a language sense and the meaningfulness of written language activities. For the student with dyslexia, write alouds should be followed by guided writing and sustained writing activities.

Writing workshops Times set aside each day in which everyone present in a classroom must write. The point of the writing workshop is to write and to use writing as a means for making sense of the world.

References

Aaron, P.G., & Baker, C.A. (1991). *Reading disabilities in college and high school.* Parkton, MD: York Press.

Aaron, P.G., & Simurdak, J.E. (1991). Reading disorders: Their nature and diagnosis. In J.E. Obrzut & G.W. Hynd (Eds.), *Neuropsychological foundations of learning disabilities* (pp. 519–548). New York: Academic Press.

Ackerman, P.T., Anhalt, J.M., & Dykman, R.A. (1986). Arithmetic automatization failure in children with attention and reading disorders: *Associations and sequela. Journal of Learning Disabilities, 19,* 222–232.

Adams, A.D., Carnine, D., & Gersten, R. (1982). Instructional strategies for studying context area texts in the intermediate grades. *Reading Research Quarterly, 18,* 27–55.

Adams, M.J. (1990). *Beginning to read: Thinking and learning about print.* Cambridge, MA: MIT Press.

Adelman, K.A. & Adelman, H.A. (1987). Rodin, Patton, Edison, Wilson, Einstein: Were they really learning disabled? *Journal of Learning Disabilities, 20,* 270–279.

Allardice, B.S., & Ginsburg, H.P. (1983). Children's learning problems in mathematics. In H.P. Ginsburg (Ed.), *The development of mathematical thinking* (pp. 319–349). NY: Academic Press.

Alley, G., & Deshler, D. (1979). *Teaching the learning disabled adolescent: Strategies and methods.* Denver: Love.

Allington, R.L. (1984). Oral reading. In P.D. Pearson, R. Barr, M.L. Kamil, and P. Mosenthal (Eds.), *Handbook of reading research.* New York: Longman.

America 2000: An educational strategy. (1991). Washington, DC: U.S. Dept. of Education.

American Education Society. (May 27, 1850). *Thirty-fourth annual report of the directors of the American Education Society.* Boston, MA: Press of T.R. Marvin.

American Psychiatric Association. (1994). *Diagnostic and statistical manual of mental disorders (DSM-IV)* (4th ed.). Washington, DC: American Psychiatric Association.

American Psychiatric Association Task Force on Vitamin Therapy in Psychiatry. (1973). *Megavitamin and orthomolecular therapy in psychiatry.* Washington, DC: American Psychiatric Association.

Ammons, R.B. (1947). Acquisition of motor skill: II. Rotary pursuit perfomance with continuous practice before and after a single rest. *Journal of Experimental Psychology, 37,* 393–410.

Anderson, R.C. (1977). The notion of schemata and the educational enterprise. In R. Anderson, R. Spiro, & W. Montague (Eds.), *Schooling and the acquisition of knowledge* (pp. 415–531). Hillsdale, NJ: Lawrence Erlbaum.

Anderson, R.C., Shirley, L.L., Wilson, P.T., & Fielding, L.G. (1984). *Interestingness of children's reading material* (Report No. 323). Urbana-Champaign, IL: Center for the Study of Reading.

Ariel, A. (1992). *Educating children and adolescents with learning disabilities.* New York: Merrill.

Arnold, L.E., Christopher, J., Huestis, R.D., & Smeltzer, D.J. (1978). Megavitamins for minimal brain dysfunction: A placebo controlled study. *Journal of the American Medical Association, 240,* 2642–2643.

Aronson, E., Blaney, N., Stephan, C., Sikes, J., & Snapp, M. (1978). *The jigsaw classroom.* Newbury Park, CA: Sage.

Ashlock, R.B. (1994). *Error patterns in computation* (6th ed.). New York: Merrill.

Atkinson, R.C. (1975). Mnemotechnics in second-language learning. *American Psychologist, 30,* 821–828.

Atwell, N. (1987). *In the middle: Writing, reading and learning with adolescents.* Portsmouth, NH: Heinemann.

Aukerman, R.C. (1981). *The basal reader approach to reading.* New York: John Wiley & Sons.

Aukerman, R.C. (1984). *Approaches to beginning reading.* New York: Wilcy & Sons.

Ausubel, D. (1960). The use of advance organizers in learning and retention of meaningful verbal material. *Journal of Educational Psychology, 51,* 267–272.

Badian, N.A. (1983). Dyscalculia and nonverbal disorders of learning. In H. Myklebust (Ed.), *Progress in Learning Disabilities.* New York: Grune & Stratton.

Bakker, D.J., & Licht, R. (1986). Learning to read: Changing horses in mid-stream. In G.T. Paulidis & D.F. Fisher (Eds.), *Dyslexia: Its neuropsychology and treatment* (pp. 87–95). NY: John Wiley & Sons.

Balow, B. (1971). Perceptual-motor activities in the treatment of severe reading disability, *The Reading Teacher, 24,* 513–525, 542.

Barkley, R.A. (1981). *Hyperactive children: A handbook for diagnosis and treatment.* New York: Guilford Press.

Baroody, A.J. (1984). Children's difficulties in subtraction: Some causes and questions. *Journal for Research in Mathematics Education, 15,* 203–213.

Baroody, A.J. (1991). Teaching mathematics developmentally to children classified as learning disabled. In D.K. Reid, W.P. Hresko, & H.L. Swanson, *A cognitive approach to learning disabilities.* Austin, TX: PRO-ED.

Barsch, R. (1965). *A movigenic curriculum* (Bulletin No. 25). Madison WI: Department of Public Instruction, Bureau for the Handicapped.

Barsch, R. (1967). *Achieving perceptual-motor efficiency* (Vol. 1). Seattle, WA: Special Child Publications.

Barsch, R. (1968). *Enriching perception and cognition* (Vol. 2). Seattle, WA: Special Child Publications.

Bartel, N.R. (1990). Problems in mathematics achievement. In D.D. Hammill, & N.R. Bartel (Eds.), *Teaching students with learning and behavior problems* (pp. 289–343). Boston: Allyn and Bacon.

Bartlett, F.C. (1932). *Remembering.* Cambridge, MA: Cambridge University Press.

Bastian, H.C. (1898). *A treatise on aphasia and other speech defects.* London: H.K. Lewis.

Bateman, B. (1992). Learning disabilities: The changing landscape. *Journal of Learning Disabilities, 25,* 29–36.

Beck, I.L., McKeown, M.G., & Omanson, R.C. (1987). The effects and uses of diverse vocabulary instructional techniques. In M.G. McKeown & M.E. Curtis (Eds.), *The nature of vocabulary acquisition* (pp. 117–156). Hillsdale, NJ: Erlbaum.

Bender, W.N. (1985). Differential diagnosis based on task related behavior of learning disabled and low-achieving adolescents. *Learning Disability Quarterly, 8,* 261–266.

Bender, W.N. (1992). *Learning disabilities—Characteristics, identification, and teaching strategies.* Boston, MA: Allyn and Bacon.

Belmont, L., & Birch, H.G. (1965). Lateral dominance, lateral awareness and reading disability. *Child Development, 36,* 59–71.

Bender, W.N. (1992). *Learning disabilities—Characteristics, identification, and teaching strategies.* Boston, MA: Allyn and Bacon.

Benton, A.L. (1987). Mathematical disability and the Gerstmann syndrome. In G. Deloche, & X. Seron (Eds.), *Mathematical disabilities: A cognitive neuropsychological perspective* (pp. 111–120). Hillsdale, NJ: Lawrence Erlbaum.

Benton, A.L. & Pearl, D. (Eds.). (1978). Dyslexia: An appraisal of current knowledge. New York: Oxford University Press.

Berenson, B. (1994). The components, functions and processes involved in model building. Unpublished paper, American International College, Springfield, MA.

Berger, C.F. (1994). *The efficacy of the Benchmark School Word Identification Program as an instructional method for teaching word recognition skills to learning disabled students.* Unpublished Doctoral Dissertation, American International College, Springfield, MA.

Bernal, E.M. (1984). Bias in mental testing: Evidence for an alternative to the heredity-environment controversy. In C.R. Reynolds, & R.T. Brown (Eds.), *Perspectives on bias in mental testing* (pp. 171–187). New York: Plenum.

Birnbaum, J.C. (1982). The reading and composing behaviors of selected fourth-and seventh-grade students. *Research in the Teaching of English, 16,* 241–260.

Bishop, D.V.M., Jancey, C., & Steel, A.Mc.P. (1979) Orthoptic status and reading disability. *Cortex, 15,* 659–666.

Black, M.M. (1993). *The structure of intelligence for a sample of African-American Learning Disabled Children across socioeconomic levels as measured by the WISC-R.* Unpublished doctoral dissertation, American International College, Springfield, MA.

Blackhurst, A.E., & Berdine, W.H. (1993). *An introduction to special education.* New York: Harper Collins.

Bley, N.S., & Thornton, C.A. (1989, 1995). *Teaching mathematics to the learning disabled* (2nd and 3rd eds.). Austin, TX: PRO-Ed.

Bobskill, L. (1991, October 11). A.I.C. team offers new evidence of physical cause of dyslexia. *Springfield (MA) Union-News,* pp. 1, 33, 35.

Boder, E. (1970). Developmental dyslexia: A diagnostic approach based on the identification of three subtypes. *Journal of School Health, 40,* 289–290.

Borasi, R. (1987). Exploring mathematics through analysis of errors. *For the learning of mathematics, 7,* 2–8.

Bousquet, K.A. (1993). *Early Screening Inventory (ESI) subtest profiles: Predictive usefulness for LD risk in preschoolers to predict later reading ability?* Unpublished doctoral dissertation, American International College, Springfield, MA.

Bozzone, M.A. (1994). The professional portfolio. *Instructor, 6,* 10–14.

Bradley, L. (1988). Making connections in learning to read and spell. *Applied Cognitive Psychology, 2,* 3–18.

Bradley, L. & Bryant, P.E. (1983). Categorizing sounds and learning to read—a causal connection. *Nature, 301,* 419–421.

Bredekamp, S. (Ed.). (1992). *Developmentally appropriate practice in early childhood programs serving children from birth through age 8.* Washington DC: National Association for the Education of Young Children (NAEYC).

Brennan, J. (1995). *America: Land of Opportunity.* Unpublished Manuscript. Springfield, MA.

Broca, P. (1865). Remarques sur le siege de la faculte du language articule. *Bulletin de la societe d'Anthropologie, 6,* 18–28.

Brown, A.L. (1978). Knowing when, where, and how to remember: A problem of metacognition. In R. Glaser (Ed.), *Advances in instructional psychology* (pp. 77–163). Hillsdale, NJ: Lawrence Erlbaum.

Brown, B., Haegerstrom-Portnoy, G., Yingling, C.D., Herron, J., Galin, D., & Marcus, M. (1983). Dyslexic children have normal vestibular responses to rotation. *Archives of Neurology, 40,* 370–373.

Brueckner, L.J., & Elwell, M. (1932). Reliability of diagnosis of errors in multiplication of fractions. *Journal of Education Research, 26,* 175–185.

Brulnsma, R. (1981). A critique of "round-robin" oral reading in the elementary classroom. *Reading-Canada-Lecture, 1,* 78–81.

Bryan, T., Bay, M., & Donahue, M. (1988). Implications of the learning disabilities definition for the regular education initiative. *Journal of Learning Disabilities, 21,* 23–28.

Bryan, T.H. & Bryan J.H. (1986). *Understanding Learning Disabilities.* Palo Alto, CA: Mayfield Publishing Company.

Bryant, P. (1995). Children and arithmetic. *Journal of Child Psychology and Psychiatry, 36,* 3–32.

Burke, E. (1855). America in 1774. In G.S. Hillard (Ed.), *A First Class Reader.* Boston, MA: Hickling, Swan, & Brewer.

Byrom, E., & Katz, G. (Eds.). (1991). *HIV prevention and AIDS education: Resources for special education.* Reston, VA: Council for Exceptional Children.

Calkins, L. (1986). *The art of teaching writing.* Portsmouth, NH: Heinemann.

Callahan, J.F., Clark, L.H., & Kellough, R.D. (1992). *Teaching in the Middle and Secondary schools* (4th Ed.). NY: Macmillan.

Cangelosi, J.S. (1992). *Teaching Mathematics in Secondary and Middle school.* New Tork: Merrill.

Cardinal, D.N., Griffin, J.R., Christenson, G.N., (1993). Do tinted lenses really help students with reading disabilities? *Intervention in School and Clinic, 28,* 275–279.

Carkuff, P.R. & Berenson, B.G. (1976). *Teaching as treatment:* Amherst, MA: Human Resource Development Press.

Carlisle, J.F. (1993). Selecting approaches to vocabulary instruction for the reading disabled. *Learning Disabilities Research and Practice, 8,* 97–105.

Carpenter, R.L. (1985). Mathematics instruction in resource rooms: Instruction time and teacher competence. *Learning Disability Quarterly, 8,* 95–100.

Carr, E. (1985). The vocabulary overview guide: A metacognitive strategy to improve vocabulary, comprehension, and retention. *Journal of Reading, 21,* 684–689.

Carver, R.P. (1992). Reading rate: Theory, research, and practical implications. *Journal of Reading, 36,* 84–95.

Casper, K.L. (August 13, 1994). *Multicultural literature in a developmentally appropriate kindergarten: A critique of ten children's books and application to curriculum.* Springfield, MA: American International College, Unpublished Paper.

Catts, H.W., Hu, C.F., Larrivee, L., & Swank, L. (1994). Early identification of reading disabilities in children with speech-language impairments. In R.V. Watkins & M.L. Rice, *Specific language impairments in children* (pp. 145–160). Baltimore, MD: Brookes Pub.

Cawley, J.F., Fitzmaurice, A.M., Shaw, R.A., Kahn, H., & Bates, H. (1978). Mathematics and learning disabled youth: The upper grade levels. *Learning Disability Quarterly, 1,* 37–52.

Cawley, J.F., Fitzmaurice, A.M., Shaw, R.A., Kahn, H., & Bates, H. (1979). LD youth and mathematics: A review of characteristics. *Learning Disability Quarterly, 2,* 29–44.

Cawley, J.F., Miller, J.H., & School, B.A. (1987). A brief inquiry of arithmetic word-problem solving among learning disabled secondary students. *Learning Disabilities Focus, 2,* 87–93.

Chalfant, J.C., Pysh, M., & Moultrie, R. (1979). Teacher assistance teams: Findings of an introspective study. *Learning Disability Quarterly, 6,* 321–33.

Cheek, E.H., Flippo, R.F., & Lindsey, J.D. (1989). *Reading for success in elementary schools.* Chicago, IL: Holt, Rinehart, & Winston.

Clark, A. (1985). Psychological causation and the concept of psychosomatic disease. In D. Stalker, & C. Glymour (Eds.), *Examining holistic medicine* (pp. 67–106). Buffalo, New York: Prometheus Books.

Clark, H.H. & Chase, W.G. (1974). On the process of comparing sentences against pictures. *Cognitive Psychology, 3,* 472–517.

Clay, M.M. (1979, 1988). *The early detection of reading difficulties.* Auckland, New Zealand: Heinemann Educational Books.

Cohn, R. (1961). Dyscalculia. *Archives of Neurology, 4,* 301–307.

Collins, A., Brown, J.S., & Newman, S.W. (1989). Cognitive apprenticeship: Teaching the craft of reading, writing, and mathematics. In L.B. Resnick (Ed.), *Knowing, learning and instruction: Essays in honor of Robert Glaser* (pp. 453–494). Hillsdale, NJ: Lawrence Erlbaum.

Coltheart, M. (1982). The psycholinguistic analysis of acquired dyslexia: Some illustrations. *Philosophical transactions of the Royal Society of London, B298,* 151–164.

Conners, G.K., Goyette, C.M., Southwick, D.A., Lees, J.M. & Andrulonis, P.A. (1976). Food additives and hyperkinesis: A controlled double-blind experiment. *Pediatrics, 58,* 154–166.

Coon, D. (1994). *Essentials of psychology.* New York: West Publishing.

Cooper, J.M. (Ed.) (1995). *Teachers' problem solving.* Boston, MA: Allyn and Bacon.

Cordeiro, P. (1993). *Whole learning-Whole language and content in the upper elementary grades.* New York: R.C. Owen Pub.

Cott, A. (1977). *The orthomolecular approach to learning disabilites.* San Rafael, CA: Academic Therapy.

Cott, A. (1985) *Help for your learning disabled child: The orthomolecular treatment.* New York: Times Books.

Council for Exceptional Children. (Winter 1992). *The Individuals with Disabilities Education Act (IDEA).* Reston, VA: Author.

Courtney, A. (1995). *The portfolio process.* Unpublished paper.

Cox, L.S. (1975a). Systematic errors in the four vertical algorithms in normal and handicapped population. *Journal for Research in Mathematics Education, 6,* 202–220.

Cox, L.S. (1975b). Using research in teaching. *Arithmetic Teacher, 22,* 151–157.

Crawford, L.W. (1993). *Language and literacy learning in multicultural classrooms.* Boston, MA: Allyn and Bacon.

Critchley, M. (1963). The problem of developmental dyslexia. *Proceedings of the Royal Society of Medicine, 56,* 209–21.

Critchley, M. (1964). *Developmental dyslexia.* Springfield, IL: Charles C. Thomas.

Critchley, M. (1970). *The dyslexic child.* London: Heinemann.

Critchley, M. (1975). Language acquisition in developmental dyslexia. In S.A. Kirk, & J.M. McCarthy (Eds.), *Learning disabilities—Selected ACLD papers* (pp. 264–270). Boston, MA: Houghton Mifflin.

Critchley, M. (1981). Dyslexia: An overview. In G. Pavlidis & T. Miles (Eds.), *Dyslexia research and its application to education* (pp. 1–11). New York: J. Wiley & Sons.

Cruikshank, D.E., & Sheffield, L.J. (1992). *Teaching and learning elementary and middle school mathematics.* New York: Macmillan.

Cunningham, R., & Shablak, S. (1975). Selective reading guide-o-rama: The content teacher's best friend. *Journal of Reading, 18,* 380–382.

Dahl, P.R. (1979). An experimental program for teaching high speed recognition and comprehension skills. In J.E. Button, T.C. Lovitt, & T.D. Rowland (Eds.), *Communications research in learning disabilities and mental retardation* (pp. 33–65). Baltimore, MD: University Park Press.

Dagostino, L., & Carifio, J. (1994). *Evaluative reading and literacy: A cognitive view.* Boston, MA: Allyn & Bacon.

D'Augustine, C., & Smith, C.W. (1992). *Teaching elementary school mathematics.* New York: Harper Collins.

Dautrich, B.R. (1993). Visual perceptual differences in the dyslexic reader: Evidence of greater visual peripheral sensitivity to color and letter stimuli. *Perceptual and Motor Skills, 76,* 755–764.

Dautrich, B.R. (1994). *Connecting texts with learners: Tips for teachers.* Unpublished manuscript.

Davenport, M. (1960). *Mozart.* NY: Charles Scribner's Sons.

Davey, B. (1983). Think-aloud-Modeling the cognitive processes of reading comprehension. *Journal of Reading, 27,* 44–47.

David, O.J., Hoffman, S., McGann, B., Sverd, J. & Clark, J. (1976). Low lead levels and mental retardation. *Lancet, 6,* 1376–1379.

Davis, R.B., Maher, C.A., & Noddings, N. (1990). *Constructivist views on the teaching and learning of mathematics.* Reston, VA: National Council of Teachers of mathematics.

deBettencourt, L.U. (1990). Cognitive strategy training with learning disabled students. In P.I. Myers & D.D. Hammill (Eds.), *Learning Disabilities* (pp. 453–466). Austin, TX: PRO-ED.

DeFries, J.C., Olson, R.K., Pennington, B.F., & Smith, S.D. (1991). Colorado reading project—An update. In D.D. Duane, & D.B. Gray (Eds.), *The reading brain* (pp. 53–87). Parkton, MD: York Press.

Deiner, P.L. (1993). *Resources for teaching children with diverse abilities.* New York: Harcourt Brace.

Dejerine, J. (1891). Sur un cas de cecite verbale avec agraphie suivi d'autopsie. *Mem. Soc. Biol., 3,* 197–201.

Dejerine, J. (1892). Contribution a l'etude anatomo-pathologique et clinique des differents varietes de cecite verbale. *Comptes Rendus des Seances de la Societe de Biologie, 4,* 61–90.

Delacato, C.H. (1963). *The diagnosis and treatment of speech and reading problems.* Springfield, IL: Charles C. Thomas.

Denckla, M.B. (1991). Academic and extracurricular aspects of nonverbal learning disabilites. *Psychiatric Annals, 1,* 717–724.

Denckla, M. (1991, February 25). *Brain behavior insights through imaging.* Paper presented at the Learning Disabilities Association National Conference, Chicago, IL.

Denckla, M.B., & Rudel, R.G. (1976a). Naming of object drawings by dyslexic and other learning disabled children. *Brain and Language, 3,* 1–16.

Denckla, M.B., & Rudel, R.G. (1976b). Rapid "automatized" naming (R.A.N.): Dyslexia differentiated from other learning disabilities. *Neuropsychologia, 14,* 471–478.

Deshler, D.D., Alley, G.R., & Carlson, S.C. (1980). Learning strategies: An approach to mainstreaming secondary students with learning disabilities. *Education Unlimited, 2,* 6–11.

Deshler, D.D. & Schumaker, J.B. (1986). Learning strategies: An instructional alternative for low-achieving adolescents. *Exceptional Children, 52,* 583–590.

Deshler, D.D., Schumaker, J., Alley, G., Warner, M., & Clark, F. (1982). Learning disabilities in adolescent and young adult populations: Research implications. *Focus on Exceptional Children, 15,* 1–12.

Deshler, D.D., Schumaker, J.B., Lenz, B.K., & Ellis, E.S. (1984). Academic and cognitive interventions for

Learning Disabled students: Part II. *Journal of Learning Disabilities, 17,* 170–187.

Dewey, J. (1899). *School and society.* New York: University of Chicago Press.

Dewey, J. (1919). *Democracy and education.* New York: MacMillan.

Diagnostic and Statistical Manual of Mental Disorders (4th ed.) (1994). Washington DC: American Psychiatric Association.

Division for Learning Disabilities. (1993). *Inclusion: What does it mean for students with learning disabilities?* Reston, VA: Division for Learning Disabilities of the Council of Exceptional Children.

Divosky, D. (1978). Can diet cure the Learning Disabled child? *Learning, 3,* 56–57.

Doehring, D.G., & Hoshko, I.M. (1977). Classification of reading problems by the Q-technique of factor analysis. *Cortex, 13,* 281–294.

Dolch, E.W. (1942). *The basic sight word test part 1 and 2.* Champaign, IL: Garrard.

Doman, R., Spitz, E., Zucman, E., Delacato, C., & Doman, G. (1960). Children with severe brain injuries (neurological organization in terms of mobility). *Journal of the American Medical Association, 174,* 257–262.

Duane, D.D., (1991). Biological foundations of learning disabilites. In J.E. Obrzut, & G.W. Hynd (Eds.), *Neuropsychological foundations of learning disabilities* (pp. 7-27). San Diego, CA: Academic Press.

Dubey, D.R. (1932). Organic factors in hyperkinesis: A critical evaluation. *American Journal of Orthopsychiatry, 2,* 353–366.

Duin, A.H., & Graves, M.F. (1987). Intensive vocabulary instruction as a prewriting technique. *Reading Research Quarterly, 22,* 311-330.

Dunlap, W.P., & Brennan, A.H. (1979). Developing mental images of mathematical processes. *Learning Disabilities Quarterly, 2,* 89-96.

Dunn, M. (Monday, March 6, 1995). Public, space shuttle link up via Internet. *Springfield Union-News, 1,* 8. Springfield, MA: Starr Pub.

DuPaul, G.J., Guevremont, D.C., & Barkley, R.A. (1991). Attention-deficit hyperactivity disorder. In T.R. Kratochwill & R.J. Morris (Eds.), *The practice of child therapy* (pp. 115–144). New York: Permagon.

Durkin, D. (1989). *Teaching them to read* (5th ed.). Boston, MA: Allyn and Bacon.

Durrell, F. (1894). *A new life in education.* Philadelphia, IL: American Sunday School Union.

Ekwall, E.E. & Shanker, J.L. (1988). *Diagnosis and remediation of the disabled reader.* Boston: Allyn and Bacon.

Ellis, A.W. (1984). *Reading, writing and dyslexia: A cognitive analysis.* New Jersey: Lawrence Erlbaum.

Ellis, N.C. & Miles, T.R. (1978). Visual information processing as a determinant of reading speed. *Journal of Reading Research, 2,* 108–120.

Ellis, N.C. & Miles, T.R. (1981). A lexical encoding deficiency. In G. T. Pavlidis, & T.R. Miles (Eds.), *Dyslexia research and its applications to education.* New York: John Wiley.

Englert, C.S., Culatta, B.E., & Horn, D.G. (1987). Influence of irrelevant information in additive word problems on problem solving. *Learning Disability Quarterly, 10,* 29–35.

Enright, B.C. (1983). *Enright Diagnostic Inventory of Basic Arithmetic Skills.* North Billerica, MA: Curriculum Associates.

Enright, B.E. (1989). *Basic mathematics.* Boston, MA: Allyn and Bacon.

Eustis, R. (1947). Specific reading disability. *New England Journal of Medicine, 237,* 243–249.

Eysenck, H.J. (1984). The effect of race on human abilities and mental test scores. In C.R. Reynolds & R.T. Brown (Eds.), *Perspectives on bias in mental testing* (pp. 249–291). New York: Plenum.

Fair, G.W. (1988). Mathematics instruction in junior and senior high school. In D.K. Reid (Ed.), *Teaching the learning disabled: A cognitive developmental approach* (pp. 378–415). Boston, MA: Allyn and Bacon.

Farnham-Diggory, S. (1987, July). *From theory to practice in reading.* Paper read at the Annual Conference of the Reading Reform Foundation, San Francisco, CA.

Farr, R. (1969). *Reading: What can be measured?* Newark, DE: International Reading Association.

Farrar, M.J. (1836). *The Youth's Letter Writer; or The Epistolary Art* (3rd ed.). Boston, MA: H & S Raynor.

Farrell, N. (1994). *The Middle School Math Project.* Unpublished Manuscript.

Federal Register (1977, December 29). *Procedures for evaluating specific learning disabilities.* Washington, DC: Department of Health, Education and Welfare.

Feingold, B.F. (1975). *Why your child is hyperactive.* New York: Random House.

Feingold, B.F. (1976). Hyperkinesis and learning disabilities linked to the ingestion of artificial food colors and flavors. *Journal of Learning Disabilities, 9,* 551–559.

Feingold, B.F. (1977). A critique of "Controversial medical treatments of learning disabilities." *Academic Therapy, 13,* 173–183.

Feingold, B.F. & Feingold, H. (1979). *The Feingold cookbook for hyperactive children and others with problems associated with food additives and salicylates.* New York: Random House.

Fernald, G.M. (1943). *Remedial techniques in basic school subjects.* New York: McGraw-Hill.

Fernald, G.M. (1988). *Remedial techniques in basic school subjects* (L. Idol, Ed.). Austin, TX: PRO-Ed (original work published in 1943).

Ferreri, C.A. & Wainwright, R.B. (1984). *Breakthrough for dyslexia and learning disabilities.* Pompano Beach: Exposition Press.

Fiore, T., Becker, E., & Nero, R. (1993). Education interventions for students with attention deficit disorder. *Exceptional Children, 60,* 163–173.

Fitch, S. J. (1900). *Educational aims and methods.* London, UK: Macmillan.

Flavell, J.H. (1976). Metacognitive aspects of problem

solving. In L.B. Resnick (Ed.), *The nature of intelligence* (pp. 231–235). NJ: Lawrence Erlbaum.

Flavell, J.H. (1987). Speculations about the nature and development of metacognition. In R.H. Kluwe and F.E. Weinert (Eds.), *Metacognition, motivation and learning* (pp. 21–39). NJ: Lawrence Erlbaum.

Forgan, H.W., & Mangrum, C.T. (1989). *Teaching content area reading skills* (4th Ed.). Columbus, OH: Merrill.

Foss, J.M. (1991). Nonverbal learning disabilities and remedial interventions. *Annals of Dyslexia, 41,* 129.

Fowler, M. (1992). *CH.A.D.D. Educators Manual:* Fairfax, VA: CASET Associates Distrubutors.

Fowler, M. (1992). *CH.A.D.D. educators manual: An in-depth look at attention deficit disorders from an educational perspective.* Plantation, FL: CH.A.D.D.

Frank, J. & Levinson, H.N. (1977). Seasickness mechanisms and medications in dysmetric dyslexia and dyspraxia. *Academic Therapy, 12,* 133–153.

Frith, U., & Snowling, M. (1983). Reading for meaning and reading for sound in autistic and dyslexic children. *British Journal of Developmental Psychology, 1,* 329–342.

Frostig, M. (1968). Education for children with learning disabilities. In H. Myklebust (Ed.), *Progress in learning disabilities* (pp. 234–266). New York: Grune & Stratton.

Fry, E.B. (1980, December). The new instant word list. *The Reading Teacher, 34,* 284–289.

Gaddes, W.H. (1985). *Learning disabilities and brain function: A neuropsychological approach* (2nd ed.). New York: Springer-Verlag.

Galaburda, A.M. (1988). The pathogenesis of childhood dyslexia. In F. Plum (Ed.), *Language, communication and the brain* (pp. 127-137). New York: Raven Press.

Galaburda, A.M. (1989). Ordinary and extraordinary brain development: Anatomical variation in developmental dyslexia. *Annals of Dyslexia, 39,* 67–80.

Garbett, R. (1993). *Can the early screening inventory be utilized to predict later reading ability?* Unpublished doctoral dissertation, American International College, Springfield, MA.

Gardner, H. (1983). *Frames of mind: The theory of multiple intelligences.* New York: Basic Books.

Gaskins, I.W. (1984). There's more to a reading problem than poor reading. *Journal of Learning Disabilities, 17,* 467–471.

Gaskins, I.W., Downer, M.A., Anderson, R.C., Cunningham, P.M., Gaskins, R.W., Schommer, M., & the Teachers of Benchmark School. (1988). A metacognitive approach to phonics: Using what you know to decode what you don't know. *Remedial and Special Education, 9,* 36–41.

Gerstmann, J. (1940). Syndrome of finger agnosia, disorientation for right and left, agraphia and acaculia: Local diagnostic value. *Archives of Neurology and Psychiatry, 44,* 398–408.

Geschwind, N. (1982). Why Orton was right. *Annals of Dyslexia, 32,* 13–30.

Geschwind, N. & Behan, P.O. (1982). Left-handedness: Association with immune disease, migraine and de-velopmental learning disorder. *Proceedings of the National Academy of Sciences, 79,* 5097–5100.

Geschwind, N. & Levitsky, W. (1968). Human brain: Left-right asymmetries in temporal speech region. *Science, 161,* 186–187.

Getman, G.N. (1985). A commentary on vision training. *Journal of Learning Disabilities, 18,* 505–512.

Gillingham, A., & Stillman, B.W. (1966). *Remedial training for children with specific disability in reading, spelling, and penmanship.* Cambridge, MA: Educators Pub.

Glaze, B. (1987). *"Learning logs," Plain talk about learning and writing across the curriculum.* Richmond, VA: Virginia Dept. of Education, Commonwealth of Virginia.

Glover, J.A., Ronning, R.R., & Bruning, R.H. (1990). *Cognitive psychology for teachers.* New York: Macmillan.

Golden, G. (1980). Nonstandard therapies in the developmental disabilities. *American Journal of Diseases of Children, 134,* 487–491.

Goodman, K.S. (1976). Reading: A psycholinguistic guessing game. In H. Singer, & R. Ruddell (Eds.), *Theoretical models and processes of reading* (pp. 497–501). Newark, DE: International Reading Association.

Goodman, K.S., Bird, L.B., & Goodman, Y.M. (1992). *The whole language catalog: Supplement on authentic assessment.* New York: SRA Macmillan.

Goodman, K., & Goodman, Y. (1982). A whole language comprehension centered view of reading development. In L. Reed & S. Ward (Eds.), *Basic skills: Issues and choices* (pp. 125–134). St Louis, MO: CEMREL.

Goodman, Y.M. (1980, January). *The roots of literacy.* Paper presented at the Annual Claremont Reading Conference. Claremont, CA.

Goodwin, M.W. (1993). *Evidence of AVIC: Conduct disordered adolescents exhibit a specific profile pattern on the WISC-R.* Unpublished doctoral dissertation, American International College, Springfield, MA.

Gough, P. (1972). One second of reading. In J. Kavanaugh & I. Mattingly (Eds.), *Language by ear and by eye: The relationship between speech and reading.* Cambridge, MA: MIT Press.

Gough, P.B. (1983). Context, form, and interaction. In K. Rayner (Ed.), *Eye movements in reading* (pp. 203–211). New York: Academic Press.

Graham, N. (1992). Breaking the visual stimulus into parts. *Current Directions in Psychological Science, 1,* 55–61.

Greene, F.P. (1970). *Paired reading.* Unpublished paper. New York: Syracuse University.

Greenleaf, B. (1846). *A key to the National Arithmetic, exhibiting the operation of the more difficult questions—for the use of teachers only.* New York: Pratt, Woodford & Co.

Greenwood, C.R., & Rieth, H.J. (1994). Current dimensions of technology-based assessment in special education. *Exceptional Children, 61,* 105–113.

Gresham, J.M., & Reschly, D.J. (1986). Social skills

deficits and low peer acceptance of mainstreamed learning disabled children. *Learning Disability Quarterly, 9,* 23–32.

Gresham, J.M., Reschly, D.J., & Carey, M.P. (1987). Teachers as "tests": Classification accuracy and concurrent validation in the identification of learning disabled children. *School Psychology Review, 16,* 549–553.

Grosser, G.S., & Spafford, C.S. (1989a). Perceptual evidence for an anomalous distribution of rods and cones in the retinas of dyslexics: A new hypothesis. *Perceptual and Motor Skills, 68,* 683–698.

Grosser, G.S., & Spafford, C.S. (1989b). Reply to Cohn's comments on cones. *Perceptual and Motor Skills, 69,* 126.

Grosser, G.S., & Spafford, C.S. (1990). Light sensitivity in peripheral retinal fields of dyslexic and proficient readers. *Perceptual and Motor Skills, 71,* 467–477.

Grosser, G.S, & Spafford, C.S. (1993a, April). *The relationship between particular visual deficits and reading problems.* In J. Donatelle (Chair), The Massachusetts Society of Optometrists. Western district meeting notice, W. Springfield, MA.

Grosser, G.S., & Spafford, C.S. (1993b, May). *A Closer Look at the Learning Disabled Child.* In C. Spafford (Chair), The Massachusetts Division of Learning Disabilities. Spring symposium meeting, Springfield, MA.

Grosser, G.S., & Spafford, C.S. (1995). *Physiological psychology dictionary.* Boston, MA: McGraw-Hill.

Grosser, G.S., Spafford, C.S., Donatelle, J., Dana, J., & Squillace, S. (in press). Contrast sensitivity responses of dyslexics and proficient readers to luminance gratings of various spatial frequencies. *Journal of the American Optometric Association.*

Grosser, G.S. & Trzeciak, G.M. (1981). Duration of recognition for single letters, with and without visual masking, by dyslexics and normal readers. *Perceptual and Motor Skills, 53,* 991–995.

Grossnickle, F.E. (1935). Reliability of diagnosis of certain types of errors in long division with a one-figure divisor. *Journal of Experimental Education, 4,* 7–16.

Gross-Tsur, V., Shalev, R.S., Manor, O., & Amir, N. (1995). Developmental right-hemisphere syndrome: Clinical spectrum of the nonverbal learning disability. *Journal of Learning Disabilities, 28,* 80–86.

Guthrie, J.T. (1973). Models of reading and reading disability. *Journal of Educational Psychology, 65,* 9–18.

Guttmann, E. (1937). Congenital aritmetic disability and acalculia. *British Journal of Medical Psychology, 16,* 16–35.

Haggard, M.R. (1986a). The vocabulary self-collection strategy: An active approach to word learning. In E.K. Dishner, T.W. Bean, J.E. Readence, & D.W. Moore, *Reading in the content areas: Improving classroom instruction* (2nd ed.) (pp. 179–183). Dubuque, IA: Kendall/Hunt.

Haggard, M.R. (1986b). The vocabulary self-collection strategy: Using student interest and word knowl-edge to enhance vocabulary growth. *Journal of Reading, 29,* 634–642.

Hale, R.L. (1983). An examination for construct bias in the WISC-R across socioeconomic status. *Journal of School Psychology, 21,* 153–156.

Hall, S.R. (1829). *Lectures on school-keeping.* Boston: Richardson, Lord, & Holbrook.

Hallahan, D.P., Kauffman, J.M., & Lloyd, J.W. (1985). *Introduction to learning disabilities* (2nd Ed.). Englewood Cliffs, NJ: Prentice-Hall.

Hallahan, D.P., Keller, C.E., McKinney, J.D., Lloyd, J.W., & Bryan, T. (1988). Examining the research base of the Regular Education Initiative: Efficacy studies and the adaptive learning environments model. *Journal of Learning Disabilities, 21,* 29–35.

Hammill, D.D. (1990). On defining learning disablilties: An emerging consensus. *Journal of Learning Disabilities, 23,* 74–84.

Hammill, D.D., & Bartel, N.R. (1990). *Teaching students with learning and behavior problems.* Boston: Allyn and Bacon.

Hammill, D.D., Goodman, L., & Wiederholt, J.L. (1974). Visual-motor processes: Can we train them? *Reading Teacher, 27,* 469–478.

Hammill, D.D., Leigh, J.E., McNutt, G., & Larsen, S.C. (1981). A new definition of learning disabilities. *Learning Disability Quarterly, 4,* 336–42.

Harnois, V.D., & Furdyna, E.J.H. (1994). *The Harnois program: Decoding skills for dyslexic readers.* Pittsburgh, PA: Dorance Publishing.

Harris, A.J., & Sipay, E.R. (1990). *How to increase reading ability* (9th ed.). New York: Longman.

Harris, K., & Graham, S. (1985). Improving learning disabled students composition skills: Self-control strategy training. *Learning Disability Quarterly, 8,* 27–36.

Harris, S.J. (1966, July 27). Strictly personal: Inglish as it kud be speld (from the Simplified Spelling Society). *Chicago Daily News.*

Hatfield, M.M., Edwards, N.T., & Bitter, G.G. (1993). *Mathematics methods for the elementary and middle school* (2nd Ed.). Boston: Allyn and Bacon.

Heckelman, R.G. (1969). A neurological-impress method of remedial-reading instruction. *Academic Therapy, 4,* 277–282.

Heddens, J.W., & Speer, W.R. (1992). *Concepts and methods in elementary school mathematics* (7th ed.). New York: Macmillan.

Heimer, R.T., & Trueblood, C.R. (1977). *Strategies for teaching children mathematics.* Menlo Park, CA: Addison-Wesley.

Helveston, E.M., Billips, W.C. & Weber, J.C. (1970). Controlling eye-dominant hemisphere relationships as a factor in reading ability. *American Journal of Ophthalmology, 70,* 96–100.

Hendrick, J. (1990). *Total learning–Curriculum for the young child.* Columbus, OH: Merrill Pub.

Henning, W. (1936). *The fundamentals of chromeorthoptics.* Actino Lab, Inc.

Henschen, S.E. (1919). Zellgerist. *Neurological Psychiatry, 52,* 273.

Heward, W.L., & Orlansky, M.D. (1984, 1988, 1992) *Exceptional children*. Columbus, OH: Charles E. Merrill.

Hinshelwood, J. (1875). Word-blindness and visual memory. *The Lancet, 2*, 1564–1570.

Hinshelwood, J. (1896). A case of dyslexia: A peculiar form of word-blindness. *The Lancet*, 1451–1454.

Hinshelwood, J. (1900a). Congenital word blindness. *The Lancet, 1*, 1506–1508.

Hinshelwood, J. (1900b). *Letter-word and mind blindness*. London: H.K. Lewis.

Hinshelwood, J. (1917). *Congenital word blindness*. London: H.K. Lewis.

Holland, A.L., & Reinmuth, O.M. (1982). Aphasia in adults. In G.H. Shames, & E.H. Wiig (Eds.), *Human communication disorders: An introduction* (pp. 561–593). Columbus, OH: Merrill.

Honert, D.V.D. (1985). *Reading from scratch/RFS*. Cambridge, MA: Educators Publishing.

Hough, R.A., Nurss, J.R., & Enright, D.S. (1986). Story reading with limited English speaking children in the regular classroom. *The Reading Teacher, 40*, 500–504.

Howell, E., & Stanley, G. (1988). Colour and learning disability. *Clinical & Experimental Optometry, 71*, 66–71.

Humphery, J.M.H. (1981). *Persistent error patterns on whole number computations and scores on Piagetian tasks as they relate to mathematics achievement of adolescents*. Unpublished doctoral dissertation, University of Texas, Austin, TX.

Hunt, N., & Marshall, K. (1994). *Exceptional children and youth*. Boston, MA: Houghton Mifflin.

Hynd, G.W. (1992). Neurological aspects of dyslexia: Comment on the balance model. *Journal of Learning Disabilities, 25*, 110–123.

Hynd, G.W. & Cohen, M. (1983). *Dyslexia: Neuropsychological theory research and clinical differentiation*. New York: Grune & Stratton.

Hynd, G.W., & Hynd, C.R. (1984). Dyslexia: Neuroanatomical/neurodiagnostic perspectives. *Reading Research Quarterly, 19*, 482–498.

Hynd, G.W., Obrzut, J.E., Hayes, F. & Becker, M.G. (1986). Neuropsychology of childhood learning disabilities (pp. 456–485). In D. Wedding, A.N. Horton, & J. Webster (Eds.), *The neuropsychology handbook*. New York: Springer.

Hynd, G.W. & Semrud-Clikeman, M. (1989a). Dyslexia and neurodevelopmental pathology: Relationships to cognition, intelligence, and reading skill acquisition. *Journal of Learning Disabilities, 22*, 204–216.

Hynd, G.W., & Semrud-Clikeman, M. (1989b). Dyslexia and brain morphology. *Psychological Bulletin, 106*, 447–482.

Hynd, G.W., & Willis, W.G. (1988). *Pediatric neuropsychology*. New York: Grune & Stratton.

Illinois Department of Rehabilitation Services. (1993). Bulletin. State of Illinois Publisher, 1201–1208.

Interagency Committee on Learning Disabilities (1987). *Learning disabilities: A report to the U.S. Congress*. Washington, DC: U.S. Department of Health and Human Services.

Irlen, H. (undated). Irlen Institute information on Scotopic Sensitivity Syndrome [correspondence].

Jackson, F.R. (1993/1994). Seven strategies to support a culturally responsive pedagogy. *Journal of Reading, 37*, 298–303.

Jackson, J.H. (1874). On the nature of the duality of the brain. *Medical Press and Circular*, 1.

James, W. (1893). *The principles of psychology*. (Vol. 1). New York: Holt.

Jarolimek, J. (1990). *Social studies in elementary education*. New York: Macmillan.

Jenkins, A.A. (1992). *Effects of a vocational mathematics curriculum on achievement of secondary learning-disabled students*. Unpublished dissertation, University of Texas, Austin, TX.

Jenkins, J.R., Matlock, B., & Slocum, T.A. (1989). Two approaches to vocabulary instruction: The teaching of individual word meanings and practice in deriving word meaning from context. *Reading Research Quarterly, 24*, 215–235.

Johansen, K. (1984, December). Man laerer at laise ved at laese-maske [you learn to read by reading—maybe]. On diagnosis and treatment of reading difficulties emphasizing some non-acknowledged methods. Unpublished doctoral dissertation, Pacific Western University, Los Angeles, CA. Also issued as Johansen, K. (1986). Dyslexia and sound therapy. *Research Abstracts, II* (Fall), 3.

Johnson, D.J., & Myklebust, H.R. (1967). *Learning disabilities: Educational principles and practices*. New York: Grune & Stratton.

Jones, B.F. (1985). Response instruction. In T.L. Harris, & E.J. Cooper (Eds.), *Reading, thinking, and conceptual developments: Strategies for the classroom*. New York: The College Board.

Junior Achievement Project Business Student Manual. (1992) Colorado Springs, Colorado: Junior Achievement Inc.

Just, M.A., & Carpenter, P.A. (1980). A theory of reading: From eye fixations to comprehension. *Psychological Review, 87*, 329–354.

Kamhi, A.G. (1992). Response to historical perspective: A developmental language perspective. *Journal of Learning Disabilities, 25*, 48–52.

Kamhi, A.G. & Catts, H.W. (Eds.) (1989). *Reading disabilities: A developmental language perspective*. Boston: College-Hill.

Kapinus, B.A., Gambrell, L.B., & Koskinen, P.S. (1988). *The effects of practice in retelling upon readers*. Thirty-sixth yearbook of the National Reading Conference. Rochester, New York: National Reading Conference.

Kaplan, R. (1983). Changes in form visual fields in reading disabled children produced by syntonic (colored light) stimulation. *International Journal of Biosocial Research, 5*, 20–33.

Katz, R.B., Shankweiler, D. & Liberman (1981). Memory for item order and phonetic recoding in the beginning reader. *Journal of Experimental Child Psychology, 32*, 474–484.

Katz, W.R., & Tarver, S.G. (1989). Comparison of

dyslexic and nondyslexic adults on decoding and phonemic awareness tasks. *Annals of Dyslexia, 39,* 196–205.

Kaufman, A.S. (1994). *Intelligent testing with the WISC-III.* NY: John Wiley & Sons.

Kavale, K.A. & Forness, S.R. (1985). *The science of learning disabilities.* San Diego: College-Hill Press.

Kavale, K.A., Forness, S.R., & Bender, M. (1988). *Handbook of Learning Disabilities: Volume II: Methods and intervention.* Boston, MA: Little, Brown & Co.

Kavale, K., & Mattison, P.D. (1983). One jumped off the balance beam: Meta-analysis of perceptual-motor training. *Journal of Learning Disabilities, 16,* 165–173.

Keller, C.E., & Sutton, J.P. (1991). Specific mathematics disorders. In J.E. Obrzut, & G.W. Hynd (Eds.), *Neuropsychological foundations of learning disabilities* (pp. 549–571). San Diego, CA: Academic Press.

Kennedy, K.M., & Backman, J. (1993). Effectiveness of the Lindamood Auditory Discrimination In Depth Program with students with learning disabilities. *Learning Disabilities Practice, 8,* 253–259.

Keogh, B.K. & Babbitt, B.C. (1986). Sampling issues in learning disabilities research: Markers for the study of problems in mathematics. In Pavlidis & Fisher (Eds.). *Dyslexia: Its neuropsychology and treatment* (pp. 9–22). New York: John Wiley & Sons.

Kephart, N.C. (1960). *The slow learner in the classroom.* New York: Merrill.

Kephart, N.C. (1963). *Perceptual-motor problems of children.* Proceedings of the First Annual Meeting of the ACLD Conference on Exploration into the Problem of the Perceptually Handicapped Child. Chicago, reprinted in S.A. Kirk & J.M. McCarthy (Eds.). *Learning disabilities: Selected ACLD papers* (1975) (pp. 27–32). Boston: Houghton Mifflin.

Kephart, N.C. (1967). Perceptual-motor aspects of learning disabilities. In Frierson and Barbe (Eds.), *Educating children with learning disabilities.* New York: Appleton-Century-Crofts.

Kephart, N.C. (Ed.) (1971). *The slow learner in the classroom* (2nd ed.). Columbus, OH: Merrill.

Kerchner, L., & Kistinger, B. (1984). Language processing/word processing: Written expression, computers and learning disabled students. *Learning Disability Quarterly, 7,* 329–335.

Kershner, J.R., Cummings, R.L., Clarke, K.A., Hadfield, A.J., & Kershner, B.A. (1986). Evaluation of the Tomatis Listening Training Program with learning disabled children. *Canadian Journal of Special Education, 2,* 1–32.

Kershner, J.R., Cummings, R.L., Clarke, K.A., Hadfield, A.J., & Kershner, B.A. (1990). Two-year evaluation of the Tomatis Listening Training Program with learning disabled children. *Learning Disability Quarterly, 13,* 43–53.

Kinsbourne, M., & Warrington, E.T. (1963). The developmental Gerstmann syndrome. *Archives of Neurology, 8,* 490–501.

Kinsbourne, M., & Warrington, E.T. (1966). Developmental factors in reading and writing backwardness. In J. Money (Ed.), *The disabled reader: Education of the dyslexic child.* Baltimore: Johns Hopkins Press.

Kintsch, W. (1980). Learning from text, levels of comprehension, or: Why anyone would read a story anyway. *Poetics, 9,* 87–89.

Kintsch, W., & van Dijk, T.A. (1978). Toward a model of text comprehension and production. *Psychological Review, 85,* 363–394.

Kirby, J.R., & Becker, L.D. (1988). Cognitive components of learning problems in arithmetic. *Remedial and Special Education, 5,* 7–15, 27.

Kirk, S.A. (1963). *Behavioral diagnosis and remediation of learning disabilities.* Proceedings of the annual meeting of the Conference on Exploration into the Problems of the Perceptually Handicapped Child, Vol 1.

Kirk, S.A., & Chalfant, J.C. (1984). *Academic and developmental learning disabilities.* Denver: Love Pub.

Kirk, S.A., & Kirk, W.D. (1976). *Psycholinguistic learning disabilities: Diagnosis and remediation.* Chicago, IL: University of Illinois Press.

Kleffner, F.R. (1964). Teaching aphasic children. In J. Magary & J. Eichorn (Eds.), *The exceptional child* (pp. 330–337). New York: Holt, Rinehart & Winston.

Konopak, B.C., & Williams, N.L. (1988). Using the key word method to help young readers learn content material. *The Reading Teacher, 41,* 682–687.

Kosc, L. (1974). Developmental dyscalculia. *Journal of Learning Disabilities, 7,* 164–177.

Krapf, E. (1937). Uber Akalkulie Schweiz. *Archives of Neurology and Psychiatry, 39,* 330–334.

Kussmaul, A. (1877). Disturbance of speech. *Cyclopedia of Practical Medicine, 14,* 581–875.

LaBerge, D., & Samuels, S. (1974). Toward a theory of automatic information processing in reading. *Cognitive Psychology, 6,* 293–323.

Laker, M. (1982). On determining trace element levels in man: The uses of blood and hair. *The Lancet, 2,* 259–262.

Landesman-Dwyer, S., Ragozin, A.S. & Little, R.E. (1981). Behavioral correlates of prenatal alcohol exposure: A four-year follow-up study. *Neurobehavioral Toxicology and Teratology, 3,* 187–193.

Landmark College. (1995–1997). *Viewbook.* Putney, Vermont: Author.

Landmark College Catalog. (1993–1995). Putney, Vermont: Authors.

Landsdown, R. (1978). Retardation in mathematics: A consideration of multi-factor determination. *Journal of Child Psychology and Psychiatry, 19,* 181–185.

Lapointe, A.F., Mead, N., & Philips, G. (1988). *A world of differences. An international assessment of mathematics and science.* Princeton, NJ: Educational Testing Service.

Lauritzen, C. (1982). A modification of repeated readings for group instruction. *The Reading Teacher, 36,* 456–458.

LaVoie, R.D. (1988). *The learning disabled child: A spe-*

cial challenge—A [booklet] guide for parents. Greenwich, CT: Chase.

Lawless, S. (1995). *An examination of addition, subtraction, multiplication, and division error patterns on the* KeyMath-Revised *as potentially helpful for early diagnosis of learning disabled children.* Unpublished doctoral dissertation, American International College, Springfield, MA.

Lazarus, B.D. (1988). Using guided notes to aid learning disabled students in secondary mainstream settings. *The Pointer, 33,* 32–36.

Lazarus, B.D. (1991). Guided notes, review, and achievement of learning disabled adolescents in secondary mainstream settings. *Education and Treatment of Children, 14,* 112–128.

Lazarus, B.D., & McKenna, M.C. (1991, April). *Guided notes: Review and achievement of mainstreamed LD students.* Paper presented at the meeting of the Council for Exceptional Children, Atlanta, GA.

Leary, C.A. (1992). *A study of the Reynolds Adolescent Depression Scale as it relates to learning disabled adolescents.* Unpublished doctoral dissertation, American International College, Springfield, MA.

LaBerge, D., & Samuels, S. (1974). Toward a theory of automatic information processing in reading. *Cognitive Psychology, 6,* 293–323.

Learning Disabilities Association of America (Summer 1993). Newsletter, pp. 341–342.

Learning Disabilities Association of America (July/August 1994). Newletter, p. 37.

Lefroy, R. (1975). Some remedial techniques for severe learning disabilities. In M. White, R. Lefroy, & S.D. Weston (Eds.), *Treating reading disabilities* (pp. 21–54). San Raphael, CA: Academic Therapy Publications.

Lerner, J.W. (March 1967). A new focus for reading research-The decision-making process. *Elementary English, 44,* 236–242.

Lerner, J.W. (1971). Children with learning disabilites. Boston, MA: Houghton Mifflin.

Lerner, J. (1975). Two perspectives: Reading and learning disabilities. In S.A. Kirk, & J.M. McCarthy (Eds.), *Learning disabilities-Selected ACLD papers* (pp. 271-285). Boston, MA: Houghton Mifflin.

Lerner, J. (1985). *Learning disabilities: Theories, diagnosis, and teaching strategies* (4th ed.). Boston: Houghton Mifflin.

Lerner, J., & Chen, A. (1992). Critical issues in learning disabilities. The cross-cultural nature of learning disabilities: A profile in perseverance. *Learning Disabilities Research & Practice, 7,* 147–149.

Lerner, J.W. (1989). *Learning disabilities: Theories, diagnosis, and teaching strategies* (5th ed.). Boston: Houghton Mifflin.

Lerner, J.W., Lowenthal, B., & Lerner, S.R. (1995). *Attention deficit disorders: Assessment and teaching.* Boston, MA: Brooks/Cole.

Lesgold, A.M. & Perfetti, C.A. (1981). Interactive processes in reading: Where do we stand? In A.M. Lesgold, & C.A. Perfetti, (Eds.). *Interactive processes in reading* (pp. 387–405). Hillsdale, N.J.: Lawrence Erlbaum.

Levin, J.R. (1983). Pictorial strategies for school learning: Practical illustrations. In M. Pressley & J.R. Levin (Eds.), *Cognitive strategy research: Education applications* (pp. 213–237). NY: Springer-Verlag.

Levin, H., & Kaplan, E.L. (1970). Grammatical structure and reading. In H. Levin & J.P. Williams (Eds.), *Basic studies on reading.* (pp. 110–133) NY: Basic Books.

Levine, M.D. (1987). *Developmental variations and learning disorders.* Cambridge, MA: Educators Publishing Service.

Levinson, H.N. (1980). *A solution to the riddle dyslexia.* NY: Springer-Verlag.

Levinson, H.N. (1988). The cerebellar-vestibular basis of learning disabilities in children, adolescents and adults: Hypothesis and study. *Perceptual and Motor Skills, 67,* 983–1006.

Lewis, R. B. (1993). *Special education technology.* Pacific Grove, CA: Brooks/Cole Publishing.

Lezak, M.D. (1995). *Neuropsychological assessment.* NY: Oxford University Press.

Liberman, I.Y., Rubin, H., Duques, S., & Carlisle, J. (1985). Linguistic abilities and spelling proficiency in kindergarten and adult poor readers. In J. Kavanagh and D.G. Gray (Eds.), *Biobehavioral measures of dyslexia.* Parkton, MD: York Press.

Liberman, I.Y., Shankweiler, D., Liberman, A.M., Fowler, C. & Fischer, F.W. (1977). Phonetic segmentation and recoding in the beginning reader. In A.S. Reber, & D. L. Scarborough (Eds.), *Towards a psychology of reading: The proceedings of the CUNY Conference* (pp. 207–225). New York: John Wiley.

Liberman, J. (1986). The effect of syntonic (colored light) stimulation on certain visual and cognitive functions. *Journal of Optometric Vision Development, 17,* 4015.

Lind, S. (1993). Are we mislabeling overexcitable children? *Understanding Our Gifted, 1,* 8–10.

Lindamood, C.H., & Lindamood, P.C. (1975). *The A.D.D. Program, Auditory Discrimination in Depth.* Hingham, MA: Teaching Resources Corp.

Livingstone, M.S., & Hubel, D.H. (1988). Do the relative mapping densities of the magno- and parvocellular systems vary with eccentricity? *Journal of Neuroscience, 8,* 4334–4339.

Lloyd, J.W., Landrum, T.J., & Hallahan, D.P. (1991). Self-monitoring applications for classroom interventions. In G. Stoner, M.R. Shinn, & H.M. Walker (Eds.), *Interventions for behavior and academic problems in regular class settings* (pp. 201–213). Stratford, CT: National Association for School Psychologists.

Lopez, R., Yolton, R.L., Kohl, P., Smith, D.L., & Saxerud, M.H. (1994). Comparison of Irlen Scotopic Sensitivity Syndrome test results to academic and visual performance data. *Journal of the American Optometrics Association, 65,* 705–714.

Lord, P.P. (1995). *A concurrent validity study of the* Test of Mathematical Abilities *and the* Wide Range Achievement Test-Revised *as the criterion.* Unpublished doctoral dissertation, American International College, Springfield, MA.

Lovitt, T.C. (1989). *Introduction to learning disabilities.* Needham Heights, MA: Allyn & Bacon.

Lubs, H.A., Duara, R., Levin, B., Jallad, B., Lubs, M., Rabin, M., Kushch, A., & Gross-Glenn, K. (1991). Dyslexia subtypes—genetics, behavior and brain imaging. In D.D. Duane, & D.B. Gray, *The reading brain* (pp. 89–117). Parkton, MD: York.

Lyon, G.R. (1988). Subtype remediation. In K.A. Kavale, S.R. Forness, & M. Bender (Eds.), *Handbook of learning disabilities: Volume II: Methods and interventions* (pp. 33–58). Boston, MA: Little, Brown & Co.

Lyons, C.A., Pinnell, G.S., McCarrier, A., Young, P., & De-Ford, D. (1988). *The Ohio reading recovery project: Volume X and State of Ohio Year 1, 1986–1987.* Volume VIII (Technical Report). Columbus, OH: The Ohio State University. (One of several reports of the impact of Reading Recovery.)

MacArthur, C.A., & Haynes, J.B. (1995). Student assistant for learning from text (SALT): A hypermedia reading aid. *Journal of Learning Disabilities, 28,* 150–159.

Maggart, Z.R., & Zintz, M.V. (1990). *Corrective reading.* Dubuque, IA: William C. Brown.

Malmquist, E. (1958). *Factors related to learning disabilities in the first grades of the elementary school.* Stockholm, Sweden: Almquist & Wiksell.

Mandler, J.M. (1984). *Stories, scripts, and scenes: Aspects of schema theory.* Hillsdale, NJ: Lawrence Erlbaum.

Manganello, R.E. (1994). Time management instruction for older students with learning disabilities. *Teaching Exceptional Children, Winter,* 60.

Mann, V. (1991). Language problems: A key to early reading problems. In B.Y.L. Wong (Ed.), *Learning and Learning Disabilities* (pp. 129–162). San Diego, CA: Academic Press.

Mann, V.A. (1986). Why some children encounter reading problems: The contribution of difficulties with language processing and phonological sophistication to early reading disability. In J.K. Torgesen, & B.Y.L. Wong (Eds.), *Psychological and educational perspectives on learning disabilities* (pp. 133–159). New York: Academic Press.

Manzo, A.V., & Manzo, U.C. (1993). *Literacy disorders: Holistic diagnosis and remediation.* New York: Harcourt Brace Jovanovich.

Markle, S.M. (1975). They teach concepts, don't they? *Educational Researcher, 4,* 3–9.

Marlowe, M., Cossairt, A., Welch, K. & Errera, J. (1984). Hair mineral content as a predictor of learning disabilities. *Journal of Learning Disabilities, 17,* 418–421.

Mason, J.M., & Au, K.H. (1990). *Reading instruction for today.* Glenview, IL: Scott, Foresman/Little, Brown Higher Ed.

Massachusetts Department of Education. (1990). *Exit facts: A report on students who left special education in school year 1988–1990.* Quincy, MA: The Division of Special Education.

Masters, L.F., Mori, B.A., & Mori, A.A. (1993). *Teaching secondary students with mild learning and behavior problems.* Austin, TX: PRO-Ed.

Mastropieri, M.A., Scruggs, T.E., & Levin, J.R. (1985). Memory strategy instruction with learning disabled adolescents. *Journal of Learning Disabilities, 18,* 94–100.

Mathes, P.G., & Fuchs, L.S. (1993). Peer-mediated reading instruction in special education resource rooms. *Learning Disabilities Research & Practice, 8,* 233–243.

Mathinos, D.A. (1991). Conversational engagement of children with learning disabilities. *Journal of Learning Disabilities, 24,* 439–446.

Mattingly, I.G. (1972). Reading, the linguistic process, and linguistic awareness. In J.F. Kavanagh, & I.G. Mattingly (Eds.), *Language by ear and by eye* (pp. 133–147). Cambridge, MA: M.I.T. Press.

Mattis, S. (1978). Dyslexia syndromes: A working hypothesis that works. In A.L. Benton, & D. Pearl (Eds.), *Dyslexia: An appraisal of current knowledge* (pp. 45–58). New York: Oxford University Press.

Maugh, T.H. (1978). Hair: A diagnostic tool to complement blood serum and urine. *Science, 202,* 1271–1273.

May, F.B. (1994). *Reading as communication.* New York: Macmillan.

McDougall, W. (1912). *An introduction to social psychology.* Boston: John W. Luce.

McEntire, E. (1981). Learning disabilities and mathematics. *Topics in Learning and Learning Disabilities, 1,* 1–18.

McGuffey's Sixth Eclectic Reader. (1896). New York: American Book Co.

McKenna, M.C., & Robinson, R.D. (1993). *Teaching through text: A content literacy approach to content area reading.* New York: Longman.

McKiernan, P. (1990). *Evidence to support the hypothesis that dyslexics exhibit an anomalous distribution of retinal receptors.* Unpublished doctoral dissertation, American International College, Springfield, MA.

McKinney, K. (1993). *Improving math and science teaching—A Report on the Secretary's October 1992 Conference on Improving Mathematics and Science Teaching and Instructional Resources.* Washington DC: U.S. Government Printing Office.

McLeskey, J., Waldron, N.L., & Wornhoff, S.A. (1990). Factors influencing the identification of black and white students with learning disabilities. *Journal of Learning Disabilities, 23,* 362–366.

McNergney, R.F., & Herbert, J.M. (1995). *Foundations of Education: The Challenge of Professional Practice.* Boston, MA: Allyn and Bacon.

Meade, J. (1994). Turning on the bright lights. *Teacher Magazine Reader, 2,* 1–5.

Melikian, B.A. (1990). Family characteristics of children

with dyslexia. *Journal of Learning Disabilities, 23,* 386–391.

Mercer, C.D. (1987, 1991). *Students with learning disabilities.* Columbus, OH: Merrill.

Mercer, C.D., & Mercer, A.R. (1989). *Teaching students with learning problems* (3rd ed.), Columbus, OH: Merrill.

Mill, J.S. (1892). *On liberty.* London: Longmans, Green & Co.

Miller, J.H., & Milam, C.P. (1987). Multiplication and division errors committed by learning disabled students. *Learning Disabilities Research, 2,* 119–122.

Monroe, M. (1932). *Children who cannot read.* University of Chicago Press.

Montague, W.E., Adams, J.A., & Keiss, H.D. (1966). Forgetting and natural language mediation. *Journal of Experimental Psychology, 72,* 829–833.

Montague, M., & Bos, C.S. (1986). The effect of cognitive strategy training on verbal math-problem solving performance of learning disabled adolescents. *Journal of learning Disabilities, 19,* 26–33.

Moore, D.W., Moore, S.A., Cunningham, P.M., & Cunningham, J.W. (1994). *Developing readers & writers in the content areas K–12.* New York: Longman.

Moreau, M.R., & Fidrych-Puzzo, H. (1994). *How to use the Story Grammar Marker.* Easthampton, MA: Discourse Skills Production.

Morgan, W.P. (1896). A case of congenital word-blindness. *British Medical Journal, 2,* 1378–1379.

Morris, C.G. (1993). *Psychology: An introduction* (8th Ed.). Englewood Cliffs, NJ: Prentice Hall.

Morris, P.E., & Cook, N. (1978). When do first letter mnemonics aid recall? *British Journal of Educational Psychology, 48,* 22–28.

Morrison, S.R., & Siegel, L.S. (1991). Learning disabilities: A critical review of definitional and assessment issues. In J.E. Obrzut, & G.W. Hynd, *Neuropsychological foundations of learning disabilities* (pp. 79–97). New York: Academic Press.

Murphy, L.A., Pollatsek, A., & Well, A.D. (1988). Developmental dyslexia and word retrieval deficits. *Brain and Language, 35,* 1–23.

Myers, G.C. (1924). Persistence of errors in arithmetic. *Journal of Educational Research, 10,* 19–28.

Myers, P.E. & Hammill, D.D. (1990). *Learning disabilities: Basic concepts, assessment practices, and instructional strategies* (3rd ed.). Austin, TX: Pro-Ed.

Myers, P., & Hammill, D. (1982). *Learning disabilities.* Austin, TX: PRO-ED.

Myklebust, H.R. (1965). *Development and disorders of written language, Vol. 1, Picture Story Language Test.* New York: Grune & Stratton.

Myklebust, H.R. (1978). Toward a science of dyslexiology. In H.R. Myklebust (Ed.), *Progress in learning disabilities* (pp. 1–40). New York: Grune & Stratton.

Nagy, W.E., & Anderson, R.C. (1984). How many words are there in printed school English? *Reading Research Quarterly, 19,* 304–330.

Naidoo, S. (1972). *Specific dyslexia.* London: Pitman.

National Commission on Aids. (1994). Preventing HIV/AIDS in adolescents. *Journal of School Health, 64,* 39–51.

National Commission on Excellence in Education. (1983). *A nation at risk: The imperative for educational reform.* Washington, DC: U.S. Government Printing Office.

National Council of Supervisors of Mathematics. (1989). Essential mathematics for the twenty-first century: The position of the National Council of Supervisors of Mathematics. *Arithmetic Teacher, 37,* 44–46.

National Council of Teachers of Mathematics. (1989). *Curriculum and evaluation standards for school mathematics (NCTM).* Reston, VA: NCTM.

National Council of Teachers of Mathematics (1991a). *A guide for reviewing school mathematics programs.* Reston, VA: NCTM.

National Council of Teachers of Mathematics. (1991b). *Curriculum and evaluation standards for school mathematics: Professional standards for teaching mathematics* (NCTM). Reston, VA: NCTM.

National Education Association. (July 6–10, 1903). *Souvenir programme—42d annual convention.* Boston, MA: Lee, Higginson & Co.

National Joint Committee on Learning Disabilities. (1988). A position paper of the National Trust Committee on Learning Disabilities [Letter to NJCLD member organizations]. *Journal of Learning Disabilities, 1,* 53–55.

National Joint Committee on Learning Disabilities. (1992). School reform: Opportunities for excellence and equity for individuals with learning disabilities. *Journal of Learning Disabilities, 25,* 276–280.

National Joint Committee on Learning Disabilities. (1993a). Providing appropriate education for students with learning disabilities in regular education classrooms. In LDA *(Learning Disabilities Association) Items of Interest on Learning Disabilities, 28,* No. 2, 7–8.

National Joint Committee on Learning Disabilities. (1993b). A reaction to full inclusion: A reaffirmation of the right of students with learning disabilities to a continuum of services. In LDA *(Learning Disabilities Association) Items of Interest on Learning Disabilities, 28,* No. 2, 3.

National Joint Committee on Learning Disabilities (1993c). Issues in the delivery of services to individuals with learning disabilities—A position paper of the National Joint Committee on Learning Disabilities, February 21, 1982. In LDA *(Learning Disabilities Association) Items of Interest on Learning Disabilities, 28,* No. 2, 3.

National Joint Committee on Learning Disabilities (1993d). Position paper on full inclusion of all students with learning disabilities in the regular education classroom. *Items of Interest on Learning Disabilities, 28,* No. 2, 3.

National Joint Committee on Learning Disabilities (1994). *Collective perspectives on issues affecting learning disabilities.* Austin, TX: PRO-ED.

National Research Council. (1990). *Everybody counts: A report to the nation on the future of mathematics ed-*

ucation (summary document). Washington, DC: National Academy Press.

Needleman, H.L., Gunnoe, C., Leviton, A., Reed, R., Peresie, H. & Barret, C. (1979). Deficits in psychologic and classroom performance of children with elevated dentine lead levels. *New England Journal of Medicine, 300,* 689–695.

Nesher, P. (1987). Towards an instructional theory: The role of student's misconceptions. *For the Learning of Mathematics, 7,* 33–40.

Newby, R.F., & Lyon, G.R. (1991). Neurological subtypes of learning disabilities. In J.E. Obrzut, & G.W. Hynd (Eds.), *Neuropsychological foundations of learning disabilities* (pp. 355–385). San Diego: Academic Press.

Newman, S.P., Karle, H., Wadsworth, J.F., Archer, R., Hockly, R., & Rogers, P. (1985). Ocular dominance, reading, and spelling: A reassessment of a measure associated with specific reading difficulties. *Journal of Research in Reading, 8,* 127–138.

Nickerson, R.S., Perkins, D.N., & Smith, E.E. (1986). *The teaching of thinking.* Hillsdale, NJ: Lawrence Erlbaum.

Norman, C.A., & Zigmond, N. (1980). Characteristics of children labeled and served as learning disabled in school systems affliated with Child Service Demonstration Centers. *Journal of Learning Disabilities, 13,* 542–547.

Novick, B.Z., & Arnold, M.M. (1988). *Fundamentals of clinical child neuropsychology.* Philadelphia, PA: Grune & Stratton.

Nunes, R.J. (1991). *Utilization of mathematical error patterns in the differential diagnosis of various disabled subtypes.* Unpublished doctoral dissertation, American International College, Springfield, MA.

Oakland, T., & Glutting, J.J. (1990). Examiner observations of children's WIC-R test-related behaviors: Possible socioeconomic status, race, and gender effects. *Psychological Assessment, 2,* 86–90.

O'Brien, J., & Forest, M. (1992). *Action for inclusion— How to improve schools by welcoming children with special needs into regular classrooms.* Toronto, Ontario: Inclusion Press.

Obrzut, J.E. (1989). Dyslexia and neurodevelopmental pathology: Is the neurodiagnostic technology ahead of psychoeducational technology? *Journal of Learning Disabilities, 22,* 217–218.

Obrzut, J.E., & Hynd, G.W. (1991). *Neuropsychological foundations of learning disabilities.* San Diego, CA: Academic Press.

Ogle, D. (1986). The K-W-L: A teaching model that develops active reading of expository text. *The Reading Teacher, 39,* 564–570.

Ojemann, G.A. (1983). Brain organization for language from the perspective of electrical stimulation mapping. *Behavioral and Brain Sciences, 6,* 189–206.

Ojemann, G.A. (1991). Cortical organization of language. *Journal of Neuroscience, 11,* 2281–2287.

Okolo, C.M. (1992). The effects of computer-based attribution retraining on the attributions, persistence, and mathematics computation of students with learning disabilities. *Journal of Learning Disabilities, 25,* 327–334.

Ormrod, J.E. (1993). *Human learning—Principles, theories, and educational applications.* New York: Merrill.

Orton, J.L. (1963). Specific language disabilities. *Bulletin of the Orton Society, 13,* 3.

Orton, S.T. (1925). "Word-blindness" in school-children. *Archives of Neurological Psychology, 14,* 581–615.

Orton, S.T. (1928). Specific reading disability— Strephosymbolia. In M. Monroe (Ed.), *Genetic psychology monographs* (1095–1099). (Reprinted from the *Journal of the American Medical Association, 90,* 1095–1099)

Orton, S.T. (1937). *Reading, writing and speech problems in children: A presentation of certain types of disorders in the development of language faculty.* New York: Norton.

Ozols, E.J., & Rourke, B.P. (1988). Characteristics of young learning-disabled children classified according to patterns of academic achievement: Auditory-perceptual and visual-perceptual abilities. *Journal of Clinical Child Psychology, 17,* 44–52.

Palinscar, A.S., & Brown, D.A. (1984). Reciprocal teaching of comprehension-fostering and comprehension-monitoring activities. *Cognition and Instruction, 1,* 117–175.

Palinscar, A.S., & Brown, D.A. (1987). Enhancing instructional time through attention to metacognition. *Journal of Learning Disabilities, 20,* 66–75.

Palinscar, A.S., & David, Y.M. (1992). Classroom-based literacy instruction: The development of one program of intervention research. In B.Y.L. Wong (Ed.), *Contemporary intervention research in learning disabilities: An international perspective* (pp. 65–80). New York: Springer-Verlag.

Paris, S.G., & Winograd, P. (1990). How metacognition can promote academic learning and instruction. In B.F. Jones & L. Idol (Eds.), *Dimensions of thinking and cognitive instruction.* Hillsdale, NJ: Lawrence Erlbaum.

Parmar, R.S., & Cawley, J.F. (1994). Structuring word problems for diagnostic teaching: Helping teachers meet the needs of children with mild disabilities. *Teaching Exceptional Children, 26,* 16–21.

Pavlidis, G.T. (1985a). Eye movement differences between dyslexics, normal and retarded readers while sequentially fixating digits. *American Journal of Optometry and Physiological Optics, 62,* 820–832.

Pavlidis, G.T. (1985b). Eye movements in dyslexia: Their diagnostic significance. *Journal of Learning Disabilities, 18,* 42–50.

Pavlidis, G.T. (1985c). Erratic eye movements in dyslexia: Factors determining their relationship. *Perceptual and Motor Skills, 60,* 319–322.

Pavlidis, G.T. (1986). The role of eye movements in the diagnosis of dyslexia. In G.T. Pavlidis, & D.F. Fisher (Eds.), *Dyslexia: Its neuropsychology and treatment* (pp. 97–110). New York: John Wiley & Sons.

Pavlidis, G.T. & Fisher, D.F. (Eds.). (1986). *Dyslexia: Its neuropsychology and treatment.* New York: John Wiley & Sons.

Pearl, R., Bryan, T. & Donahue, M. (1983). Social behaviors of learning diabled children: A review. *Topics in Learning and Learning Disabilities, 3,* 1–14.

Pearson, P.D., & Fielding, L. (1991). Comprehension instruction. In R. Barr, M.L. Kamil, P. Mosenthal, & P.D. Pearson (Eds.), *Handbook of reading research* (Vol. 2, pp. 815–860). New York: Longman.

Perfetti, C. (1985). *Reading ability.* New York: Oxford University Press.

Perfetti, C.A., & Lesgold, A.M. (1979). Coding and comprehension in skilled reading and implications for reading instruction. In L.B. Resnick & P. Weaver (Eds.), *Theory and practice of early reading* (Vol. 1). Hillsdale, NJ: Lawrence Erlbaum.

Perino, J. & Ernhart, C. (1974). The relation of subclinical lead levels to cognitive and sensorimotor impairment in black preschoolers. *Journal of Learning Disabilities, 7,* 616–620.

Pesce, A. (1995). *Pesce's Papers.* Unpublished manuscript.

Peterson, P.L., & Knapp, N.F. (1993). Inventing and reinventing ideas: Constructivist teaching and learning in mathematics. In G. Cawelti (Ed.), *Challenges and Achievements—1993 Yearbook of the Association for Supervision and Curriculum Development.* Alexandria, VA: Association for Supervision and Curriculum Development.

Peterson, S.K., Mercer, C.D., & O'Shea, L. (1988). Teaching learning disabled children place value using the concrete to abstract sequence. *Learning Disabilities Research, 1,* 52–56.

Petrauskas, R., & Rourke, B. (1979). Identification of subtypes of retarded readers: A neuropsychological, multivariate approach. *Journal of Clinical Neuropsychology, 1,* 17–37.

Piaget, J. (1952). *The child's conception of number.* London, England: Routledge & Kegan Paul.

Pianko, S. (1979). A description of the composing processes of college freshmen writers. *Research in the Teaching of English, 13,* 5–22.

Pirozzolo, F.J., Dunn, K., & Zetusky, W. (1983). Physiological approaches to subtypes of developmental reading disability. *Topics on Learning & Learning Disabilities, 3,* 40–47.

Polya, G. (1945). *How to solve it.* Princeton, NJ: Princeton University Press.

Porter, N. (1896). Wise Tidbits from Yesteryear. In McGuffey's Sixth Eclectic Reader (pp. 8–20). New York: American Book Co.

Posamentier, A.S., & Stepelman, J. (1990). *Teaching secondary school mathematics* (3rd Ed.). Columbus, OH: Merrill.

Posner, M.I. (1979). Applying theories and theorizing about applications. In L. Resnick & P. Weaver (Eds.), *Theory and practice in early reading* (Vol.1, pp. 331–342). Hillsdale, NJ: Lawrence Erlbaum.

Post, T.R. (1992). *Teaching mathematics in grades K–8: Research-based methods* (2nd ed.). Boston, MA: Allyn and Bacon.

Powers, H.W.S. Jr. (1975). Caffeine, behavior and the LD child. *Academic Therapy, 11,* 5–11.

Prater, Ma., Serna, L.A., Sileo, T.W., & Katz, A.R. (1995). HIV disease. *Remedial and Special Education, 16,* 68–78.

Pressley, M., Johnson, C.J., Symons, S., McGoldrick, J.A., & Kurita, J.A. (1989). Strategies that improve children's memory and comprehension of text. *The Elementary School Journal, 90,* 3–32.

Pressley, M., & Levin, J.R. (1987). Elaborative learning strategies for the inefficient learner. In S.J. Ceci (Ed.), *Handbook of cognitive, social and neurological aspects of learning disabilities.* Hillsdale, NJ: Lawrence Erlbaum.

Pressley, M., Levin, J.R., & Miller, G.E. (1981). How does the keyword method affect vocabulary comprehension and usage? *Reading Research Quarterly, 16,* 213–225.

Public Law 94–142. (1975, November 29). Education for All Handicapped Children Act. U.S. Congress.

Purves, A.C., Rogers, T., & Soter, A.O. (1995). *How porcupines make love III–Readers, texts, cultures in the response-based classroom.* New York: Longman.

Radencich, M. (1985). Writing a class novel: A strategy for LD students? *Academic Therapy, 20,* 599–603.

Rayner, K.(1983). Eye movements, perceptual span and reading disability. *Annals of Dyslexia, 33,* 163–173.

Rayner, K. (1986). Eye movements and the perceptual span: Evidence for dyslexic typology. In G.T. Pavlidis, & D.F. Fisher (Eds.), *Dyslexia: Its neuropsychology and treatment* (pp. 111–130). New York: John Wiley & Sons.

Ray's Modern Elementary Arithmetic (1879). New York: American Book.

Reading Report Card (1985). (Report #15-R–01). National Assessment of Educational Progress. Princeton, NJ: Educational Testing Service.

Reid, D.K., & Hresko, W.P. (1981). *A cognitive approach to learning disabilities.* New York: McGraw-Hill.

Reid, R., Maag, J., Vasa, S., & Wright, G. (1994). Who are the children with ADHD: A school-based survey. *The Journal of Special Education, 28,* 117–137.

Rief, L. (1991). *Seeking diversity: Language arts with adolescents.* Portsmouth, NH: Heinemann.

Report of the Committee on the Function of Mathematics in General Education (1940). New York: Appleton-Century Co.

Reutzel, R.D. (1985). Story maps improve comprehension. *The Reading Teacher, 38,* 400–405.

Reyes, B.J. (1986). Teaching computational estimation: Concepts and strategies. In H.L. Schoen, & M.J. Zweng (Ed.), *National estimation and mental computation: 1986 yearbook.* Reston, VA: National Council of Teachers of Mathematics.

Richardson, J.S., & Morgan, R.F. (1994). *Reading to learn in the content areas.* Belmont, CA: Wadsworth.

Richman, N., Stevenson, J. & Graham, P. (1982). *Preschool to school: A behavioral study.* London: Academic Press.

Ricks, D. (1986). Dyslexia: Disorder that might have its good points. *Los Angeles Times,* 1.

Riddell, P.M., Fowler, M.S., & Stein, J.F. (1990). Spatial discrimination in children with poor vergence control. *Perceptual and Motor Skills, 70,* 707–718.

Rittner, M. (1982). Error analysis in mathematics education. *Special Education in Canada, 56,* 4–8.

Roberts, R., & Mather, N. (1995). The return of students with learning disabilities to regular classrooms: A Sellout? *Learning Disabilities Practice, 10,* 46–58.

Robinson, H.M. (1946). *Why pupils fail in reading.* Chicago, IL: University of Chicago Press.

Rogers, J. (1993). The inclusion revolution. *Research Bulletin—Phi Delta Kappa, 11,* 1–5.

Ross, A.O. (1976). *Psychological aspects of learning disabilities and reading disorders.* New York: McGraw-Hill.

Ross, D.D., Bondy, E., & Kyle, D.W. (1993). *Reflective teaching for student empowerment.* New York: Macmillan.

Rourke, B.P. (1985). Overview of learning disability subtypes. In B.P. Rourke (Ed.), *Neuropsychology of learning disabilities* (pp. 3–14). New York: Guilford.

Rourke, B.P., & Strang, J.D. (1983). Subtypes of reading and arithmetical disabilities: A neuropsychological analysis. In M. Rutter (Ed.), *Developmental neuropsychiatry* (pp. 473–488). New York: Guilford Press.

Rubin, D. (1991a). *Diagnosis and correction of reading difficulty.* Boston, MA: Allyn and Bacon.

Rubin, D. (1991b). *Diagnosis and correction in reading instruction.* Boston, MA: Allyn and Bacon.

Ruddell, M.R. (1993). *Teaching content reading and writing.* Boston: Allyn and Bacon.

Rumelhart, D.E. (1977). Toward an interactive model of reading. In S. Dornic (Ed.), *Attention and Performance* (pp. 573–603). Hillsdale, NJ: Lawrence Erlbaum.

Rupley, W.H., & Blair, T.R. (1989). *Reading diagnosis and remediation.* Columbus, OH: Merrill.

Rutter, M., Tizard, J. & Whitmore, K. (1970). *Education, health and behavior.* London: Longmans.

Rutter, M., & Yule, W. (1975). The concept of specific reading retardation. *Journal of Child Psychology and Psychiatry and Applied Disciplines, 16,* 181–197.

Ryder, R.J., & Graves, M.F. (1994). *Reading and learning in content areas.* New York: Merrill.

Sachs, J. (1988). Teacher preparation, teacher self-efficacy, and the Regular Education Initiative. *Education and Training in Mental Retardation, 23,* 327–332.

Salpeter, J. (1988). Answers to your questions about CD-ROM. *Classroom computer learning, 8,* 18.

Samuels, S.J. (1979). The method of repeated reading. *The Reading Teacher, 32,* 403–408.

Samuels, S.J., & Miller, N.L. (1985). Failure to find attention differences between learning disabled and normal children on classroom and laboratory tasks. *Exceptional Children, 51,* 358–375.

Sasso, G.M. (1988). Service arrangements. In K.A. Kavale, S.R. Forness, & M. Bender (Eds.), *Handbook of learning disabilities: Vol. III: Programs and practices* (pp. 85–101). Boston, MA: College-Hill.

Sattler, J.M. (1992). *Assessment of children* (3rd ed.). San Diego, CA: Jerome M. Sattler.

Satz, P. & Morris, R. (1981). Learning disabilities: A review. In F.J. Pirozzolo, & M.C. Wittrock (Eds.), *Neuropsychological processes in reading* (pp. 109–141). New York: Academic Press.

Satz, P., Morris, R., & Fletcher, J. (1985). Hypotheses, subtypes, and individual differences in dyslexia: Some reflections. In D.B. Gray & J.F. Kavanagh (Eds.), *Biobehavioral measures of dyslexia* (pp. 25–40). Parkton, MD: York Press.

Schachter, S.C., Ransil, B.J. & Geschwind, N. (1987). Associations of handedness with hair color and learning disabilities. *Neuropsychologia, 25,* 269–276.

Schank, R.C. (1979). Interestingness: Controlling inferences. *Artificial Intelligence, 12,* 273–297.

Scheid, K. (1990). *Cognitive-based methods for teaching mathematics to students with learning problems.* Columbus, OH: LINC Resources.

Schmidt, H.P., Kuryliw, A.J., Saklofske, D.H., & Yackulic, R.A. (1989). Stability of WISC-R scores for a sample of learning disabled children. *Psychological Reports, 64,* 195–201.

Schmidt, M.C., & O'Brien, D.G. (1986). Story grammars: Some cautions about the translation of research into practice. *Reading Research and Instruction, 26,* 1–8.

Schneider, W., & Shiffrin, R.M. (1977). Controlled and automatic human information processing: I. Detection, search, and attention. *Psychological Review, 84,* 1–66.

Schumaker, J.B., Deshler, D.D., Alley, G.R., Warner, M.M. & Denton, P.H. (1982). Multipass: A learning strategy for improving reading comprehension. *Learning Disability Quarterly, 5,* 295–304.

Schumm, J.S., Vaughn, S., Gordon, J., & Rothlein, L. (1994). General education teachers beliefs, skills, and practices in planning for mainstreamed students with learning disabilities. *Teacher Education and Special Education, 17,* 22–37.

Schunk, D.H. (1987). Self-efficacy and motivated learning. In N. Hastings & J. Schwieso (Eds.), *New directions in educational psychology: Vol. 2. Behaviour and motivation in the classroom.* (pp. 233–252). Lewes, Sussex, UK: Falmer Press.

Schwartz, E., & Sheff, A. (1975). Student involvement in questioning for comprehension. *The Reading Teacher, 29,* 150–154.

Science News (1991). 140, 189.

Scruggs, T.E., Mastropieri, M.A., Bakken, J.P., & Brigham, F.J. (1993). Reading versus doing: The relative effects of textbook-based and inquiry-oriented approaches to science learning in special education classrooms. *Journal of Special Education, 27,* 1–15.

Scruggs, T.E., Mastropieri, M.A., McLoone, B.B., Levin, J.R., & Morrison, C.R. (1987). Mnemonic facilitation of learning disabled students' memory for expository prose. *Journal of Educational Psychology, 79,* 27–34.

Searfoss, L.W. (1975). Radio reading. *The Reading Teacher, 29,* 295–296.

Searfoss, L.W., & Readence, J.W. (1994). *Helping children learn to read.* Boston, MA: Allyn and Bacon.

Semrud-Clikeman, M., & Hynd, G.W. (1991). Specific non-verbal and social-skills deficits in children with learning disabilities. In J.E. Obrzut & G.W. Hynd (Eds.), *Neuropsychological foundations of learning disabilities* (pp. 603–629). San Diego, CA: Academic Press.

Sgroi, R.J. & Sgroi, L.S. (1993). *Mathematics for elementary school teachers.* Boston, MA: PWS-Kent.

Sharma, M.C. (1986). Dyscalculia and other learning problems in arithmetic: A historical perspective. *Focus on Learning Problems in Mathematics, 8,* 7–45.

Sharpley, C.F., & Edgar, E. (1986). Teacher's ratings versus standardized tests: An empirical investigation of agreement between two indices of achievement. *Psychology in the Schools, 23,* 106–111. Boston: Birkhauser.

Shaywitz, B.A., Shaywitz, S.E., Liberman, I.Y., Fletcher, J.M., Shankweiler, D.P., Duncan, J.S., Katz, L., Liberman, A.M., Francis, D.J., Dreyer, L.G., Crain, S., Brady, S., Fowler, A., Kier, L.E., Rosenfield, N.S., Gore, J.C. & Makuch, R.W. (1991). Neurolinguistic and biologic mechanisms in dyslexia. In D.D. Duane, & D.B. Gray (Eds.), *The reading brain* (pp.27–52). Parkton, MD: York Press.

Shaywitz, S.E., Shaywitz, B.A., Fletcher, J.M., & Escobar, M.D. (1990). Prevalence of reading disability in boys and girls. *Journal of the American Medical Association, 264,* 998–1002.

Sieben, R.L. (1977). Controversial medical treatments of learning disabilities. *Academic Therapy, 13,* 133–147.

Siegel, S. (1956). *Nonparametric statistics.* New York: McGraw-Hill.

Siegel, E., & Gold, R. (1982). *Educating the learning disabled.* New York: Macmillan.

Silver, A.A. , Hagin, R.A., Beecher, R. (1978). A program for secondary prevention of learning disabilities: Results in academic achievement and in emotional adjustment. *Journal of Preventive Psychiatry, 1,* 77–87.

Silver, L.B. (1987). The "magic cure." A review of the current controversial approaches for treating learning disabilities. *Journal of Learning Disabilities, 20,* 498–504.

Simpson, M.L., Hayes, C.G., Stahl, N., Connor, R.T., & Weaver, D. (1988). An initial validation of a study strategy system. *Journal of Reading Behavior, 20,* 149–180.

Slavin, R.E. (1992). *Student team learning: A practical guide to cooperative learning.* Washington DC: National Education Association.

Slingerland, B.H. (1976). *A multi-sensory approach to language arts for specific language disability children: A guide for primary teachers.* Cambridge, MA: Educators Publishing Service.

Smith, F., & Goodman, K.S. (1971). On the psycholinguistic method of teaching reading. *Elementary School Journal, 71,* 177–181.

Smith, D.D., & Luckasson, R. (1995). *Introduction to special education.* Boston, MA: Allyn and Bacon.

Smith, D.D., & Rivera, D.P. (1991). Mathematics. In B.Y.L. Wong (Ed.), *Learning about learning disabilities* (pp. 345–374). San Diego, CA: Academic Press.

Smith, T.E.C., Polloway, E.A., Patton, J.R., & Dowdy, C.A. (1995). *Teaching students with special needs in inclusive settings.* Boston, MA: Allyn and Bacon.

Snowling, M. (1980). The developmental of grapheme-phoneme correspondence in normal and dyslexic readers. *Journal of Experimental Child Psychology, 29,* 294–305.

Snowman, J. (1986). Learning tactics and strategies. In G.D. Phye & T. Andre (Eds.), *Cognitive classroom learning: Understanding, thinking, and problem solving.* Orlando, FL: Academic Press.

Solan, H.A. (1990). An appraisal of the Irlen technique of correcting reading disorders using tinted overlays and tinted lenses. *Journal of Learning Disabilities, 23,* 621–626.

Solman, R.T., Dain, S.J., & Keech, S.L. (1991). Color-mediated contrast sensitivity in disabled readers. *Optometry and Vision Science, 68,* 331–337.

Spache, G.D. (1976a). *Diagnosing and correcting reading disabilities.* Boston: Allyn and Bacon.

Spache, G.D. (1976b). *Investigating the issues of reading disabilities.* Boston: Allyn and Bacon.

Spafford, C.S. (1989). Wechsler digit span subtest: Diagnostic usefulness with dyslexic children. *Perceptual and Motor Skills, 69,* 115–125.

Spafford, C.S. (1992). *The Adventures of Dr. McKite.* Unpublished pilot project. East Longmeadow, MA: Author.

Spafford, C.S. (1994). *Detective Q. Squirt—A metacognitive approach to study skills management.* Unpublished paper.

Spafford, C.S. (1993, Fall). *The 3 Rs generated from sharing our rich cultural diversity—Responsibility, respect, and relating.* In Hampden County Teachers Association, Workshop Program. Workshop conducted at the annual Hampden County Teachers Association workshop program, Chicopee, MA.

Spafford, C.S. (1995). *Concurrent and predictive validity study of the TOMA in examining math grades of students at-risk for learning disabilities.* Submitted Manuscript.

Spafford, C.S. & Grosser, G.S. (1991). Retinal differences in light sensitivity between dyslexic and proficient reading children: New prospects for optometric input in diagnosing dyslexia. *Journal of the American Optometric Association, 62,* 610–615.

Spafford, C.S. & Grosser, G.S. (1993). The "social misperception syndrome" in children with learning disabilities: Social causes versus neurological variables. *Journal of Learning Disabilities, 26,* 178–189, 198.

Spafford, C.S., Grosser, G.S., Donatelle, J.R., Squillace, S.R., & Dana, J.P. (1995). The use of chromatic lenses during visual search and contrast sensitivity among proficient and disabled readers. *Journal of Learning Disabilities, 28,* 240–252.

Spafford, C.S., Pesce, A., & Grosser, G.S. (in press). *Original American Cyclopaedic Dictionary of Education.* Boston, MA: Allyn & Bacon.

Spafford, C.S., & Stanley, C. (1995). *Gender gap reversal presents new light on curricular mathematics interventions based on gender-specific differences in language for 8th grade students in an urban setting.* Submitted Manuscript.

Spalding, R.B. with Spalding, W.T. (1957, 1962, 1969, 1986, 1990). *The writing road to reading.* Author.

Spencer, H. (1861). *Education: Intellectual, moral, and physical.* New York: D. Appleton & Co.

Spiers, P.A. (1987). Acalculia revisited: Current issues. In G. Deloche, & X. Seron (Eds.), *Mathematical disabilities: A cognitive neuropsychological perspective* (pp. 1–25). Hillsdale, NJ: Lawrence Erlbaum.

Spinelli-Nannen, T., (1995). Social learning: The role of the school. *The Connecticut School Psychologist, 2,* 14–15.

Spitler, H.R. (1941). *The syntonic principle.* College of Syntonic Optometry.

Spradlin, J. (1967). Procedures for evaluating processes associated with receptive and expressive language. In R. Schiefelbusch, R. Copeland, & J. Smith (Eds.), *Language and mental retardation* (pp. 118–136). NY: Holt, Rinehart, & Winston.

Spring, C. & Sandoval, J. (1976). Food additives and hyperkinesis: A critical evaluation of the evidence. *Journal of Learning Disabilities, 9,* 560–569.

Sprinthall, R.C., Schmutte, G.T., & Sirois, L. (1991). *Understanding educational research.* Englewood Cliffs, NJ: Prentice-Hall.

Sprinthall, R.C., Sprinthall, N.A., & Oja, S.N. (1994). *Educational psychology* (6th Ed.). New York: McGraw-Hill.

Stanford, L., & Hynd, G. (1994). Congruence of behavioral symptomatology in children with ADD/H, ADD/WO, and learning disabilities. *Journal of Learning Disabilities, 27,* 243–253.

Stanley, C., & Spafford, C.S. (1995). *Closing the mathematics gap between minority and non-minority urban education students via data analyses of math-language achievement performances.* Submitted Manuscript.

Stanovich, K.E. (1986a). Cognitive processes and the reading problems of learning-disabled children: Evaluating the assumption of specificity. In J.K. Torgesen, & B.Y.L. Wong (Eds.), *Psychological and educational perspectives on learning disabilities* (pp. 87–131). New York: Academic Press.

Stanovich, K.E. (1986b). Matthew effect in reading: Some consequences of individual differences in the acquisition of literacy. *Reading Research Quarterly, 21,* 360–407.

Stanovich, K.E. (1994). Romance and Reality. *The Reading Teacher, 47,* 280–289.

Staton, J. (1980). Writing and counseling: Using a dialogue journal. *Language Arts, 57,* 514–518.

Stein, J. (1989). Visuospatial perception and reading problems. *Irish Journal of Psychology, 10,* 521–533.

Stein, J. & Fowler, S. (1985). Effect of monocular occlusion on visuomotor perception and reading in dyslexic children. *The Lancet,* 69–73.

Stein, N.L., & Trabasso, T. (1981). *What's in a story: An approach to comprehension and instruction* (Technical Report No. 200). Urbana-Champaign, IL: University of Illinois.

Stice, C.F., Bertrand, J.E., & Bertrand, N.P. (1995). *Integrating reading and other language arts.* Boston, MA: Wadsworth Pub.

Stone, C.A., & Forman, E.A. (1988). Differential patterns of approach to a complex problem-solving task among learning disabled adolescents. *The Journal of Special Education, 22,* 167–185.

Storey, R.K. (1995). *Utility of the* Wechsler Intelligence Test for Children-Revised *in screening for Attention Deficit Hyperactivity Disorder.* Unpublished doctoral dissertation. American International College, Springfield, MA.

Strauss, A.A., & Lehtinen, L. (1947). *Psychopathology and education of the brain-injured child* (Vol. I). New York: Grune & Stratton.

Strauss, A., & Werner, H. (1938). Deficiency in the finger scheme in relation to arithmetic (finger agnosia and acalculia). *American Journal of Orthopsychiatry, 8,* 719–725.

Strayer, G.D., & Norsworthy, N. (1917). *How to teach.* New York: Macmillan.

Strichart, S.S., & Mangrum, C.T. (1993). *Teaching study strategies to students with learning disabilities.* Boston: Allyn and Bacon.

Struempler, R.E., Larson, G.E. & Rimland, B. (1985). Hair mineral analysis and disruptive behaviors in clinically normal young men. *Journal of Learning Disabilities, 18,* 609–612.

Suydam, M.N. (1984). Microcomputers in math instruction. *The Arithmetic Teacher, 32,* 35.

Swanson, H.L. (1988). Memory subtypes in learning disabled readers. *Learning Disabilities Quarterly, 11,* 342–357.

Swanson, H.L. (1989). Strategy instruction: Overview of principles and procedures for effective use. *Learning Disability Quarterly, 12,* 3–14.

Swanson, H.L. (1993). Principles and procedures in strategy use. In L.J. Meltzer (Ed.), *Strategy assessment and instruction for students with learning disabilities* (pp. 61–92). Austin, TX: PRO-ED.

Swanson, H.L., Cochran, K.F., & Ewers, C.A. (1990). Can learning disabilities be determined from working memory performance? *Journal of Learning Disabilities, 23,* 59–67.

Symons, S., & Pressley, M. (1993). Prior knowledge affects text search success and extraction of information. *Reading Research Quarterly, 28,* 251–259.

Taba, H. (1967). *Teacher's handbook for elementary social studies.* Reading, MA: Addison Wesley.

Tallal, P., Sainburg, R.L., & Jernigan, T. (1991). The neuropathology of developmental dysphasia: Behavioral, morphological, and physiological evidence for a pervasive temporal processing disorder. *Reading and Writing: An Interdisciplinary Journal, 3,* 363–377.

Task Force on DSM-IV American Psychiatric Association (1994). *DSM-IV Draft Criteria.* Washington DC: Author.

Tatsuoka, K.K. (1984). Changes in error types over learning stages. *Journal of Educational Psychology, 76,* 120–129.

Taylor, J.S. (1912). *Principles and methods of teaching reading.* New York: Macmillan.

Taylor, K.K. (February 1984). Teaching summarization skills. *Journal of Reading, 27,* 389.

Taylor, S.E., Frankenpohl, H., & Pettee, J.L. (1960). *Research and Information Bulletin, No. 3.* Educational Developmental Laboratories, 1960.

Taylor, W. (1953). Cloze procedure: A new tool for measuring readability. *Journalism Quarterly, 30,* 415–433.

Teale, W.H. (1984). Reading to young children: Its significance in literacy development. In H. Goelman, A. Oberg, & F. Smith (Eds.), *Awakening to literacy.* Exeter, NH: Heinemann.

Thatcher, R.W. & Lester, M.L. (1985). Nutrition, environmental toxins, and computerized EEGs: A mini-max approach to learning disabilities. *Journal of Learning Disabilities, 18,* 287–289.

Thomas, E., & Robinson, H.A. (1972). *Improving reading in every classroom.* Boston, MA: Allyn and Bacon.

Thomas, P.J. (1985). Techniques for determining cognitive qualities. In J.F. Cawley (Ed.), *Cognitive strategies and mathematics for the learning disabled.* Rockville, MD: Aspen Pub.

Thornton, C.A., Tucker, B.F., Dossey, J.A., & Bazik, E.F. (1983). *Teaching mathematics to children with special needs.* Menlo Park, CA: Addison-Wesley.

Tierney, R.J., Carter, M.A., & Desai, L.E. (1991). *Portfolio assessment in the reading-writing classroom.* Norwood, MA: Christopher-Gordon.

Tierney, R.J., & Cunningham, J.W. (1984). Research on teaching reading comprehension. In P.D. Pearson (Ed.), *Handbook of Reading Research* (pp. 609–656). New York: Longman.

Tierney, R.J., Readence, J.E., & Dishner, E.K. (1990). *Reading strategies and practices—A compendium.* Boston, MA: Allyn and Bacon.

Tomatis, A.A. (1963). *L'Oreille et le langage.* Paris, France: Le Rayon de la Science, Edition du Sevil.

Tomatis, A. (1978). *Education and dyslexia.* France-Quebec: Les Editions, AIAPP.

Topping, K.J. (1995). Cued spelling: A powerful technique for parent and peer tutoring. *The Reading Teacher, 48,* 374–383.

Torgesen, J.K. (1988). Studies of children with learning disabilities who perform poorly on memory span tasks. *Journal of Learning Disabilities, 21,* 605–612.

Torgesen, J.K. & Kail, R.V. (1980). Memory processes in exceptional children. In B.K. Keogh (Ed.), *Advances in special education. Vol. 1: Basic constructs and theoretical orientations.* Greenwich, CT: J.A.I. Press.

Traub, N., (with Frances Bloom). (1992, 1990, 1975, 1973, 1972). *Recipe for Reading.* Cambridge, MA: Educators Publishing.

Travers, J.F., Elliot, S.N., & Kratochwill, T.R. (1993). *Educational psychology.* Madison, WI: William C. Brown Communications.

Trelease, J. (1982). *The read-aloud handbook.* New York: Penguin Books.

Troutman, A.P. & Lichtenberg, B.K. (1987, 1995). *Mathematics—A good beginning—Strategies for teaching children.* Pacific Grove, CA: Brooks/Cole Pub.

United States Office of Education (1977, August 23). *Education of handicapped children: Implementation of Part B of the Education of Handicapped Act,* Federal Register I, Part II. Washington, DC: U.S. Department of Health Education and Welfare.

United States Department of Education. (1989). *Eleventh annual report to Congress on the implementation of the Education of the Handicapped Act.* Washington, DC: U.S. Government Printing Office.

United States Department of Education (1995). *Sixteenth annual report to Congress on the implementation of the Individuals with Disabilities Education Act.* Washington DC: U.S. Government Printing Office.

U.S. Department of Education. (1991, September 16). Clarification of policy to address the needs of children with attention deficit disorders within the general and/or special education. *Memorandum.*

Valeri-Gold, M. (1987). Previewing: A directed reading-thinking activity. *Reading Horizons, 27,* 123–126.

Vansittart, P. (1964). *The lost lands.* London: Macmillan & Co.

Vargo, F.E., Grosser, G.S., & Spafford, C.S. (1995). Digit span and other scores on the WISC-R in the diagnosis of dyslexia in children. *Perceptual and Motor Skills.* In press.

Varnhagen, C.K., & Goldman, S.R. (1986). Improving comprehension: Causal relations instruction for learning handicapped learners. *The Reading Teacher, 39,* 896–904.

Vaughn, S. (1991). Social skills enhancement in students with learning disabilities. In B.Y.L. Wong (Ed.), *Learning about learning disabilities* (pp. 407–440). San Diego, CA: Academic Press.

Vaughn, S., & LaGreca, A.M. (1988). Social skills of LD students: Characteristics, behaviors, and guidelines for intervention. In K. Kavale (Ed.), *Handbook in learning disabilities* (pp. 123–140). San Diego, CA: College Hill.

Veit, D.T., Scruggs, T.E., & Mastropieri, M.A. (1986). Extended mnemonic instruction with LD adolscents. *Journal of Educational Psychology, 78,* 300–308.

Vellutino, F. (1977). Alternate conceptualizations of dyslexia: Evidence in support of a verbal deficit hypothesis. *Harvard Educational Review, 47,* 334–354.

Vellutino, F.R. (1987). Dyslexia. *Scientific American, 256,* 34–41.

Vogel, S. (1987). Issues and concerns in LD college programming. In D. Johnson, & J. Blalock (Eds.), *Adults with learning disabilities* (pp. 239–275). New York: Grune & Stratton.

Vogel, S.A. (1990). Gender differences in intelligence, language, visual-motor abilities, and academic achievement in students with learning disabilities: A review of the literature. *Journal of Learning Disabilities, 23,* 44–52.

Vygotsky, L. (1962). *Thought and language.* Cambridge, MA: MIT Press.

Wade, S.E., & Adams, B. (1990). Effects of importance and interest on recall of biographical text. *JRB: A Journal of Literacy, 22,* 331–353.

Wade, S.E., Schraw, G., Buxton, W.M., & Hayes, M.T. (1993). Seduction of the strategic reader: effects of interest on strategies and recall. *Reading Research Quarterly, 28,* 93–111.

Walker, B.J. (1992). *Diagnostic teaching of reading: Techniques for instruction and assessment* (2nd ed.). New York: Merrill.

Walker, D.K., Singer, J.D., Palfrey, J.S., Ozra, M., Wenger, M., & Butler, J. (1988). Who leaves and who stays in special education: A 2-year follow-up study. *Exceptional Children, 54,* 393–402.

Walker, N. (1985). Impulsivity in learning disabled children: Past research findings and methodological inconsistencies. *Learning Disabilities Quarterly, 8,* 85–94.

Wallace, G., Cohen, S.B., Polloway, E.A. (1987). *Language arts.* Austin, Texas: PRO-Ed.

Wallace, G., Larsen, S.C., & Elksnin, L.K. (1992). *Educational assessment of learning problems: Testing for teaching* (2nd ed.). Boston, MA: Allyn and Bacon.

Wallach, M., & Wallach, L. (1976). *Teaching all children to read.* Chicago, IL: University of Chicago Press.

Warrington, E.K. (1987). The fractionation of arithmetic skills: A single case study. In G. Deloche & X. Seron (Eds.), *Mathematical disabilities: A cognitive neuropsychological perspective* (pp. 235–256). Hillsdale, NJ: Lawrence Erlbaum.

Watson, J.M. (1876). *Independent third reader.* New York: A.S. Barnes.

Watson, R.J. (1994). *Analysis of WISC-R Composite and WISC-R Coding subtest scores in reading disabled and emotionally handicapped children.* Unpublished doctoral dissertation, American International College, Springfield, MA.

Waugh, N.C., & Norman, D.A. (1965). Primary memory. *Psychology Review, 72,* 89–104.

Webster, R.E. (1979). Visual and aural short-term memory capacity deficits in mathematics disabled students. *Journal of Educational Research, 72,* 277–283.

Weiner, B., Frieze, I.H., Kukla, A., Reed, L., Rest, S., & Rosenbaum, R.M. (1971). *Perceiving the causes for success and failure.* New York: General Learning Press.

Weiten, W. (1995). *Psychology—Themes and variations.* Boston, MA: Brooks/Cole.

Weller, C. & Strawser, S. (1987). Adaptive behavior of subtypes of learning disabled individuals. *The Journal of Special Education, 21,* 101–115.

Wender, P.H. (1987). *The hyperactive child, adolescent, and adult.* New York: Oxford University Press.

Wentworth, G., & Smith, D.E. (1912). *Work and play with numbers.* Boston, MA: Ginn & Co.

Wernicke, C. (1874). *Der aphasiche Symptomenkomplex.* Breslau, Germany: Cohn and Weigert.

White, Dianne L. (1995). *Identifying error patterns of students with learning disabilities using subtraction and division computations from the KeyMath-Revised.* Unpublished doctoral dissertation, American International College, Springfield, MA.

White, M. (1988). Dyslexia and thinking disorders. *Transactional Analysis Journal, 18,* 141–147.

White, N.C. (1989). *The Slingerland approach: An effective strategy for teaching spelling.* Cambridge, MA: Educators Publishing.

White, O. R. & Haring, N.G. (1980). *Exceptional teaching* (2nd ed.). Columbus, OH: Charles E. Merrill.

White, W., Schumaker, J., Warner, M., Alley, G., & Deshler, D. (1980). *The current status of young adults identified as learning disabled during their school career* (Research Report No. 21). Lawrence: University of Kansas, Institute for Research in Learning Disabilities.

Whittey, P., & Kopel, D. (1936). Factors associated with the etiology of reading disability. *Journal of Educational Research, 29,* 449–459.

Wiederholt, J.L. (1974). Historical perspectives on the education of the learning disabled. In L. Mann & D.A. Sabatino (Eds.), *The second review of special education* (pp. 103–152). Austin, TX: PRO-ED.

Wiederholt, J. (1978). Adolescents with learning disabilities: The problem in perspective. In L. Mann, G. Goodman, and J. Wiederholt (Eds.), *Teaching the learning disabled adolescent.* Boston: Houghton-Mifflin.

Wiederholt, J.L. (1989). Restructuring special education services: The past, the present, the future. *Learning Disability Quarterly, 12,* 181–191.

Wiederholt, J.L., & Bryant, B. (1987). *Assessing the reading abilities and instructional needs of students.* Austin, TX: PRO-ED.

Wiederholt, J.L., Hammill, D.D., & Brown, V. (1983). *The resource teacher* (2nd ed.). Boston, MA: Allyn and Bacon.

Wiig, E.H. (1990). Linguistic transitions and learning disabilities: A strategic learning perspective. *Learning Disability Quarterly, 13,* 128–140.

Wiig, E.H., & Semel, E.M. (1980). *Language assessment and intervention for the learning disabled.* Columbus, OH: Merrill.

Wilkinson, I. Wardrop, J.L., & Anderson, R.C. (1988). Silent reading reconsidered: Reinterpreting reading instruction and its effects. *American Educational Research Journal, 25,* 127–144.

Will, M.C. (1986). Educating children with learning problems: A shared responsibility. *Exceptional Children, 52*, 411–415.

Williams, M.C., & LeCluyse, K. (1990). Perceptual consequences of a temporal processing deficit in reading disabled children. *Journal of the American Optometric Association, 61*, 111–121.

Wilsher, C., & Taylor, J. (1987). Remedies for dyslexia: Proven or unproven? *Early Child Development and Care, 27*, 437–449.

Winograd, P.N. (Summer 1984). Strategic difficulties in summarizing text. *Reading Research Quarterly, 19*, 400–425.

Witmer, J.M., Bornstein, A.V., & Dunham, R.M. (1971). The effects of verbal approval and disapproval upon the performance of third and fourth grade children on four subtests of the Wechsler Intelligence Scale for Children. *Journal of School Psychology, 9*, 347–356.

Wolf, M. (1986). Rapid alternating stimulus naming in the developmental dyslexias. *Brain and Language, 27*, 360–379.

Wolfarth, H. & Sam, C. (1982). The effect of color psychodynamic environmental modification upon psychophysiological and behavioral reactions of severely handicapped children. *The International Journal of Biosocial Research, 1*, 10–38.

Wolfe, D., & Reising, R. (1983). *Writing for learning in the content areas.* Portland, ME: J. Weston Walch.

Wolraich, M.L., Lindgren, S., Stromquist, A., Milich, R., Davis, C., & Watson, D. (1990). Stimulant medications use by primary care physicians in the treatment of attention deficit hyperactivity disorder. *Pediatrics, 86*, 95–101.

Wong, B.Y.L. (1980). Activating the inactive learner: Use of questions/prompts to enhance comprehension and retention of implied information in learning disabled children. *Learning Disability Quarterly, 3*, 42–47.

Wong, B.Y.L. (1991). The relevance of metacognition to learning disabilities. In B.Y.L. Wong (Ed.), *Learning about learning disabilities* (pp. 231–258). San Diego, CA: Academic Press.

Wong, B.Y.L., Butler, D.L., Ficzere, S.A., Kuperis, S., Corden, M., & Zelmer, J. (1994). Teaching problem learners revision skills and sensitivity to audience through two instructional modes: Student-teacher versus student-student interactive dialogues. *Learning Disabilities Research & Practice, 9*, 78–90.

Woolfolk, A.E. (1993). *Educational Psychology.* Boston, MA: Allyn and Bacon.

Worrall, R.S. (1990a). Detecting health fraud in the field of learning disabilities. *Journal of Learning Disabilities, 23*, 207–212.

Worrall, R.S. (1990b). Neural organization technique— treatment or torture? *Skeptical Inquirer, 15*, 40–50.

Yates, F.A. (1966). *The art of memory.* Chicago: University of Chicago Press.

Young, N. D. (1993). *WISC-R patterns among the dyslexic population: Should Bannatyne be banned?* Unpublished doctoral dissertation, American International College, Springfield, MA.

Ysseldyke, J.E. & Algozzine, B. (1990). *Introduction to special education,* 2nd ed. Boston, MA: Houghton Mifflin Co.

Zaragoza, N. (1987). Process writing for high-risk learning disabled students. *Reading Research and Instruction, 26*, 290–301.

Zentall, S.S., & Ferkis, M.A. (1993). Mathematical problem solving for youth with ADHD, with and without learning disabilities. *Learning Disability Quarterly, 1*, 16.

Zigmond, N.K. (1967). Auditory processes in children with learning disabilities. In L. Tarnopol (Ed.), *Learning disabilities: Introduction to education and medical management* (pp. 196–216). Springfield, Il: C.C. Thomas.

Zigmond, N. & Sansone, J. (1986). Designing a program for the learning disabled adolescent. *Remedial and Special Education, 7*, 13–17.

Zigmond, N., & Baker, J.M. (1994). Is the mainstream a more appropriate educational setting for Randy? A case study of one student with learning disabilities. *Learning Disabilities Research & Practice, 9*, 108–117.

Index